DRIVING FORCE

The McLaughlin Family and the Age of the Car

HEATHER ROBERTSON

M&S

Cloth edition published 1995
Trade paperback edition printed 1996

Canadian Cataloguing in Publication Data

Robertson, Heather, 1942-
Driving force : the McLaughlin family and the age of the car

Includes index.
ISBN 0-7710-7556-1 (bound)   ISBN 0-7710-7557-X (pbk.)

1. McLaughlin, Robert Samuel, 1871-1972.   2. McLaughlin family.
3. General Motors of Canada – History.   4. Automobile industry
and trade – Canada – History.   I. Title.

TL140.M35R6 1995   338.7'629222'092271   C95-931235-8

The publishers acknowledge the support of the Canada Council and the
Ontario Arts Council for their publishing program.

Typesetting by M&S, Toronto
Printed and bound in Canada

McClelland & Stewart Inc.
The Canadian Publishers
481 University Avenue
Toronto, Ontario
M5G 2E9

1 2 3 4 5   00 99 98 97 96

CONTENTS

ACKNOWLEDGEMENTS

This book could not have been undertaken without the assistance of the City of Toronto Arts Council and the Writers' Reserve Program of the Ontario Arts Council.

Among the many people who contributed to *Driving Force*, I am particularly grateful to all the members of the McLaughlin and Mowbray families who provided letters, documents, clippings, photographs, and their personal recollections. General Motors of Canada generously gave me access to its plants and company archive as well as to important initial research by Philip Smith. I appreciate the guidance of Tayce Wakefield, Stew Low, and Charles McGregor of the public-relations staff, Robert Henesey of the communications department, and the co-operation of Locals 222 and 303 of the Canadian Auto Workers union. My special thanks to Gayle Wotten, Howard Knapp, Perry Krygsman, Hildegard Tischler and Oleh Perun, who saved my life on the line.

John Bonnett and Lorraine Li helped with archival and bibliographical research. Norman Penner and David Sobel unravelled the byzantine complexities of union politics. Richard Scharchburg, archivist of the GMI Alumni Foundation's Collection of Industrial History, Flint, Michigan, and Lawrence Gustin of the Buick Motor Company, Flint, contributed their valuable expertise. Personal assistance was provided by Marion O'Donnell, Brian Malcolm, Sophie Drakich, and the staff and volunteers of Parkwood; Ruth Brooking and Brenda Carrigan of the McLaughlin Public Library, Oshawa; Joan Murray and the staff of the Robert McLaughlin Gallery, Oshawa; Mike Foley of the Canadian Automotive Museum, Oshawa; Nora Herd of the Oshawa Historical Society; collectors Ron Bouckley, Harry Schoon, Bill Sherk, and the late Ian McNab; General Motors of Canada engineer and McLaughlin–Buick historian Boyd Wood; Dave Mitchell and Vern Bethel of the McLaughlin–Buick Club; Charles Taylor and employees of Windfields Farm; John M. Lewis, Toronto; David Monaghan, curator of transportation, National Museum of Science and Technology,

Ottawa; Leon Warmski, Archives of Ontario; Maureen Hoogenraad and Barbara Wilson, National Archives of Canada. Specific acknowledgements are given to other individuals and archives in "Notes and Sources."

My thanks to Anne Collins, former senior editor at *Saturday Night*, who originally commissioned this as a magazine story, and to my calm, capable editor, Dinah Forbes.

Introduction

SAM AND ME

December 18, 1991: Perry Krygsman is sitting in the cafeteria at General Motors of Canada's Car Plant #2 in Oshawa, Ontario. He is on his morning break from the line, and the cafeteria is quiet. The television set in the corner is usually tuned to cartoons or talk shows, but this morning the screen is occupied by the big, homely face of General Motors chairman Robert Stempel delivering his year-end "Report to the GM Team." Perry's experience in his eight years with GM is that whenever management talks to the workers it's bad news, and if the head honcho is beaming into Oshawa from the fourteenth floor of the General Motors building in Detroit, the news will be worse than usual.

Stempel's voice is urgent, his tone ominous. He speaks of a "dramatic loss in consumer confidence" and an accelerated need for GM to cut costs, improve productivity, and achieve "lean capacity" through "restructuring and resizing." Perry knows what these words mean and finally Stempel gets to the point: "A number of U.S. and Canadian plants will be idled or consolidated over the next few years." They include, he says, six car-assembly plants: the number producing mid-sized cars will be reduced from five to four.

Car Plant #2 is one of those five mid-sized-car plants, and rumours have been flying for months that it's in for the chop. Perry waits to hear the worst, but Stempel goes on: "At this time we are *not* announcing plants involved in further consolidation." Oh, terrific. Let everybody twist in the wind. Perry hasn't time to hear more. He dodges through the conveyor belts of car bodies and grabs his rivet gun from the relief worker without missing a beat. He's scared as hell. It's a week before Christmas; his wife is expecting a baby and they are carrying a big mortgage on a new house in Peterborough. Perry would quit GM tomorrow, but there are no jobs out there, *nothing* for a young guy with a high school diploma. Perry hates being jerked around, but what bugs him the most is the way Stempel delivered his message: *he didn't even stop the line.*

I catch a clip from the GM video in Toronto on the 6 p.m. television news. Stempel's manner is aggressive, his language alarmist. He makes sawing motions with his right arm like the tomahawk chop. He irritates me. Why the sudden panic? General Motors of Canada has a reputation as a solid, profitable company, a good citizen. I don't like being intimidated by Americans, and when the announcer explains that Plant #2 manufactures the Buick Regal, I jump up from the couch and shout in Stempel's face: "*You can't do that! That's the McLaughlin–Buick!*"

Where did that primal memory come from? What is the McLaughlin–Buick? The name McLaughlin disappeared from the Buick before I was born. My only knowledge of General Motors comes from *Roger and Me*, Michael Moore's angry, satirical film about Roger Smith, the GM chairman who began a ruthless process of plant closures that devastated Michigan. I am haunted by the film's images of deserted, decaying workers' houses, and I remember now another image, a photograph in my mother's album, taken in Saskatchewan *circa* 1916, of children standing beside an open-topped car in a sunny field. My mother, Margaret, is among those children. Her father, Maurice Duncan, managed the Yorkton branch of the Dominion Bank, and my mother vividly remembered Saskatchewan's golden age, before the Crash, when driving a McLaughlin–Buick was the epitome of class. It was an exotic car, but not ostentatious (it was made in Ontario), elegant and expensive. The Royal Canadian Mounted Police drove McLaughlin–Buicks, and so did the bootleggers, although the

American gangsters preferred Studebakers. The McLaughlin–Buick was a Canadian car, wasn't it?

I hit the road to investigate the imminent disappearance of a legend. Oshawa is fifty-five kilometres east of Toronto on a desolate, dangerous stretch of highway bordered by a brown crust of strip malls and housing developments. I pass steel-clad office towers owned by Mazda and Toyota, and I feel embarrassed to be driving a second-hand 1988 Nissan Pathfinder: basic black, no chrome, no trim, no trouble. I love this car. I learned to drive on a 1953 Morris Minor, then moved on to a 1959 Nash Rambler, a second-hand 1960 Chevrolet, a 1968 Ford Galaxie convertible, and the only new car I have ever owned, a 1972 Triumph Spitfire. Since then, with the brief exception of a Renault 18, I have driven a succession of Japanese models. The only Buick in my life was an ice-green 1958 Limited owned by a boyfriend's father. It was as long as a hearse, and the padded interior was upholstered in a shiny, pleated material similar to that used in caskets. Riding in the front seat, I felt embalmed.

That feeling comes over me again as I enter the McLaughlin Public Library, a gift to Oshawa from Colonel Robert Samuel McLaughlin in 1954. McLaughlin's round, pale face beams down from a colour photograph hanging on the wall of the reading room. His eyes are expressionless, his smile enigmatic. A portrait of his wife, Adelaide, hangs on the other side of a tall window, the way photos of the King and Queen used to be displayed. They have both been dead for years.

Historical photographs of the McLaughlin family are mounted in a permanent exhibit near the front entrance, and below them glass cases glitter with medals and ribbons and silver cups won by McLaughlin horses. This little shrine is only one of many monuments to Colonel Sam, the city's patron saint. Next door, the Robert McLaughlin Gallery, named for Sam's father, houses within its collection paintings by Sam's daughter Isabel. On the lake shore, Colonel Sam Drive leads to the new headquarters of General Motors of Canada, perched like a spaceship next to McLaughlin Bay. The McLaughlin family motto, "One Grade Only, and That the Best," is inscribed over the entrance.

I find Paul, the last McLaughlin in the family business, in a rambling old rabbit warren of a plant built in 1926. Paul, a thirty-three-year-old plastics engineer with the Lighting and Bumper Business Unit of GM's

Automotive Components Group, is the great-grandson of George, Sam's older brother and business partner when they built the first McLaughlin–Buicks in 1908. The McLaughlins sold their motor-car company to General Motors in 1918, and Paul, a graduate of the General Motors Institute in Flint, Michigan, has worked his way up through the ranks as his father, E. R. S. "Dick" McLaughlin, did before him. Paul is as apprehensive about his future as everybody else: GM is laying off hundreds of engineers and office staff. Paul has no privileges, and no regrets.

"If the McLaughlins hadn't sold, they would have been pushed aside," he says. "The situation was similar to some of the decisions we are facing today. We have to be competitive. I think working for GM is an opportunity right now, but I don't believe Stempel's got the answers."

I tour Car Plant #2 on February 14, 1992. It is part of a vast complex by the lake, a moonscape of grey, windowless factories with ventilators mushrooming from their roofs. Inside, I encounter a legacy of Roger Smith: robots. In the mid-1980s, GM spent $3.5 billion automating the Oshawa car plants – Plant #1 makes Chevrolet Luminas – a droplet of the $45 billion Smith invested in robotics in his obsession to transform GM into a futuristic corporation of "peopleless plants." Big robots do most of the welding and smaller ones, guided by computers, trundle about on fixed paths carrying partly built cars to and from the work stations. The Automated Guided Vehicles, called AGVs, are as busy as the Seven Dwarfs, and this plant has four thousand people.

I pass an automated stamping press and, next to it, a stack of curved steel fenders, delicate and finely moulded as shells. In 1908, my other grandfather, Henry Robertson, was doing the work of this machine. He was a pattern maker in the Winnipeg shops of the Canadian Northern Railway, and he worked in wood, shaping patterns that were pressed into fine sand to mould the steel when it was poured. He apprenticed in the Scottish shipyards on the Clyde, and he came to Canada a Labour man. I have inherited his battered wooden tool chest with the initials "H.R." and, from his library, a leather-bound copy of Robert Louis Stevenson's *Kidnapped* and volume one of *Capital* by Karl Marx.

On February 24, 1992, General Motors Corporation announces a 1991 loss of $4.5 billion; General Motors of Canada reports a profit of $323 million. The profit margin – 1.7 per cent – is painfully narrow; the Canadian company sold 1 million vehicles worth $19.3 billion to make $323 on each one. The employees, on the other hand, earned $1,880 per unit, exactly the amount GM is estimated to be losing on every car it builds. Who is running this company?

The fate of Plant #2 depends on what Stempel calls "employee relations." Toyota can build a car in half the time, and if GM's efforts to match Japanese productivity are crippled by strikes, slowdowns, or sabotage, everybody will be out of work. GM is demanding compulsory overtime; it is cheaper to eliminate jobs and pay workers time-and-a-half for the extra hours. A lot of workers like the money, but others resent the arbitrary dislocation in their lives and fear the erosion of rights they have fought for generations to acquire. Why should they share the pain of Detroit's disasters? "I visited GM's Canadian operations on three different occasions," wrote Roger Smith's speech writer, Albert Lee, in 1988, "and was repeatedly surprised each time by the workers' antagonism or utter indifference to the U.S. parent. Dropping names of the chairman or president did no good, as the average factory worker claimed not to know who they were."

Scuffles break out in the union hall. Police seize the ballot boxes during a rowdy election for a new plant chairman; a scrutineer is accused of concealing 160 phony ballots in his sock. Local 222 of the Canadian Auto Workers has a reputation for being fractious and cranky, and the squabbles seem to have more to do with personalities and patronage than with the issues. Local 222's grizzled president, John Sinclair, remains calm, almost indifferent. Sinclair has been around for thirty years, and I get the impression he has been through all this before. The American tyrannosaur is bellowing and lashing its tail; keep still, and it will eat somebody else. He's right. A Lumina van plant at Tarrytown, New York, is taken out, and, in Ontario, a foundry and engine plant in St. Catharines. A van plant in Scarborough will close in 1993, at a cost of $131 million and a loss of three thousand jobs, but that decision was made in 1989 by Roger Smith. The Buick is reprieved.

It is early March, and the snow is melting in the sunken gardens of Sam McLaughlin's estate, Parkwood. Parkwood is a National Historic Site, and the house is open for tours year-round. The rear of the twelve-acre property is surrounded by a solid, six-foot wooden fence, and, in front,

I pass through wrought-iron gates set in a low stone wall. The rough stucco facade of the house looks much like Sam's face, plain and uncommunicative. The house is old, shrouded by cedars and spruces, and the broken slats in the black shutters remind me of a movie about a businessman of even greater *hubris*: *Citizen Kane*.

Inside, a greenish dappled light filters through louvres, lowered blinds, layers of heavy damask draperies, and the pleated silk shades of exquisite lamps. Sounds are hushed, and I feel I have wandered into a strange, painted wood. I walk on a floor of planked oak, and above, like a canopy of branches, the arched ceiling is patterned with trailing ivy. In the hall, the walls are painted with murals of birch trees, fauns, nymphs, and rosy-cheeked children; the carpet in the sun room glimmers like a lily pool. Silver candelabra gleam on the long mahogany dining table; Sam's old briar pipes stand in a rack beside his chair, and upstairs, on Adelaide's French-style dressing table, her gilded combs and brushes rest where she left them. Time has stopped, but everything is dusted and polished. Vases are filled with fresh flowers, and soft cushions on the antique chairs have been plumped up for guests. I am in a darkened theatre. Am I too early for the play, or too late?

April 1, 1992: I am in a procession of about two thousand GMC trucks heading for the Oshawa arena. The bumper sticker in front of me says: "The way to a man's heart is through his fly." These guys have just come from work, and they look tough, tired, and surly. Bobby Orr's picture is on the arena wall, but CAW president Bob White is on the ice. White has struck a deal on compulsory overtime: maximum two hours during the week, and six hours on Saturdays with a week's notice. The sweetener: Plant #2 stays in business.

"We're going back seventy-five years!" one woman yells. Feet pound, and the boards reverberate to the sound of whistles and catcalls. "Brothers and sisters," White pleads, his quaint words a poignant echo of the days when workers sang for bread and roses. Bread wins: the deal is approved.

April 8, 1992: I am at the Moose Lodge for the third annual reunion of the employees of department 32, the cutting and sewing room. They are a lively bunch of women and they know each other well; GM segregated women into the sewing and wiring departments until 1970, when equal-rights legislation and feminist agitation within the union gave them the right to work anywhere in the plant. A lot of these women worked together for years. "It was an old building with rows and rows of Singer sewing machines," recalls Elsa Goddard. "There would be 150 women stuck in between piles of material, in a trough of material. There were windows, but there was no air-conditioning, let me tell you. In the summer it would get up to one hundred degrees. We'd take salt pills. Very seldom would they let you go home." Elsa and her two sisters, Joan and "Bubbles," got on at "The Motors" as teenagers in the 1940s and '50s after learning their craft sewing longjohns at the local knitting mill. Their father, Maurice Cardinal, worked in the GM plant, but Bubbles laughs: "You had to get by old lady Baxter at the unemployment office. If she didn't like you, you didn't get in. I started at ten to twelve dollars a week and I thought I was making such big money!"

These women have strong hands and their arms are muscular from years of yanking heavy carpets, car linings, and seat covers through double-needle machines at breakneck speed. Their work was timed. "Sure, you got your finger caught sometimes," shrugs Bubbles. "You'd just wait for the mechanic to come and take the machine apart." She didn't find it monotonous: "It was a lot of fun. I hated to quit." Women used to be dismissed when they married; some stayed single or lived common-law, and childbirth qualified them for sick leave. The "Singer girls" looked out for each other, flirted with the cutters, razzed the foreman, and kibitzed about parties, clothes, and guys. "I'd daydream," says Joan. "I could sew like a bugger and my mind would be fifty miles away. Maybe it was because I was uneducated. It worked, anyhow."

Windfields Farm, May 20, 1992: It's a soft, sunny day and young colts are frisking in the paddocks. I am standing by a grave. The granite headstone reads:

Northern Dancer

1961 – 1990

Canada's greatest racehorse is buried here. Northern Dancer was bred by E. P. Taylor, the Toronto financier who bought this 450-acre farm from Sam McLaughlin in 1951. Taylor liked to describe McLaughlin as "a man with a voice of brass, a grip of iron, and a heart of gold," and Taylor's son Charles, who now owns Windfields, remembers that at the age of ninety-nine Colonel Sam had "a handshake like a vise." Taylor encountered Sam, accompanied by his nurse, at the Ontario Jockey Club, where Sam was on the board of directors. "He told me with great glee that his nurse was not allowed in the directors' room, so he could sneak in there to have a cigar and glass of brandy. 'I'm in my one-hundredth year,' he told me. He was very proud of that."

Colonel Sam is buried in Union Cemetery not far from Windfields. A gravedigger points me toward the mausoleum, a smooth block of black granite that reminds me of Lenin's tomb. It is landscaped with cedars and yew, and two dried carnations are tucked through the handles of its polished Art Deco doors. Flowers for whom? The tomb's walls are devoid of inscriptions. The name "McLaughlin" appears nowhere. Is this modesty, or arrogance? In Oshawa, Colonel Sam's image peers out everywhere, as ubiquitous as the Cheshire Cat, or Chairman Mao.

August 18, 1992: Car Plant #2 will remain open until the end of the 1995 model year. The Buick Regal sells well in a depressed economy. Quality is good; a J. D. Power consumer survey ranks Plant #2 seventh out of forty-six North American plants, five places behind the rival Toyota plant in Cambridge, Ontario. Cars are cheaper to build in Canada: wages are paid in Canadian dollars and governments heavily subsidize medical, pension, and training programs. So what *is* wrong with Plant #2?

Cryptic answers come in technospeak: synchronous production, *kaisen* (continuous improvement), Total Quality Management, focus groups, just-in-time, win-win. It is Japanese, translated into English by the American guru who taught it to the Japanese in the first place, Dr. W. Edwards Deming. The ascetic face of ninety-one-year-old Dr. Deming hovers over General Motors of Canada via video satellite. Deming is leading management seminars on his fourteen-point "Deming philosophy." It contains elements of Fordism ("the work and the work alone controls us"), McLuhanism ("the medium is the message,") Marxism ("a commodity has a value because it is a crystallization of social labour,") Harry Truman ("the buck stops here"), and the common sense of Benjamin Franklin, who cautioned in 1748: "Remember that time is money." In Deming's voice I hear the ethic of a New England puritan, Ralph Waldo Emerson, who put it this way: "If a man can make a better mousetrap than his neighbour, though he builds his house in the woods the world will make a beaten path to his door."

September 18, 1992: I have decided that I cannot write a book about making cars without making them myself, and my request to work a week or so on the line in Plant #2 has finally worked its way through General Motors. It has been years since the company hired anyone off the street and there seems to be no training program I can fit into. Assembly-line jobs are defined as "unskilled," and any able-bodied person is expected to get the hang of things in a couple of days. There are some areas of the plant where women are not welcome, and, at fifty, I have reached an age at which employees are eligible to retire if they have thirty years' service. Where to place me in the plant poses a problem, and there are delays due to layoffs and booting up the line for the 1993 models. This is my first day on the job.

GM insists that I sign a waiver relieving the company of liability in case I am killed or injured on the job. I also have to promise not to reveal any production secrets during my term of employment. Who am I, Rosie the Riveter or James Bond? Local 222 doesn't mind me working as long as I don't take anybody's job or pay, so I will work for free alongside full-time employees, giving them a rest in return for putting up with me. I take the day shift in the Buick body shop, 6:48 a.m. to 3:13 p.m.; the night shift runs 5:48 p.m. to 2:13 a.m. (Maintenance takes over between shifts.) The shifts change every two weeks.

On my first day, I drive into a scarlet sunrise; a necklace of oncoming headlights sparkles on the black asphalt. I find a spot in the parking lot across from the plant and join the crowd streaming toward the gate. I am wearing my best shop rat gear: black jeans, a denim shirt, running shoes, and my son's castoff high school jacket. I carry my lunch in a brown paper bag. Nobody pays any attention to me.

I report to the main office. I am introduced to four or five big, pleasant men in white shirts who live in little brown offices with nameplates on the doors. The white shirts size me up. Nobody has yet told me where on the line I am going to work or what job I'll be doing. I am given a GM employee card. My number is 1347, and my name is misspelled "Roberts." To get in the electronic gate to the plant, I insert the card in the time clock; I punch it in again to get out. The wallet-sized booklet of plant rules that comes with the card states that "leaving work assignment or plant during working hours without permission" is "sufficient grounds for disciplinary action ranging from reprimand to immediate discharge depending on the seriousness of the offence in the judgement of Management."

Management assigns me to "prime," whatever that is, and Mike, the supervisor, leads me up a steel staircase to the body trim line on the second floor. Car bodies seem to pop out of nowhere, like a row of giant jelly beans. Their painted shells have been fitted with doors, but not much else, and, secured by a hidden drag chain, they ride waist-high under a canopy of plastic air hoses as thick as Spanish moss. Men and women walk beside them, making mysterious, ritualized gestures with their arms. Prime is at the end, where the drag chain rises and makes a sharp curve to the left. Four women, one on each corner, stand on a raised dais, and as they bend and sway under the brilliant lights, they look like Botticelli angels.

The job seems simple enough: paint black goop around the edges of the window openings to help cement the glass to the steel body. The bonding agent adheres better to the goop than to paint, and black cuts glare. I have some skill and experience with house painting, so I am feeling confident, but there's a hitch: the chemicals used in the prime and solvent are so toxic that I have to take an isocyanate tolerance test before I am allowed in the work area. It's a breath test and I am assured that this is merely a precaution; the woman I will work with, Hildegard, has been there for twenty years. Hildegard appears to be my age or older, a gentle-looking woman with a welcoming smile.

I have to wait. The foreman is off sick, and it seems that nobody else has been told to expect me. It doesn't matter; I am only a spare part. Mike walks me down the line, explaining the jobs: door handles go in here, vinyl trim on there. I smile at the workers; they glare at me with cold hostility. What's wrong? Do they think I'm a company spy? They don't look too tough; most of them are younger than I am. That's it: "Heather Roberts" looks like an old babe with thirty years' seniority. She can pick any job she wants; the worker she bumps bumps the next, and at the end of the line some kid is out of a job.

I pause to watch a woman with a round, ruddy face and red-gold hair that flows down her back. She gives me a fierce look, grabs an air gun dangling at the end of a long hose, yanks it, and rivets a piece of metal on to the inside of a door. She is beautiful, earthy, and when she brushes a strand of hair off her sweaty face I see that she is tired. Why don't I help out here? Mike explains to her who I am; she takes a breath and nods. I hang my jacket up beside her windbreaker. Her name is embroidered on the front: Gayle.

Gayle installs window regulators in the left rear doors of Buick Regals and Chevy Luminas. Four different regulators are layered on cardboard in big bins behind us: Chevy standard and automatic; Buick standard and automatic. They look like sharp-edged boomerangs with holes and notches where cranks and panes of glass will eventually be fitted, and my first job is to remember which boomerang comes from what bin.

I am issued a heavy denim apron. This is to protect the cars. I tie a canvas pouch full of rivets around my waist and pull on a pair of tight, green vinyl gloves. I peer up the line. The cars all look alike to me. Each one, however, carries a white computer printout on the left front fender with specifications coded in large black letters: B4 means a four-door Buick with standard windows; B4 A31 is automatic windows. Chevrolet is C4. We can pass on the two-doors.

I fish the proper regulators out of the bins and hand them to Gayle. They are covered in clear, odourless grease that soaks into my gloves. Our work space is only about ten feet long and six wide, but we are making 450 cars this shift and that's a lot of trips to the bins. As each car slowly passes, Gayle has sixty seconds to wiggle the regulator into the interior door panel, insert and drive four rivets, then stick a rubber patch over the hole in the floor that anchors the seat belt. The patches come in long strips and we wear them looped over our pouch strings.

The atmosphere is hot and stuffy. Fans in the catwalk above the cars bathe us in gusts of cool air. I hear their faint whirr over the white glare of inaudible sound that beats against my body. I am aware of the roar of the machinery only when Gayle has to shout her instructions into my ear. The plant pulsates with heavy-metal rock music. Headphones are not permitted, but radios are, and two or three are going full blast across the floor on the door line. A lot of people wear yellow earplugs and bring the morning's *Toronto Sun*: the *Sun* has the Sunshine Girl and stories short enough to read in a few seconds between jobs. Gayle stows a paperback in her cupboard, and when the line slows down, as it tends to do, she reads a sentence or two.

We share a work station: one small battered table with a tiny cupboard and attached stool. The stool is too small and uncomfortable to be of any use. "If you sit down too much," Gayle warns, "they'll find a harder job for you to do." We are watched. Supervisors in their white shirts are easy to pick out, and there are the team and group leaders, union stewards, engineers in blue coveralls, and frequent flying wedges of suits. Beware of people carrying clipboards. These are Dr. Deming's soothsayers examining the dinosaur's entrails for omens, offering human sacrifices to the gods of Total Quality Management. To the workers, TQM means what it did to Henry Ford: speed up.

Word that I am a writer spreads down the line. Everybody loosens up. I meet Perry across the way installing right rear door regulators. He's short and stocky, with a sleeveless T-shirt, spiked hair, and a big grin. He does a great Bob Stempel imitation. Perry introduces me to Howard, a white-haired man of about sixty who is covering the cars' most exposed bulges with padding. It's an easy job, but Howard has been injured – he was knocked down by a robot run amok – and he finds it hard simply being on his feet for eight hours. GM is obliged to find suitable jobs for people recovering from work-related illnesses at the same time as it is trying to eliminate meaningless tasks; as a result some workers wander around the plant with nothing to do.

A thin blonde in a pink shirt spends a few aimless minutes brushing Howard's stack of pads, then she's off to the cafeteria for coffee followed by a cigarette in the smoking area; later she drifts along the line chatting and flirting with a dark-eyed young man who ought to be a K-mart greeter. The "leeches," as Howard calls them, bug the hell out of their brothers and sisters who get only a fifteen-minute break twice a day and thirty minutes for lunch. I try to be useful, but I am fearful of tripping over or banging into something. I am in the middle of a perpetual motion machine: robots run about, lights flashing, and forklift loaders zoom up and down the aisles. The drag line lurches and grinds, hoses lash the air, and, behind me, the bodies of unpainted cars float through the gloom like sightless silver whales.

At noon we dodge the whales to reach the cafeteria. I am not very hungry. Gayle fills a big Pepsi container with crushed ice; the water will ease her thirst in the afternoon. She has been doing this job for only three weeks: she was bumped out of the technical stores department where she had been ordering and tracking equipment on computer. Her work experience is in office management, except for her first month at GM in 1981:

"I put in carpets," she says. "Me and two men. We'd roll up the carpet, shove it in the car, tack it down. You had to lie in the trunk, and you had to leave one leg out or they'd lock you in the trunk and you wouldn't get out all the way down the line. I lost forty pounds. I was skin and bone. It takes a month to learn how not to kill yourself on this job."

Gayle's gun arm aches. She is afraid of developing tendinitis, and I notice that her arms are slim, her hands and wrists narrow and more finely boned than mine. She doesn't complain. She likes to work hard, and the pay at GM is $20.53 an hour. After taxes and deductions it totals about twenty-one hundred dollars a month, more than twice what she would earn anywhere else around Oshawa, and GM's pension and dental benefits are excellent. Her husband, Al Wotten, is a bus driver. She dreams of being able to buy a small farm with a stable where she could board horses and give riding lessons.

I go to the medical centre for my test. I answer a questionnaire about smoking, allergies, asthma, hives, pneumonia, hay fever, dust, wheezing, and medications. I breathe into a tube until my eyes pop. I pass. I feel cocky. I haven't fired a gun since I tried a friend's .22 when I was a kid, but I remember the smooth feel of the barrel and the force of the recoil against my shoulder. My trigger finger itches. Tomorrow I will go to work.

The next day I arrive just after 6:30 a.m. The lights are dimmed, the machinery at rest. I feel as if I am walking through a silent, shadowy cathedral. Where is everybody? I find Perry lying face down on his table, asleep; Howard is sitting in his place, paging through the *Sun*. I look around, and I see people tucked away in their work stations, reading or meditating, acolytes at their morning devotions. The cars appear to be where we left them yesterday, except the colours and numbers are different; the night shift has polished them off. We're looking at bodies that were barely born a day ago, and now they seem to stretch to infinity.

The man who installed door handles yesterday has been taken off his job. "He doesn't like anybody watching him," Gayle says. "He goes crazy." Losing it is one of the innumerable infractions for which workers can be disciplined. The rule book puts it this way: "distracting the attention of others or otherwise causing confusion by unnecessary demonstration of any kind on Company premises." Apart from criminal acts such as assault, theft, sabotage, and selling drugs, workers can be reprimanded for, among other things, distributing literature or soliciting contributions, littering, loitering in toilets, carelessness, carrying weapons, horseplay, scuffling, running, throwing things, failure to follow instructions, stopping work, "failure to open and disclose the contents of lockers, vehicles, purses, handbags, briefcases, lunch pails or other containers on request," and, simply, "restricting output."

The lights go up; the line lurches to life. When it's running smoothly, Gayle inserts a rivet and passes me the air gun. It feels clumsy and surprisingly heavy, and I have to pull hard on the cord to drag the hose back to meet the oncoming car. C4. Standard. I grab the greasy regulator in my left hand and try to wiggle it inside the door, dragging the rivet gun into place with my right arm. *Get in there, get in.* I struggle with it, trying to line up the rivet holes. The car drags me along. I'm losing time. My hands are shaking. I get the rivet in a hole and pull the trigger. It makes a dull bang. I feel the shock in my hand. My left hand gropes in my pouch for the next rivet. They slither around in my greasy glove. *I can't get a grip on one.* I pinch a rivet between my thumb and forefinger and try to insert it in the gun. My right arm is trembling with the strain of pulling on the cord. *I can't get it in.* I pull on the car, trying to make it stop. *Wait a minute. Stop. I'm not finished. Stop this car!* The car drags me along. How much time do I have? Where am I? I can't look up. My glasses are fogging. I can't see. *I'm not going to make it.*

I am, literally, at the end of my rope. Gayle grabs the gun and drives the last rivets. She does the next few cars while I get my bearings. It looks so *effortless!* I try again. The gun is slippery, the regulator feels like an eel. *Damn bloody grease.* The rivets slip out of my fingers. My hands shake, my heart is pounding. *How do I get this damn thing in?* I am so slow that I run into the guy ahead who installs the front door regulators. He doesn't appreciate it. I don't blame him.

Who am I, Gerald Ford? Can't I walk and chew gum at the same time? Isn't this an unskilled job? I realize that I have never before performed different tasks simultaneously with each hand, in less than a minute, on a moving object, while I am in motion. I'm in behaviour therapy. I struggle on, doing every fifth or tenth door, fearful of defeat as the next car looms up beside me. By noon I'm breathing hard, my face is flushed; the *bang* of the gun throbs in my head, my hand is stiff, and I suffer from searing thirst. This, I know now, is *manual labour.*

"I thought I had to learn it all in three days," Gayle reassures me. "I got into a state like panic. My arm was so sore, I got so tired. I thought, 'I can't do this. I'll never be able to do this.' The guys on the line really helped pull me through. After the weekend, I came back and it was okay."

I am grateful for her kindness and patience. Having me screwing up isn't making her job any easier, although I am providing a good deal of merriment for everyone else. I am the plant fool, a wandering troubadour, and I spend more time talking to people than learning my job. Howard Knapp tells me about the thirty-three years he worked for Oshawa's Houdaille foundry making bumpers and bathtubs; it was hard, filthy work and when the plant announced it was closing the workers had to stage a sit-in strike to get their pensions. Howard is proud of that; his father, he says, was one of the first union men in GM.

"I'd really like to study criminology," Perry yells at me. Perry dropped out of community college and he can't afford to start again. He has a cool, cynical style, but despair is in his eyes: "I don't want to retire from this place," he says. "I don't think I'm gonna make thirty years here." Perry's gun goes down. He waves and jumps around. A repairman scrambles up the guy wires to replace it. Four or five doors go by with dangling right rear window regulators. Perry winks: "The customers will be getting the quality to which they are accustomed: one grade only, and that the best." Not to worry: the regulators will be installed by experts at the end of the line who do, and undo, whatever has to be done. I am glad they are there.

Wednesday morning, September 30, 1992: I am feeling aggressive. I can stay on my feet, my gun hand is okay, and I am flexing muscles I didn't used to have. I am getting used to the grease, and I am learning how to scoop a rivet into the palm of my glove and feed it to the gun like a minnow to a fish: bang — bang —— bang — bang. A siren goes off. I look around for the fire exit but nobody else pays attention: a car is stuck in the hoist on its way downstairs and the alarm is summoning the maintenance crew. Later, a robot carrying doors gets squashed in the upstairs hoist. Another robot lands on top of it. Their lights flash frantically and their alarms emit little squeals of pain. A knot of clipboard carriers gathers around them, trying to figure out how to descramble their codes. Nobody much likes the robots. One is called "Lou Ann" in memory of the worker she replaced.

Perry brings me a paperback novel, *The Killing Line* by Carl Clark. "It's about this place," he says. I lend him *Rivethead* by Ben Hamper, the Flint auto worker who inspired *Roger and Me*. Gayle gives me her mother's phone number. "She grew up with the McLaughlins' grandchildren," Gayle says. "She knows all the gossip." Gayle's maiden name is Gray; her friends call her "Gee-Gee." The line is baulky today; it slows, stops, lurches on again. We get an extra six minutes for lunch. A shaft of bright sunlight shines through a crack in an outside door. I feel intense nostalgia.

The group leader comes by to warn me I'm popping my rivets; I have to hold the regulator tighter against the metal plate before pulling the trigger. The damn things get heavier as the day wears on, and I push myself to see how many cars I can do without needing a rest. I engage each door in mortal combat: take *that* you sonofabitch. I know I'm wasting a lot of energy, and by 2 p.m. I am flushed and dizzy with fatigue. My hand is so stiff I am afraid it will seize up. Gee-Gee offers me some of her Blue Ice gel painkiller. It helps, but I wonder how long I can last: eighteen hundred rivets a day is a lot of punishment. Is there any way I could do this job for eight hours, five days a week? Who am I kidding?

Perry is right: Plant #2 is the location for *The Killing Line*, a fast-paced thriller featuring sabotage, sexual assault, theft, a brutal beating, a gory accident, and a bunch of foul-mouthed sleazeballs with names like Mule. At the end, the plant goes up in flames. Things must have been a lot crazier around this place in 1986, when the novel was published. "Heck," says Perry, "you can't even call someone a space cadet any more." Harassment and abusive language are not tolerated, and alcoholics, drug addicts, and psychos are supposed to receive treatment and counselling.

"There are still some wackos around," Gee-Gee says. She is afraid to shower at the plant after work for fear of being accosted. Maintenance workers have washroom keys, and guys who work double shifts can catch a few hours' sleep on stacks of cardboard. "People *lived* here," she says. "They'd sleep in the basement or in a car seat. They'd have coffee makers, microwaves, steal lunches. Some guys had gyms and barbecues up on the roof. They'd cook you breakfast to order. A homeless person could live very well at GM for years." Television sets were hidden in lockers, and the plant supported a thriving black market. One entrepreneur installed a popcorn machine beside his workbench: he sold popcorn for seventy-five cents a bag and rented out pornographic magazines. He called it his "Corn and Porn" stand.

Thursday, October 1, 1992: I decide maybe prime is safer after all. It's quieter here, although somewhere a radio is blaring "You ain't nothin' but a houn' dog." The stubby paintbrush is attached to a long green tube. As the car swings around the corner, Hildegard leans over, squeezes the trigger, and, as the car sways by, swirls a strip of black goop around the lip of the rear window opening. If she slops over it will show, and a drop on the car body has to be wiped up immediately with solvent.

"Don't inhale this stuff," she warns me. It's high in lead, she says, and I notice the warning signs on the big cans: "Vapours can explode. Harmful or fatal if swallowed." Hildegard wears surgical gloves. I try the paintbrush. Too much goop comes out, or not enough. I am terrified of drips. A sign on Hildegard's desk says: "Due care should be exercised to prevent damage to any part of the vehicle. This is especially true where painted surfaces are concerned. Paint repair is a difficult and costly procedure that can rarely match the original finish of the vehicle."

I drip on a white Buick, grab the solvent rag, wipe, dash ahead to finish, can't reach. Oh, hell. "Everything in here is moving, everything vibrates," Hildegard says. "It can make you nervous. You have to follow the curve of the car, step back so the car comes at you." White cars make me extremely nervous. I get paint on my left glove, put my hand on the car and get paint on the car. Solvent. New glove. I feel terrible. Would I buy a car made by Heather Roberts? Dave, our team leader, calls me "Heather Allan Poe." He should call me "Drippy."

I practise on the lower rim of the rear window. Hildegard asks my opinion of her favourite *Sun* columnist, Douglas Fisher, and poet Irving Layton. "I think he likes his own work best," she says of Layton. She tells me that the McLaughlin mausoleum was broken into last night. Adelaide's casket was smashed and her remains disturbed. The vandals were looking for jewellery. Where did they think they were, King Tut's tomb?

I can't smell anything, but the air seems full of fumes. I feel queasy. I am trying to learn a whole different set of motions from what I learned yesterday. I am a hopeless failure. Today is a nine-hour day: mandatory overtime. Hildegard refuses to work it. "They're not going to force me," she says. "I work every day. I do my job." Gee-Gee sticks it out. She urges me to leave. Her mother, Peggy, will pick up her two-year-old son, Cody, from day care.

Peggy Gray grew up in Oshawa's "social set," a circle of well-to-do families that gravitated around the golf club. "It was right out of *The Great Gatsby*," she laughs. "They played the piano, danced the Charleston. They all partied together. I remember some of the dress-up parties. I saw my father once in a blue sequined dress and a blond wig. A lot of drinking went on. *All* that group drank. It was a gay life."

Peggy's father, Dr. F. L. Henry, was a dentist and a prominent Liberal. In 1925, five-year-old Peggy Henry presented a bouquet of flowers to Prime Minister Mackenzie King on one of his rare visits to Oshawa, and among her favourite possessions is his charming, handwritten thank-you note. The Henrys were close friends with the McLaughlins, and they didn't take a back seat; Thomas Henry had settled here in 1812 when the lake shore was still virgin forest.

Peggy drives me down to the harbour to see his stout stone house, restored as the Sydenham Museum and archives of the Oshawa Historical Society. Thomas Henry married twice and raised sixteen children; he fought with Sir Isaac Brock in the War of 1812, served as harbour master, and travelled the county as a circuit preacher and elder in the Methodist church. Elder Henry was so revered when he died in 1879 that eighteen ministers attended his funeral and eighty-five carriages lined the road in front of the church. Around the corner, an unknown carriage maker, Robert McLaughlin, was starting up in business. When it comes to founding fathers, Gee-Gee Wotten, sweating it out on body trim, has an ancestry as distinguished as Sam McLaughlin's, and on her mother's mantelpiece are displayed the ribbons and trophies she has won at equestrian events.

Friday, October 2, 1992: Our partner on the night shift has managed to switch our gun for one that is lighter and easier to hold. A good omen.

"Okay, let's go!" Gee-Gee says.

"Fridays are better than other days," Perry grins. It's payday. Dave comes by handing out cheques. Even the stub has a slogan: "Take time out for safety."

I look at my watch: 9 a.m. Somewhere people are starting work, sipping coffee, gazing out the window. I feel tired and claustrophobic. "Don't fight it," Gee-Gee shouts. "You have to dance with the car."

Of course. The car calls the tune here. I must yield, submit to the embrace of my mechanical bridegroom, swing and sway to the rhythm of the chain. Line dancing. Simple. Pull back, crouch forward, four steps, four shots, patch floor, pull back, twirl away, a little do-si-do by the regulator bins, then curtsey to my next white whale. I surrender my identity. I relax. I can breathe. My arm loosens up. I lean my weight against the car, letting it absorb the pressure of the recoil. My confidence begins to grow: *maybe I can do this job after all.* I look around. We are doing a kind of graceful maypole dance, and some of the workers are so in step they hardly seem to move at all.

We are a carnival crowd; women in eye shadow and bright lipstick, two guys who look as if they're off to the beach. Big hair, biker biceps, colourful T-shirts. People dress up for this job, play a role. "You spend so much time together," Gee-Gee says. "You never get close, but you do know a person really well. It's like a family. It's a weird world, but I like it here." An older man in a blue coverall pushes a broom along the aisles, stopping from time to time to dance a little jig and give somebody a playful poke in the ribs. Workers with the most seniority pick the choicest jobs; he must be the plant therapist.

I hear bellowing over on the window line. Baboons in rut. What is it? Gee-Gee shrugs. "Sometimes when a woman comes through on a tour, it's like the Sunshine Girl. The guys can be real animals. When you've worked here a while, you get used to it. People in different areas of the plant talk a different slang, have different values. It's like going to a new little village. You have to learn the customs. Here, we tell jokes." The guy on the front door pulls the string on her rivet pouch. She grabs it in the nick of time.

By 2:30 p.m. the line is running fast and the beat of heavy-metal music rolls through the plant. I catch the rhythm and surf along on a tidal wave of sound. I can rivet now, rest on the car, ease up a little. This village has been good to me. I arrived as a stranger. These people have taught me, tolerated me, taken care of me. I will miss them. I don't feel locked in anymore, I feel safe. I am in a warm, incandescent underworld practising magical rituals unknown to everyone outside. I am among the Little People. We make pretty toys for good children, but we have to be placated with coins and dishes of food. It is said here that retired auto workers die soon: like the Irish who dance with the fairies, we are enchanted.

3:05 p.m. Another howl from the Neanderthal camp. I hear the voice of the beast, and in that roar the primordial echo of the cave.

PART ONE

I

AWAY

The graveyard of the old Presbyterian church lies in the centre of the village of Enniskillen, on the west side of a road leading south to Lake Ontario, north to Lake Scugog. The church was torn down years ago, a sacrifice to union with the Methodists, but its yard is kept neat and tidy, separated from the roadside ditch by a wrought-iron fence. A dozen white marble headstones are arranged in a flat semicircle facing the gate; they form a cosy, convivial company much as, in life, the people they commemorate must have gathered around a kitchen table.

McLaughlin is the name on all but three of the stones, and their old bones now mingled with the earth represent as many as five generations. Minnie, the youngest, died on August 29, 1873, aged twenty-two months, and her sister Ida Jane followed on February 19, 1874, aged seven years, eight months, and nineteen days. They were "the children of William and Sarah Ann." The oldest McLaughlin is also named William; the Abraham of the McLaughlin clan, this patriarch died on January 26, 1866, at the age of ninety-five.

A tough nut, old William, proud and sentimental. His stone is carved with a swirling leaf motif that frames a clenched fist, its index finger pointing heavenward, and underneath a verse is inscribed:

An aged saint lies here in peace
For here the storms of life all cease
His lot was not through life to glide
His faith and patience long were tried
Wave after wave secure he passed
And rose in triumph until the last

His wife Jane lies nearby. Jane died on June 17, 1858, at seventy-seven. Her headstone is carved with the same motif as William's, and an inscription beneath her name reads: "A native of Co. Cavan, Ireland." The call of the pipes can be heard in that brief phrase. A tribute to the home she left behind was the most significant way her family could remember Jane McLaughlin.

Letters and numbers chiselled on weathered stones or scribbled by census takers on ruled sheets of paper, ownership inscribed with the flourish of a quill pen on land-registry forms, these graven images create the shadows of a dynasty almost obliterated by time. The McLaughlins were farmers, humble members of what the Victorian gentry were pleased to call the "lower classes," a large family whose members were so indistinguishable and indifferent to individuality that interlocking generations shared the same paucity of names: William, Elizabeth, John, Mary, James, and Jane. They were people of few words, and their Word was the Bible; it would have been presumptuous of them to record their own exodus as if old William dared compete with Moses. However, with a characteristic sense of timing, the McLaughlins left Ireland in the spring of 1832, a year, in all its grisly horror, that is one of the most vividly recorded in Canadian history.

It was not the clan's first migration; their Scottish ancestors had been "planted" in County Cavan generations earlier, enticed, as now, by the promise of land. The family took root, but their Presbyterian religion did not, and with the resurgence of Irish Catholic nationalism the McLaughlins were part of a tiny, besieged minority in Cavan. They were not Orange; their ties to the Church of Scotland would incline them to resist fanatical allegiance to a British monarch, an English church, or Anglo-Irish landlords. The men belonged to the Free-masons, an international secret society that abhorred the bigotry and violence of Irish politics.

Cavan was a landlocked county of mountains and bogs. The McLaughlins were tenant farmers, and over the years their land had virtually disappeared, divided and subdivided until each branch of the family eked out a subsistence living from eight or ten acres of barley and potatoes. In good years, the landlord raised the rent; in bad years, the government imposed a poor tax to feed the destitute. No matter how hard they worked or how frugally they lived, the McLaughlins faced a future of degrading poverty. At worst, landlords drove their tenants out and turned their land to pasture. Starving families straggled along the country roads toward Dublin or Belfast, but Ireland's great textile mills were silent.

"Their desire for land was intense, single-minded and beyond mere economic considerations," Canadian historian Donald Akenson writes of the Irish Protestants. "Irish Protestants shared no consistent ideology but instead an attitude, one of assertiveness. They were as capable of being left-wing as right, democratic or authoritarian, revolutionary or reactionary. The one thing they were not likely to be was quiet."

The McLaughlins were able to save a little money, or raise it by selling off their livestock and household furnishings. Their passage to Canada was likely arranged and paid for by the church – the Presbyterians had established a synod in Upper Canada in 1831 – and their land may have been chosen in advance through an agent of the Canada Company. Two Protestant families from County Cavan had already settled in Upper Canada – the Parrs near Peterborough, the Henrys in Darlington township on Lake Ontario – and the McLaughlins could be sure of a welcome. Like the other Irish Protestants who came to Canada at this time, they had resources, hope, ambition, and a profound conviction that God was with them.

Old William is over sixty in 1832 when he strikes off for the New World, a small grizzled figure trudging away from his thatched stone cottage. Jane is beside him, and his fifty-two-year-old brother, James, with his wife, Elizabeth, and their son, William. Twenty-eight-year-old Thomas is in the crowd with his wife and children, as well as George and his wife, Mary. The younger children ride on horse-drawn carts piled high with sacks of oatmeal and potatoes, kegs of butter and pickled eggs, pots and kettles and rolls of bedding, but the older ones walk: Alex, age twelve, James, seventeen, and twenty-year-old John.

John's nickname, "Broghie," distinguishes him from the others. He has a talent for making and mending the thick, hobnailed boots favoured by Irish farmers. He is a small man, like the rest of the family, with unkempt sandy hair, a high forehead, and deep-set pale eyes that give his face an expression as severe as his religious views. Like the other men, he wears dark homespun, but the women look cheerier in their red petticoats and colourful patterned shawls. Among the women, one fair, good-natured face stands out: Eliza Rusk, John's betrothed, is walking close by with her family.

The McLaughlin–Rusk clan is lost to sight in the mob of emigrants, sailors, and hucksters thronging the docks. (Few emigrant ships bothered to keep passenger lists, and the name of the McLaughlins' ship is unknown.) Anxious faces in a crowd, they stand silently by the ship's rail as she drifts downriver on the ebb tide, her sails cracking and filling as a cold breeze off the north Atlantic swings her bow to the west. Night falls; they descend into the hold. The hatches are closed; faces are hard to see by the light of a few guttering candles. Surrounded by their worldly goods, hundreds of nameless castaways are stowed into tiers of wooden bunks the size of coffins. Their voyage will last from eight to twelve weeks.

The Irish emigrant vessels were judged to be worse than the ships working the African slave trade. In *The Great Migration*, Edwin Guillet quotes British naval historian Basil Lubbock: "The typical emigrant packet was little better than a hermetically sealed box; as deep as it was long, with clumsy square bows and stern, with ill-cut, ill-set sails and with a promenade deck no longer than the traditional two steps and overboard." As for the crews, they were commonly composed of "rum-soaked, illiterate, bear-like officers, who could not work out the ordinary meridian observation with any degree of accuracy, and either trusted to dead reckoning or a blackboard held up by a passing ship for their longitude; whilst they were worked by the typically slow-footed, ever-grousing Merchant Jack of the past two centuries."

Families cooked their meals on deck, and if their food ran out, they starved. Some captains confined their steerage passengers to the hold for the entire trip, and in rough seas battened down the hatches. "Water leaked through from the deck in such quantities that the beds were soaked and the floor ankle deep, so that many thought the vessel was sinking," writes Guillet. "Candle lanterns could not be lighted. The crashing of casks, tinware and dishes as the ship pitched and heaved, the shrieking and crying of women and children, and the wild noise of the storm combined to create a time of horror which could never be effaced from memory."

John McLaughlin had at least the comfort of his Bible, and the story of Jonah and the whale must have impressed itself on his imagination. With the Bible in his hand, John could manage without a preacher or a church. The power of Presbyterianism was its democracy; Christ was present in any group of believers, however poor and forlorn, gathered together in His name, and His word was written for anyone to read. John McLaughlin could read. Was it the gift of a country schoolmaster, or a local preacher? Was he taught by his mother, or did he puzzle the words out himself? In the rural, feudal society of County Cavan, the ability to read was revolutionary.

At sea, the McLaughlins and Rusks were able to form their own congregation, read aloud from the scriptures, and pray together. Rats and lice infested the ships, and epidemics of smallpox, measles, and dysentery swept through the cramped and fetid berths; the stench of vomit and excrement, rotting food, and decaying bodies was so foul it was said that an emigrant ship could be smelled a mile away. Polluted drinking water, scooped up from the rivers in the Irish ports, spread typhoid and "ship fever" among the passengers, and in the summer of 1832 these infections were joined by a virulent new pestilence: cholera.

Asiatic cholera was identified by its victim's ghastly pallor, agonizing cramps, vomiting, and diarrhea; it led to death within hours. Cholera was so contagious it seemed to ride on the wind, and it turned the emigrant ships into floating charnel houses where the uninfected shared food and bedding with the sick and dying, and the dead were fed to the fish.

During the first week of June 1832, an armada of four hundred ships bearing twenty-five thousand British emigrants sailed up the St. Lawrence River to dock at the quarantine station on Grosse Île; another thirty-five thousand emigrants landed before freeze-up. Old William's clan was part of a wave of humanity so overwhelming it became a phenomenon, like Niagara Falls, to be observed, measured, inspected, examined, analyzed, explained, and described. Ships' captains, doctors, immigration agents, and newspaper reporters all had something to say, but among the most acute witnesses were two inquisitive young English authors, the Strickland sisters, Susanna, Mrs. Moodie, and Catharine, Mrs. Traill. Their husbands, officers in the British army, had been pensioned off with tracts of wilderness in Upper Canada, and the Moodies and Traills sailed separately for Canada in the summer of 1832.

Mrs. Moodie, in the privacy of her comfortable cabin on the upper deck, takes no notice of the "live cargo" beneath her feet until the ship drops anchor on August 30. At dawn the next day the steerage passengers are ferried ashore on Grosse Île: "I watched boat after boat depart for the island full of people and goods, and envied them the glorious privilege of once more standing firmly on the earth after two long months of rocking and rolling at sea." By afternoon, she had arranged a tour of the island:

"Never shall I forget the extraordinary spectacle that met our sight the moment we passed a low range of bushes which formed a screen in front of the river. A crowd of many hundred Irish emigrants had been landed during the present and former day and all this motley crew – men, women and children who were not confined by sickness to the sheds (which greatly resemble cattle pens) – were employed in washing clothes or spreading them out on the rocks and bushes to dry.

"The men and boys were *in* the water, while the women, with their scanty garments tucked above their knees, were tramping their bedding in tubs or in holes in the rocks, which the retiring tide had left half full of water. Those who did not possess washing tubs, pails or iron pots, or could not obtain access to a hole in the rocks, were running to and fro, screaming and scolding in no measured terms. The confusion of Babel was among them. All talkers and no hearers – each shouting and yelling in his or her uncouth dialect, and all accompanying their vociferations with violent and extraordinary gestures, quite incomprehensible to the uninitiated. We were literally stunned by this strife of tongues. I shrank, with feelings almost akin to fear, from the hard-featured, sunburnt women as they elbowed rudely past me."

The first suspected cases of cholera were reported at Grosse Île on June 6; by June 15, a hundred people were dying every day in the town of Quebec, 150 daily in Montreal. Quebec was quarantined, and ships sailed upriver to Montreal, where the passengers were put ashore on the riverbank. "We were struck by the dirty, narrow, ill-paved or unpaved streets of the suburbs, and overpowered by the noisome vapour arising from a deep open fosse that ran along the street behind the wharf," writes Catharine Traill. "This ditch seemed a receptacle for every abomination, and sufficient in itself to infect a whole town with malignant fevers."

The city's grey stone houses were shuttered and draped with crepe, and the sullen tolling of the church bells deepened her gloom: "Whole streets had been nearly depopulated. Those that were able fled panic-stricken to the country villages." By September, the death toll from the epidemic had reached more than ten thousand and Susanna Moodie went ashore with a feeling of dread: "The day was intensely hot. A bank of thunder clouds lowered heavily above the mountain, and the close, dusty streets were silent, and nearly deserted. Here and there might be seen a group of anxious-looking, care-worn, sickly emigrants, seated against a wall among their packages, and sadly ruminating upon their future prospects."

The Moodies travelled on by stagecoach to Prescott, where they boarded a paddlewheel steamer, *William IV*, for Cobourg, a village halfway between Kingston and York, and the jumping-off place for settlers pushing north into the bush. The *William IV* reached Cobourg at midnight, in the rain. By the flickering light of the ship's lanterns, Mrs. Moodie could see that the noisy crowd on the wharf were porters and draymen, one of whom would, for a price, unload the Moodies' baggage and find them lodgings. She may have noticed, in the glare of a shower of sparks from the smokestack, the tired, sunburned face of John McLaughlin.

He was glad enough to be alive, and on dry land. Too frugal to pay for passage on a steamer, the McLaughlins had travelled in an open boat, one of hundreds of clumsy, flat-bottomed barges that brought freight down to Montreal and took immigrants to Belleville, Kingston, Cobourg, York, and Niagara. These primitive *bateaux* were equipped with oars, a rudder, and a single sail, and the immigrants, with what little remained of their baggage, were crammed aboard for a journey more perilous than the Atlantic crossing.

Twenty miles was a good day's voyage in an open boat; it could take two weeks to drag the boat through the rapids from Lachine to Prescott. In shallow water, the boatmen poled the barge along, inches at a time, and when winds were contrary, they rowed to the rhythm of their *chansons*. At sunset, when the boats put in to shore, the immigrants had to fend for themselves; the boatmen built a cosy campfire, ate their dinner of salt pork and ship's biscuit, and smoked their pipes. "They eat often, and drink quantities of lake water," Mrs. Thomas Stewart observed, adding wistfully: "In the morning, before setting out, they always have hot pea soup." Shivering in his coat – the boatmen enjoyed the shelter of their canvas sail – John Howison watched them "reclined around the fire, talking barbarous French, and uttering the most horrid oaths; others sat in the boats and sang troubadour songs; and a third party was engaged in distributing the provisions. They resembled a gang of freebooters. For three days I had been disgusted with the dirtiness, noise and grossness of the Canadian boatmen, and, during as many nights, had been prevented from sleeping by the fumes of rum and tobacco, the bites of musquetoes [sic], and the hardness of the planks which formed my bed."

Lake Ontario was cold and featureless. The shore was rocky, and ancient trees grew to the water's edge, a black forest of swamps and miasmal mists. Settlements were scarce, farms few and far between. Occasionally the boat people could buy a little bread and milk and sleep on a farmhouse floor, but more often than not doors were slammed in their faces: fear of cholera had come before them, and cholera came with them. The charnel houses of the ships became the charnel houses of the immigrant sheds, and in the dirty, lousy shanty towns of Upper Canada, the Irish died of hunger, exposure, exhaustion, and disease.

How many of his family did old William lose? It is not remembered. "Follow me, and let the dead bury their dead," Jesus told St. Matthew, and McLaughlin was a man who took Jesus at his word. Tossing about on the choppy waters of Lake Ontario in a boat Peter the Fisherman himself might have rowed, the McLaughlins would have recognized the Sea of Galilee, and prayed for salvation.

Somewhere east of Cobourg, the McLaughlins' boat capsized; John salvaged only his wallet and his Bible. It was a significant combination, and John's rough baptism became the seminal story in the family legend; all earlier memories went to the bottom of the lake with his baggage. Stripped of his past, John was also separated from his family; the others went on to Darlington, he remained in Cobourg.

Work was plentiful for a keen young man with a strong back. English gentlemen like John Dunbar Moodie and Thomas Traill, clinging desperately to their tattered respectability, squandered the last of their gold to hire farmhands and servants from among the Irish immigrants; the Irish charged what any fool would pay. John McLaughlin could earn ten dollars a month and more, a small fortune in a land where butter had recently displaced the beaver skin as common currency.

Once he had bought new clothes and stout boots, John walked north on the rutted road that led to Peterborough. Peterborough was a rude hamlet of log shanties, but the road to it was as crowded as the pilgrims' road to Canterbury, and perhaps for a mile or two John fell in beside a wagon carrying a young woman seated on buffalo robes looking about her with appraising eyes: "We left Cobourg on the afternoon of the 1st of September," writes Catharine Traill. "The afternoon was fine – one of those rich, mellow days we often experience in the early part of September. The warm hues of autumn were already visible on the forest trees, but rather spoke of ripeness than decay. The country round Cobourg is well cultivated, a great portion of the woods having been superseded by open fields, pleasant farms and fine, flourishing orchards, with green pastures, where abundance of cattle were grazing. . . . As you advance further up the country, the land rises into bold, sweeping hills and dales. About halfway between Cobourg and the Rice Lake there is a pretty valley between two steep hills. Here there is a good deal of cleared land and a tavern. The place is called the 'Cold Springs.'"

Near the springs, in Cavan township, John McLaughlin stopped at a settlement later named Millbrook. He did not buy land here, and he may have been taken in by the Parrs as a hired hand. During the winter he could have made boots and mended harness, worked in the mill, or hired himself out as a logger. He saved his money. In 1833, John made a down payment on two hundred acres twenty-five miles west of Millbrook in concession 7, Darlington township, a few miles east of the lots settled by old William and the rest of the McLaughlin family. John's land, the north and south halves of lot 11, was priced at twelve shillings, six pence an acre, and on June 23, 1834, he made a deal with the owner, John Mahaffy, to pay it off in six instalments, plus interest. John McLaughlin had committed himself to an investment of 125 pounds (about five hundred dollars), at a usurious interest of nearly 30 per cent. He was already, at twenty-two, the financier of the family.

John remained in Millbrook after he and Eliza were married in 1835, and their first son, Robert, was born there on November 17, 1836. John paid his first instalment to Mahaffy in January 1837. The next payments followed at regular intervals, beginning in May, indicating that John moved his family to the Darlington farm that summer.

Cavan township, a hotbed of Orange fanaticism, was no place for a man of John McLaughlin's liberal views in the anxious summer of

1837. The Presbyterians were staunch Reformers, and their fiery little leader, William Lyon Mackenzie, was stumping the countryside stirring up agitation against the corrupt, arrogant regime of the lieutenant-governor of Upper Canada, Sir Francis Bond Head. The Patriots, as Mackenzie's men came to call themselves, carried pikes and muskets to protect themselves against gangs of Tory toughs, and they travelled on foot and by horseback in cavalcades bearing a flag proclaiming "Liberty or Death."

Support for Mackenzie's cause was strong in Darlington, where circuit preachers rained fire and brimstone on the heads of the wicked colonial aristocracy, but, like their neighbours, the McLaughlins drew the line at armed rebellion. Their caution was wise. When Mackenzie led his ragtag troops down Toronto's Yonge Street on December 6, 1837, they broke ranks and fled into the bush as soon as the first shots were fired.

Along the freezing creeks and ravines of Darlington township, the weary, frightened men who tapped on certain doors at night were given food and a bed, then guided to hiding places in the marshes. Some Patriots made their way across the lake by canoe and rowboat; others took refuge with Thomas Henry at the mouth of Oshawa Creek. Henry was a man of such staunch Christian principles he was never suspected of being a rebel supporter.

"His house, barn and even cellar were often occupied by those who dared not be seen abroad," recalled Mrs. P. A. Henry. "Here they were concealed, fed and comforted until an opportunity could be found for them to cross the lake and take refuge on Republican soil. More than once his sons and his team met the lonely wanderers at appointed places along the shore and brought them to a safe retreat. And the same agents conveyed them to out of the way places, where they could embark on some American vessel bound for the 'other side.'"

Had Elder Henry been caught, he could have been deported to Australia, or hanged, like his good friends, Samuel Lount and Peter Matthews, whose public executions he witnessed the following spring. Henry saved a rebel neighbour, Dr. James Hunter, by testifying that he was visiting Hunter on the evening of the rebellion, and in the spring he concealed Hunter in a shanty in the marsh at the mouth of Oshawa Creek until he could be smuggled aboard a schooner. Henry's seventeen-year-old son, John, who will play a prominent role in Robert

McLaughlin's life, masterminded the fugitive doctor's daring escape.

"Between 12 and 1 o'clock that night," writes Mrs. Henry, "two figures instead of one emerged from the shanty, and proceeded cautiously towards the point where the red skiff was concealed. It was a wild, dark night, but the young man's accustomed feet led the way, and the doctor followed with nervous tread. They reached their destination safely, and found the skiff where he had left it. They looked out over the water, and for a moment stood silent, almost irresolute. The wind was blowing almost a gale, breaking the water into yeasty waves, mixed with fragments of floating ice. The dauntless young man launched his boat among the seething waves, and ordered the doctor to lie flat on the bottom. The gentleman at first demurred at this arrangement, but being bluntly informed that he must obey orders or he would be left to look after himself, submitted, and the frail craft was soon tossing among the breakers.

"Clouds of inky blackness enveloped the sky, and entirely hid the schooner from their view, but the intrepid oarsman held on his way until a fiercer gust of wind made a rift in the clouds, and gave him a glimpse of the masts of the vessel. As they passed the outlet of the marsh, cakes of ice were floating seaward, and a large piece came in contact with the little skiff, threatening to capsize it. The doctor made a move to rise, but an assurance from John, that a blow from his oar would quiet him if he did not keep quiet, caused him to lie still, until they drew up on the lee-ward side of the vessel, and the little red skiff was made fast to a rope, which John knew would be hanging in a convenient place near the stern of the boat.

"Shortly after this, two dark figures might have been seen climbing into the schooner, if anyone had been there to see them. They stood on the stern deck, and a dark hole, just about large enough to admit a man's body, was before them. This led down into a small, dark place only a few feet square, where odds and ends which were desirable to have out of sight were usually thrown. John, taking his hand, helped him lower himself into his snug quarters, and then putting on the 'hatch,' was soon after in the berth with the mate, to whom he dared to communicate his success only by a *nudge*, which was answered in the same way. After waiting until certain that no one had been disturbed, Billy Barrow crept softly on deck, and proceeded to put large bolts in the corners of the 'hatch,' to give it the appearance of great security.

Then he closed the cracks with oakum and pitch, having previously prepared a place for ventilation from the freight room." The schooner passed inspection in the morning, and, says Mrs. Henry, Dr. Hunter "reached the Republic in safety."

The Americans were more than allies in the Reformers' fight against the Family Compact; they were family. Thousands of Yankees had moved north since the 1776 Revolution; some were Loyalists, some had fled for safety, but many came to take up free land offered by Canada's first governor, John Graves Simcoe. Sailing ships of all sizes plied back and forth across the lake, enmeshing the frontier villages on both sides in a dense, invisible web of mutual self-interest; commercially, the traffic across Lake Ontario was as important as that creeping along its coasts, and free trade was encouraged by the fact that Canadian ports seldom bothered to open a customs house.

John McLaughlin felt at home among enterprising men like the Henrys. By 1840, he had title to both his lots and he became, at the age of twenty-eight, the largest landowner in his family. His farm was beautiful land, high and rolling, bordered on the east by a stream that widened into a millrace for the mill in the village of Tyrone, and, on the south, by concession road 7. The hardwood forest was so dense that when he went out to chop wood he had to blaze a path to find his way home.

"We plunged at once into the deep forest, where there was absolutely no road, no path, except that which is called a blazed path, where the trees marked on either side are the only direction to the traveller," wrote Irish author Anna Brownell Jameson in the summer of 1837. "How savagely, how solemnly wild it was! So thick was the overhanging foliage, that it not only shut out the sunshine, but almost the daylight; and we travelled on through a perpetual gloom of vaulted boughs and intermingled shade. There were no flowers here – no herbage. The earth beneath us was a black, rich vegetable mould, into which cart wheels sank a foot deep; a rank, reedy grass grew around the roots of the trees, and sheltered rattlesnakes and reptiles. The timber was all hard timber, walnut, beech, and bass-wood, and oak and maple of most luxuriant growth; here and there the lightning had struck and had shivered one of the loftiest of these trees, riving the great trunk in two, and flinging it horizontally upon its companions. There it lay, in strangely picturesque fashion, clasping with its huge boughs their outstretched arms as if for support. Those which had been hewn to open a path lay where they fell, and over their stumps and roots the cart had to be lifted or dragged."

Mrs. Jameson, an avid reader of Goethe, saw Canada through the eyes of the Romantic poets; the bush was Nature, and Nature was Sublime, although she was disappointed in Niagara Falls. For pastoral people like John McLaughlin, the Canadian wilderness had no resonance in personal experience, no metaphor in the desert stories of the Bible; the darkness at noon evoked a pagan, pre-Christian Celtic Britain before the sacred groves were chopped down. For a Presbyterian, it was also the domain of Beelzebub, lord of the flies, black-flies, wasps, mosquitoes, gnats, and no-see-ums that bit chunks of flesh from McLaughlin's neck and made his hands swell to twice their normal size.

"The axe of the chopper relentlessly levels all before him," Catharine Traill observed. "Man appears to contend with the trees of the forest as though they were his most obnoxious enemies; for he spares neither the young sapling in its greenness nor the ancient trunk in its lofty pride; he wages war against the forest with fire and steel." The forest was clear-cut, the stumps left to rot. Mrs. Traill, a bird-watcher and collector of wild flowers, took delight in this wilderness holocaust:

"We had a glorious burning this summer after the ground was all logged up; that is, all the large timbers chopped into lengths, and drawn together in heaps with oxen. My husband, with the men-servants, set the heaps on fire; and a magnificent sight it was to see such a conflagration all round us. If the weather be very dry, and a brisk wind blowing, the work of destruction proceeds with astonishing rapidity; sometimes the fire will communicate with the forest and run over many hundreds of acres. This is not considered favourable for clearing, as it destroys the underbrush and light timbers, which are almost indispensable for ensuring a good burning. It is, however, a magnificent sight to see the blazing trees and watch the awful progress of the conflagration, as it hurries onward, consuming all before it, or leaving such scorching mementoes as have blasted the forest growth for years."

Potash from the burning of the Canadian forest could be traded with the local merchants for seed and tools, and the seed, broadcast by hand or worked in with a primitive harrow, produced crops of miraculous abundance. Grain prices were good, and by 1841, when Canada West's first census taker knocked on the door of John and Eliza McLaughlin's log house, he noted in his cramped, spidery hand that they had one hundred acres in potatoes, thirty acres each in barley, oats, and wheat, and five in corn. They owned five head of cattle, four hogs, but no horses – oxen weren't counted – and they had made forty pounds of maple sugar the previous year. Eliza had also woven twenty-two yards of fine cloth, an indication that she equalled her husband in skill and industriousness, and she had given birth to two more children. No one in the family was reported to be "blind, idiots or lunatics."

John McLaughlin served as a tax assessor for Darlington township, testimony to his intelligence and integrity, and in politics he was an avid disciple of George Brown, publisher of the Toronto *Globe* and scourge of Tory corruption. McLaughlin was also a thorn in the flesh of the backwoods distillers and tavern-keepers.

"You could get whiskey, and the very best of it, at twenty cents a gallon," Robert McLaughlin recalled years later. "Whiskey was drunk at most of the 'raising bees' at that time, though few took it to excess. My father never touched it, and would not have it at his 'bees,' and the neighbours used to say that they would not come to them. But they were all good-hearted people, and would be sorry for their stand, and when the time came would all turn in and help."

McLaughlin marched to his own drummer, and many must have found him a self-righteous pain in the neck: in later years, his grand-son, Sam, thought him crotchety, but Sam could be stubborn too. A perceptive portrait of John McLaughlin is provided by his friend and fellow Presbyterian, J. B. Fairbairn, in his *History and Reminiscences of Bowmanville*:

"He lived near Tyrone, and was indefatigable in his efforts to keep the congregation together after it was established at Enniskillen. He gave liberally of his time and means for that purpose, was for years a leading elder and was looked up to by the membership and held in the greatest respect. He was a most useful citizen, well educated and well informed, an original thinker and thoroughly independent in his opin-ions. He was at one time jointly with the late James McClellan, Bowmanville, appointed Census Commissioner for the township. They resolved at whatever place they were entertained overnight they would have family worship. They adhered to that resolution. It wanted moral courage thus to avow their principles. Both were the kind of men to act on their convictions."

This was likely John McLaughlin, whose neat script recorded his family still living in their single-storey log house in the census of 1851. There were five children: Robert, William, James, John, and Mary Jane. Robert, now fifteen, was described as a "labourer," but the younger children were all in school. The presence of a local school was another tribute to McLaughlin's zeal. Public money for education in Upper Canada had for years been monopolized by the Church of England, and as a consequence the heretic population was largely illiterate. Ignorant parents often begrudged the hours school took from their children's chores, and resented the money they had to pay toward a teacher and a schoolhouse they saw no use for. Schools were shacks equipped with a few hard benches and, with luck, some dog-eared British primers praising the glories of Empire. "I passed some school-houses built by the wayside," wrote Mrs. Jameson. "Of these several were shut up for want of a schoolmaster, and who that could earn a subsistence in any other way would be a schoolmaster in the wilds of Upper Canada? Ill fed, ill clothed, ill paid, or not paid at all – boarded at the houses of different farmers in turn, I found some few men, poor creatures! always either Scotch or American, and totally unfit for the office they had undertaken."

Robert McLaughlin vividly recalled his schooling: "There were some teachers who applied the rod too freely," he told a *Globe* reporter, "but others did not run to that extreme. I think my first teacher was a man named Brady. He was a good-natured fellow. In the spring when we had studied pretty well – there were not many of us in those days – he would say: 'Well, boys, you have done good work, so you can all go fishing.'"

Mr. Brady, Robert remembered, "was firmly convinced that the world did not revolve around the sun. He took his scientific fact from the Bible. When the scholars would ask why we could not see the sun at night, the answer always was that the sun had moved, not the earth." In Free Kirk Enniskillen, Mr. Brady no doubt found God to be a safer authority than Copernicus.

Robert's penmanship would always be crabbed, his grammar and spelling idiosyncratic, but he acquired a forceful command of the English language, enough arithmetic to keep accounts, and a healthy scepticism. Robert, lean and sinewy like his father, was an introspective young man with shaggy blond hair and a penetrating stare. Robert cared nothing for the past; he looked to the future, and he had an idea that was revolutionary in its simplicity.

2

FLASH

"My father wanted me to follow the farm," Robert McLaughlin reminisced to the *Globe* reporter in 1919, "but somehow or other I had a feeling I should not do that. I always seemed to have a sort of mechanical turn about me. When I was a young fellow I used to spend a good deal of my time in making axe handles. Everybody used the axe then, and I did quite a business selling them. What I got for them I would take into Bowmanville and buy tools. I kept at it until I obtained a real set of tools. Then I was happy. With the tools I did all the carpentry and repair work needed about the place."

Although a boy in the backwoods, Robert McLaughlin had a clear grasp of industrial economics. Other farmers regarded the giant hardwood trees as worthless impediments to be cleared from the land and reduced, at best, to potash. Robert, however, saw the trees as a valuable crop, but, like flax or hemp, the wood first had to be manufactured into something useful for people to buy. What could be better than axe handles? He could sell axe handles to farmers to chop down trees so he could fashion them into axe handles to sell to farmers to chop down trees *ad infinitum*. Axe handles were not only in demand, they broke and had to be replaced. Robert, whittling and sanding in a corner of the McLaughlin barn, had, in a single stroke, hit upon the principles of value-added manufacture, consumer demand, mass production, and planned obsolescence. And he reinvested his profits to upgrade his technology.

Robert McLaughlin boldly proclaimed that his axe handles were the best in Bowmanville. They certainly established his reputation, and they were not easy to make; the wood had to be prime, free of faults, and shaped to get the proper weight and heft. Robert marked each handle with his initials; he took pride in his craftsmanship and his talent for advertising would soon match his genius as a capitalist.

On his trips to Bowmanville to trade for tools, Robert bought artist's oil paints. "I had the knack of handling the brush," he told Floyd Chalmers of the *Financial Post*, "and I liked to do that." He had no art lessons – there was no one to teach him – and he copied illustrations from books and newspapers onto scrap boards. His landscapes bear no resemblance to the countryside around Tyrone. They are weird, murky, surreal dreamscapes featuring pale, humped mountains, scrawny spruce trees, and flat, melancholy lakes. McLaughlin was no Krieghoff or Paul Kane, but he was learning a great deal about the chemistry of paint, knowledge, as the *Globe* noted, "that stood him in good stead in the years to come."

Robert's *beaux arts* would have been appreciated by a family accustomed to manufacturing almost everything it needed, from soap, salt pork, and pickles to quilts, cloth, chairs, and candles. John McLaughlin's household was a self-contained cottage industry, and while they were now property owners, and their prosperity had increased a thousand-fold, they still lived in a rural culture not all that different from the one they had left. In the early years, they didn't own a wagon or a cart: the oxen dragged their bags of grain to the grist mill on a stone boat. Robert walked the seven miles to Bowmanville and back; everybody walked. Only the circuit preacher, Dr. Thornton, owned a horse. Once a month he held a service in one of the farmhouses, standing with his back to the roaring fireplace, his congregation seated before him in a parable of Hell: in the first circle, they roasted; in the outer circle, they froze. The settlers' lives were governed by God, the sun, and the seasons; their rituals and beliefs were closer in time to 1651 than 1851.

Tradition determined that Robert, the eldest son, would inherit the farm, whether he wanted to or not, and in return he was expected to help the younger boys strike out on their own. It was John McLaughlin's ambition to establish all his sons on farms in the neighbourhood, creating a dynasty in one generation, but all the cheap land had been taken up and prices were rising; their money would have to be carefully hoarded and cleverly spent, and the backbreaking toil of earning it fell to the boys themselves.

"My father tried to make a farmer out of me," Robert told Chalmers. "I made a very poor farmer. I got very tired of it." Robert, however, was an obedient son, a strait-laced puritan who shared his father's phobia of whisky. Robert's one vice was chewing tobacco, a habit among men that was almost universal in rural areas, perhaps because it was the only indulgence the preachers did not condemn. Unlike his father, Robert had little interest in acquiring money; his pride lay in his reputation for quality work and honest dealing.

It was the third son, James, who had the good fortune to be sent to Toronto to study medicine. Robert educated himself, reading whatever newspapers or magazines he could get his hands on – *Blackwood's* and the London *Illustrated News* for style and engravings, the *Globe* for its Liberal politics, and the local papers for gossip – and by 1864, the year Dr. James McLaughlin opened his practice in Bowmanville, Robert was reading by the bright yellow light of a new coal-oil lamp.

In 1859, a well had been drilled in the black ooze near Oil Creek, Pennsylvania, and a fountain of oil spouted out of the ground. While the gusher had created a frenzy of speculation, crude oil, like timber, had to be refined, and in Cleveland, Ohio, Robert's young contemporary, John D. Rockefeller, was cautiously laying the foundations for Standard Oil. Nobody as yet knew exactly what oil was good for, except it burned like hell; gas was so dangerous it was burned off in the drilling or refining stages, and for the next fifty years, gasoline would be used primarily as a lighting and dry-cleaning fluid.

Unlike Cleveland, the streets of Bowmanville were not slick with oil, and John McLaughlin's territorial ambitions had gone awry: no neighbour would sell him land for the low price McLaughlin was willing to pay. Like all the families in the township, the McLaughlins faced the predicament they had come to Canada to escape: small farms and big families. They were landlocked. John McLaughlin was fortunate to have two hundred acres of good soil; many large families had one hundred acres or less, and, once cleared, much of the land turned out to be sandy or swampy. After thirty years of continuous cropping, all of the farms were becoming exhausted, but their owners were reluctant to leave them for an uncertain future in the cities.

Famine in Ireland, coupled with an aggressive British emigration policy, had brought hundreds of thousands of new settlers to Upper Canada – now called Canada West. The Crimean War, 1853 to 1856, followed by the outbreak of the American Civil War in 1861, had created a boom market for Canadian grain, and the newly prosperous farmers, eager to acquire more land, drove up the price of real estate. Grain merchants and land speculators made fortunes, and John McLaughlin became a backwoods banker.

Cash was monopolized by the Conservative merchants of Toronto and Montreal, who lent it to themselves, and kept their banknotes, as much as possible, out of the soiled hands of the rural rabble, especially Liberal rabble. Banks were few and far between in the countryside, and those that did exist had an unpleasant habit of going broke when some financial bubble burst. Farmers wisely kept their cash in a tobacco tin, and if the tin was empty, they borrowed from the miller, tavern-keeper, or a friend. The exchange was usually sealed with an IOU specifying the rate of interest and expiry date, and the "notes," bits of paper endorsed with a series of signatures, were passed from hand to hand in lieu of hard currency. These paper pyramids tended to collapse: when the bottom dropped out of the wheat market at the end of the Civil War in 1865, it ruined Oshawa's leading merchant, John Warren, and swallowed the savings of the farmers who had trusted him to manage their financial affairs.

John McLaughlin was more adept at managing this informal economy: he had at least $3,500 invested in farm mortgages. Nobody defaulted, and when Robert left home in 1864, he too became mortgaged to his father. John sold Robert fifty acres on the western boundary of the family farm for $800; he had purchased the property in 1849 for $400. John was not a generous man: the land would have made a fine wedding present for Robert and his bride.

Robert married his neighbour, Mary Smith, on February 5, 1864. Mary was 21, a lovely young woman with an oval face, a wide, expressive mouth, and a roguish glint in her eye. The Smiths were Scots, and from now on the McLaughlins would identify themselves more with Canada's highland merchant princes than with the Roman Catholics, Fenians, and factory workers whose endless "troubles" had come to define the Irish identity in North America.

Mary, Robert's wife.
(*Ewart McLaughlin Collection*)

Robert built a house of sawn lumber on his land. He felled the trees, cut them to length, hauled them to the sawmill, then hauled the lumber back to the site and put up the house. Beside it, he made a barn to store his hay and tools. He didn't own very much, and his barn was really a woodworking shed. Robert loved the smell and feel of wood, the subtle patterns of the grain and the soft, golden browns of walnut, oak, and ash, but he had no training as a cabinetmaker, and he was losing his market for axe handles to the factories.

Robert turned his hand to making whiffletrees. Farmers were trading in their oxen for horses, and there was a growing demand for wagon parts. Robert needed the money. By 1867, the year Canada became a nation, he and Mary had two children, John James, age two, and an infant daughter, Mary Jane. The McLaughlins had no particular reason to rejoice in Confederation. A despised Tory government was led by the drunken reprobate, Sir John A. Macdonald, and Liberal leader George Brown had been defeated by an Oshawa Conservative, T. N. Gibbs. To the True Grits, Confederation was still a pig in a poke, politics a game for boodlers and lawyers.

Robert was much more interested in the activities of Joseph Hall in Oshawa and the Massey family in nearby Newcastle. Hall and the Masseys, both from New England, were buying American patents and manufacturing agricultural machinery that could do the work of a dozen men in a fraction of the time. The mechanical binder was a marvel, and even tight-fisted farmers were willing to pay cold, hard cash for a machine that combined Progress with Practicality. Canada had entered the Age of Iron.

"Iron was the universal material of the late nineteenth century," writes historian William Kilbourn. "It stood for all that was good and rich and strong and modern. Sleep was sounder on an iron bedstead, learning more solid on a school desk anchored on cast iron grills."

The fashion for iron began with the invention of the kitchen stove, a cleaner, safer, and more efficient device for cooking and heating than an open fireplace. The steam locomotive – the "iron horse" – symbolized speed, power, and adventure. Iron standards for gas lamps were decorative as well as modern, and for Canada's new Gothic Revival houses of parliament, wrought-iron ornamentation was de rigueur. Iron also came to represent the most sacred of all Victorian virtues: hygiene. Iron pipes kept water purer and made underground sewage possible; the Queen herself patronized Mr. Crapper's flush toilet, and the modesty of bathing in a private room was preferable to sharing the communal kitchen washtub. As Kilbourn observes: "The iron bathtub in the home became associated with progress, morality and the sacred right of individual free enterprise."

Joseph Hall had established his iron works in Oshawa, fifteen miles southwest of Tyrone, in 1857. The Joseph Hall Iron Works was Canada's first American branch plant – Hall's main factory was in Rochester, New York – and it produced everything from engines, farm machinery, and printing presses to castings and carriage parts. Moulded iron was plentiful in Oshawa and, for a hard bargainer like Robert McLaughlin, cheap. But Robert wasn't a blacksmith, or a machinist, and there wasn't much demand for buggies in the back concessions. Farmers used their wagons in the summer; in spring and fall the roads were impassable and in the winter people travelled by sleigh. The deep snow drifted in the concession roads, and once the streams and rivers froze, a sleigh could zip across country with wonderful speed.

"We had splendid fun," Robert later remembered. "There were parties every week. One household would ask all their neighbours in for an evening. Then a few days later, one family of all the guests would in their turn have all to their place, and so the round would go." There would be fiddling and singing, games of euchre, a step dance, tea served with doughnuts and cakes, and, late at night, the cold, exhilarating ride home. Winter was the time for courtship and marriage, and for marketing.

"I stood at my window today watching the sleighs as they glided past," Anna Jameson wrote in *Winter Studies and Summer Rambles in Canada.* "They are of all shapes and sizes. A few of the carriage-sleighs are well appointed and handsome. The market-sleighs are often two or three boards nailed together in the form of a wooden box upon runners; some straw and a buffalo skin or blanket serve for the seat; barrels of flour and baskets of eggs fill up the empty space. Others are like cars, and others, called *cutters,* are mounted on high runners, like sleigh phaetons; these are sported by the young men and officers, and require no inconsiderable skill in driving."

Anybody could make a sleigh, but Robert McLaughlin grasped the logic behind Mrs. Jameson's observations: if sporty young men drove cutters, then cutters were driven by sporty young men, however dirty, gnarled, and grizzled they may appear to others. Robert decided he would build a "dream" machine. "I made my first cutter in the old log cabin on the farm in 1863," he told Floyd Chalmers. "Even when I settled down on the 50-acre farm in 1864, I continued to make cutters in one corner of the barn. I painted them up and added little decorations that looked nice. I got more fun out of that than out of the farming."

Robert had acquired an old bound set of Volume II of *The Coach Maker's Illustrated Monthly Magazine,* published by C. W. Saladee in Columbus, Ohio, in 1856. The magazines carried detailed articles on every aspect of carriage-making, and gave precise specifications for building a variety of fancy buggies and sleighs. Robert adapted the drawings to his skill and resources and designed his own cutter: a scallop-shell body slung in an *art nouveau* frame as strong as it was graceful. The body was painted vermilion, the padded seat upholstered in green twill, and the runners shod with iron. The McLaughlin cutter, with its curled dashboard, was fast, light, and a perfect place to steal a kiss.

It was deceptively difficult to make. For the body, Robert soaked poplar boards in water, bent them to achieve their curved shape, then glued and bolted them together. The wood had to be dried, sanded, puttied, painted, and coated with varnish. He hired a travelling upholsterer, J. B. Keddie, who drove out to the farm with a wagonload of horsehair and dry moss. Keddie did an excellent job, but the real work lay in the cutter's frame and runners, and for that McLaughlin had to rely on a blacksmith. He was probably James Best of Oshawa, who later claimed to have made the ironwork for the first McLaughlin carriage – Robert rarely gave public credit to his collaborators – and Best irritated McLaughlin by arriving days late. Nonetheless, while still rough and homemade, the cutter was, to use one of Robert's favourite expressions, the "tastiest" job of work ever seen on concession road 7.

A neighbour offered to buy it right out of the shed, but Robert refused to sell his prototype. He built another cutter, sold it to his neighbour, then, as word spread, he built another, and another, and another. The Enniskillen hotelkeeper, however, was not satisfied with McLaughlin's standard one-horse model. "He came to me and said he wanted one with 'a real flash to it,'" Robert said. "I offered to paint on the panels a landscape scene, and he said 'Go ahead.' When he bought that cutter, and began to go round the country with it, you could see that landscape scene a quarter of a mile away. Everybody began asking who made the cutter, and he told them all. That is the first advertising I ever got."

According to legend, the scene depicted William of Orange crossing the Boyne River on his white horse. (A McLaughlin cutter with this handpainted logo is preserved at Upper Canada Village). Robert, having anticipated the custom spray-painted van, began to make wagons, and decorated them to order with landscape scenes. "When I made my first wagon, I pounded every rivet until I knew it was perfect," he said, "and I shaped every spoke until I knew it too was perfect." He spared no expense – he took parts to Toronto to get the work properly done – and he exhibited his finished products at the Bowmanville fair. Robert discovered that his customers willingly paid a higher price for products they believed to be better, and if McLaughlin's name was on his product, so was his reputation.

In 1867 Robert McLaughlin faced a critical choice: his expensive sideline was taking too much of his time, and his shed had become too small for his volume of work. He had to decide if he should remain a local handyman, the poor farmer who makes wagons and cutters for his neighbours, or if he had the "push" to go into business. The venture would require capital, and he would lose caste in the community as well as disappoint his father. Robert was calling himself a "carriage-maker," but duty, and the fear of losing his land, much as he hated it, kept him rooted until 1869, when he moved his family four miles west to the village of Enniskillen. Robert built his first carriage works, a rough-hewn, two-storey shed, on the main street a few yards south of the Methodist church (a strategy that guaranteed his merchandise a good crowd of gawkers on Sundays), and his family lived in a small log house beside the Presbyterian church across the road. Robert had a staff of four: "one Blacksmith, one Body and Wheel Maker, one Apprentice, and the proprietor."

In Toronto, another daring young Irish Protestant, Timothy Eaton, employed five people in his new dry-goods store on Yonge Street, and, to the horror of the merchant establishment, Eaton *sold his wares for cash.* Cash was vulgar; a gentleman's credit was as good as his signature, and the greater his credit, the higher his standing in the community. Bills were confidential: they were paid discreetly at the end of the month, or not paid at all. Coins were given to the poor: cab drivers, newsboys, servants, labourers, and prostitutes. Money was associated with filth and vice, and men who traded in coin were regarded as usurers or thieves.

But Eaton was astute: Ontario farmers, careful and frugal by habit, had hoarded their gold for thirty years. They had cash, and a powerful craving to spend it. They built new brick houses with running water and gingerbread trim, and displayed their overstuffed, factory-made furniture in their front parlours. The parlour door was kept shut, and the heavy drapes were drawn to keep the sun from fading the wallpaper. Only clergymen were entertained in the parlour, and corpses were laid out there before interment. The parlour was a shrine to the pagan gods of the ruined woodland: the floor was planked pine or maple, painted or covered with an Axminster rug; the straight-backed chairs were made of golden oak; the desk was burled walnut; and the horse-hair sofa, carved with ornamental figleaves, was flanked by marble-topped tables of cherry or bird's-eye maple. Every respectable parlour had an upright piano, and its walls were decorated with formal portrait photographs or framed etchings, cut from magazines, of Scottish highland scenes. Robert McLaughlin's cutters and carriages were extensions of the Ontario parlour, a mobile, practical, and highly visible way the country bourgeoisie could advertise its prosperity.

Robert was also poised to capitalize on the mass exodus from the land of farmers' sons now forced to seek work in cities and villages. Good jobs were few. Ontario's economy was dependent on British financiers so infatuated with corrupt and foolish railway speculations they bankrupted entire municipalities. Trade with Great Britain was assumed to be the sole purpose of Canadian enterprise; industrialization smacked of disloyalty and republicanism. The republic to the south, however, was pushing energetically westward, and hundreds of thousands of young Canadians crossed the Great Lakes to boom towns in Michigan, Indiana, Ohio, and Wisconsin: even immigrants to Canada travelled on to the United States.

The homeless who remained were called "tramps," a contemptuous word used by Thomas Conant to denounce "a class of persons whose filth and foul diseases are the result of laziness and their own vices." This proletarian army – critics called it "an irrepressible stampede" – tramped from town to town, sleeping in haystacks and begging for food. Tramps were accused of stealing chickens, freeloading in jail, and setting fire to barns by surreptitiously smoking their pipes. "Bums" included alcoholics, thieves, and ne'er-do-wells, but most of them were looking for honest work. The "underemployed" would spend the winters in the northern logging camps, then move to the sawmills in spring; summer would bring them south for the harvest, and in the fall they would pick apples. The tramps carried all their worldly possessions on their backs, and with virtually no expenses, many of them were able to live as well, or better, than the employed.

Wages in Ontario were pitifully low. The bottom line was set by the farmers: a hired hand worked an eighteen-hour day for scarcely more than his room and board, if he got fed at all. "The labourer had no rights save to the pay agreed between him and his employer, who usually considered it only common sense and responsible financial management to shave that pay in any way he could," writes W. H. Graham in *Greenbank*, a social history of a rural community fifteen miles northwest of Enniskillen. "The labourer had no recourse save to a local Justice of the Peace, whose interests coincided only too often with those of the farmers. Until 1879, the labourer could not join with his peers to demand a better deal because that was against the law. The Master and Servant Act forbade 'any tavern keeper, boarding house keeper or other person' to persuade servants or labourers to 'confederate for demanding extravagant or high wages.' No tavern or boarding house keeper could seize more than six dollars worth of a man's clothing to cover his bill; the practice of taking all a debtor's clothing prevented him from going out to work."

Among the gangs of men on the roads were skilled tradesmen who carried their own tools from job to job. Robert could hire an experienced man for a dollar or two a day, a labourer for much less; apprentices, usually boys of twelve to fourteen, lived in virtual bondage. The sale of one cutter, at a going price of fifty dollars, paid a month's wages for Robert's three employees. How many cutters could they make in a month? One? Three? Ten? The principle of the assembly line was in place; McLaughlin was already noting exactly how much time each man spent on a job: "C. N.: Wed. Sept 8th, half past three; finished Monday 20th at 10 a.m. less one-half day mending, one-half day on wheel, one-half day absent." He records that C. N. began a new job on Tuesday the twenty-first at 11 a.m. and finished Thursday night, the twenty-eighth.

Labour was a significant expense. One ledger itemizes the cost of a ladies' phaeton. Out of a total of $117.44 for the body and ironwork, the ironwork comes to $60.25, the wheels $18.50, the body $12 and painting $11.50. Labour on the ironwork accounts for $29 out of the $60.25. On the trim and upholstering, labour comes to $15 out of $36.80. McLaughlin's attention to detail was microscopic: 70 cents for tacks and thread, 37 cents for a whipholder, 30 cents worth of cotton cloth and 6 cents for buttons. He adds a $30.84 profit to the total to bring the selling price to $185. This rig may have won prizes at the Bowmanville fair, but McLaughlin could see that the time involved was more than his business could bear, and he got out of building phaetons fast.

A photograph taken at the Enniskillen factory about 1872 shows that McLaughlin is prospering. His employees have increased to seven, and they stand proudly, feet apart, hands on hips. The handsome fellow in the centre, sporting a pocketwatch, a starched collar, and a loud checked shirt, may be the blacksmith, cleaned up for the event, and the cocky little man staring at the camera could be the clerk, whose quill calligraphy immortalized McLaughlin's daily accounts. The shabbiest man in the group is the proprietor: Robert McLaughlin's eyes peer out from above a bushy, unkempt beard, and he wears a shapeless tweed suit, but his jaunty, nautical cap declares his position as Enniskillen's captain of industry.

Robert's enormous left hand rests on the head of his son, George. George William, the third child, was born in 1869; another boy,

The employees of Robert McLaughlin's Enniskillen factory, c. 1872. Robert is second from left, his hand on the head of his son George. (*General Motors of Canada/McLaughlin Public Library*)

Robert Samuel, followed on September 8, 1871; and a daughter, Elizabeth, arrived in 1874. Little Sammy must have been too young to run around the factory; this was one of the rare photo opportunities that Sam McLaughlin ever missed.

A severe depression began in 1873, the aftershock of a financial panic in the United States. Banks collapsed, credit evaporated, grain prices fell, and merchants with overdue accounts went bankrupt. Robert made ends meet by doing repairs: he replaced broken iron pieces and spliced runners, repainted carriage bodies, and made new spokes for old wheels. His bookkeeper's entries for January 20, 1874, record that the factory put a new tongue in William Wedge's bobsleigh for $1.25, sold Ira Livingstone a new axe handle for 10 cents, sharpened William Pollack's saw for 15 cents, and put two new beams in Wedge's knee sleigh for $1.40.

No job was too small for McLaughlin: he made fork handles and wagon tongues, repaired whiffletrees, mended chairs, sold paint and hardware, and kept a meticulous record of every transaction. His father and brothers sent work his way – William was his steadiest customer – and he wasn't too proud to make a deal: on June 5, 1874, he sold James Madill a new buggy for $125, and took Madill's old buggy for $25.

Robert was also prepared to barter: on December 23, 1876, he sold Dean Sawyer one cutter for $40 "to be paid in good waggon sides, at $12 per m. at mill or $13 per m. at Enniskillen or $15.50 at Oshawa, $10 to be delivered this winter, balance in July, 1877." The next year, he contracted with Roland Campbell to build a wagon within three weeks on condition that Campbell "agrees to deliver for said waggon 76 cords good dry birch or maypole wood in winter of 1877–78."

McLaughlin had made a virtue of his location in the backwoods: "I was known in Bowmanville as the 'Country Carriagemaker,'" he told the *Globe*. "I don't know why my business was successful. I never considered that I had exceptional ability. The only reason I can think of is that I insisted from the start that only the best workmanship would go into my product. It cost more, but I never let this motto be broken. I was brought up amongst the trees, and I knew all about lumber, and had a good knowledge of varnishes and paints. I did my own buying, and watched all incoming material closely to see that I always got the quality I wanted."

It was a good thing Robert paid attention: in October 1877, he found that thirty-three of his customers owed him money. In some cases, it was a matter of one or two dollars, but other debts were substantial: Ezra Gifford owed $21, the Reverend Mr. Large $31, and John Munson $54.15. Robert sent the whole list "to I. Elford for collection." Mr. Elford was effective: by November 14 he had nabbed $32, and he brought in another $90 by the following March. Robert McLaughlin was winding up his business in Enniskillen. His shop was too remote – all his wood, iron, cloth, and leather had to be hauled in by wagon from Bowmanville or Oshawa – and the local market was saturated. The country carriage-maker was ready to go to town – and take a new wife.

Mary died on March 10, 1877. She was thirty-four. She had borne Robert five children in ten years, and had become thin and feverish, worn out by a persistent, hacking cough. The McLaughlins tried to pretend that Mary was frail, her illness a nagging chest cold: to call it by its real name would break a terrible taboo. Tuberculosis, the "white plague," was a deadly epidemic more tenacious than cholera. It was mysterious, highly infectious, and incurable. "Consumption," as tuberculosis was called, seemed to strike at random, and its victims, however long they survived, were treated as the living dead.

There are two significant entries in Robert's fragmentary housekeeping ledger for 1875: in May he paid a $14 doctor's bill, and on July 16 paid $1.35 "cash to Miss Parr" to bring her total to $5.35. Miss Parr was likely Sarah Jane, a spinster in her late thirties who was helping Mary with the household chores (Robert's secretary was a Miss Coffin). Unmarried women eked out a penurious existence as nannies and servants, and the five rambunctious McLaughlin children were a handful, especially Sam, a noisy little urchin with a talent for trouble.

"One day when I was five I wandered into the room where the wheels were hung from the ceiling to dry," Sam recalled later. "A wheel fell on me, knocking me out and opening a deep gash in my head. I was carried into my father's office – howling lustily as soon as I recovered my breath, I have no doubt – and while everyone else fussed around wondering what should be done next, the Governor solved the problem simply: he produced one of those brown-striped humbugs and gave it to me. The pain and tears stopped miraculously. After that, the family always said I had 'wheels in the head.'"

Sam's accident occurred the year his mother died. He grew up with no memory of her, but his vivid recollection of this sudden blow, a story he often repeated in his old age, suggests his injury became a parable to express the inarticulable pain he felt at his mother's loss. Sam placed himself at the centre of his own universe, a characteristic he shared with his father. Robert describes his response to Mary's death in a letter to a bereaved friend some years later: "I note what you say in reference to your not sleeping since your loss. I had precisely the same trouble. It was over four months in my case before I got a whole night's sleep. You should by this time have overcome your difficulty."

There is a chilling selfishness in the word "difficulty." Mary's death disturbed Robert's equanimity: he was tired and distraught; no one tended to the children at night; no one kindled the fire before sunrise; no one slept beside him, her harsh, hot breathing eased by opium. How could he keep his mind on business? Mary's illness was an inconvenience, her death a betrayal; Robert felt helpless and resentful. On January 17, 1878, less than a year after Mary's funeral, Robert McLaughlin married Sarah Jane Parr in St. Andrew's Presbyterian Church, Oshawa.

Apart from her will, written in 1896, Sarah Jane has left no personal record, no letters or snapshots, no children of her own, and she has been exorcised from McLaughlin history to such an extent that few people know she ever lived. Sarah Jane, obviously a woman of some gumption, was living alone in 1871 when the census recorded her working for a milliner in East Whitby township. She came from Brantford, Ontario, where her father was a carpenter, and she was a niece of the Parrs of Cavan township. By marrying her, Robert may have been repaying a family obligation, and securing an emotional bond with his birthplace.

His hasty wedding was unseemly in a Presbyterian community. Mourning customarily lasted at least a year, often a lifetime, and while McLaughlin had a young family, he also had the means to pay someone to keep house. Miss Parr's presence in his home must have caused talk – the country carriage-maker was very conscious of his public image – and Robert was infatuated enough to disregard the outrage of his children, who called their new mother "Steppie." An unpopular marriage was also a good way of propelling himself out of a claustrophobic environment, and in 1878, Robert McLaughlin and his family left Enniskillen, a move everyone predicted would be his ruin.

3

A BETTER BUGGY

"McLaughlin will last six months," scoffed Oshawa's carriage-maker, William Bambridge, when Robert set up his new buggy works on Oshawa's Simcoe Street. Bambridge's gloomy prediction was accepted wisdom, and even Robert's father and brothers had pleaded with him to settle in Bowmanville. Oshawa, a raw, rough village hacked out of a black ash swamp, was infamous for its bankruptcies and bottomless mud; Bowmanville, where the McLaughlins had done business for forty years, was a solid red-brick town. Robert was well-known and highly regarded there, and his brother, Dr. James McLaughlin, a Liberal, a sport, and a crack shot, had become, at thirty-eight, one of Bowmanville's most prominent citizens.

Dr. James McLaughlin lived at Rathskamory, an ugly country house in a four-acre park on the north edge of town. Rathskamory had been built by his predecessor, Dr. G. H. Low, as a model of an Irish gentleman's estate, and Dr. James was vain enough to pay for an illustration in Belden's Historical Atlas for 1878. The clumsy drawing shows a sketchy house surrounded by a glassed-in veranda and a conservatory, and a carriage rolls along a driveway curving through manicured lawns dotted with gazebos and artfully planted trees. The atlas misspells the name:

"Rathskamery: Residence of J. W. McLaughlin Esq. M.B. L.R. C.P. L.R.C.S. Bowmanville, Ont. Canada."

Robert, who until the end of his life signed himself simply "R. McLaughlin," had no desire to live in the shadow of "J. W. Esq." Robert was forty-two; his hair was thinning, his shoulders stooped, and he was ready to break free from his family's control. The Masseys were building an immense new factory in Toronto – a curious place to make farm machinery – and while he wasn't bold enough to leap that far, he realized that Bowmanville was too conservative, too rooted in the colonial past, to be the "pushing" kind of place he needed for his business to grow.

Besides, Bowmanville already had six carriage-makers, Oshawa only one, and Oshawa was nine miles closer to Toronto, a hustling little city that would soon dash Bowmanville's hopes of becoming anything more than a station stop on the railroad to Montreal. Oshawa had other attractions for McLaughlin: a Presbyterian congregation, a new public school for his children, a rabid Grit newspaper, the *Ontario Reformer*, and old allies in the families of Elder Thomas Henry and his son John. Oshawa's factories and tanneries provided ironwork, cabinetry, and leather, and, most significantly, a pool of highly skilled workmen who had come from the industrial cities of Ireland, Scotland, and the New England states.

The deciding factor was credit. The Ontario Bank in Bowmanville was Conservative and Methodist – banking, like everything else in Ontario, was a function of politics and religion – but Oshawa had a branch of the new Dominion Bank, owned by Liberal Presbyterians in Toronto, as well as a small local bank, the Western, whose president, John Cowan, was a man after McLaughlin's own heart.

Cowan, also an Irish Protestant, owned the Ontario Malleable Iron Company, with which Robert did business, and the two men shared a puritanical attitude to work: Cowan never missed a day at the office, or a Sunday at church, and the only other place he was known to go was the bank. He was modest and taciturn, a bachelor of scrupulous honesty and public charity whose greatest joy was his private library. McLaughlin was exactly the sort of man Cowan would lend money to, and Robert borrowed three thousand dollars from the Western Bank using his fifty-acre farm at Tyrone as collateral. With another three thousand dollars from the sale of a piece of his property in Enniskillen, he was able to erect in Oshawa a three-storey brick workshop with

Robert's children. Clockwise from left:
John James, Mary Jane, Sam, George,
and Elizabeth.
(McLaughlin Public Library)

large display windows in the front and a separate shed on one side for
the blacksmith. He employed eleven men.

Robert found a house near the Albert Street School, and he had his
children's photograph taken not long after they moved to town. A
more miserable, heartsick little group of waifs would be hard to find.
The boys are skin and bone, their suits too grown-up and big for them.
Mary Jane is only eleven, but her long blond hair, her pride and joy, is
pulled severely back from her forehead and her dress, already too
small, looks to be patched together from hand-me-downs. Lizzie, the
baby, is recovering from scarlet fever; her hair had been cut short
during her illness, and Steppie decided to keep it that way. Steppie
later cropped Mary Jane's hair too, because it was "easier," and Mary
Jane was cruelly ridiculed for looking like a boy.

The McLaughlins' frame house, like most in Oshawa, was set in a
large yard with an outhouse, a well, and a shed for chickens, firewood,
and a cow. The well water in the village was foul – typhoid was a perennial scourge – and sewage made its way into the roadside ditches and
creeks. Some families kept pigs, and they all took pride in their vegetable gardens. The gardens were a necessity for the factory workers.
Wages were poor enough, but when work was slow, men were laid off
without pay, and they would peddle eggs and potatoes, haul freight,
and do odd jobs for the boss. With no income tax and no property tax
– even levies for schools were bitterly debated – a village family could

get by on less than three hundred dollars a year, and many of them did. For a man of Robert's penny-pinching habits, Oshawa was ideal.

Oshawa set its watches by the sound of the noon whistle, and the village smelled of smoke, raw lumber, fresh paint, and tanning hides. Robert's new enterprise, grandly named the "Oshawa Carriage Works," was right in the middle of the action, halfway between the Hall Iron Works and the Gibbs Bros. Furniture Factory, two blocks north of the Kingston Road.

The Kingston Road, hacked out of the bush between 1816 and 1817, was Upper Canada's first serious attempt at road building, and its purpose was military. Britain's war with the United States in 1812–13 had been a near thing for the Canadian colonies, and in the event of future American naval aggression, Canada needed a safe overland supply route linking Montreal and Niagara. The Kingston Road ran inland from an overgrown lake-shore trail built in 1799 by an American contractor, Asa Danforth. The Danforth, as the western remnant of the road is still called in Toronto, began at the end of King Street with a sign that read "Road to Quebec" with a arrow pointing east. Early settlers found it quicker to walk along this trail than to travel by boat, but since no money was ever allocated to keep it in repair, the trestle bridges washed out and remote stretches reverted to swamp.

"The procedure in opening a road was always the same," Edwin Guillet writes in *Early Life in Upper Canada*. "An explorer went ahead, closely followed by two surveyors with compasses; blazers then notched trees intended to be the boundaries of the road, and woodmen chopped down those which were in the course of the roadway; gangs of men followed to clear away the trunks and the brush. It was quite usual to leave the stumps until they had rotted, and consequently the roadway was seldom absolutely straight even over small sections."

Stagecoach passenger Anna Jameson complained: "We often sank into mud-holes above the axle tree; then over trunks of trees laid across swamps, called here corduroy roads, where my poor bones dislocated. A wheel here and there, or broken shaft lying by the wayside, told of former wrecks and disasters. In some places they had, in desperation, thrown huge boughs of oak into the mud abyss, and covered them with clay and sod, the rich green foliage projecting on either side. By the time we arrived at Blandford, my hands were swelled and blistered by continually grasping with all my strength an iron bar in front of my vehicle, to prevent myself from being flung out, and my limbs ached woefully."

The Royal Mail was carried on the Kingston Road by foot, mule, horse, stagecoach, and sleigh, and as the freight increased, the farmhouses where the postmen stopped to rest grew into inns: Farewell's Tavern, between Whitby and Bowmanville, was one of the most popular. The inns, their beds so verminous wise travellers slept on the floor, offered dubious food and whisky, but the news was hot, even if it was months old, and the talk entertaining. The inns attracted peddlers and speculators, and in 1835 a Scottish merchant, Edward Skae, opened a general store on the Kingston Road one mile west of Farewell's Tavern. Skae occupied the southwest corner of the Simcoe Street crossing; a hotel, a tavern, and a rival store took up the other three corners, and the "Four Corners" became the commercial hub of Oshawa.

Simcoe Street was the brainchild of its namesake, Governor Simcoe, and its purpose was to open up the Canadian interior to traders and settlers. British army engineers, ignoring the well-worn Algonquin trail along the high banks of the Oshawa Creek (Oshawa, roughly translated, means "the place where the stream becomes the path") ran their road straight north through quicksand until it vanished into the Scugog marsh.

Oshawa was an unpromising place to sell carriages, and shipping was difficult because McLaughlin's shop was more than a mile north of the Grand Trunk Railroad station. The railway had been built from Montreal to Toronto in 1854, and its investors, finding all the property around the Four Corners already in private hands, had run their line through vacant land they had secretly purchased at bargain prices. Standing on the wooden sidewalk in front of his shop, McLaughlin could watch an endless procession of wagons laden with merchandise plod up and down Simcoe Street between the factories and the freight sheds, and ponder the greed and idiocy that made Canada such a hard place for an honest man to earn a dollar.

Robert lasted more than six months – it was the boastful Bambridge who went broke – but the Ontario economy remained in the grip of depression and the carriage trade was failing. Between 1871 and 1881, the number of carriage works in South Ontario County shrank from 30 to 22, their employees from 89 to 71. Total wages

Sporty John Beare, Greenbank farmer, in his old McLaughlin cutter, c. 1885. (G.K. Beare)

dropped from $28,000 to $18,300; value of production from $63,000 to $50,000. It was an anxious time, and McLaughlin sold the vacant north corner of his Simcoe Street lot to the town for a new city hall, fire hall, and jail.

There was little to distinguish McLaughlin's carriages from his competitors'. He dropped his curvaceous cutter – it was expensive to build – and he no longer painted landscapes on his carriage bodies. His English-style designs were square, standard, and utilitarian, and like everyone else he imported most of his parts from American suppliers. McLaughlin could control the quality of work produced by his own men, but not parts manufactured in Buffalo or Indianapolis, and it was Robert's irritation with carriage mechanics that prompted him to build a better buggy.

"It was, strangely for my father, whose great concern had been with the woodwork and who had hired others for the metal parts, an invention made of metal," Sam said later. "It was a new gear for buggies and carriages. The gear is all that part of a carriage between the body and the wheels – the springs, couplings, chassis and the mechanism that permits the front axle to turn and steer the vehicle. The McLaughlin gear had long flexible springs, couplings of Norway iron, brass and rubber washers, but the most important part was the turning mechanism. There's an old saying, 'as useless as a fifth wheel,' but the Governor belied that saying by incorporating a fifth wheel into the turning mechanism of his gear, and he patented it."

McLaughlin's gear, patented in 1880, made his carriages more comfortable and the horses easier to manoeuvre. Robert had a healthy respect for horses: he avoided them. In a letter to D. S. Brown in

Cannington, who offered a horse in trade, Robert frankly replied: "As I am no horseman, I don't know that I could handle a horse."

One of McLaughlin's biggest suppliers was a Guelph company, Kloepfer and Walker, and their travelling salesman, Tony Foster, was a popular caller at the Oshawa shop. Says Sam: "Tony Foster was a memorable and colourful figure, and we were always glad to see him come to the shop, dressed in a soft tweed hat, braided velvet coat, horse-blanket vest, yellow gloves, and carrying a cane. Tony sold upholstering material and hardware items, and he was always sure of an order from the Governor, even when we weren't really low on inventory. But this day Tony didn't have time for a sales talk. He took a look at a McLaughlin gear, leaned his ample weight on the springs, tested the fifth wheel steering mechanism and said:

" 'By Jove, Mr. McLaughlin, that's a fine-looking gear. I could sell some of those to my customers now.'

"The Governor thought of this idea for a moment, then said: 'All right, Tony, if you can sell them, we'll sell them to you.'

"Tony waited to hear no more. He hurried back to Guelph and described the gear to his boss, Chris Kloepfer. A couple of days later both Tony Foster and Mr. Kloepfer arrived early in the morning. They looked the gear over again, then spent the rest of the morning in the Governor's office.

"When my father came home at noon he held a solemn conference with his sons, two teenagers and me not yet in my teens. 'Boys,' he said, 'I have had an offer to sell the gear patent.' He paused. 'Ten thousand dollars.' Pause. 'That's a lot of money.' Pause. 'Will I take it?'

"I suppose that since he had done us the honour of consulting us on this very important matter we should have thought over the question for a minute or two. But we didn't. In one voice we chorused: 'No, don't sell it.' "

Robert instead offered Kloepfer exclusive rights to sell the McLaughlin gear across Canada, provided he took five hundred gears a year for two years. It was a deal.

"Until then our sales had been almost entirely local," said Sam. "Often a buyer would come to our shop with a horse and drive away in a new carriage. Now orders for gears and carriages started to come in from places that our shipper had never heard of, places far beyond Ontario in eastern and western Canada."

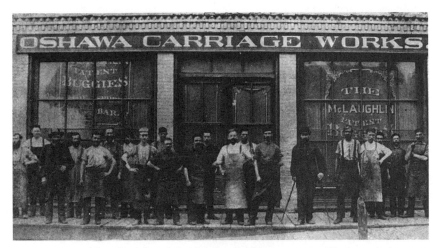

Robert McLaughlin, third from left, with his employees in 1887. His first upholsterer, J. B. Keddie, now foreman of the trim shop, is sixth from left. (*General Motors of Canada/Thomas Bouckley Collection, Robert McLaughlin Gallery*)

On his showroom window, in foot-high letters, Robert advertised "The McLaughlin Patent Buggy Gear." The gear looked like a skeletal steel grasshopper. It was inexpensive to make – McLaughlin sold them to Kloepfer for twenty-two dollars each – and it introduced to his shop the principle of mass marketing. Robert had been in the habit of touring the rural fall fairs to advertise his carriages; now his gear did the job.

"Carriage factories all over the country advertised their products as 'equipped with the wonderful new McLaughlin gear,'" said Sam. "That meant they were advertising *us*. People figured, 'If we're buying a carriage with a McLaughlin gear, why not buy the whole McLaughlin carriage?'"

Robert was fiercely protective of his patent rights: the discovery of imitations would provoke him to write vituperative letters denouncing "bastards and counterfeits" and threaten the offenders with court injunctions. His work was the great love of Robert's life, and an affectionate portrait is provided by his old friend, Dr. D. S. Hoig:

"Those early days, especially those spent in the first narrow quarters on Simcoe Street, where everyone knew everyone else – a lot of the men had come over from Enniskillen – were, I think, very happy ones for the Chief. The business had not yet grown beyond the point where it was within his personal control. He was very close to all the old

Interior of the carriage factory. (McLaughlin Public Library/Thomas Bouckley Collection, Robert McLaughlin Gallery.)

employees, and for many years it was his custom to walk through the shop, stopping here and there for a word or a joke, of which latter he was very fond. The travellers were always on the lookout for a good story to bring home to the 'Old Man,' as he was affectionately called by the office staff, and his hearty laugh of appreciation amply repaid their trouble. He was very popular with the men, particularly the older ones who knew him to be entirely fair in his dealings with them. I have heard men say – men who worked in the Enniskillen shop – that at that early period he gave every job a final inspection and that the slightest defect – a loose bolt or a rattling spoke – would ensure its being sent back for repair."

McLaughlin applied the same standards to his suppliers. "Please find note enclosed less price of glue which I have returned freight prepaid," he wrote to A. Ramsay & Sons, Montreal, in 1884. "I mistook the price quoted by your agent or he quoted wrong. I understood him to say it was $1.75 per gal. $3 per gal. is too high. Besides my body makers don't like to use it. They say they can make surer work with other glue."

Robert wrote hundreds of orders and remonstrances every year, scrawling them in black ink in letterpress books equipped with onion-skin copy pages. This one, to A. L. Farewell in June, 1885, is character-istic: "If your note due November 18/84 is not paid immediately I shall proceed at once to put it into court. Amount of note: principal – $51.70, interest – $4.05. Total: $55.75. Respectfully, R. McLaughlin."

McLaughlin usually sold his carriages for a cash down payment, the balance due in three to six months. Bad debts were a chronic misery, especially since Robert was in debt himself. On December 5, 1885, he wrote to R. Haney in Pickering apologizing for missing the due date on two loans for $55 and $35. "I find I am overdue at the bank and behind

$178. I have not found it so difficult to get along in a long time. I find that long credit is closing in on me. I pay 16 men every Saturday in cash. I get four months on material. Profit's very small. I have to scratch around to pay all I can when due. I am getting tired of it." Robert's optimism, however, shines through: "The darkest hour is before the daylight. Keep each tub on its bottom."

Haney was only one of McLaughlin's many sources of cash, and the previous November 13, Robert had failed to meet a $192 debt. "From the first part of this month I have had to pay $1,006. Before the first of next month I have got to pay over $600 more. I have to discount every dollar, collect all I can and borrow to get me over this month. You can guess I can ill afford to pay but as we are in the scrape we must get on with it and not squeal about it."

Robert was fighting back from ruin. "I am burned out," he wrote to Kloepfer on July 21, 1884. "Main building was set on fire in showroom. We saved only 4 finished buggies slightly damaged, 1st and 2nd storey gutted, all of 3rd storey damaged. Some no good. Not much we can use."

McLaughlin was fully insured, but Kloepfer was getting cold feet about the buggy gear. It had been harshly criticized by the competition, so McLaughlin added new rubber washers and advertised a "nicer gear than last year, solid improvement." He told Kloepfer that since Canada produced fourteen thousand buggies a year, Kloepfer would have to sell a gear to only one in twenty-eight buggies.

Threatening, pleading, hectoring, McLaughlin's business letters reveal his rigorous methods. In an 1881 letter to a prospective trimmer, William Wilwood, he wrote: "I will give you what you ask for, 11 months at the rate of $550 for 12 months. In the dead of winter there will be months that I could not make it pay to keep the trimming shop open. I would want you to fill in time helping me with office work such as keeping books, posting and making out accounts and various little things you could help me with by making yourself agreeable should you not be fully employed in the trimming shop. Should you accept my offer and things between us be suitable and agreeable very likely you would have a steady job for a number of years. My offer of course will be subject to the unforeseen calamities that would render it impossible to run my shops. If you accept my offer I would want it to be business as I want to notify my present man."

McLaughlin's search for the perfect workman was uncompromising.

To buggy-painter David Moore of Chatham, Robert wrote on December 13, 1884: "I want a good man that can do a good job and durable with push and strictly temperate. I also want a man to *settle down* and stay." Moore did not bite, or suit, and on January 17, 1885, McLaughlin wrote to W. H. Bosley in Belleville: "I want a man of energy and push, a first class striper and finisher, *strictly sober* and *reliable* in *word and principle*, careful in stock, keeps the shop in good order, a man that will want to settle down and make himself at home." Robert offered him $11.20 per week for winter, $12 for summer: "If times were not so very poor and money so tight I would not ask it." Yet five days later he wrote to a Mr. Plews in Toronto: "I am now all right and find I can sell all I can make easily. If you can give me security for 10 to 20 buggies I have no doubt we can do good business."

In a letter to J. C. Knox of Carlton Place, McLaughlin revealed he had taken a page from Timothy Eaton's book: "I have a good buggy and I enclose pamphlet and circular description of same. I will put the matter before you straight and square. If you want to handle the best buggy in the country and will secure me against any loss in the deal I will send you further particulars and quote you prices. Owing to losses in the house commission style we have been running, I have adopted the cash and security system, giving a little more profit to the dealers, making it a certainty there will be no losses."

By recruiting his best customers as his dealers, McLaughlin was able to expand his sales exponentially. He could sell a buggy to a dealer for seventy or ninety dollars, about thirty to fifty below retail price, allowing the dealer a substantial margin and relieving himself of the financial risk. McLaughlin was very choosy about the people who bought his buggies. In a letter marked *private* to dealer G. W. Hunt in Mohr's Corners, he wrote: "Regarding your man Lee, I know but little about him. If you had sold him a buggy I would call you a poor agent. I saw Lee in Toronto. He was talking buggy but I did not ask him for a deal because I did not know if he was good on credit. I would not sell to any unless I was sure except for cash. I got a letter about 10 days ago asking if I would sell him a buggy on six months. I did not answer it as I found he was not good. *Do not sell to him.* Perhaps I need not say to you, unless you can sell to perfectly good marks better keep them [the buggies] over. I am glad you were shrewd enough not to get beat with Lee. This is private. Don't quarrel with him. He could do us harm through the country. Don't mention to anybody anything I have wrote."

McLaughlin had a large network of informants who warned him about the finances and peccadilloes of his prospective dealers and employees, and he did not hesitate to entice a new "mark" into a cut-price deal with the admonition that "the price will be only between ourselves." The secret of McLaughlin's success was his vigilant and aggressive marketing, and he understood hard-sell advertising. On September 22, 1884, he scribbled this advertisement for *Grip* magazine in Toronto: "MCLAUGHLIN, Manufacturer of the Celebrated McLaughlin Patent Buggy Gear and Business Buggy. The simplest in construction made, easiest in motion, noiseless in use."

As his production increased, McLaughlin hired travelling salesmen to hustle advance orders. On February 22, 1886, John Henry was on his way to Orillia, where McLaughlin sent him a report that he had received orders for fifty-six gears in one week: "Don't you think the Old Man ought to have a twinkle in his eye? I mean, Henry, the next five miles is how we get them out if it keeps pouring down like this. The smith shop is now like a beehive. All busy as nailers. Don't stay to talk to doubtful marks. Go for the good ones. Keep cool and quiet unless you come across more chipmunks. I leave the matter with you. You know our margin is small. We can't run any risk. In case an agent only wanted a buggy for his own use, put five dollars more on our quotation for a single buggy. One thing I know, we will have all we can do unless the bottom falls out of our tub sooner than I seem to think."

Two days later, McLaughlin cautioned Henry again: "Don't call on doubtful men. Don't yield too far in terms. I think we will have our hands full with work. Don't push that end spring too much as it puts us out sometimes to drop off. Keep down all you can varnish buggies and varnish gears. It is very hard to get all white timber. More at present."

McLaughlin had learned all the tricks of the carriage trade, and the more work, the better. He never took a day off sick, or travelled anywhere except on business. In late summer, he shut the shop for two or three weeks to allow his men to pick apples and harvest their vegetable crops; only slackers complained that the Old Man could have afforded to pay them for their vacations. Men who disagreed with McLaughlin didn't last long. On March 7, 1885, Robert wrote to Thomas Chapman: "As I understand you to say you feel you cannot comply with the rules laid down in the shop the same as my other men do, and if you still feel unable to do so, you may consider yourself not in my employment after tonight. I am sorry to be forced to this to me unpleasant alternative but I cannot possibly avoid it especially in a foreman."

McLaughlin was always in the shop before the men arrived at 7 a.m., and he left long after the 6 p.m. whistle.

On January 9, 1885, he is bent over his desk in the office, rapidly writing out the last of the day's orders. The fire in the grate is low; his hands are getting cold. His heart is not in his work tonight, and as the twilight deepens, Mary's ghost slips into the room, silent as the snow sifting in on the windowsill. Robert abruptly turns a page, dips his nib in the inkwell, and begins a letter to his eldest son, now a young man of nineteen and a student at the Ontario College of Pharmacy in Toronto.

"Dear Johnny. Your grampa is gradually sinking. He might drop off any time. You will have to go to the funeral. I think you had better go. You would do well to remember that you are now passing through a critical period. The next five years will determine whether you will be spared to be a strong, healthy man or a weak one. It is largely in the care of you to take care of yourself. Get to bed as early as possible and get up early so that you can get the fresh atmosphere in the morning. I have noticed that you have a cough I don't like. Talking it over after you left with your Ma, she told me you did not wear drawers. This surprised me very much. In a climate like this such a course is suicidal to health. If it is so that you don't I am surprised to think you are so very foolish. It will surely tell on your health, if not now, later on. You have not good underclothing up there, shorts and drawers, and if they are not here buy some and put them on at once.

"Notice the various men that have risen in the world. You will find they have good sound bodies as a rule. About one-half the human race is pulling through life with pain more or less and to a disadvantage at getting along on account of weakness of constitution caused by indiscretions in youth, want of knowledge, hygiene, improper food etc. You will see others hardy and strong, models of manhood whose life is a pleasure to them who in their youth have escaped the evils and dangers to which all are subject. A very simple and safe recipe against those evils can be found in the last words of a man who had everything in this world at his command and tried them all. He said, 'The conclusion of the whole matter is this, to enjoy life as long as it is to fear God and keep His commandments.' This as you are aware is Ecclesiastes by Solomon. Let this be your guide and you need fear nothing in time or eternity. To do so will not deprive you of an atom of pleasure or good times even as far as this world goes. Yours affectionately, R. M."

It is doubtful that Johnny put on his longjohns, or believed that his cough was a sign of indiscretion, ignorance, dirt, hunger, or evil. Jack was a brilliant student – he would win the gold medal in the spring – and his intelligence was matched by his warm heart, good looks, and sense of humour. Jack had probably discarded his drawers to spite snoopy Sarah, and he encouraged his younger brothers and sisters to rebel against their stepmother. The children called themselves "The Five Hell Cats," an epithet bestowed on them, no doubt, by Steppie herself.

Sarah may have meant well. The belief that illness was linked to immorality had a solid foundation in the Victorian era: venereal disease was a common consequence of sex, and in Ontario, alcoholism killed as many young men as did syphilis or consumption. To be healthy, the McLaughlin children would have to be *good*, and to expiate the curse of Jack's cough, they would have to do penance. Sarah appears to have treated the children like workhouse orphans. They did all the chores: the boys sawed cordwood, hauled water, and looked after the horse and cow; Mary Jane and Lizzie did the housework. Sarah demanded obedience, and if the children didn't do as they were told, she threatened to tell their father. Robert was as quick with the birch as most fathers were – the belief that obedience should be beaten into children was unchallenged – but the children dreaded a tongue-lashing more, and if they dared tell on Steppie, she promised that Robert would make their lives a living hell.

Sarah went to extreme lengths to enforce her power. Lizzie liked to read in bed late at night, and when she heard Steppie coming up the stairs, she blew out her lamp and hid under the covers: whenever Sarah came into Lizzie's room, she sniffed the coal-oil lamp for telltale traces of smoke. Steppie refused to have cats in the house, but the Hell Cats smuggled them in under their clothes. When George and Sam, who shared a bed, heard Steppie's heavy tread on the stairs, they stuffed their cat into a pant leg and hung it out the window on a rope.

Robert approved of this Spartan regime. Lizzie and Mary Jane were offered none of the advantages normally showered on the daughters of flourishing businessmen: no dancing or painting lessons, no debutante parties, ballgowns, or finishing schools, no trips to theatres or visits to meet eligible young men in Toronto and Buffalo. They did play the organ. Robert enjoyed popular music, in his own way: "He plays up-to-date pieces on the player piano," the *Globe* reporter noted in 1919. "His mechanical genius is shown when he takes the records from the player piano and, stretching them out on a table, alters them until they record the music as he thinks they should. And if anyone says anything to him about it, he replies that that is how he likes to hear the piece played, and played that way it is, accordingly."

"I wish I were a man!" cried Mary Jane. At sixteen, she enrolled in a business course, and, at eighteen, she ran away. Her escape was planned and executed by the Hell Cats. After graduation, Jack had found a job with a druggist in Brooklyn, New York, and he sent home postcards showing off the amazing new Brooklyn Bridge, Grand Central Station, the Statue of Liberty, the Metropolitan Opera House, and the Vanderbilts' white marble mansions on Fifth Avenue. Perhaps Johnny tactlessly compared the exquisite carriages of the New York *nouveau riche* with the plain McLaughlin Business Buggy, or unwittingly aroused the country carriage-maker's hostility to cities, but when Mary Jane asked her father's permission to visit New York, his answer was no.

Jack secretly sent her a train ticket, and Mary Jane arranged to stay with her namesake, Aunt Mary Jane, in Bowmanville. In the dead of night, she crept out through her bedroom window, suitcase in hand, and ran to the station just in time to catch the express. Mary Jane stayed in New York two years, sampling soda water.

Carbonated water had been a mainstay of the druggist's trade since 1867, when Atkinson's Drug Store in Oshawa advertised: "The New York board of health says: 'We regard soda water as the only innocent drink of all the mineral waters in use,'" and a Dr. Maxwell of Calcutta added: "In the treatment of cholera, I found soda water both grateful and beneficial." Jack must have been frequently dosed with soda water flavoured with fruit syrups, a cure definitely preferable to cod liver oil, and in Brooklyn he was learning to run a soda fountain. A new tonic had taken New York by storm. "It relieves fatigue," the advertisements said. Jack had discovered that this fizzy syrup didn't make him drowsy or drunk, and drinking it became a habit. Its kick was no secret: cocaine was advertised in the tonic's name, Coca-Cola. Jack may have been looking for a cure for his cough, but he was poised to cash in on North America's insatiable thirst for a soda "pop."

His choice of profession had been partly determined by his father.

Robert had decided Jack's health was too frail for him to practise medicine, and he was determined that his three sons would eventually join him in the carriage business. While Jack was still jerking soda in Brooklyn, Robert drew up a contract making Jack, along with his blacksmith, William Parks, junior partners in a new company called the McLaughlin Carriage Company. The company was capitalized at $33,000; Robert would put up $28,500, the value of the present factory, Parks $3,000, and Jack $1,500. Jack never signed it. Instead, he set himself up in the wholesale soda-fountain business in Toronto, and Mary Jane, in utter misery, returned to Oshawa.

Robert, thwarted by his oldest son's independence, turned to his surrogate son. In 1884, Robert had hired a twenty-three-year-old Oshawa teacher, Oliver Hezzelwood, to bring order to the chaos of his financial records, and Oliver soon became the Old Man's confidant as well as his bookkeeper. A descendent of John Hazelwood, commodore of the Pennsylvania navy during the War of Independence, Oliver had grown up on a farm in Raglan, Ontario, and he was a man of means in his own right: his mother's family, the Fosters, were wealthy merchants in Buffalo, and every Christmas the Hezzelwoods received a cheque for $10,000 to be divided among the family members.

Oliver was generous and modest, an abstainer from both alcohol and tobacco, and his head for figures was matched by a talent for writing verse. He had taught the McLaughlin children, and his authority proved invaluable when Robert's two younger sons were conscripted into the carriage works.

George, Robert's second son, was apprenticed at fourteen in 1885, the day he finished school. Soft-spoken and self-effacing, with a playful sense of humour, George, the most accommodating of Robert's brood, took a genuine interest in the business. Sam did not.

"I had no great urge to go into the carriage business," Sam told *Maclean's* magazine in 1954. "I thought that one second-generation carriage maker in the family was enough. Besides, there were other things I wanted to try. I thought I might want to become a hardware merchant, and I worked in Dan Cinnamon's store for five months. I thought of becoming a lawyer – I fancied I looked a little like one. I knew from George that apprenticeship with the Governor was no rest cure. It meant working practically from dawn until after dusk, six days a week, and that would interfere with the bicycling I was so keen on."

Sam McLaughlin, age nineteen, with his penny-farthing bicycle. (*McLaughlin Public Library/ Thomas Bouckley Collection, Robert McLaughlin Gallery*)

Sam was short, loud, and strong, an aggressive, hyperactive boy who drove his parents to distraction. Sammy didn't walk; he ran, jumped, somersaulted, swam, skated, fished, and hunted rabbits on the farm at Tyrone. "I can never forget the many, many happy days we kids put in at the old homestead," Sam reminisced toward the end of his life. "George, our cousin Arthur (son of Dr. McLaughlin of Bowmanville) and I literally spent weeks out there. I shall never forget 'Jack,' the old Arabian horse which my uncle, Dr. McLaughlin, drove for years in his country practice. He was basically white, with a lot of brown spots, and was some horse, with a temper, and if he ever got a chance he would nip you and almost tear a piece of flesh off.

"George and Arthur and I one day had orders from Grandfather McLaughlin to take a message to Bowmanville, and the only horse available in that busy season was 'Old Jack.' We hitched him up to grandfather's nice old phaeton. We were really feeling a little bit gay, and going up a grade on the way to Bowmanville, we touched the old horse up with the whip. Lo and behold, the results were disastrous! Up went his tail and he literally smothered us with what shot out of his rear end.

"When we arrived in Bowmanville, our aunt would not let us in the house. She gave us something to eat out in the woodshed. So we delivered our message and drove back to the farm, but the whip stayed in the socket."

When bicycle mania hit Canada in the 1880s, Robert, out of desperation, bought Sam a $140 penny-farthing model, and Sam bicycled as furiously as he did everything else. "The fascination usually wears off in a year or two," Jack wrote their anxious father. "It seems to stick to Sam longer, but it's a mistake for him to travel such long distances."

Said Sam: "Long distances? Once for a holiday I rode from Oshawa to Brockville and back over dirt roads, a distance of more than three hundred miles. Often I rode the thirty miles to Toronto and back in one day. That was a toll road, but being on a bicycle I didn't have to pay. I entered races at all the fairs and meets I could get to, with pretty fair success. In fact, George said jokingly that I brought home so many cups and cruets and pickle dishes that I would be able to furnish a house when I got married. I knew the answer to that one. I wasn't ever going to marry. I was going to be too busy to be anything else but a bachelor."

As soon as Sam finished school, the family put a quick end to his lollygagging. He says: "I received a pleasant but firm letter from Jack, in which he persuaded me it was my duty to enter the family business. So in 1887 I became an apprentice in the upholstery shop. I soon found that George had not been exaggerating when he said it was no advantage to be the boss's son. I swept the floors and did all the other menial work that apprentices have hated from time immemorial."

George was promoted to the office, although it was next to the paint shop and reeked of turpentine and varnish, and his father was grateful for help with the paperwork. As early as January 16, 1884, George had been assigned to take inventory of the company's assets, and he did so with exceptional thoroughness. He counted every bolt and screw, every coupling, axle, and spool of thread, noting in his clear, minute script that they had on hand: 4,217 pounds of side and end springs worth $38.68; 100 select wagon poles at 50 cents each; one set new wheels, tired and painted, worth $20, and 4,074 feet of basswood valued at $57. George added it all up to the last penny for a total of $10,436.55. When improvements to the shop were added on, the company's assets came to $25,619.38. Liabilities, not specified, were $7,862.23. The McLaughlin Carriage Company was small, but it was healthy, and it was growing.

In the summer of 1887, Robert bought the shop next door and

several empty lots, and he enlarged both the blacksmith and the body works. He now had a separate room to build his gears, and a covered bridge connecting the shops allowed him to move his buggies quickly from one stage to the next. The most significant addition was an engine house, with a boiler ($225), smokestack ($43.60), and whistle ($7.75.) He was getting mechanized: an inventory for August 1887 includes a steam-powered bandsaw, a sander, and two drills. The assets of his company totalled $39,896.14, and they included his house, which Robert listed as part of the company: the carriage works appears to have been tax exempt, one of the many "bonuses" the town of Oshawa offered its leading industries. Robert also listed the contents of his house: carpets and curtains, $42.40; cruets and forks, $20; bedroom set, $37.50; cow, $30. Perhaps Sarah objected to the smell of paint, because McLaughlin's office inventory includes, along with two dollars in blotting paper, a quart of ink and ten pounds of brass tacks, "artist's tubes, brushes & canvas" valued at eight dollars. Robert had developed the habit, which would last the rest of his life, of dabbing away at his canvases during spare moments at work.

Robert's liabilities – loans and unpaid bills – totalled $14,781.09, leaving him with a net worth of $25,115.05. His ledgers for profit and loss have disappeared, but the list of accounts receivable shows that McLaughlin was owed $523.03 in overdue payments, and $7,033.59 on carriages and cutters he had sold retail, on credit. One of his assets was a mortgage on his fifty acres in Tyrone: he had sold it to his brother William in 1879, taking back a mortgage of two thousand dollars at 8 per cent interest.

The Governor was no more generous to his sons. "As an apprentice I was paid $3 a week," Sam said, "and every payday the Governor solemnly deducted $2.50 for room and board. I had fifty cents a week to spend as foolishly as I wished." Sam's tastes, however, were simple, and a penny would buy a smoked herring, a chunk of toffee, or a handful wintergreen candies.

Sam showed an unexpected enthusiasm for upholstery. "Trim" was the glamorous part of the buggy, but the cushions were laborious to cut and stitch by hand. Waxed thread had to be worked through leather or thick cloth, the openings stuffed with dry moss, then the cushion buttoned and tacked firmly to the body. Upholsterers held the tacks in their mouths to save time, and learning to spit tacks was

A corner of the trim shop, photographed by Sam McLaughlin when he became foreman in 1892. Sam sent the picture with the following note to a member of the Trimmers' Social Club in 1957: "Extreme left, Jack Kyle; next to him 'Red' Hastings; standing at attention, holding the broom, Jimmy Reinhardt; Will Cook was in the background, then Andy Thompson; sitting at a bench, tufting a seat back, are Charlie and Will Simmons; the handsome-looking man with the mustache, just about under the clock, was Alf Parker, my assistant and the wiggly looking fellow who never could keep still a minute was 'Scout' Wigg. The other man I cannot identify, although it looks like Alf Parker's brother Henry, one of my journeymen. The frame which is drawn up to the ceiling, which has cords across it every square foot, was my measuring rack which I used to check in the hides. A buggy top is shown on the left of the picture." (*General Motors of Canada*)

an art in itself. In 1890 Sam became a journeyman upholsterer; his salary was six dollars a week.

Top wages were $1.75 a day, and Sam decided to test his skill in the United States: "I wanted to make sure I was good enough to make a journeyman's full pay in carriage shops other than McLaughlin's. I wanted to find out that I wouldn't be paid all that money just because I was the Governor's spoiled brat."

Sam got a job with H. H. Babcock in Watertown, New York, for the top wage. It was a reconnaissance trip: Babcock was larger and more up-to-date than the McLaughlin operation, and the factory superintendent, who came from the village of Brooklin, five miles west of Enniskillen, gave Robert's inquisitive young son the run of the plant. Sam learned all Babcock knew in two months, then moved on to check out in shops in Syracuse and Binghamton. Before he came home, Sam said: "I took my savings, went to New York City and 'did the town.'"

McLaughlin and Babcock had nothing to fear from each other; a tariff of 35 per cent virtually prohibited the sale of buggies across the Canadian–American border and McLaughlin was free to snap up all the Canadian business he could get. In his 1891 catalogue, McLaughlin advertises "the best equipped and most extensive facility in the Dominion": a three-storey brick factory, five times as much stock and double the capacity in his workshops. He states that all his buggy bodies will be painted black, their gears black or wine, but "other coloured vehicles can be furnished at a variation in prices." McLaughlin already practised the golden rule of standardization – any colour, so long as it's black – that would be associated with Henry Ford, and he knew the secret of making the customer pay for everything else. The earliest version of the McLaughlin motto is expressed in this catalogue: "We shall, as formerly, confine ourselves to one grade of goods only, viz. – A 1 or the best grade. No Number 2 or B work will be furnished. We justly claim that no one can undersell us without reducing the quality of the goods."

The McLaughlin Carriage Company now occupied the old Gibbs Bros. Furniture Factory on the corner of William and Mary streets, a move that demonstrated Robert's ability to capitalize on the financial misfortunes of others. Thomas and William Gibbs, merchant bankers and members of Parliament as well as furniture-makers, had been the political and commercial kingpins of Oshawa until they were ruined by an unwise speculation in barley futures in the winter of 1878. The Gibbses fled Oshawa, and the furniture factory sat vacant for some years before the town made McLaughlin an offer: if he would buy the building for $5,000, the town would lend him the money. McLaughlin's property on Simcoe Street was worth more than $5,000. Why not trade for a plant three times as big, with no cash down, and make a profit on the deal? Doomsayers predicted that McLaughlin would have to rent out the top two floors, but he built an addition. In 1892, he made George and Sam junior partners; George's investment was $5,000, Sam's $4,000. Robert, whose own investment was $53,000, apparently took the money out of their wages: when George married Annie Hodgson the next year, he had to borrow from his father-in-law to buy a house.

The McLaughlin factory as it was in 1893 is described in the July 1929 issue of *News and Views*, a house magazine published by the General Motors' Acceptance Corporation: "It is early morning – almost seven o'clock, and winter is hard upon the town. Everything is in full blast. A dozen men weave in and out through a pattern of smoke and flame about five great forges. The wind-song of bellows rises to a roaring over-all. Men in great leather aprons, made from single sheep-skins, stoke up the fires, provoking them to a crackling heat that gradually is to make the forges into molten ovens. Intermittent puffs of white, sulphurous smoke find their way out a large open window, through which the burnt orange of sudden flame licks casually the frozen winter morning. The day is just beginning in the McLaughlin Carriage Company and there's a man's work to be done. When the forges are ready, practically every metal part of a buggy will be turned out smooth in the perfection of a blacksmith's art. Close by, trip hammers, operated by hand, are ready for other metal parts not forged by the smiths. One man slides the sheet metal into the die while another pulls the lever which trips the hammer with the measured regularity of modern machinery."

The heat was welcome in the winter, but on summer afternoons it could be unbearable. Windows were the only ventilation, and, in daytime, the only source of light. On dark winter days, the men worked by the dim light of guttering gas lamps or primitive electric bulbs dangling from the ceiling. Health and safety regulations were unknown, and in the carpentry and upholstery shops, dust was so thick that George, as an apprentice, wore a facemask with a sponge when he swept the floor.

The paint shop was segregated from the rest of the factory. Said *News and Views.* "Every body gets as many as fifteen coats. First comes a coat of 'rough stuff' to protect the wood from moisture. Then every inch of the surface is rubbed over with pumice-stone made from Mount Vesuvius lava until it is as smooth as slate. Coats of paint follow, then varnish, and rubbing varnish and rub-downs with pumice-stone and felt. Between certain coats of paint the body stands for a month or more. The last coat is often put on only after the carriage has been ordered, and then it stands for a final four or five days before delivery."

Robert ran a tight ship, but there was always room for a joke. George's most hated job was washing out the glue pot, and one day he could not resist dumping its sticky contents over a dozen workmen sunning themselves on the ground outside an open window. He fled to the roof and battened the hatches as the men howled below.

"Oh, it was all very happy and carefree," George remembered. "Every employee knew everyone from the boss down by his first name. Responsibility did not hang too heavily on anyone. Most of the customers, when they came to take delivery of their carriages, would find an excuse to take the shippers across the road, where in the local hotel a long and foaming glass of beer, costing five cents, would seal the bargain. Sometimes, perhaps, the potation would make the carriages look more beautiful than they really were. The story is told of one farmer who appeared for his new carriage on the eve of a local holiday. The wheels were to be red, and alas, only three could be found. But when the customer re-appeared, after sealing the sale in the usual way, the carriage stood against the wall of the factory, all ready. The farmer drove off. Next time he returned to town, however, he informed Mr. McLaughlin that he had discovered that the left rear wheel – the one which had stood nearest to the wall – was black. Apologies were made for the inadvertent mistake, a new wheel supplied, and the customer completely satisfied."

McLaughlin's 1893 catalogue advertises fourteen basic buggies with names like Kensington, Mikado, and, in honour of Canada's new governor general, Aberdeen. They are equipped with steel springs and axles, rubber washers, and the McLaughlin Patent Lever Top, made of twenty-eight-ounce rubber ("leather tops supplied at the usual advance in price.") The wheels are hickory, and "the seats are trimmed with the best No. 1 Select soft finished Leather, (either Dark Green, Dark Plum Blue or Russet) or with fine, heavy All-Wool English Broadcloth (dyed in the wool) and improved Spring Cushions. All Carriages are supplied with Floor Cloth and removable Carpet; Boot on back of Body, improved Rubber Apron and Rein Pocket, and a Silver Dash Rail."

The catalogue claims: "Purchasers of carriages cannot lay too much stress on the fact that the Proprietors of our Factory are all first-class mechanics, and have all branches under their direct supervision." In fact, Sam and George knew nothing about mechanics, and McLaughlin's other claims were exaggerated. Says his catalogue: "Dealers in, and purchasers of our goods, should fully understand that the small amount extra asked for our vehicles does not go into our profits, but is spent in the Superior Stock used, and the consumer gets

George and Annie
McLaughlin with their
sons, Ewart and Ray,
c. 1898. (*Marion
O'Donnell*)

full advantage by having a Buggy that will last very much longer than a
lower grade of work."

His customers, however, might have been shocked to discover that
the buggy they bought for $90 cost McLaughlin $46.97 to make.
McLaughlin itemized everything that went into a rig. The gear cost
$9.48; the wheels, $8.52; shafts, $1.61; the body, $1.92; the seat, 70
cents; top, $7.36; trimming, $5.36; fixings, $4.52; painting, $7.50;
silver hub bands were 50 cents extra. The cost of labour, coal, electricity, crating, and cartage was included, and Robert built in a profit
margin of 12.5 per cent to bring the net cost to $53.24.

The cheapness of McLaughlin's materials suggests that he got enormous discounts from his suppliers, or he was using a flashy paint job and
clever craftsmanship to sell a run-of-the-mill product. His wheels were
Standard B grade, the body was made primarily of basswood, a soft,
punky wood inferior to elm or maple, and the seat cushion had no
springs; the floor cloth cost a meagre seventeen cents, the carpet, eighteen cents. A black piano-box cutter with red plush upholstery and
crimson runners could be manufactured for $14.59; it sold for $36. The
McLaughlin Carriage Company manufactured 590 cutters in 1893, for
a clear retail profit of $12,000.

The trick to selling a better buggy was to convince customers, as
McLaughlin instructed his dealers, that "QUALITY REMAINS LONG
AFTER PRICE IS FORGOTTEN." He emphasized the care that went
into his products: "We use nothing but the best NO. 1 HAND BUFFED
Trimming Leather throughout. For stuffing XXXX moss and hair is used

exclusively – not an ounce of sea grass or excelsior – wooden shavings." Carriage bodies painted black looked like steel (some customers demanded a clear-varnished body, a taste that resurfaced in the next century in station wagons trimmed with vinyl "wood") and McLaughlin hired painters who could do beautiful striping and scroll work. Like the sewing machine he purchased for Sarah, Robert's best rigs were decorated with delicate traceries in crimson and gold.

By October 1894, the McLaughlin Carriage Company was worth $165,700, including $103,000 in accounts receivable; it had $50,000 in debts. Robert paid out $42,883 in wages during the year; he paid himself $16,430, George $1,550, and Sam $1,240. He invested in the Oshawa Street Railway, a private corporation that built a streetcar line up Simcoe Street from the lake shore and a spur connecting the McLaughlin factory to the Grand Trunk Railway. Streetcar service meant McLaughlin's men could get to work more quickly, and by loading his buggies directly into boxcars on the spur line, he could sell by the carload from coast to coast. McLaughlin was ready to do business on a national scale, and on December 14, 1896, George was dispatched to Saint John, New Brunswick, to open the company's first branch office.

"At night went to attend prayer meeting at 3 churches – found no one at either – weather a little stormy," George wrote in his diary on December 16. It was characteristic of the Governor to exile his son to New Brunswick for Christmas, and it was also typical of him to send George, on Christmas Eve, a gold pocketwatch engraved "From Father," with the date and George's initials. For the next two months, George whistlestopped from village to village through the Maritimes, smoking out no-goods, signing up new dealers, and trying to take business away from the competition.

"Met J. A. Simpson, local builder," George recorded in Springhill, Nova Scotia, on January 22, 1897, "who kept me until the train had left in the hope of getting his order which he never intended to give. Met Mr. Mills who is a farmer and would not make a good agent." The next day in Oxford he took an order from J. Harvey Treen. "Treen was at one time in the furniture business & failed. There is an impression that he has money some place. Is not popular." On January 26, George arrived in New Glasgow, where he sold Graham Fraser a boxcar-load: "He is flighty & will require watching. Is quoted worth 5 to 10 thousand." George was armed with credit reports published by the Dun company

Oshawa town council, 1897. Oliver Hezzelwood is seated second from the right, Sam McLaughlin kneels in front. (*Thomas Bouckley Collection, Robert McLaughlin Gallery*)

(later Dun & Bradstreet) in Toronto, weekly estimates of the bank balances of Canada's businessmen spiced with juicy speculation about their drinking habits and infidelities. George stuck close to the Scots Presbyterians; he scored a carload with the McKay brothers in Sydney after a five-hour sales pitch, but struck out with J. S. O'Brien in Antigonish: "O'Brien would not handle. Tried Floyd and Stewart, egg man. No go. Promised to stop on return and see O'Brien again. Stayed at Merriman's. Drunken bum made racket at night. Try Smith's hotel next time. $1.50."

The McLaughlins piggybacked on the farm-equipment dealers. Agents could sell binders in the spring, buggies in the summer, and cutters in the winter, and the biggest market was in the west, where hundreds of thousands of immigrants from Ontario, the United States, Britain, and Europe were pouring in to take up free homesteads on the prairies. Robert began shipping carriages to towns he couldn't find on a map, and George was sent west to scout sales in places with names like Moose Jaw and Medicine Hat.

By 1899, Robert McLaughlin was advertising himself as "the largest carriage factory in Canada." He was making twenty-five hundred cutters and sleighs a year and an equal number of carriages. He had branch offices in Saint John, Montreal, and Winnipeg, and he had refined his motto to "One grade only, and that the best." His success was not unique. Central Canada's economy was becoming industrialized, and McLaughlin was a member of a powerful new class of brewers and distillers, sugar refiners, flour millers, cement makers, and steel manufacturers. Oshawa promoted itself as the "Manchester of Canada," proof that the local boosters had never been to Manchester, and in 1899 the mayor of Oshawa was Robert McLaughlin.

It was Robert's *annus horribilis* and *annus mirabilis*, an end to the old century fraught with promise for the new. Sarah died in April. Her crabbiness may have been caused, at least in part, by chronic illness. A decade earlier, Robert wrote an angry letter to his brother James, revealing a good deal of his own psychology as well as details of his wife's complaints. "I cannot see how you make out I wrote 'with bitterness,'" Robert said. "My intention was to write what I believed to be simply business facts. It is about 3 years since Sarah's trouble commenced with some disorder in her stomach or bowel producing a sort of diarrhea. For about 18 months she could not eat meat or vegetables of any kind. Two years ago last November she got a severe blow with the end of the cutter shaft on the back between her shoulders. A year ago she was so weak she was unable to get in the buggy alone. I thought then she would not get better. She rallied and overcame to a great extent her bowel troubles, yet the wound or soreness remained in her back. She visited you several times and inferred from what you said there was nothing seriously wrong. Then I took her down twice myself and had a talk with you, and you told me there was not much wrong, that at her age many women were much the same and a great deal of her trouble arose from imagination.

"On account of your absence, I had to employ Drs. Rae and Hoig, and now after 2 years and 6 months, her back is as bad or worse than it ever was. Not one of you three has been able to tell me what is wrong or whether there is any help for the trouble. I am now of the opinion that no cure will be accomplished as the trouble is of such long standing. I am also of the opinion that neither you, Rae nor Hoig has got to the bottom of it. While I can see the policy of not giving your opinion even if you believed there was no remedy for her but to remain a partial invalid for life, it would be proper for me to know so that I can arrange my domestic affairs accordingly. I find in my own case that if I were disabled so that I would have to abandon the pleasure of active work and industry it would, I believe, be one of the severest punishments that could be inflicted upon me. I have to admit that active work has always been a real pleasure to me, and it is well it is so. Her case is a similar one. She has been a constant hard worker all her life, never at rest, neither in mind nor in body. To give this up with its hopes and pleasure

Top left: The McLaughlin factory the morning after the fire. (*McLaughlin Public Library/Thomas Bouckley Collection, Robert McLaughlin Gallery*)

is no easy job, and it convinces me that for her to succumb to imaginary troubles in order to get rid of work or active life has very little insight in it.

"In reference to what I wrote about certain of our friends coming to a conclusion that she has exercised cruelty and tyranny over the children, those who arrived at this conclusion have done us both a wrong. 1st: It is wrong for any person to arrive at a judgement by hearing only one side of the story. 2nd: For near friends to settle down to a conviction and keep it in for years and at the same time keep up an outward appearance as usual and not have the straightforward courage to let me know, I don't think it is friendly or faithful. We should as near friends and Christians faithfully tell each other of their faults and obey scriptural command. It would have been much better if we could have talked these things over but as brothers we appear to have no time for social intercourse which I think is not the best way."

Robert was a dangerous man to cross. As an elder in St. Andrew's Presbyterian Church, he wielded a good deal of moral authority, and he regularly denounced his neighbours as liars and scoundrels in vitriolic letters to the *Reformer*. Only his daughter Lizzie dared to stand up to him. Lizzie graduated from the Whitby teacher's college at age sixteen, and found a job in Longford Mills, a rough lumber town near Orillia, about as far away from home as she could get. Robert was horrified, but Lizzie, who weighed barely ninety pounds, had learned discipline the hard way, and she soon had the school louts whipped into line. Lizzie taught for two years, and when her father finally begged her to return home, she agreed, on condition that Steppie's tyranny come to an end.

Steppie left. When Sarah, "wife of Robert McLaughlin, Carriage Maker," made her last will on October 29, 1896, she was living alone in Port Hope. The decision to separate may have been hers: Lizzie had demanded, among other privileges, use of the carriage, and Robert, suspicious now of Sarah's behaviour, had sided with his daughter. Sarah bequeathed her entire estate to her sister Mary and brother Henry Parr of Brantford, and on her death, her worldly possessions amounted to a thousand-dollar promissory note and $479 in cash. Lizzie did not allow Steppie's death to ruin her wedding plans: on September 27, 1899, Lizzie married John Owens, a clerk with the Western Bank.

About 3 a.m. on December 7, fire broke out in the wood-drying room of the McLaughlin Carriage Company. By dawn the old brick building was no more than a blackened shell. The Oshawa fire brigade was ineffectual. Robert should have known: as mayor he had just approved a by-law partially exempting the town's largest industries, including his own, from a tax to pay for waterworks.

The McLaughlin works employed three hundred men. With their families, they made up a third of the town's population, and without work in winter, they would be destitute. The mayor of Gananoque, 200 miles to the east, offered McLaughlin free accommodation for his business in an empty building next to one of McLaughlin's suppliers, the Gananoque Spring and Axle Company, and Sam hopped on the next train east. A citizens' committee, fearful that Oshawa might lose the carriage works, proposed a $50,000 loan from the town to assist McLaughlin to rebuild. Robert was in a ticklish position: could the mayor lend money to himself? He resigned, and accepted the $50,000.

It was a windfall. His loss on inventory was minimal – most of his cutters had been shipped for the Christmas trade – and the building was heavily insured. Robert was able to use his misfortune as a bargaining chip to negotiate cheaper freight rates with the Grand Trunk Railway, and he contracted to put up a new factory in time for the summer rush. The McLaughlin Carriage Company entered the twentieth century in style. By the spring of 1900, the McLaughlins were too busy making buggies to pay any attention to a queer little contraption chugging around Toronto, a carriage without a horse.

4

BUICK

Toronto, April 25, 1904: A few moments before eight o'clock in the evening, Oliver Hezzelwood slips into the showroom of the Canadian Cycle and Motor Company at the corner of Bay and Temperance streets. He is surprised to find the room so crowded, but relieved to see that his presence may go unnoticed. Hezzelwood is in enemy territory. CCM, teetering on the brink of bankruptcy since the bicycle craze collapsed, is now advertising itself as Toronto's "Automobile Corner." In the Old Man's book, the automobile is a worthless toy, and the owner of CCM, Joe Flavelle, a crook. However, after twenty years with the carriage company, Oliver is only too aware of Robert McLaughlin's more pig-headed prejudices.

"Hezzelwood!" A hand clasps Oliver's arm, and he turns to face CCM's new manager, Tommy Russell. "Ready to move up to a little more horsepower?" Russell says with a wink. "Come over here. I'll show you twenty-four horses, and you won't have to clean the stable." He leads Oliver toward an automobile the size of a fire engine. It was made in the United States by a mechanic named Packard, Russell says, and runs like a top at fifty miles an hour. The Packard's red leather seats are so steeply banked they remind Hezzelwood of Massey Hall, a box to be seen in for certain, and he notices young Jack Eaton inspecting the Packard's upholstery. Is Eaton going to start selling automobiles? He feels a twinge of anxiety. Eaton has stayed out of the buggy business. What if he jumps in with this new rig?

"We've got Eaton almost sold," Russell whispers. "And once the swells take it up, automobiling will be the rage." Hezzelwood is unimpressed. Who would buy something this ungainly? It must weigh a ton. The wheels are thick and squat; the steering lever looks as if it could snap like a toothpick. And the engine starts with a crank! "How much are you asking for it?" he asks. "Only eight thousand dollars," Russell beams. "Top and tires included. A windshield costs extra." Hezzelwood hopes his face does not betray his shock. "It's a steal," Russell assures him. "You pay more than ten thousand for a European make."

"I don't want to put McLaughlin in the shade," Oliver quips. He sidles away. "Go take a look at the Ford," Russell calls after him. "Fastest machine in the world: ninety-two miles an hour! Ford built it himself. Don't leave before you hear him speak."

Hezzelwood vaguely recalls the stunt. When was it, January? Ford drove some homemade contraption a mile across the ice in almost half a minute. Americans are always doing this crazy sort of thing, walking tightropes across Niagara Falls, locking themselves in trunks, sawing women in half, and Hezzelwood had dismissed Ford as another circus performer in it for his share of the bets. There's a sucker born every minute, he thinks, and about two hundred of them are in this room, including me. The crush of people is so great Hezzelwood can hardly make his way to the door, and he is trapped when the music stops and Russell leaps on the stage to pitch "the joy of touring" in a Peerless, a Packard, a Thomas Flyer, an Autocar, a Duryea, an Ivanhoe, or a Ford. Hezzelwood has imagined Henry Ford as a Houdini-like creature in goggles and a leather helmet, and he is amazed when a gaunt, greying man about his own age walks forward to shake Russell's hand. Henry Ford is wearing a threadbare black suit, and he talks about his machine in a flat, Midwestern twang.

Ford's voice is almost a croak, and he blurts out words, strange words like *carburetor* and *magneto* that Hezzelwood has never heard before. Ford's use of *ain't* offends Oliver's literary sensibilities, but he likes the mechanic's bluntness, and by the time Ford describes how he set the world speed record in a cigar-shaped wooden box powered by a one-hundred-horsepower engine, Oliver is all ears. To make his track, Ford says, he dumped loads of hot cinders on the ice of the St. Clair flats, then scraped the cinders into a smooth, frozen straightaway:

"I had the course gone over carefully, so there was not an obstruction the size of a marble in the way. The slightest lump would send the machine flying in the air. I took a mechanic with me. He lay down in the front of the box and managed the throttle; I was on the seat, steering with a wheel. We had a running start of about a mile and a half, and when we hit the track the throttle was wide open and we were going like the wind.

"We were racing against time, and it was wildly exciting while it lasted. Have you ever dived into deep water? Well, that mildly describes the sensation. There was a roaring in my ears like a thousand fiends let loose, and the force of the wind felt like the pressure of tons of water. After we covered the course, we ran along the ice for over two miles, clear into Canada, on the machine's own impetus. I kicked my man as a signal to shut off the throttle, and we ran the machine into the snow. The air was full of flying snow until we came to a stop. For the last mile, the rear wheels were simply sliding on the ice."

The hair rises on the back of Oliver's neck, and as soon as Ford's speech ends, he pushes through the throng to see his exhibit. He is disappointed. The racing car is not here, and Ford's two-cylinder runabout is a flimsy little rig, no bigger than a fifty-dollar buggy. The engine is under the seat. What if it blows up? He raps his knuckles against the body: basswood. The trim and paint job aren't anywhere up to McLaughlin standards. "One thousand cash and you can drive it home, Mr. Hezzelwood," a voice says in his ear. It takes Oliver a moment to place the face: McGregor, Gordon McGregor of the Walkerville Wagon Works. Oliver has heard the McGregor shop has fallen on hard times.

"You're selling for Ford?" he asks, incredulous. "No sir," grins McGregor, "we're going to be building Fords." McGregor says he is selling the wagon works to Ford, but he and a group of Ontario investors are buying a 49-per-cent interest in the Ford Motor Company of Canada. "The Gray works in Chatham will build our bodies. Ford'll make the engines and chassis in Detroit, ship 'em across the river, and we'll put the whole job together. Presto! One made-in-Canada car."

Ford's machines look like red ants. "I brought six to Toronto on

Saturday," McGregor says. "The only one not sold yet is this two-seater here. I'll throw in the tires." Isn't there a risk of explosion? Not at all. McGregor explains that combustion is confined to the cylinders, and the gasoline tank is steel. "The only danger would be in the event of a collision, but you'll be thrown clear in plenty of time." Hezzelwood is silently calculating the profit McGregor will make manufacturing Fords.

"How do I learn to drive?"

"Come by in the morning. We'll go for a spin."

On Tuesday morning, perched up beside McGregor in the Ford's little bucket seat, Oliver feels like an egg in a crate. He could fall out at the next corner. He grips the side, and pictures himself splattered all over the road.

"Where's the door?"

"Door? What for?"

The car chugs south on Bay, and an astonishing scene opens up before Oliver's eyes: the old city of Toronto has vanished. A week ago, the corner of King and Bay was a canyon of factories and warehouses; three days ago, the factories were charred skeletons; today, all that remains after the great fire is a field of rubble stretching as far east as the customs house on Parliament Street. It smells like hell, but as they turn the corner, Oliver feels a breeze off the lake. He can see almost to Buffalo. They pass a solitary brick wall; seconds later, it crashes in a cloud of dust.

McGregor drives west on King. The traffic thins out, and the Ford's engine is running smoothly. It has pleasant, soothing sound. Hezzelwood loosens his fingers from the seat. He is in one piece, and so far the horses they have passed have not run amok. "We'll head out to the lunatic asylum," McGregor says. "You can take the wheel and nobody'll notice."

Aaarrrgggh! Why won't this bloody perverted piece of stinking ill-begotten wreckage *start?* Hezzelwood has his coat off. His arm aches from cranking and his shirt is stained with grease. In front of the asylum, the Ford had stopped. Jets of steam shot out of the radiator. "She needs a rest," says McGregor, checking the oil. "Automobiles have personalities. They're temperamental."

"This one is dead," says Hezzelwood.

"Overheated."

In about twenty minutes, the engine sputters to life and Hezzelwood nervously takes the wheel. "Are you sure I'm not too old for this?" he says, cautiously lowering the brake lever. He circles the driveway of the asylum and points the Ford back toward Toronto. It steers as easily as a bicycle, and he has to be careful not to weave all over the road. He can count every pebble and tuft of grass as they pass beneath his feet, but the car's weight gives him a feeling of stability, and he doesn't bounce up and down.

"How fast am I going?"

McGregor licks a finger and sticks it in the air. "'Bout eight or nine miles an hour. Limit's ten."

Hezzelwood sticks close to the centre of the road, as far as possible from the delivery horses plodding along by the ditch, but the ancient nags hardly raise their heads from their nosebags. At Bathurst, he catches up to a streetcar. The driver opens his throttle and rattles away, dinging his bell indignantly; Oliver catches him at the next stop and whizzes by, giving the streetcar two blats from his horn. A boy leans out and shouts: "Get a horse!" McGregor tips his hat. "Ford customer of the future," he says.

The noise of the engine makes Oliver's ears ring and the gas fumes are going to his head. It's not an unpleasant sensation. He feels like Pooh Bah perched up here, and although he has often ridden down Queen Street to the Metropolitan Methodist Church, today the street looks unfamiliar, as if he is seeing it for the first time. It looks like a panorama, one of those curved pictures photographers put together, and he can see the whole street at once. As he puzzles over this, a carriage pulls up on his right. The horse rolls its eye and curls its lip; Oliver can feel its hot breath on his neck and smell the pungent reek of its sweating hide. It's unnerving, being up here hobnobbing with a horse. In a buggy, you're behind.

"You know what I like about this machine?" Oliver shouts at McGregor. "I don't have to look at the world from a horse's ass!"

His new automobile makes Hezzelwood the laughingstock of the county, and his friends fear for his sanity. Oliver has been bitten by the "automobile bug," an irrational obsession that transforms otherwise sober and careful men into monomaniacs. How else to explain the fact that Hezzelwood spends every spare moment, *even on Sundays*, chugging around the countryside, splattered with mud, apparently determined to break his neck? Robert McLaughlin finds Hezzelwood's antics so amusing he makes automobile accidents the focal point of two carriage-company calendars; the automobiles are depicted wrecked in

The McLaughlin company calendar, 1905. (*General Motors of Canada/Parkwood*)

the ditch, their passengers injured and frightened, while fashionable young couples whiz by in their smart new McLaughlin buggies.

Hezzelwood pays no attention to the jokes. Ontario is full of people who complain that streetcars run too fast, and electric lights are too bright, but who wants to go back to a world without electricity or machinery? McLaughlin has been using machinery to manufacture buggies for years. Why not use machinery to run the buggy? Oliver intends to drive his Ford until it falls apart, then put it together again to find out how it works.

Mud is the problem. It flies up from all directions until he is completely plastered with it, and from time to time he has to stop to wipe his goggles. He persuades the boys in the trim shop to cut him a sheet of rubber big enough to cover the entire car, with two holes in it through which he and his passenger can put their heads, but the rubber sheet makes steering difficult, he can't free his hands to wipe his goggles, and the spectacle of two disembodied heads floating down Simcoe Street in a self-propelled black blob sends pedestrians into hysterics.

Oliver soon discovers that, apart from its engine, his thousand-dollar Ford has about forty dollars' worth of parts. The McLaughlin Carriage Company could build a body with a proper dashboard, mud-guards, and a buggy top for less than twenty dollars. Oliver figures that the price of a motor car is calculated on the basis of a hundred dollars for every horse in the engine, and if, as Ford claims, he has sold four thousand motor cars, he is a millionaire.

Hezzelwood has money to invest, and he is a director of the carriage company. Robert McLaughlin incorporated his business in 1901 with a capital of $400,000 divided into 4,000 shares of $100 each. Oliver, with 120 shares, is the only outsider on the board; the other directors, in addition to Robert, are four of his five children: George, Sam, Lizzie, and Mary Jane. Not one of them cares a fig for automobiles. The buggy business is booming, and with an annual production of about fifteen thousand gears and rigs, Robert McLaughlin boasts of being the biggest carriage-builder in the British Empire. Robert's hair and beard are white, but he still puts in the same brutal hours, and only a year ago he married again.

Eleanor McCulloch was an English-born widow of Robert's age with a grown family. Physically, she was fearsome, with a short, thick neck and beetle-browed face, but her good-natured disposition made her popular with everyone, including the McLaughlin children, although by the time of their father's third marriage they had all left home. Mary Jane was the last, but in 1901, at age thirty-four, she married John, a younger member of the McCulloch clan. There may have been induce-ments: John McCulloch was twenty-eight, an accountant in the office of the carriage factory, and Mary Jane, for all her prickliness, was an heiress. The Governor, however, was not about to put on the dog. Robert built a frame bungalow with an English garden for Eleanor on Simcoe Street, and they lived there, a stone's throw from the carriage works, in almost monastic simplicity.

Young Sam is Hezzelwood's best bet. Sam likes to spend money, and by 1904, the rough-and-tumble little boy with wheels in his head has become a sharp wheeler-dealer. Mr. Sam, as he is now respectfully known, is rumoured to play poker and take a glass of whisky on occa-sion. Mr. Sam fancies Cuban cigars and has his suits custom-tailored in New York City. He wears leather shoes, with spats, an affectation

Adelaide Mowbray, centre back row, with her pupils at S.S. #2, Whitby, 1896. (*Parkwood*)

almost unheard-of in Oshawa, and he changes his shirt every day. Yet Sam is still a rough diamond. His manner is blunt, his language crude, and his gloss of sophistication is attributed to his wife, Adelaide. Everybody, including Sam himself, agrees that it was a lucky day when he met Miss Mowbray.

"I bicycled out to Tyrone one Sunday to visit my uncle on the old homestead," Sam told *Maclean's* in 1954. "I had no inkling of my fate when my uncle asked me to go to church with his family. The only person I really saw in the church that day was a vision of beauty in the choir, but the strange part of it was that I had known her previously. She had visited in our home – she and my younger sister had gone to normal school together – but I had never paid any attention to her. Somehow that morning, as my uncle's pew was well forward in the church, I could get a ringside view of her. So absorbed was I that my uncle had to nudge my elbow when they passed the collection plate."

Sam waited at the church door to invite Miss Adelaide out for a walk, but she had to teach a Bible class. Sam made a date for the next Sunday, and this time he drove out in his buggy: "I believe I made some progress, for I asked for another date the next Sunday and on that day

I proposed to her. In those days I sported a big, sandy-coloured moustache and a Vandyke beard. Although Miss Adelaide had not said anything against them, I reluctantly decided they must go, for nothing should interfere with my chances."

Adelaide Louise Mowbray bore a strong resemblance to Sam's mother, Mary, and she was the type of big, rosy-cheeked country girl Sam liked to call "a fine heifer." Adelaide, at five feet, nine inches, was almost two inches taller than Sam. At the time of his proposal in the summer of 1897, she was twenty-two and she was teaching school in Tyrone. Sam's visit to church may have been less fortuitous than he supposed: Adelaide was exactly the wife the McLaughlins believed Sam needed to "settle down," and his Uncle William may have conspired with Lizzie and the rest of the family to make a match of it.

The Mowbrays were Methodists and strict teetotallers. Ralph Mowbray, Adelaide's father, farmed nearby at Kinsale; he had served as warden of Ontario county and for several years as deputy reeve of Pickering township. Her mother, Victoria, could trace her lineage back to the *Mayflower*. Adelaide was a lady. Her posture was erect, almost regal, her virtue impeccable. She was better educated than her eager little suitor, and every bit as intelligent, yet she wasn't stiff or standoffish like the girls Sam had met in Toronto. Adelaide had a natural warmth and friendliness that drew people to her; she was talkative and, like Sam, brimming with vitality. If Adelaide had a fault, it was tardiness: her nickname was "Always Late Mowbray."

Sam pursued Adelaide with the same relentless, obsessive energy he had devoted to cycling. For all Sam's bad habits – the Mowbrays disapproved of smoking and playing cards as well as drinking – Adelaide found his boyish charm irresistible. More than fifty years later, when Adelaide was awarded an honorary doctorate by Queen's University, rector Leonard Brockington described her as "playing Wendy to Sam's Peter Pan," the most perceptive remark ever made about this oddly matched couple.

Adelaide accepted Sam's proposal in October; they were married at the Mowbray farm on February 2, 1898, in the midst of a howling blizzard. Two clergymen officiated, one Methodist and one Presbyterian, and because of the snowstorm Sam had to drive his Presbyterian minister to the wedding himself. By the end of the ceremony, the snow had blocked the roads and covered the fences. Sam bundled his bride into his sleigh; they dashed over the drifts to Whitby, caught the train, and spent a week in New York on their honeymoon.

Sam bought a big brick house on the Old Kingston Road about a block from the carriage works. The McLaughlin men were accustomed to walking home for their midday meal, and woe betide the wife who did not have their food hot on the table exactly twenty minutes past the noon whistle. Sam had reconciled himself, somewhat reluctantly, to working for the Governor. He didn't have a choice. "I had wanted, among other things, to become a draftsman," he told *Maclean's.* "But the Governor put his foot down. 'If I want a draftsman,' he said, 'I can get a draftsman. I want you to stay here and learn the business.'"

Sam had earned his spurs in the spring of 1900. After the fire had wiped out the carriage company's entire stock of patterns, machinery, and materials. Sam set up a temporary shop in Gananoque, brought in the men from Oshawa, boarded them all in local homes and hotels, and worked them, and himself, around the clock. By the time the McLaughlins moved into their new building in June, Sam had been able to fill three thousand outstanding orders from his makeshift operation. He was still, however, in the Governor's pocket. "I was thirty years old, and a family man, before I decided I had come up in the world enough to start going to the office at the luxuriously late hour of eight o'clock," he remembered. "The first morning I did so my conscience grew more and more bothered the nearer I got to the plant – and finally I sneaked in the back door, thoroughly ashamed of myself."

By 1904, when Oliver Hezzelwood took Sam for a spin in his Ford, Sam was looking for adventure. He had little to do at the plant, and being a family man meant prams and diapers. Sam and Adelaide had three daughters – Eileen, four; Mildred, two; and Isabel, not yet a year old – but Sam wanted a son, and he was going to keep trying until he got one. His hair was thinning, and he was fearful that he would spend the rest of his life as "Mr. Sam," the Governor's youngest boy.

Your car is crap, Sam told Hezzelwood. I could do better. Oliver knew Sam was hooked, and Sam's competitive instincts may have been piqued by a story in the *Cycle and Automobile Trade Journal.* The writer, Hugh Dolnar, described a ride in a car driven by the inventor's son, Tom Buick:

"At first, Buick drove with some decent regard for law and prudence, but the road was hard, the clear air was intoxicating, and after one request to 'push her' up one steep hill, which the car mounted at 25 miles speed, Buick began to be proud of his mount and drive for fun.

David Buick. (*National Automotive History Collection, Detroit Public Library*)

The car simply ran to perfection, and is extremely easy, especially in sharp side crooks of the road wheel ruts, and has very little bounce over short road depressions. The writer never went so fast on a rough, hilly road. The rear brakes were not connected and what braking was done was with the reverse. But the brake was not used. The car flew down the hills and flew up the hills, all the same rate, and the engine purred and the wind whistled past and the soft September sun smiled benignly on the fine farms we ran by, and it was all delightful."

The Buick was manufactured at the Flint Wagon Works in Flint, Michigan. Sixteen cars had been sold, and the company had orders for eleven more. Dolnar described the body as "a 'solid job,' that is, not detachable. The upholstering is the best grade of 'machine buff' leather. The standard body color will be indigo blue, with yellow running gear, any colored leather."

If Sam had contacted James Whiting, the owner of the Flint works, he could have bought Buick outright. Whiting had sunk $100,000 into his automobile venture; he was $75,000 in debt and despaired of ever seeing a penny in return. Whiting was actively looking for a younger man with money who could take over the business, and control its stubborn creator, David Buick.

Buick was fifty, a short-tempered, rough-spoken Scottish immigrant who had been apprenticed at age fifteen to a Detroit manufacturer of plumbing fixtures. Buick rose to foreman, then bought the company with a partner, William Sherwood, when it went bankrupt in 1882. Over the next ten years, Buick invented a lawn sprinkler and flushing devices – the company's stationery featured a logo of a toilet – and he patented a means of bonding porcelain to cast iron. David Buick was the father of the American Standard bathroom, but building a better bathtub held no appeal for Buick, and he and Sherwood sold out for $100,000 in 1899. Buick established the Buick Auto-Vim and Power Company to manufacture gasoline engines. He specialized in marine engines – he was commodore of the Detroit Yacht Club – and began experimenting with an automobile.

The first Buick was built between 1899 and 1901 by the company's brilliant but temperamental manager, Walter Marr. A former racing cyclist, Marr had a knack with engines, and like Ford, with whom he discussed valves and carburetors on the street corner, Marr became a crank about his invention. Marr was an obsessive tinkerer, a drifter who never stayed on a job for long, and he fought violently with Buick. He quit in a rage not long after his automobile was finished, and in April 1901 Buick sold Marr "all my right, title, and interest" in the car for $225.

Buick heard about a compact, fast-burning, valve-in-head engine that produced more horsepower than any other gasoline engine its size. He hired its young French inventor, Eugene Richard, and purchased Richard's patent with the little money he had left. Buick had sold his own plumbing patents along with his shop, and by 1903 he didn't have enough cash to finish his second car. Buick had been borrowing small sums from his sheet-metal supplier, Benjamin Briscoe, and he offered to sell Briscoe the car if Briscoe would advance him the rest of the money. Briscoe got the car for about $1,300, and for another loan of $1,500 he got Buick's company too.

The Buick Motor Company was incorporated on May 19, 1903, with $100,000 in capital stock: Briscoe held $99,700; Buick, $300. "It was an unusual contract," comment Buick historians Terry Dunham and Lawrence Gustin. "Buick, as president, was given the option of repaying what he owed Briscoe – about $3,500 – and receiving in return all the stock – or, failing that, relinquishing control of the Buick Motor Company to Briscoe by September 1903."

Briscoe immediately sold the Buick company to the Flint Wagon Works for $100,000, and on July 4, 1903, he entered into a partnership with another mechanic, John Maxwell, to form the Maxwell–Briscoe Motor Company. In their authoritative history, The Buick, Dunham and Gustin speculate that Briscoe "figured that if Buick couldn't pay, at least he would have the Buick shop which Maxwell could use as a nucleus for a factory to produce the Maxwell car. Knowing Buick as he did, Briscoe must have assumed he would end up with the shop."

However, Buick borrowed the $3,500 from his new owner, James Whiting, and paid his debt to Briscoe with interest and a bonus. A man of scrupulous honesty, Buick naively assumed his partners would be the same, and when Whiting insisted that Buick repay his loan before he could receive his shares in the reorganized company, Buick agreed. Without dividends from his shares, however, Buick had no means to pay back his debt. He had been cheated out of everything but his name.

The Buick Motor Company's financial crisis was Whiting's fault. One of their first auto workers, Albert Calver, gives this account of the Buick production line: "They gave us some blueprints to go by, but a lot of the design had to be made up as we went along. Whenever we got stuck, we just did things the way we had done with the buggies. Sounds funny to say we lined up the wheels with an old pine yardstick and the frame with a piece of string, but that's the way we did it – same as we'd lined up thousands of buggies. There was no such thing as welding, so all the parts had to be joined with rivets. And none of the bolts we used were cut to size. We just went around to the barrel and hunted around for bolts we thought might fit. If they were too long, we just cut them off.

"The biggest job, though, was getting the motor to fit into the frame. When we got the frame done, the motor was just too big. We spent some long hours with cold chisels hacking away at those angle irons to make room for the motor. When we finally finished getting the frame and motor together, we had to carry it all across the street by hand. It was a job."

Robert McLaughlin would have been horrified; he was horrified enough that his boys were wasting his time and money on automobiles. He informed Sam, George, and Hezzelwood that they could build a motor-car on their own time, with their own money, and he figured no banker in Canada would go near such a harebrained proposition.

The McLaughlin motor-car scheme languished until the summer of 1905, when a catchy new tune had everyone singing: "Come away with me, Lucille, in my merry Oldsmobile." Ransom E. Olds's little curved-dash runabout was a runaway bestseller, and it was perfect for the McLaughlins: simple to build, easy to run, and cheaper than a Ford. Timothy Eaton had featured the Oldsmobile on the cover of his 1901 catalogue, and Olds claimed to have sold twenty thousand cars in the previous four years, more than all other American makes put together.

The Oldsmobile runabout, however, was no longer being made, and Ransom Olds had left the company, pushed out by a clique of Detroit financiers determined to build big cars. Olds was working on a new car, the Reo, but he insisted on owning his Canadian factory outright. Sam was desperate to run his own shop, and when he discovered that CCM had purchased Canadian rights to the Thomas Flyer, Sam realized that the McLaughlin boys were losing out in the automobile game.

Hezzelwood's contacts in Buffalo got Sam in the door of Richard Pierce's Arrow works. Said Sam: "Mr. Pierce took me to lunch at his club and afterwards showed me around his plant where the Pierce Arrow was being manufactured, painstakingly by hand operations, piece by piece, part by part. This stately courteous gentleman of the old school then made a startling statement in a quiet, matter-of-fact voice: 'Cars like this have no future, Mr. McLaughlin. I would advise you against trying to make them.'"

It was the best advice Sam ever got, and it may have persuaded him to ignore Henry Leland's Cadillac. Instead, Sam and Hezzelwood took the train to Jackson, Michigan, to visit one more inventor, Charles Lewis. "He was a fine old gentleman, genial and courteous and ready to do anything in the world for us," Sam said. "He was enthusiastic over the possibilities of our manufacturing cars in Oshawa and outlined how it could be done. We could manufacture the engines and many of the parts, he would supply us with an engineer and certain parts. He proposed an arrangement whereby we would pay him a certain amount in cash for the benefits we would derive from our connection with him."

Sam and Hezzelwood bought two Jackson cars and tested them on the Oshawa roads. "Suffice to say," Sam recalled, "as automobiles they were a poor job of plumbing." Sam, however, had already been looking at a better offer: "While we had been eating breakfast in Jackson, William Durant and his factory manager had walked into the dining room. 'Sam, what on earth are you doing here?' Durant asked. I told him. He thought for a moment, then said: 'Charlie Lewis is a dear friend of mine. You get his story, then if you're not satisfied, come and see me.'"

Durant had recently purchased the insolvent Buick company from Whiting, and he was building cars in Jackson. Sam had often met "Billy," as Durant was affectionately called, at carriage shows. The Durant–Dort Carriage Company in Flint produced 150,000 rigs a year, ten times McLaughlin's output, and Durant had created this colossus

William C. Durant seated to the driver's left in a 1906 Model F Buick. (*Buick Motor Corporation/National Automotive History Collection, Detroit Public Library*)

from a fifty-dollar investment in a road cart. Now, Billy said, he intended to do bigger things with Buick.

Durant disliked cars: they were noisy, smelly, dirty, and always breaking down. Making an automobile was merely a means of making money, and Durant was driven by a consuming passion for speculation. He was still young, not yet forty-five, wealthy, and, as a grandson of industrialist Henry Crapo, a former governor of Michigan, a blue-chip member of Flint's frontier establishment. Billy was also a black sheep: he had deserted his wife, and was often seen in the company of his beautiful young secretary, Catherine Lederer.

Slight, soft-spoken, with luminous brown eyes and a dazzling smile, Durant possessed mesmerizing charm, absolute self-confidence, and the sales genius of P. T. Barnum. He had no difficulty persuading Flint businessmen to invest in Buick – most of them were his uncles and cousins – and he audaciously valued the company's stock at $500,000 before he had made a single car. In January 1905, Durant exhibited the old Buick at the New York auto show, and took orders for more than a thousand new cars. By the time he bumped into Sam McLaughlin, his plant was producing two cars a day, and Durant was ready to boost the value of his company's stock to $1.5 million.

Sam was smartening up, and before he went back to see Durant, he bought a 1906 Model F two-cylinder Buick for $1,650 from Durant's Toronto agent, the Dominion Automobile Company. "Before I was halfway to Oshawa, I knew it was the car we wanted to make," he told *Maclean's* in 1954. The test was probably the steep Rouge Hill west of Pickering: the Buick, with its light frame and powerful engine, could take the hill in stride, and it went forty miles an hour on a straightaway. It was Sam's kind of car: strong and fast, and its broad, swooping fenders kept the mud off. The Buick sold for $1,250 in the United States; if Sam made the car in Canada, he could match the American price or pocket the four-hundred-dollar difference he saved in customs duties.

Sam went to see Durant. Billy was eager to make a deal, and Sam spent more than two days investigating the Buick operation: "We worked out a tentative plan we thought would be fair to both sides. Then Durant and I sharpened our pencils, agreed on most points – and then reached an impasse. We just couldn't agree on final details of the financial agreement." The sticking point appears to have been who would have majority ownership of the Canadian company. "I guess we were both stubborn," Sam said.

"I went home to Oshawa and told the Governor and George about my failure. I half-expected my father to say, 'All right, that's over; now let's get busy making carriages.' But he didn't. He listened while George and I worked out our alternative plan – to make our own car. All the Governor said was, 'If you think you can make a go of it, go ahead.'"

The Old Man had been sniffing the wind, and he must have been intrigued by the financial information Sam had uncovered at the Buick company. In a *Maclean's* story published on September 1, 1924, J. Herbert Hodgins gives this version: "It is told of Sam that he returned to Oshawa, and in conference with his father and brother, pictured the possibilities of the new industry. 'The first year,' he argued, 'we will be making so and so, and the second year so and so and the third year . . . we'll be wearin' diamonds!'"

Profits were so enormous automobile manufacturers went to great pains to conceal them, but Ransom Olds's records are illuminating. Between March and September, 1905, Olds sold 864 Reo cars for $955,905; his profit was $323,457 and he paid a 10-per-cent dividend on his stock; in 1906, he sold 2,458 Reos and paid a 50-per-cent dividend, plus a 35-per-cent cash bonus. Olds's profit that year must have been close to $1 million. Buick's production was equivalent. By comparison, the McLaughlin Carriage Company, with an annual output of about 15,000 rigs, would be lucky to clear $100,000.

In February 1907, the McLaughlin Carriage Company attempted to hire three Detroit mechanics to design and build "the running gear or chassis of three automobile cars of the highest grade in finish, workmanship and design, and of a thoroughly practical, useful, elegant and marketable kind of about the value of two thousand dollars each." The McLaughlin cars would be designed by Wayne Dunstan and built in Detroit by A. Moorehouse; Harry Nicholds would act as purchasing agent, superintendent, and accountant, and McLaughlin would pay for the parts. The chassis were to be shipped to Oshawa by the following March, and the three Americans would spend the next three years overseeing production in Oshawa.

Sam McLaughlin always maintained that his father had no involvement in the automobile business, but a stipulation that the contract would be void if any of the men "become addicted to, or indulged in, the excessive use of intoxicating liquor," indicates that the offer was drafted by the Governor, and Robert later told the *Financial Post* that he had thought automobiles were a good "sideline" for his buggy business. The contract gave Dunstan, Moorehouse, and Nicholds free rein to construct automobiles operated "by means of gasoline engines, steam engines or electricity, or any combination of them, or other motive power." They would each be paid $125 a month. This paltry wage was ridiculous enough, but McLaughlin intended to hold on to $50 of their monthly wages until the men had moved to Oshawa. They were offered no shares in the company, only a tiny royalty on the wholesale selling price of each automobile: on a car valued at $1,500, the three contractors would share $50. McLaughlin reserved the right to substitute a profit-sharing arrangement – this was struck out by the Americans' lawyer – and demanded a $10,000 bond for "faithful performance" of their duties.

The agreement was never signed, and Sam hit the road in search of another engineer. The McLaughlins seem to have had no idea what kind of car they wanted to make, no grasp of automobile economics – Pierce had already warned Sam against a high-priced car – and their arrogant, cheapskate attitude toward mechanics indicates ignorance of the complexities of automobile technology. The McLaughlins were already lagging far behind the Canadian competition. The Masseys had experimented with automobiles in 1900, and in 1905 CCM jumped in with the Russell: "The Thoroughly Canadian Car; Canadian Material, Canadian Labour, Canadian Capital." Tommy Russell's car was made in Toronto – with an imported Flyer engine – and his five models were priced between $1,300 and $2,500. The Russell had the style of a cockroach, but the low-priced model was better than the Ford and cheaper than a Buick, and by 1906 Tommy Russell was selling cars in England, Australia, and New Zealand.

Back-yard inventors were springing up as quickly as Michigan millionaires. In Montreal, automobile dealer George Foss claimed that he sold Sam McLaughlin a Stanley Steamer, a car that worked like a locomotive. Foss should have sold himself to Sam McLaughlin; in 1897, Foss had built a gasoline-powered car that looked not unlike the rigs Olds and Ford were tinkering with, and it ran like a top. A local bank president offered to finance commercial production, but Foss, to his later regret, backed out.

McLaughlin's best bet was William Still, a Toronto electrician who had patented a lightweight, high-energy battery. In 1893, Still's attorney, Frederick Featherstonhaugh, had installed a battery-powered, four-horsepower motor in a two-seater carriage. His electric car was smooth and silent, without heat or smell, and it was steered with a simple lever. The car's body, designed by Featherstonhaugh, had the graceful lines of McLaughlin's first cutter, and it was fitted with a collapsible buggy top. The car had been built, however, at the rival Dixon carriage works in Toronto, right across Temperance Street from CCM, and CCM provided its wire wheels and pneumatic tires.

Featherstonhaugh's electric was going strong in 1907, and Still had formed his own company, but while his battery was strong enough to get Featherstonhaugh to his home in Mimico and back, it would not get Sam McLaughlin to Oshawa. Sam had not given up on Buick, and negotiations to buy Buick chassis were still active. A letter from the Buick Motor Company dated May 17, 1907, offers to sell to the McLaughlin Carriage Company a "completed chassis, tested out and ready to finish," for $525. "This would be without tires, body, dash, hood, storage battery, tools, lamps, horn, etc." The rest of the letter has been lost, but the writer points out that, with duty and freight, the chassis would cost the McLaughlins $700, and the estimated total cost with parts added would be $1,050. He apologizes for the "annoying" but unavoidable delay in responding to the "peculiarities" of the

The buggy greets the car: a 1908 McLaughlin company calendar advertises the car that was never built, the McLaughlin Model A. (*General Motors of Canada/ Parkwood*)

McLaughlins' proposition, and the last enigmatic words on the surviving page, "To be perfectly . . . ," are not encouraging.

Two months later, July 12, the McLaughlins hired an American engineer, Arthur Milbrath, and began to build a gasoline car. Said Sam in 1954: "We brought him to Oshawa and installed him in one of our buildings which had been set aside as the automobile shop. We equipped it with automatic lathes and other machine tools, planers and shapers – dozens of machines. From a Cleveland firm we ordered cylinders, pistons and crankshafts to our own specifications, and engine castings to be worked in our own shop. I put all I had into designing the most beautiful car I could dream of – the bodies, of course, would be made by the same artisans who had been making our carriages for years. The car was to be more powerful than the Buick."

Milbrath was paid $155 a month, and he was to supervise production of two hundred Model A McLaughlin automobiles by spring. According to George, the McLaughlin Model A was to be a car "of the Buick type." It appears that the McLaughlins intended to "adapt" the American Buick into a car they could call their own. A drawing of the McLaughlin Model A, featured on the company calendar for 1908, certainly looked like a Buick, except the car was painted bottle green with crimson wheels and chassis and matching leather upholstery; it sported four polished brass lamps and a horseshoe-shaped brass radiator.

"We had everything we needed for our first hundred cars," Sam said, "and had the first cars all laid out and practically ready for assembly, down to the beautiful brass McLaughlin radiator on which I had spent so many hours, when disaster struck. Arthur Milbrath became severely ill with pleurisy."

The Model A was never built, and Arthur Milbrath left the company at the end of September. Milbrath's pleurisy seems to have been a case of "diplomatic flu," an opportunity for the McLaughlins to bail out of a ruinous mess when a deal with Buick presented itself. The events surrounding the disappearance of the McLaughlin Model A are shrouded in secrecy and disinformation, but correspondence between the McLaughlin Carriage Company and the Buick Motor Company recently unearthed in a McLaughlin family vault indicates that Sam McLaughlin's version of events cannot be taken at face value.

A letter from George McLaughlin to William Durant dated October 11, 1907, reveals that the McLaughlins, far from making everything themselves, had ordered their parts from independent suppliers, and they had very little stock on hand. "None of the transmissions has been shipped to us as yet, altho' they are nearly all completed in Detroit," George wrote, and George was optimistic about being able to cancel contracts for other parts that had not been shipped. The "Automobile Department" of the McLaughlin Carriage Company was months – even years – away from being able to manufacture a car.

"Without an engineer we were helpless," said Sam. "The automobile shop, so ready to produce its harvest, lay idle – dead. In this plight I thought of William Durant and his goodwill towards the McLaughlins. I wired him, asking him if he could lend us an engineer. His answer came back promptly: 'Will you be home tomorrow? I'm coming over.'"

According to Sam's standard story, he contacted Durant during the first week of September, barely two days after Milbrath suffered his "severe attack of pleurisy," and the next morning Durant arrived in Oshawa by train with his manager, Bill Little. "We went into my father's office with my brother George and Oliver Hezzelwood and in five minutes we had the contract settled," Sam said. "Chiefly it covered the terms under which we had 15-year rights to buy the Buick engine and some other parts. We would build and design our own bodies."

In an interview for the National Film Board movie, *The Oshawa Kid*, however, Sam put another spin on the story: "He [Durant] came over and sold me the idea that it was just putting your head into a furnace to try to build a hundred cars, that you'd go bust. They sold me the idea that it was foolishness because the demand in Canada was very limited. And we'd never have great volume. And he sold me the idea that he would sell me his Buick engine, and let me have any parts of the Buick car I wanted."

Durant was selling hard, and he may have initiated the meeting himself. The American automobile industry was on the verge of collapse. Buick was facing bankruptcy. Automobile investors, panicked by bank failures and predictions that the motoring craze had peaked, dumped their stock and called their loans. Car buyers decided to wait. Many companies, pushed to the wall, shut down production, but Durant kept churning out Buicks, gambling that when the depression passed, only Buick would have cars to sell. Durant desperately needed cash to meet his payroll and stave off his creditors, and a sale to the McLaughlins would dispose of some of the hundreds of unsold Buicks he had stockpiled in vacant lots.

Durant had them over a barrel. George and Sam had borrowed heavily from the Dominion Bank, and Oliver Hezzelwood had persuaded his uncle in Buffalo, O. E. Foster, to invest $100,000. They had advertised a car they didn't have, and they didn't have a licence to clone a Buick. Durant's proposition allowed the McLaughlins to get into the business quickly with a good product, at minimum expense, and with little risk. The official agreement, dated October 3, 1907, was signed, on behalf of the Buick Motor Company, "W. C. Durant, general manager," and for the McLaughlin Carriage Company, "R. McLaughlin, president." For the rest of his life, Sam McLaughlin would take sole credit for founding the McLaughlin Motor Car Company, but it was the Governor's name on the bottom line, and the automobile company was a subsidiary of the McLaughlin Carriage Company: George was vice-president, Sam secretary-treasurer. The scissored half-page bearing the signatures is all that can be found of the agreement that changed Canadian automotive history, but three letters between the two companies in October reveal that it was more than just a purchasing contract.

"We have dispensed with the services of our chief engineer superintendent and all of our workmen," George wrote to Durant on October 11, "so we are now in a position to start with a clean sheet." Milbrath had been dismissed, and George does not mention illness as the cause. In his closing paragraph, George also makes this request: "Please

Workmen seated in the body of the first McLaughlin–Buick, 1908. Left to right,
Mr. Tanton, foreman; Norman Thomas; Tanton's son; and George Parsons, Oshawa's first
motorcycle policeman. (*Thomas Bouckley Collection, Robert McLaughlin Gallery*)

forward as early as possible a sample 1908 body, as we wish to make our
moulds and forms and be getting on with this work."

The McLaughlins were buying the complete Buick, body design and
all, and they were required to purchase all their wheels, lamps, radiators, axles, springs, and other parts from Buick suppliers. All the stock
they had on hand had to be sold or junked. "We will send you as
quickly as possible parts for five completed Model F cars," Bill Little
wrote to Sam McLaughlin on October 22. "Before shipping we will
completely assemble and test each car, afterwards removing the axles
and shipping them separately. While all the parts used by us are interchangeable, we consider it advisable to number the parts so there can
be no mistake in reassembling after the goods reach you. Assembled
drawings are being made showing the different views of the car
completely assembled which should prevent the possibility of error
once you get underway yourselves." The first five Buicks came from a
total order of one hundred; Little promised them by November 9, "the
others to follow shortly after."

The 1908 assembly line, McLaughlin Motor Car Company. The cars were pushed backwards by hand as each operation was completed. (*McLaughlin Public Library/Thomas Bouckley Collection, Robert McLaughlin Gallery*)

The only purpose in shipping the cars across the border in pieces was to shave a bit off Canadian customs duties: a complete car was taxed at 35 per cent, but an engine could be imported at 27.5 per cent and a frame at 30 per cent. These small savings on metal parts were eaten up by the cost of putting the Buick back together in Oshawa, but the McLaughlins could economize by building their own wooden bodies from Buick patterns. Sam McLaughlin was now committed to a paint-by-number automobile, and his fantasy of inventing a Canadian car was carted off to the scrap heap along with his brass radiator. Even the McLaughlins' advertising was integrated with Buick's: "Some considerable saving could be effected by having your catalogue printed at the same time and by the same parties making ours," Durant wrote on October 22. "If you will advise us how many you will require, we will obtain an estimate which will include the necessary changes in wording with your own special cover design and frontispiece."

The McLaughlin Motor Car Company was incorporated in Ontario on November 20, 1907 with a capital of 5,000 shares valued at $100 each. All five directors – Robert, George, and Sam McLaughlin, Oliver Hezzelwood and O. E. Foster – bought one share each. Company executives were Robert, George, and Sam McLaughlin, but their silent partner soon made his presence felt: early in 1908, Billy Durant bought 1,000 shares of the McLaughlin Motor Car Company in trust for Buick. Robert McLaughlin, on behalf of the carriage company, owned 2,650 shares. Robert's son-in-law, J. B. McCulloch, and Oliver's younger brother George bought one share each, giving the McLaughlin interests an investment of $265,700, and a comfortable majority; the extra shares were apparently set aside for future investors. As president and chief shareholder of the carriage company, Robert McLaughlin owned a controlling interest in the McLaughlin Motor Car Company. Sam became president, but by the time the first claret-red Model F chugged off the assembly line, all Sam had left of his design was the name: McLaughlin–Buick.

5

GENERAL MOTORS

The McLaughlin Motor Car Company manufactured 154 McLaughlin–Buicks in 1908. The Model F, the only model the factory seems to have made that year, sold for a list price of $1,400, $200 more than a Buick cost in the United States, but less than it would cost to import one. Assuming a profit of 20 to 30 per cent, the McLaughlins would have cleared about $50,000. Even though a McLaughlin–Buick cost almost three times as much as an auto worker earned in a year, twice as much as the average salary for a bank clerk or schoolteacher, the cars sold like hot cakes.

Dr. Hoig was one of the earliest and most enthusiastic owners of a McLaughlin–Buick, and he explains why: "The village doctor, keeping only one or two animals, had usually only a part time man, and had to do the night work in the stable himself. And mighty disagreeable work it was, especially in the winter. From the moment when, in the course of harnessing, you tried to force the cold bit in his reluctant mouth, until some hours later, when with half frozen fingers you unbuckled the harness and bedded him down for the night, and, if not too sleepy, waited up to give him a drink, all with the dim light of an oil lamp, each minute held its own peculiar misery. From such

A proud family in their new 1908 McLaughlin–Buick, Bowmanville, Ontario. The first thing to do after buying a car was to have its picture taken. (*Ontario Archives 2368 S5197*)

conditions, even the imperfect motors of those early days, with poor springs that seemed to break like cheese, poor lights that necessitated stopping every time they were lit, cranking the car every time you started, the dreadful roads, the change seemed like a deliverance from slavery."

Fear and loathing of horseflesh was a strong incentive to switch to gasoline. Ford dreamed of liberating farmers from the drudgery of the horse-drawn plough; Olds promoted his runabout with this slogan: "It never kicks or bites, never tires out on long runs, and during hot weather you can ride fast enough to make a breeze without sweating the horse. It does not require care in the stable, and only eats while it is on the road, which is no more than at the rate of 1 cent per mile." Spirited carriage horses were hard to control; flimsy buggies afforded their occupants no protection if they hit a ditch or crashed into a tree. Buggy accidents were frequent and often fatal; even Sarah McLaughlin's life may have been shortened by the blow she received from the cutter shaft.

Hoig's misadventures with his McLaughlin–Buick created as much hilarity in Oshawa as had Oliver Hezzelwood with his Ford: "Once I left my car on Mary Street where there is a steep grade. My brake wouldn't hold, so I put the gear in reverse, which held it satisfactorily;

but, unfortunately, on coming out of the house, I forgot its being in reverse, and started to crank it. What was my amazement to see it back away from me, like a shy maiden, and project itself through the fence of Newton Johns' house, and attempt to enter the home. And this provided an opportunity for the only 'bon mot' that I had ever known Mr. Johns, who is a rather serious appearing gentleman, to indulge in. He telephoned me to say that he had just heard of the occurrence, and that he hoped I did not propose to charge it up as a visit."

Hoig's next mistake was less amusing: "I forgot that I had left the car in gear, and when I started to crank, it sprang forward like a wild beast, with me on the bumper, through the trees, until stopped by a big maple, smashing the car effectually. I was thought to be dead, but escaped with some smashed ribs."

Doctors could afford to buy cars – Ford was plugging his new Model T as "the doctor's car" – and they provided the manufacturers with priceless publicity. The doctor's car was seen everywhere, and its idiosyncrasies provided fresh anecdotes to entertain and distract anxious patients. The automobile became identified with health and fresh air, science and social prestige. A British physician praised the car's jolting for "a healthy agitation" of the liver, and claimed that "much benefit to nervous patients is caused by the air blowing on the face." Windshields were still optional, and it would be more than ten years before the closed car began to catch on.

The invention of the automobile followed on the heels of the discovery of germs, and a radical change in public attitudes to health. Disease was no longer an arbitrary act of God, placated by poultices and prayer, but a human misfortune that could be both prevented and cured. Responsibility shifted from God to man, but the devil was still Beelzebub. Houseflies were identified as carriers of typhoid and other contagious diseases, and the source of contamination was not hard to find: "Fattening on the horse droppings on the street, and in the stable, and in other much more objectionable extramural structures, they would swarm into the house in the warm spring days through the open windows and doors, remaining for the whole season," says Dr. Hoig.

The elimination of horse manure became part of a passionate public-health crusade – air pollution from automobile exhaust would not be recognized for more than forty years – and the liberation of overworked dray horses was encouraged by animal-welfare activists. The magazine *Horseless Age* predicted: "In cities and towns the noise and clatter of the streets will be reduced. Streets will be cleaner, jams and blockades less likely to occur, and accidents less frequent, for the horse is not so manageable as a mechanical vehicle." Farmers, resentful of being pushed to the side of the road by a speeding motor car, then begged to drag the car out of the ditch, hauled rocks and logs onto rural roads to discourage automobile traffic, but since farmers refused to pay taxes to improve the roads, they had little support from teamsters or carriage owners.

The rival automobile and tire manufacturers promoted their products by organizing race meets, hill climbs, and long-distance endurance tests. Durant loved this kind of showmanship, and he challenged Barney Oldfield's dominance of the racetrack with a Buick team of drivers led by "Wild" Bob Burman and a swarthy Swiss mechanic, Louis Chevrolet. Burman, driving a McLaughlin–Buick, set Canadian speed records at races in Montreal and Winnipeg between 1908 and 1910. The competitions created a buzz of excitement among the sporting crowd, particularly wealthy businessmen who aped European aristocrats by employing chauffeurs to drive, and repair, their powerful cars.

Rich men bought electric cars for their wives. Electrics had closed tops, windows, and the odourless engines started with a twist of the wrist. Miss Daisy Post of New York drove an electric as early as 1899, followed, with haste, by Mrs. William K. Vanderbilt and Mrs. Stuyvesant Fish. "These women do not drive their own autos," a reporter pointed out, "but use them for paying calls, for shopping and for riding on the Avenue, and the style of vehicles which they choose are the Victoria and the brougham. The automobile Victoria, with two men in livery on the box, is certainly a very smart appearing vehicle."

Louis Chevrolet in a Buick racer. (*Buick Motor Corporation*)

In Flint, Durant's daughter Margery was driving a Buick. "So simple a child could sell it," was Durant's pitch, and Margery was barely twenty. "I had broken clutches and flat tires, burned-out bearings and short circuits, valve rattles and piston knocks from one end of the country to the other," Margery writes in her memoir, My *Father*. "I came to know where all the good-natured farmers with the strongest mules lived. I found out just where the deepest mud puddles lay. I learned to look out for ugly stumps hidden like rattlesnakes in the grass beside our narrow country roads. I walked miles to get some grinning farmer to crank my engine. I ruined half the dresses I possessed trying to find out why my engine wouldn't start – when night was coming on and I was miles from home. I wanted to be driving all the time! There was nothing like it!"

Margery was the Buick's most demanding test-driver, and she and her father logged hundreds of miles along the twisting back roads of Michigan and New York state. "Sudden stops with old-fashioned brakes were painful events," she recalls. "You drew up with a fearful jerk. Or else there was an imperceptible change of speed culminating in a sharp rear-back that felt exactly as if the car were shying at something in the road. We took turns driving in order to give each other a rest. The driver today has little idea of the way one's shoulders used to be taxed by the continual jerking of the wheel and whipping of the car's front end."

Durant made careful notes about the Buick's faults and he never despaired, even when, as Margery discovered on one trip, "the whole back end of our driving mechanism was falling off!" A broken-down Buick was left to the mercies of a local mechanic or shipped back home on the train: "Father knew that while we may have given one village a bad sample of what the motor car could do, there were a score of other villages through which we had driven as serenely as if our vehicle were being run by a perpetual motion machine. He was stubbornly driving his horseless carriage through villages so that the plain people of the country could see its worth."

A pretty girl at the wheel turned heads, and sold Buicks, but, like Boadicea in her chariot, Margery Durant was leading a rebellion. She was proving to women that they could drive, and they could drive alone, by themselves, wherever they wanted to go. Only the most able or eccentric horsewomen drove buggies. Except on Sundays, when their husbands or fathers drove them to church, women went about

Cranking a car, Winnipeg, Manitoba, c. 1912. (*Western Canada Pictorial Index, Winnipeg*)

on foot, by streetcar or cab, or they hired a man to drive them. In Ottawa, Laura Borden, the very proper wife of Conservative MP Robert Borden, drove her own electric car, and it was no accident that the roof of the electric car was high enough to accommodate a lady's hat.

No respectable woman ever left the house without her hat, and Edwardian hats had reached magnificent proportions. A framework of straw more than two feet wide, piled equally high with everything that took a milliner's fancy – ostrich feathers, silk roses, bows, ribbons, veils, and wisps of lace – was perched like a nesting bird on the top of a lady's upswept hair. The hat was held in place by long pins, and if a lady's hair was insufficient, a hairpiece or "transformation" was added.

Buggies and electrics were excellent vehicles for showing off hats, but gasoline automobiles went too fast: hats flew off, hairpins came out, hair fell down, or off, and ladies were left *déshabillé*. The solution, to tie the hat on with scarves wrapped around the neck, could be fatal if the scarves became tangled in the wheels – dancer Isadora Duncan was dramatically strangled in this way. For a brief period, women were persuaded to wear voluminous white cotton "dusters" to protect their clothes and cover their hats, and some dusters shrouded a woman's entire head, leaving her a small gauze opening to peer through. Dusters were hot, hideous, and stupid. What was the point of wearing a hat if no one could see it? And why drive in the country if you had to breathe through a veil? Women had a choice: give up driving, or change their style.

The dusters disappeared, and ladies began sporting little peaked "chauffeur" caps and sleek felt helmets modelled on the leather-and-goggles style of race-car drivers. They began to cut their hair, and raise their skirts above their ankles: dresses that dragged on the ground were too clumsy for clambering in and out of cars, especially when you had to stand in the ditch while the driver changed a tire, or change it yourself. The bicycle craze had introduced women to the freedom of bloomers and divided skirts; now the honk of the automobile horn sounded the death knell for bustles, stiff-necked blouses, and wasp-waist corsets. Women who slit their hobble skirts became known as "flappers" from the pieces of fabric left waving in the wind, and not long after Canadian women learned to drive, they got the vote.

Margery Durant's Canadian husband, Dr. Edwin Ruthven Campbell, was a pivotal figure in the relationship between Sam McLaughlin and Buick. Campbell had been born near Port Perry on Lake Scugog, one of Sam's favourite cycling spots, and Sam often spoke of Campbell as his closest friend. It may have been Campbell who persuaded Durant to let the McLaughlins retain majority ownership of their Canadian Buick plant, a favour Durant granted to no one else.

Campbell was a romantic, mysterious figure. The records of the University of Toronto show that an "E. Campbell" graduated from the Faculty of Medicine in 1887, but seven or eight years later, Dr. Edwin Campbell was practising in a remote lumber camp in northern Michigan. He apparently encountered the Durant family on vacation, and Sam McLaughlin later joked that it was Campbell's skill at poker, not surgery, that caught Durant's attention. A handsome, suave young bachelor, Campbell moved to Flint soon after, and cut a swath through Flint society. "He made his winter rounds in a red sleigh, his lap covered with furs," says Lawrence Gustin. "It was said that to be well born, a child had to be delivered by Dr. Campbell." Campbell became the Durants' personal physician in 1896, when Margery was nine, and they married when she was eighteen; Campbell gave his age as thirty-two. Unless he had earned his medical degree at age thirteen, he seems to have knocked nearly ten years off his age. Even so, Campbell's age caused Flint tongues to wag that he was nothing but a fortune-hunter – Durant's wedding gift was $150,000 of his carriage-company stock – but this scandal paled beside Durant's divorce on May 27, 1908, and his marriage to Catherine Lederer in New York the next morning. Durant set Catherine up in a hotel suite, and spent his time commuting between New York and Flint. Dr. Campbell gave up his practice and joined Durant in New York to help promote a bold new scheme: a monopoly of the American automobile industry.

On July 14, 1971, two months before his one hundredth birthday, Sam McLaughlin dictated an astonishing letter to Lee Mayes, general manager of General Motors' Buick division in Flint. "I was sitting in Mr. Durant's little office in Flint with Dr. Campbell, after Mr. Durant had bought the Buick company," Sam said. "The three of us were alone there when we started gossiping and talking about things in general. During the course of the conversation we decided we should form a company, calling it General Motors, and Dr. Campbell was directed to go to Chicago to sell the first million dollars worth of stock. He did so, and had no trouble whatever selling the stock; so that was really how General Motors was formed and started."

Never, in the course of countless interviews, had Sam McLaughlin once mentioned being in on the organization of General Motors, nor is he mentioned in any of the accounts left by the participants, including Durant's own extensive notes. In extreme old age, Sam seems to have compressed several incidents into one, and it is possible that Durant did sound Sam out at an early stage. Certainly Durant's small investment in the McLaughlin Motor Car Company was his first step in assembling an automobile conglomerate, and the McLaughlins' success in Canada was encouraging. Ford was already selling his Canadian-built cars to Great Britain, Australia, and other countries in the British Empire at preferred tariff rates, and Durant could envision himself ruling a worldwide automobile empire more powerful than Standard Oil or the House of Morgan.

J. Pierpont Morgan had cast an acquisitive eye on the automobile industry as early as 1901, when his New York banking house loaned Benjamin Briscoe $100,000 to build radiators for the new Oldsmobile. By 1907, Morgan had a substantial investment in Briscoe's own automobile, the Maxwell–Briscoe, and idea of a merger of companies originated with a Morgan partner, George Perkins. Four makes were involved – Buick, Maxwell–Briscoe, Reo, and Ford – and negotiations with Durant, Briscoe, Ransom Olds, and Henry Ford began in the spring of 1908. They were a prickly, hard-nosed quartet, and hopes of a merger quickly foundered on the shoals of pride and suspicion. Ford and Olds pulled out – Ford wanted no truck with Morgan or any other banker – and the deal collapsed when the Morgan bankers got cold feet.

Durant was left holding the bag. "The Buick stock had been deposited and if released could never again be collected in the same form," Durant told Morgan's lawyer, Herbert Satterlee, "nor would I have the courage, or care, to make another attempt. I must have a consolidation." Durant, as usual, had a card up his sleeve: the Detroit investors who had pushed Ransom Olds out of his company were facing ruin, and Oldsmobile was for sale. Satterlee agreed to incorporate Durant's new company. What would they call it? Morgan had claimed the "International Motor Car Company" as the name of his stillborn venture, and a "United Motors Car Company" was already in existence. "We suggest the name, 'General Motors Company,' which we have ascertained can be used," Satterlee wrote to Durant on September 10, 1908. Durant liked it, and the General Motors Company of New Jersey came into being six days later. Incorporating in New Jersey offered the advantage of almost no restrictions on a company's activities.

General Motors was capitalized at $12.5 million, and on September 29, it bought Buick for $3.75 million in stock. "The price was remarkably low," observe Dunham and Gustin, "but since Durant was selling it to himself, it didn't matter much." On November 12, General Motors bought all the Olds Motor Company stock for $3 million in General Motors stock, and Durant supplied Oldsmobile with a hot new model, a Buick Model 10.

"I sent to the Oldsmobile factory by truck one of these bodies in the white [unpainted], following with my engineer and production manager," Durant said later. "Arriving, at the plant, I had the body placed on two ordinary saw horses and asked the plant manager if there was a cross-cut saw. When it was produced, I asked to have the body cut lengthwise from front to rear and crosswise in the center from side to side (bodies at that time were made of wood), giving me an opportunity to widen and lengthen the body, changing the size and appearance completely. When finished, it was a handsome creation, painted and trimmed to meet the Oldsmobile standard and priced to the trade at $1,200 ($200 more than the Model 10). This gave to the dealers a very handsome small car without interfering in any way with the Buick Model 10. A very happy solution – placing the Oldsmobile Division of General Motors immediately on a profitable basis."

A "McLaughlin" car near Sarnia, Ontario, c. 1910. (*Ontario Archives 16856 - 1659*)

In Canada, the McLaughlin Motor Car Company advertised the Buick Model 10 in French grey for $1,050, and imported some of these sporty two-seaters from Flint, but the Oshawa works concentrated on building the standard, five-passenger Buick Model F. Like Ford's Model T, it was a family car, with four cylinders and twenty-two horsepower. It came with three brass oil lamps, gas headlights, generator, horn, repair outfit, and jack. Extras: lined top with blizzard front and dust hood, $100; glass windshield, $50; extra gas tank, $40. The wheel base was ninety-two inches, and the engine was connected to the rear axle by a "heavy, strong and substantially built roller chain." Each brake drum was fourteen inches, and "the braking surface is lined with camel's hair felt, which can be renewed at a very slight expense when necessary."

The differences between a McLaughlin–Buick and a Buick were almost imperceptible. Rather than cut a hole in the floor to sink the battery, McLaughlin's engineer, William Moyse, raised the body about an inch and a half, filling the space with a strip of wood. The Buick's upholstery had an extra tuck under the buttons, but the McLaughlins designed their own unique "glass front," a split windshield that allowed the driver to crank up the top half to form a visor. Said the catalogue: "This is the only front we have seen which, when driving against the

Four generations: J. J. McLaughlin with his infant son, Allan, flanked by his father, Robert, on the left, and grandfather, John. *(McLaughlin Public Library)*

rain, can be adjusted by the driver so that he can see out clearly, and at the same time be thoroughly protected from the wet." Robert's craftsman's touch can be seen again at work: "Handsome East India Mahogany, selected grain. Beautifully finished in varnish and oil. Brass finished. Heavy English Plate Glass. This is a high grade front in every particular. No better can be made."

The Old Man had become something of an expert on industrial glass as a shareholder and director in his eldest son's firm, J. J. McLaughlin, Manufacturing Chemists. In the eighteen years since he had returned to Toronto from Brooklyn, Jack McLaughlin had developed a successful wholesale business, manufacturing and selling soda-fountain products to drugstores in Ontario and western Canada. J. J. McLaughlin specialized in "Hygeia" Distilled Water, "Real Fruit" juices, and "Sanitary" Soda Fountains, but the company also made and imported mineral waters, carbonated beverages, syrups, creams, cordials, extracts, fountain fruits, ice-cream machinery, and soda-fountain supplies.

Jack had started in a small plant on Berti Street, but soon moved to 145–155 Sherbourne Street, an industrial area near the waterfront. There was nothing particularly sanitary about the outside of his factory, a red-brick warehouse with a huge, belching smokestack, but Jack's advertising cleverly played on the public craze for cleanliness. His soda fountains were made of onyx and chrome, hard materials that had an antiseptic shine when wiped with a wet cloth, and the gleaming counter and spigots were reflected in a long plate-glass mirror behind the fountain.

The soda fountain was modelled on the bar of a saloon, and its purpose was to offer a non-alcoholic alternative to whisky and beer. Unlike the saloon, the soda fountain was a respectable meeting place, especially for young women, and its popularity increased in direct proportion to temperance agitation. In Toronto the Good, where members of the Women's Christian Temperance Union flailed at hotelkeepers with their rolled umbrellas, selling soda fountains was a highly profitable act of Christian duty. When J. J. McLaughlin Ltd. was incorporated on October 25, 1905, it was valued at $250,000, and Jack McLaughlin's family lived in the fashionable new suburb of Rosedale.

Jack had married Maud Christie, a red-haired New Yorker of such intimidating *hauteur* she terrified almost everyone who met her. Maud was a *Christie*, as she frequently reminded her colonial in-laws, and she had scant time for the countrified McLaughlin sisters. Maud's dowry probably helped Jack set up in business, and he could afford to build a rambling frame summer home on Lake Rosseau in Muskoka. The clean, cool air of Muskoka was the last hope for tubercular patients, and Jack had already spent some time at the sanatorium in Gravenhurst. At his cottage on Worthington Point, he could enjoy the summers with his three children, Donald, Margery, and Roland: Jack and Maud's first son, Allan, had died in infancy.

Jack was forty-three, and although his body was skeletal, his mind was feverish and inventive. After more than ten years of experiments, he had developed a new formula for ginger ale. His first product, "McLaughlin's Belfast Style Ginger Ale," based on an old Irish recipe, was too dark and syrupy for Canadian tastes, but by 1904 he had lightened the colour and sharpened the taste. He called it "McLaughlin's Pale Dry Ginger Ale," and the next year he applied for a patent for "Canada Dry Pale Ginger Ale." Maud, her husband's taste-tester, came up with the slogan: "The Champagne of Ginger Ales." The name was a marketing inspiration, and Jack's sparkling new soda pop, pungent with fresh Jamaican ginger, found eager customers with the Robert Simpson Company of Toronto and the Hudson's Bay Company in Edmonton, Alberta. J. J. McLaughlin's Canada Dry trademark was registered on January 18, 1907. The label pictured a map of Canada crowned with a beaver.

Jack followed his father's example, shipping boxcar-loads of bottled ginger ale to a Winnipeg warehouse for distribution throughout the Prairies, and in the spring of 1907 J. J. McLaughlin Ltd. opened a second

The J.J. McLaughlin Pharmacy

First Canada Dry label, 1906

J. J. McLaughlin's first Toronto soft drink factory, and his first label for Canada Dry ginger ale. (*Cadbury Beverages*)

bottling plant in Edmonton. That summer, six months before the first carloads of disassembled Buicks arrived in Oshawa from Flint, J. J. McLaughlin had shipped his first boxcars of Canada Dry across the American border to Buffalo, Brooklyn, and Detroit.

"The Champagne of Ginger Ales" gave a high-class image to a workingman's drink, and champagne was a popular tonic for invalids, teetotal or not. Jack drank champagne: he also put whisky in his eggnog. Coca-Cola no longer contained cocaine – the drug was banned in 1903 – and while caffeine was an effective substitute, whisky had a bigger kick. It wasn't long before Canadians discovered that an ounce or two of rye in a glass of Canada Dry was a miraculous cure for everything that ailed them, and who could tell the rye from the Dry?

Canada Dry was sold in pint- or quart-sized green bottles; it was legal and portable, and its simple, hygienic packaging capitalized on the public's fear of contaminated water. Soda pop could be purchased at the grocery store, and it could be drunk at home, at the curling rink, and the baseball game, or it could be packed with a picnic in the family's new car. The bottles were returnable: each one was embossed with McLaughlin's name and some early ones bore the stern reminder: "This bottle is my property. Anyone using, destroying or retaining it will be prosecuted."

With its standard formula and uniform quality, bottled pop was the most significant innovation in mass production since the photograph, and it introduced the moving production line to North American industry. Henry Ford usually attributed his inspiration for his automated assembly line to a visit to an abattoir, where animal carcasses swung by the butchers on pulleys, but one of Ford's earliest jobs had been in a bottling plant. He introduced his moving chain only in 1913, when the parts of each Model T had been simplified and standardized to the point where they were as interchangeable as pop bottles.

Technologically, J. J. McLaughlin was years ahead of his younger brothers. Early automobiles were manufactured much as carriages had been. The bodies were constructed in one part of the shop, the chassis in another, and the engines elsewhere. As completed, parts of each vehicle were pushed or carried from one station to another, and when the body, engine, and chassis all reached the back door, they were bolted together in "marriage" and the car sent on its way. The pace was set by the workmen, and it depended on their skill, enthusiasm, and the respect they had for their foreman. Each man owned his own tools, and if there was a foul-up, he put his tools down until it was resolved.

In 1908, Oliver Hezzelwood opened the first McLaughlin–Buick dealership in Toronto. It was housed in a handsome building of buff-coloured brick at the corner of Church and Richmond streets, and the location, a block south of all the city's biggest churches, drew a good Sunday congregation of window shoppers. There was nothing else to do on the Lord's Day in Toronto, and for most of the pedestrians who gathered in front of the main-floor display windows, a shiny red McLaughlin–Buick with its polished brass headlamps was the most magnificent object they could ever dream of owning.

In England, the indolence and appetites of King Edward VII gave a glitter of dissipation to the twilight years of the British Empire, but Canada was sunk in gloom. The most popular colour for carriages, apart from black, was drab green. Drab blue was a close second. Muddy shades of ochre and red were copied in carpets and wallpapers; in clothing, tweed was ubiquitous. Furniture was varnished a dark, sticky brown. Frame houses were usually left unpainted, and buildings of brick and stone became blackened with soot. Coal dust from the furnaces turned curtains brown in the winter, and in the summer, dirt blew in from the unpaved roads. Few families could afford crystal or silver, and even the fashion in women's hats was black. Electric

An early car wash. (*National Archives of Canada, PA 86110*)

lights were dim, and careful towns turned the power off at midnight.

The gloom was psychological too. The poor knew only work and sin; the rich pulled long faces, read their Bibles, and collected paintings of buffalo or English sheep. A McLaughlin–Buick stuck out like a Mississippi gambler at a prayer meeting: vulgar, extravagant, all flash and Yankee "show." Its brass suggested saloons and spittoons, its red upholstery brought a whiff of the brothel, and it wasn't long before the Canadian government slapped a "luxury" tax on automobiles. This fortuitous association with vice made an automobile intensely desirable, and for the opportunity to park such a provocative piece of modern machinery in front of his humble home, the average man would make a lifetime of sacrifices.

Caressing the automobile was one of the joys of ownership, and enchanted motorists spent as many happy hours wiping, polishing, and washing as they did driving. This outpouring of affection caused a headache for the manufacturers: rubbing the body dulled the varnish and soap turned the paint milky. Owners were admonished to wipe the car with a flannel cloth or wash it in clear, cold water. Motorists who lived near a lake or a creek with a firm bottom drove their cars into the water up to the hubcaps and washed them there; the soaking also swelled the wooden spokes and gave the car a smoother ride.

An open car had to be kept indoors, and most people used their stable or carriage house once the horse and buggy had been sold. Some owners covered their car's radiator with a blanket at night, and it wasn't uncommon to see a car roaring down the street with its distraught driver yelling, "Whoa! Whoa!" An automobile took at least as much care and worry as a horse. Brass lamps and trim had to be polished, folding tops oiled, gasoline fetched in cans from the hardware merchant and poured into the tank through a chamois filter. Underneath, the drive chain had to be cleaned, frame bolts tightened, and the moving parts oiled. Motorists who neglected their automobiles were chastised by the manufacturers. "Look the car over carefully and you will find numerous oil holes, oil cups and grease cups," instructed a Cadillac manual. "Remember that these are placed there for a purpose. THAT PURPOSE IS OIL. Oil holes frequently become stopped up. When they do, be careful not to overlook them."

Most American-made automobiles until 1914 had the steering wheel on the right, although in most Canadian provinces, cars, like carriages, drove on the right-hand side of the road. Nova Scotia and British Columbia stuck to the British custom of driving on the left, and Prince Edward Island banned automobiles until 1913. Country roads were so narrow that cars followed the wagon ruts down the middle. There were no stop signs or traffic lights. Speed limits varied from five to ten miles per hour in cities and towns, although Winnipeg, influenced by a powerful automobile lobby, permitted fifteen miles per hour in residential areas. Manitoba had no speed limit for country roads so long as the driver used "reasonable care." The maximum fine was fifty dollars, and the offender's car could be impounded by a magistrate, but in rural areas, police were so scarce drivers could go as fast as they dared. In Ontario, the provincial police convicted eleven motorists of offences in 1910, six the following year, two in 1912 and one in 1913.

Automobiles were licensed for a fee of five or ten dollars, and the licence had to be prominently displayed on the car. Provincial governments published the names of automobile owners, their licence numbers, addresses, and the makes of their cars. Thieves could pick and choose, and since cars could not be locked, popular models disappeared in the middle of the night. In 1910, 372 McLaughlin–Buicks were registered in Manitoba and Saskatchewan, a close second to Ford's 398. Reo trailed a distant third. Everybody else drove an astonishing variety of makes: Auburn, Overland, Pope–Waverly, E.M.F., Flanders, Autocar,

Office staff, McLaughlin Carriage Company, 1909. The factory manager, E. W. Drew, is in the centre, flanked by Robert and George McLaughlin. Sam McLaughlin stands well back, behind Drew, a position that reflects his junior rank in the company. *(McLaughlin Public Library/Thomas Bouckley Collection, Robert McLaughlin Gallery)*

International Auto Buggy, Brush, Stoddart–Dayton, Tudhope–McIntyre, Hupmobile, Chalmers, Kissel Kar, Metz, Zimmerman, and "Self Made." The automobile did not agree with everyone: out of 823 registered licences in Saskatchewan, forty-five drivers stated that they had "disposed of" their cars. One was "no longer operating," one was "defunct," and one had been "destroyed by fire."

The McLaughlin Motor Car Company manufactured 423 Buicks in 1909 and 847 in 1910, a puny output compared to Buick's American production of 30,525 in 1910. Buick was now the largest automobile company in America, outselling Ford and Cadillac combined, and General Motors had mushroomed into a conglomerate of more than twenty-five companies with sales totalling $50 million. Durant had tried, and failed, to buy Ford Ford's price, $8 million in cash, was too steep for Billy's bankers – but he bought Cadillac for $4.75 million in the summer of 1909. Says Durant biographer, Bernard Weisberger, in *The Dream Maker*: "Stimulated, energized, almost intoxicated with the sense of how easy it was to buy motor companies, Durant rushed ahead, sweeping up new firms as if they would rot left unpicked."

"They say I shouldn't have bought Cartercar," Durant said later. "Well, how was anyone to know that Cartercar wasn't going to be the thing? It had the friction drive and no other car had it. Maybe friction drive would be the thing. And then there's the Elmore, with its two-cycle engine. That's the kind they were using on motorboats; maybe two cycles was going to be the thing in automobiles. I was for getting every car in sight, playing safe all along the line."

Durant picked up Oakland, Ranier, Welch – an automobile the size of a locomotive – Marquette, Ewing, Randolph, and Reliance trucks, the National Motor Cab Company, the Novelty Incandescent Lamp Company, and a dozen more obscure manufacturers, including Bedford Motors of London, Ontario. Durant's method was simple and inexpensive: he traded shares in General Motors for shares in the company he was buying. Since General Motors was valued at more than $60 million and its shares were trading at close to $100, his offer was attractive to struggling manufacturers looking for security.

The McLaughlins took advantage of Durant's spending spree. On September 17, 1909, the capital of the McLaughlin Motor Car Company was increased to $1.2 million by adding 7,000 shares at $100 each to the original 5,000. Durant bought 5,000 shares of the reorganized company in trust for Buick; the McLaughlin Carriage Company increased its holding to 5,000 shares and the remaining stock, valued at $197,000, remained unsold. Robert, George, and Sam McLaughlin owned six shares each; Oliver and George Hezzelwood, O. E. Foster, and J. B. McCulloch three shares each. Durant did not join the board of directors of the McLaughlin Motor Car Company or the McLaughlin Carriage Company, but Buick had increased its ownership significantly, and in exchange, Durant had given the McLaughlins 5,000 shares of Buick stock. The value of the carriage company was inflated to $1.2 million, giving the two McLaughlin enterprises in Oshawa a capitalization of $2.4 million, about 3 per cent of the paper value of General Motors. In November 1909, General Motors declared a 150 per cent dividend on its stock, and Sam and George McLaughlin raised their salaries by $500 to $3,000 a year.

Durant had acquired an almost mystical reputation as a financial wizard, and he cultivated a Napoleonic style. "It was quickly made plain that General Motors was a 'one-man institution,'" a reporter for Motor World wrote early in 1910. "Durant dominated it from top and bottom and brooked no interference. He is a prodigious worker and the wonder is how he attended to so many details, great and small, and lived through it all. He kept one eye on his factories and another on the stock ticker, and the while he dreamed of world conquests."

Billy, as his friends still called him, radiated boyish enthusiasm, and his confidence was infectious. He was able to raise millions in an afternoon, and his investors trusted him implicitly. He seemed never to sleep. He summoned his managers to conferences in the middle of the night, rarely remained in town more than a few hours, and kept all the details of his innumerable business transactions in his head. Apart from his personal secretary, Winfred Murphy, Durant didn't bother with staff, files, records, or correspondence. "We're going to New York," he would announce, meaning that the train left Flint in ten minutes. "He was in constant motion among his companies, rushing from outpost to outpost," writes Weisberger in *The Dream Maker*. "He needed to maintain a desperate pace simply to keep up with his own inspirations."

"It was like the visitation of a cyclone," recalled Lee Dunlap, manager of the Oakland plant in Pontiac, Michigan. "He would lead his staff in, take off his coat, begin issuing orders, dictating letters, and calling the ends of the continent on the telephone, talking in his rapid, easy way to New York, Chicago, San Francisco. It put most of us in awe of him. On this visit, I expected he would stay several days as we were to discuss the whole matter of plant expansion. But after a few hours, Mr. Durant said, 'Well, we're off to Flint.' In despair I led him on a quick inspection of the plant. Instantly he agreed we would have to build, and asked me to bring the expansion plan with me to Flint the next day. There wasn't any plan, and none could be drawn on such short notice, but his will being law, and our need great, something had to be done."

Dunlap and his staff spent all night constructing a miniature cardboard layout of the factory, including the proposed new buildings. "Feeling like a small boy with a new toy, I took this lay-out to Flint and rather fearfully placed it before the chief. He was pleased pink. We had a grand time fitting our new buildings into the picture as it was spread on his desk. We placed those new buildings first here, then there, debating the situation. When we agreed as to where they should go, he said, 'Glue them down and call W. E. Wood.' Mr. Wood came in after a few minutes and received an order for their construction. In the whole history of America up to that time, buildings had never risen as swiftly as those did. Contractor Wood had men, materials and machinery moving towards Pontiac within twenty-four hours, and we were installing machinery in part of the structures within three weeks. But, of course, we could not be equally swift in paying for them. That was something else. But for the time being none of us worried too much over that; we figured the 'Little Fellow' would find the money somewhere. Which he did, in the end, though we know there was plenty of trouble before the bills were receipted."

It was typical of Durant that he would spend hours playing with toy buildings, and authorize a new factory, without inspecting the car he was making. Durant's philosophy was the opposite of Henry Ford's. The Ford company existed to manufacture cars; for Durant, a car was a vehicle to build General Motors. As Durant's lawyer, John Carton, said later: "Billy never thought that General Motors would become the big manufacturer that it did; what [he] desired, most of all, were large stock issues in which he, from an inside position, could dicker and trade."

Durant trusted his hunches, and some paid off. He had bought the rights to a new sparkplug invented by a French immigrant, Albert Champion; Cadillac's profits were quickly repaying his investment; and Oldsmobile was proving the power of a $3 million name. The public, however, was becoming wary, and the market was glutted with junk. The Oakland plant had been failing when Durant bought it; it continued to founder, and most of Durant's other acquisitions were worthless. In January 1910, Durant had paid John Heany $7 million in General Motors stock and $112,759 cash for his electric-headlamp company. Heany's dubious patents were being challenged by General Electric, and Heany had barely escaped conviction for tampering with the dates on his applications. Soon after the purchase, Heany's patents were voided. How had Durant made such a blunder?

Says Weisberger: "John Carton had a hard suspicion, shared by others. It was that Durant knew that he was buying a false front and did not care. The purchase furnished an excuse for issuing extra GM shares that would find their way to market disguised as representatives of objects of value. The practice of authorizing issues with nothing behind them, known as stock-watering, had a long and dishonorable entry in the annals of deceiving investors."

Durant protested that the Heany lamp was exactly what he wanted, but his reputation had been tarnished, and Wall Street financiers turned a cold, appraising eye on General Motors. The company was earning an annual profit of $10 million, but this was far from sufficient to cover the costs of runaway expansion, and the "wild man," as Durant was now called, was borrowing frantically from more than two hundred financial sources. He had stripped Buick to buy Cadillac at an inflated

price, and by the spring of 1910, he had run out of cash to pay his suppliers and his workmen. Production ground to a standstill at the Buick
plant in Flint; forty-two hundred auto workers were laid off, and layoffs
and shutdowns followed in other GM plants in Michigan.

Durant mustered his troops for a last, desperate stand, and among
the loyalists were the McLaughlins of Oshawa. Their friendship was
not without calculation. A memo to "R. S. McL." dated August 25,
1910, and initialled by George, notes a twelve-month loan of
$52,935.25 from Canada's Standard Bank "to cover loan of $50,000
sent W. C. Durant, for which W. C. D. is to give his own note secured
by stock certificates of Durant & Dort Cge. Coy. He is also to *give* 500
shares General Motors Coy. stock (Common). This to be placed with
Standard Bank as security for loan."

The McLaughlins gambled that General Motors would survive.
Although their loan small – Durant needed $15 million – it was a vote
of confidence at a time when the richest men in the United States were
refusing to lend Durant another penny. On September 30, 1910,
Robert McLaughlin exercised his option to buy twenty-three shares of
General Motors stock for $100 each. It was a trivial sum, but the shares
were trading at $25 and the word on Wall Street was that GM was a
scrap heap.

The McLaughlins appear to have been in on a secret rescue plan
negotiated by two members of the GM board, J. H. McClement and
Wilfrid Leland, who convinced two banking houses, Lee, Higginson of
Boston and J. & W. Seligman of New York, that Buick and Cadillac
were well worth saving. On September 26, the bankers offered to lend
General Motors $15 million for a five-year period, on condition that
Durant relinquish control of the company for the term of the loan. The
deal had been negotiated without Durant's knowledge or consent, and
the price was steep. The banks took a commission of $4.25 million in
cash and $6 million in GM stock; they charged 6 per cent interest on
the loan, and held a mortgage on all GM property. A board of five
trustees, including Durant, would be appointed to run the company,
but authority would rest with the new president, Boston banker James
J. Storrow.

Durant was humiliated, but the agreement was signed on November
11, 1910. To make way for the bankers' appointees, eleven members of
the GM board were forced to resign, among them Sam McLaughlin,
who had been appointed in May. It was an embarrassing end to Sam's

fledgling boardroom career, and for the rest of his life Sam skipped over the crisis that nearly put him out of business. "We began to have a little fun with our creditors," Sam joked on the occasion of General Motors of Canada's seventy-fifth anniversary. "They [the bankers] thought [Durant] was too much of a plunger."

The McLaughlin Motor Car Company escaped the carnage as GM's insolvent companies were ruthlessly shut down or sold off. The McLaughlin–Buick was still in business – 962 cars were built in Oshawa in 1911 – but consumer confidence was shaken. To help mend fences, Oliver Hezzelwood joined the Ontario Motor League, a militant and politically influential automobile lobby that included John Craig Eaton and millionaire whisky distiller George Gooderham.

An avid motorist, Gooderham was organizing a group of contractors to build Ontario's first concrete highway between Toronto and Hamilton. The old dirt road to Niagara Falls was already crowded, and, in the apparent absence of traffic police, Gooderham took it upon himself to enforce the law.

"Shortly after passing through Beamsville I was overtaken and passed by a car being driven in a most reckless way," he wrote to the provincial secretary. "Fortunately the roads were not dusty and I was able to distinguish the number. Mrs. Gooderham, who was with me, was very much alarmed at the way the car was being driven and I can honestly say that I believe a speed of 50 miles an hour is well within the mark. Both Mrs. Gooderham and myself were convinced that the man who drove the car must have been intoxicated, as the car bounded from one side of the road to the other and finally landed up in the ditch at the side of the hill just this side of Jordan.

"I drove into Jordan and tried to get a constable in order that the man might be placed under arrest, but as usual when required, no constable was to be found. I then motored on to St. Catharines hoping to stop the car there, but again I was unsuccessful. I was very much surprised later to find the car leaving Ridley College field with two of the School boys riding in it, and on enquiry as to who the boys were I got additional information. On returning home, I made enquiries as to the owner of car License No. 19993 and found that while this number belonged to Mr. W. G. Tretheway, it was on a car which did not belong to him, nor did the car belong to the man by whom the chauffeur was employed.

"I am of the opinion that from the conduct of this man he is not a proper person to hold a chauffeur's licence, and I understand under the Act your department has the right to cancel this licence if you see fit. In addition to this, I think some action should be taken against the people who permitted the licence number to be put on a car which it did not belong to. The chauffeur's name: George Avery; employed by Andrew Wilson."

It was unsporting of Gooderham to take his grievance to the minister, not to Wilson, and the hapless Avery no doubt lost both his job and his licence. Gooderham's indifference to Avery's accident is typical of the time: accidents were the fault of those involved in them, and they could take the consequences. Victims could expect very little help from the police, as this 1915 report from Inspector John Miller of the Norfolk county OPP amply demonstrates:

"In my inquiry so far as to who it was who ran into Mrs. G. Hetherington, on the 6th of Oct. on the road between Courtland and Langton, I have only been able to get a trace of one car. This was driven by a young man called Doc. Robbins, who was working at the time for the Norfolk Garage in Simcoe. But who has since left Canada, and I believe living in Detroit. I was not able to see him. The owner of the car does not know anything about the matter, he had asked the boy if he had ran into anybody, and he said he did not. At the time this happened, the car was taking a lace traveler to the different places, this traveler I believe lives in Toronto, and works for a house that handles laces. I will have to see this man before I can conclude if this is the car that ran over the woman.

"I have another man selected for the job, if the other falls down, and I am more inclined to think that this is the more correct. The man is James Craig of Wyecombe, and he is in the habit of going into Courtland and getting drunk. He had a Ford car, and when he gets drinking, he does not know when to stop. And when he gets that way he does not know what he is doing, and he would run his car along the road, and never bother to look out for other rigs, and I am told he might do such a thing and never know that he did. When he is sober he is a very fine man, and it is said if he did do anything like that he would be the first to stand by anything he did. I saw Jim Craig, and put it to him very strongly, but he could not say that he did run over a woman, as he had no knowledge of it, and is very sure that it was not him.

"I will have to hunt up this traveler, and get his statement. I will locate him today, or tomorrow, and if this fails it is about all I can do in the case."

Justice was even more callous in Winnipeg, where Sir John A. Macdonald's aging, alcoholic son, Hugh John, was police magistrate. Under the headline, "THE OAKES MATTER," the Winnipeg motoring magazine, Gas Power Age, gives a glimpse into the reasoning of automobile fanatics:

"Arthur H. Oakes, a prominent real estate operator in Winnipeg and a citizen of long standing, one of the most energetic and successful of our business community, had the misfortune to knock down an old lady on a dark street on July 13 at about 9:55 p.m. A coroner's inquest was called, and the jury found that the speed of the automobile was in excess of a mile in six minutes. Wonderful. Ninety-nine out of 100 of the automobilists in the city and every city in world, as well as the most out-of-the-way villages, exceed this speed limit a thousand or more times a day. Why? Because it is a ridiculous one and makes the motor vehicle obsolete. The municipal commission at once convicts Mr. Oakes before a trial and prejudices his case by cancelling his licence. Noble act! The case came to trial by Mr. Oakes being arraigned for manslaughter. No evidence was produced other than it was a case of misfortune, and Magistrate Macdonald discharged the defendant."

Automobile drivers viewed traffic regulations as a personal insult, a conspiracy concocted by old ladies and the police to steal their money and ruin their fun. The Ontario Motor League was quick to exploit this paranoia. On August 16, 1912, president Frank Mutton sent a circular to club members promising that the league "will endeavor to protect you from traps on the different highways, because of the fact that many of our members have been fined recently through their operation. This is a method of prosecution which we deem most unfair, particularly for the reason that, in the vast majority of cases, only the prosecutor's word seems to be the evidence accepted. We have decided to post a man in the vicinity of traps over the week-ends. He will advise members of the League carrying the official badge on the radiator cap, when they are approaching the trap. You will be signalled by his swinging his arm straight up and down. Only automobiles bearing the Ontario Motor League badge will be signalled. Tell your friends who are not members of the League and they will soon become members. Every member should secure at least one more member."

A speed trap was a constable on a motorcycle hiding in a clump of bushes, timing passing cars with a stopwatch. It was an arbitrary, and probably inaccurate, method, but a motor-league vigilante caught flailing his arms at passing traffic could be arrested for obstructing police, creating a hazard, and causing a disturbance. The police already had the upper hand, as the editor of *Gas Power Age*, E. W. Rugg, discovered to his chagrin in the fall of 1911:

"Evidently the Inspection Department is out to get our money for criticizing their work. Car 116 was left on a street broken up by 'traffic improvements' between two piles of sand and the driver was detained on business longer than contemplated. The car was standing on the street at 5:40 p.m. without lights. The defendant drew to the attention of the judge that over 60 percent of the MOVING VEHICLES in the city of Winnipeg carry NO LIGHTS, that official sunset is known to few persons, that business occupation is likely to cause forgetfulness for a time of a MONSTROUS IMPEDIMENT TO TRAFFIC in the shape of a motor car without lights, and in addition drew the attention of the judiciary to the contemptible conduct of the Chief Inspector in forcing his way into the private office of the defendant while engaged with business associates and serving his summons – and incidentally making ANOTHER FIFTY CENTS."

Governments quickly perceived the automobile's potential as a source of revenue, but the petty fees and fines they collected didn't begin to cover the cost of building and improving roads. Canada's enormous investment in railroads, and the political clout of the railway tycoons, had stifled the development of highways. More than seventy years after her summer rambles, Anna Brownell Jameson would have found Ontario's rural roads painfully familiar, and Boadicea, accustomed to England's paved Roman highways, would have been outraged. Two thousand years of highway technology had passed Canada by, and catching up was expensive: in 1911 Manitoba's roads commissioner estimated the cost of building a twenty-foot-wide gravel road with drains and culverts to be $3,224 a mile.

"Good Roads!" was the battle cry of automobile owners, and it grew in volume and intensity as car sales increased. Yet the fault was equally with the automobiles. Few cars were equipped to be driven in the rain, and because of their weight they sank into mud or sand. On hard roads, their rubber tires, wrapped in canvas, punctured or shredded so often that changing at least one flat tire was part of an everyday excursion. No matter. Automobile drivers were determined to go where they wanted, when they wanted, and as fast as they liked.

The automobile was the quintessential expression of individualism: the driver was in control of a machine that magnified human speed and power to a degree that no one had never before experienced. Walking, by comparison, was tedious and laborious; even cycling was too much work. Sam McLaughlin, who had once cycled sixty miles in one day, now drove sixty miles in one hour, and arrived refreshed. Sam didn't have to worry about speed traps: he carried a VIP card courtesy of the OPP, and he drove fast. Isabel McLaughlin remembers excursions with her father at the wheel of the family car; if Sam spotted a railway train, he would race it to the next crossing, and win.

Motorists hired teams of horses to grade the roads; they also put up the first signposts. Before the automobile, farmers and townspeople had seldom travelled farther than the next village by road, but now rural roads were full of sightseers wondering where in the devil they were. Towns didn't bother with signs, and unless the name was advertised on a post office or storefront, visitors had to stop to ask. Road maps were virtually unknown, and motorists had to rely on guidebooks. The *Official Automobile Guide of Canada* gives these instructions for driving from Moncton, New Brunswick, to Truro, Nova Scotia:

"0.0 Moncton RR station. East on Main Street. Cross RR 0.1, past P.O. on left 0.5. Cross RR 0.8 and iron bridge 1.1. 1.7 diagonal 4-corners, turn right with poles, road becoming rough and stony. Avoid right hand road 6.2. Follow main wires through covered bridge 13.7 and across RR 13.8.

"13.9 Memramcook, end of road in village, turn right, passing St. Francis Xavier college (over to right). Pass Upper Dorchester station on right 18.5 . . ." And so on for ninety miles.

A. C. "Ace" Emmett, secretary of the Winnipeg Automobile Club, marked his own routes and published Manitoba's first highway maps: "All the routes were indicated by colour, such as the Red Route, Blue Route, Yellow Route. The highway markings consisted of colour bands painted on or around various objects at a point where a turn was to be indicated. The work was carried on by volunteer crews who were supplied with paint brushes and stencils cut for R (right) and L (left.) A greater part of the marking was on telephone poles, for which the Manitoba Telephone System gave permission."

Motorists rarely travelled alone, and for long excursions they joined together in caravans. A town with a comfortable hotel, gasoline, a skilled mechanic, and a freshwater creek for a swim could do a booming trade in touring traffic. One of Manitoba's first gravel roads was built along the west bank of the Red River to Winnipeg Beach. The beach was already served by an electric railway, but in an automobile a family could carry enough supplies for a weekend, and after the road went in, cottages sprang up around the south shore of Lake Winnipeg. Camping was already a fad. An automobile's trunk was exactly that: a large metal or leather box strapped on the back of the car. Boxes of dried and canned food could be tied onto the running boards, and waterproof gear such as air mattresses and canvas cots strapped to the top: seat cushions were easily replaced by tents, blankets, and pillows, and dunnage bags full of clothes were stuffed into corners. Campers didn't mind looking wrinkled, greasy, or poor: nobody could see them, and because camping was healthy, living like a hobo was perfectly respectable. Women became sunburned and freckled; men took off their shoes and socks and rolled up their pant legs, although their hats would be the last to go. Even Robert McLaughlin loved Muskoka, where he could fish and swim with his grandchildren.

Touring liberated Canadians from their cramped, airless houses, and from a stagnant social circle constrained by relatives and religion. In a motor club, people who otherwise would never have met shared an interest no one else understood, and a club picnic was a lot more fun than a night out at the Masonic Lodge. Children came along, and far from the prying eyes of their neighbours, motorists indulged in everything forbidden by the Lord's Day Act.

Where there were no roads, automobiles made them. On the Prairies, cars followed the rutted tracks left by Métis buffalo hunters, and while cars were faster, the noise and dust they created were no improvement on the Red River cart. The old trails meandered south to the United States, west to Regina and Moose Jaw, then north toward the new settlement of Saskatoon. On the high prairie, the unbroken sod was dry and firm, the summer weather sunny; an automobile could be driven across country as easily as an Indian rode a horse, and in the summer of 1911 George McLaughlin hired an Indian to help guide his McLaughlin–Buick from Winnipeg to Victoria, British Columbia.

The incentive was provided by the Pacific Highway Association, which offered a gold medal to the first automobile to make it to the west coast from Winnipeg. There were no roads through the Rockies,

George McLaughlin and his Indian guide near Qu'Appelle, Saskatchewan, 1911. In the rear sits Richard McKenzie, manager of the McLaughlin agency, Winnipeg. Mechanic L. M. Brooks of Oshawa, next to the car, is wearing goggles and a white duster. (*Thomas Bouckley Collection, Robert McLaughlin Gallery*)

but cars could be fitted with flanges to run on railroad tracks through the mountains. It was a publicity stunt. Buick had dropped out of automobile racing to save money and the McLaughlins were scrambling to stay in the public eye. The run to Victoria had enough novelty and adventure to make headlines, and a gold medal would be a sales bonanza.

George was an unlikely adventurer. Decked out in a sporty cap and Harris tweeds, he looked more like Toad of Toad Hall. He was accompanied by his mechanic, L. R. Brooks, a man of gargantuan girth swaddled in a white duster that gave him a medical air, and his two Prairie managers, Richard McKenzie of Winnipeg and J. G. Cline of Regina. For George, it was a business trip: he would scout sales prospects, and check in on his sister Mary Jane and John McCulloch in Calgary, where McCulloch was setting up a new McLaughlin–Buick dealership. They took along a camera to record their progress, and Cline kept a daily log which was published in the August issue of *Gas Power Age*:

"Leaving Winnipeg Monday, July 10th, a good run was made to Portage, with the exception of about four miles of very heavy grade which gave us axle deep plugging. Portage was reached in three hours, where a stop of three hours was made, driving on to Carberry for supper and on to Brandon for the night. Leaving at 1:30pm, Elkhorn was reached for supper, and Moosomin for the night." In Whitewood the

"Left Moose Jaw Friday morning and encountered the first heavy mud." When digging didn't help, a farmer pulled the McLaughlin–Buick out of the mud with his team of horses. (*Ewart McLaughlin Collection*)

next day, they hired their Indian guide for some sightseeing in the Qu'Appelle Valley before going on to Regina and Moose Jaw. "Left Moose Jaw Friday morning for the north and encountered the first heavy mud, but was not delayed very long owing to a team being handy. After crossing the Qu'Appelle Valley, we went north to Craik on the CNR, and drove on to Hanley for the night. Just before reaching Hanley we encountered a small creek which refused to let us through and it was necessary to use the block and tackle (which works fine) and let us out in short order."

They left Saskatoon at 10 a.m. on July 18, crossed the Saskatchewan River by ferry at Radisson, and reached Battleford at 8 p.m. "The roads were fairly good," Cline reported, "but found a lot of new trails which are rough. The old trails are fenced off in a number of places, and the

Culture shock: The McLaughlin–Buick pulls up to a Saskatchewan homesteader's sod hut. (*Ewart McLaughlin Collection*)

trail keeps changing every few weeks. It is impossible to get a map of the road which would be any good at a later date. Left Battleford the next morning with very poor directions and everyone telling us that we would likely get stuck. We took the best trail and had a very good run, only through very rough and sandy country, with the roads in such condition that it was impossible to make any time. Our speedometer reading was 121 miles for the day when we pulled up at a small place called Islay. Thursday the 20th was a bad day for us, the roads getting worse, and it was necessary to stop for a number of times for sloughs and mud holes. The roads were also very rough."

Battered and covered with mud, the McLaughlin–Buick lurched into Edmonton at 3 p.m. on July 21, eleven days and 1,152 miles after leaving Winnipeg. "Here the trip had to be abandoned," Cline reported, "having omitted to make registration every 100 miles as required." It hardly mattered. Later that summer, a Wright aeroplane, piloted by Frank Coffyn, flew into Winnipeg. It was the first aircraft to land in the city, and Coffyn's flights became the sensation of the Winnipeg Exhibition. The highlight was a two-mile race around a half-mile track featuring the aeroplane, a motorcycle, and a Knox automobile. Coffyn's flying machine won in two minutes, thirty-nine seconds, one second ahead of the motorcycle; the car was dead last.

"The last day Coffyn made an ascent, he returned with a passenger, which was also the first passenger flight," reported *Gas Power Age*. "The passenger was a noted speed artist in the Western automobile world, and the holder of all records from one to twenty miles in Western Canada. Mr. W. C. Power of the McLaughlin Motor Car Co., the gentleman who accompanied Mr. Coffyn, has announced his retirement from future automobile racing events."

6

THE OFFER

"Yesterday we walked or biked, today we automobile, and tomorrow we will fly," predicted *Gas Power Age*, although as a personal consumer item, an aeroplane "just now comes both a little high in price and unsettled in stability." To a spectator at the Winnipeg Exhibition in 1911, the prospect of flitting about the sky in a private aeroplane seemed no less plausible than roaring down the road in a motor car had been ten years earlier, and the McLaughlins were alert to the sales potential of a mass-market flying machine. The loss of W. C. Power to the aircraft industry was a hard blow for the McLaughlin–Buick. Only the year before, Power had captured three trophies in the Winnipeg Auto Club's annual meet, including the Dunlop Cup for covering twenty-five miles in 25 minutes, 19 seconds. Buick, however, had cancelled its racing program to save money – Durant had spent $1 million on advertising in 1910 – and the McLaughlin–Buick's sales began to suffer: between 1911 and 1914, the McLaughlin Motor Company built fewer than a thousand cars a year.

The McLaughlins' relationship with the new regime at General Motors was insecure. Durant, feeling that he had been treated shabbily, distanced himself from the corporation and was actively developing several competitors, including a car designed by Louis Chevrolet. In 1912, 4,998 of Durant's shares in the McLaughlin Motor Car Company were placed in the hands of Central Trust of New York; the two remaining shares were purchased by Buick executive Thomas Neal and the new president of General Motors, Charles Nash. Nash, the former manager of the Durant–Dort Carriage Company, had come from humble rural origins, and he was the sort of clever, honest, "pushing" man the McLaughlins liked to do business with. If they were tempted to buy back their company at this opportunity, they let it pass. The name Buick, however, quietly faded from McLaughlin advertising, replaced by a pitch for a "Canadian automobile guaranteed by the stability and integrity of the house of McLaughlin." The McLaughlins also hedged their bets by selling two rival imports, a Pierce Arrow and a Rausch & Lang electric.

General Motors had scrapped Buick's little Model 10 "White Streak," leaving the McLaughlins without a cheap, snazzy car in a market already saturated with luxury limousines – Eaton had jumped into competition with the ponderous Chalmers – and every year the Buicks grew bigger, more powerful, and more expensive. In 1912, McLaughlin was advertising a forty-horsepower, five-seat Model 43 "with complete electric light equipment" for $2,350; a Ford Model T sold for $850. Gordon McGregor's Canadian-made Ford was leaving McLaughlin in the dust. In 1909, the Ford Motor Company of Canada and McLaughlin each produced about 450 cars, but by 1913, Windsor was turning out 11,586 Canadian Fords, and McLaughlin managed only 881 Buicks. Everybody, it seemed, drove a Model T, or wanted to, and unlike the Buick, the price of the Model T kept going down. Henry Ford boasted that the Model T was the cheapest, lightest, strongest car in the world, and if Tin Lizzie broke down, fixing her was a cinch. This was not true of the McLaughlin Buick.

The McLaughlins' ninety-day warranty on their cars was valid only if broken parts were shipped to the factory at the owner's expense, and freight for the replacements had to be prepaid. "We make no warranty whatever in respect to tires, rims, radiators, coils, batteries or parts not manufactured by us. If the motor vehicle is altered, or repaired, outside of our factory, our liability shall cease," the company warned.

On February 22, 1911, W. H. Haycraft of Brooklin, Ontario, ordered a $1,300 cherry-red Model 33 McLaughlin–Buick to be delivered "on or about" May 1. The car had a twenty-two-horsepower engine and a wheel base of one hundred inches; it came with a speedometer, tire chains, a mohair top, and a "butcher's body" to replace the back seat. Haycraft paid $100 down. Terms were $600 cash on delivery, $300 on October 1, and $300 December 1. His licence, number 5418, cost $4 extra.

Haycraft picked up his car on May 19. On August 30, he brought it back to the factory to have the pistons cleaned, valves ground, and radius rods tightened. Labour: $4.60. On September 11, he bought a new Goodyear tire for $33.85, and four days later, an inner tube. On October 16, he had a front spring replaced free of charge, and a coil repaired on October 23. The car needed cylinder oil three days later, and a plug on November 7. On May 6, 1912, less than a year after he took delivery, Haycraft left his car at the factory for a tune-up. The mechanic "took motor out of frame, put in new helical gears, new oil pump, drive pinion, rebedded crank shaft, took up big end bearings, ground all valves and cages, cleaned carbon out of cylinders and pistons, put in new piston pins, magneto coupling, new pump and magneto drive shaft, repaired magneto and transmission, repaired radiator and brake, put on new brake lining, adjusted steering column and tightened oil springs." The car had its paint touched up and was given a fresh coat of varnish. Total cost, including labour: $96.49.

Haycraft raised hell. On July 4 the McLaughlins allowed him a credit of $7 on parts, followed by a $16.49 credit on labour. On August 9, he was back again for an $18 box coil and on August 26 he paid $26.70 for repairs to his carburetor and new sparkplugs. Haycraft returned the coil in October, and his saga ends on November 2, with a receipt for $25.

All of Haycraft's invoices, including the order for the car, are typed on the letterhead of the McLaughlin Carriage Company; the word "Buick" appears once, as half the name of the car. Not only was Robert McLaughlin still running the show, but he wasn't shy about backing the Buick with his own company's reputation for quality. There was little else to distinguish the McLaughlin–Buick from the Russell, Tudhope, Winnipeg Flyer, or a dozen more Canadian-built automobiles that were jostling for scraps of a market dominated by the Model T. On days when the McLaughlin–Buick's prospects looked particularly gloomy, the Governor would say with a wink to his youngest son, "Where are all those diamonds, Sam?"

At seventy-five years of age, Robert was at the peak of his fame and power. The McLaughlin Carriage Company manufactured nearly twenty thousand cars, carriages, cutters, and gears a year, and claimed to be the largest in the British Empire. McLaughlin cars and carriages were shipped to Australia, New Zealand, and Great Britain, and in India, modern maharajahs traded in their elephants for McLaughlin–Buicks. The Old Man's shoulders were stooped, and he wore spectacles, but he was as alert as ever, and Eleanor kept his beard neatly trimmed. His habits had changed very little. He hated vacations: a trip to California ended in three days when Robert, disgusted at having nothing to do, took the train home. He gave generously to St. Andrew's Church and local charities, especially the Salvation Army and the YMCA, but he abhorred the public spotlight and frivolous society. Robert sought no honours, and received none. He was not knighted or appointed to the Senate, although Prime Minister Laurier rewarded many younger and less deserving Liberals, and the reason, apart from Robert's dislike of puffery, may have been his hostility to free trade with the United States.

As an ambitious young craftsman, Robert had hated the high American tariffs that excluded his cutters and gears from U.S. markets, but now, as the president of the McLaughlin Carriage Company, he feared that cheap American competition would cut into his profits. Protection, or Canada's National Policy, had been the inspiration of Sir John A. Macdonald's Conservative government, but after Macdonald's death and the defeat of the Conservatives in 1896, the Liberals hung on to high tariffs to appease the manufacturers of Ontario and Quebec. Canada's sheltered industrial economy created thousands of jobs, and enormous private fortunes, but the arrival of the automobile challenged the patriotic assumption that Canadians should pay higher prices for made-in-Canada products. Why should a Ford made in Windsor, or a Buick built in Oshawa, cost two or three hundred dollars more than one manufactured in Detroit or Flint?

A free-trade crusade was launched by Western farmers squeezed between CPR freight rates and Massey–Harris profits, and since most of the farmers owed their homesteads to Liberal immigration policies, they formed an important bloc of Liberal support. Laurier's finance minister, W. S. Fielding, began to negotiate with Washington to lower or eliminate reciprocal tariffs on a few "natural" products. Although manufacturing was not directly affected, Robert took alarm. On June 27, 1910, he let Laurier know his views in a terse letter:

"If your Government can see their way clear, in any dealing there may be hereafter with Washington on reciprocity, to simply allow the tariff on manufacture to remain as it is at the present time, in order that none of our industries would be injured by a lowering of the tariff against them, I think it would be the wisest policy in the interests of your Government when the time arrives for the next election." Realizing that he had perhaps been a little blunt Robert added: "I ask your pardon if I am undertaking too much by infringing on your valuable time." Two days later, Laurier dictated a breezy reply: "You owe me no apology for having written me; on the contrary, I welcome this expression of your opinion. I can assure you that I will be happy at all times to receive communications from you, on this or any other subject, my Dear Mr. McLaughlin."

Laurier didn't respond to a letter McLaughlin had enclosed, a copy of a three-page, single-spaced denunciation of free trade that Robert had mailed, with a personal note, to the editor of the Toronto *Globe*. Robert had intended his letter to be published, then changed his mind, but it is an eloquent expression of the McLaughlins' business and political philosophy. Pointing out that the Prairie price of wagons, buggies, and farm equipment had been cut in half since the National Policy went into effect in 1880, Robert turned on the Americans:

"For thirty or forty years, a great and powerful nation of seventy or eighty millions of people, through the Republican party, have absolutely refused to deal with Canada by raising a wholly prohibitive tariff against us, but, now when there is serious trouble in the Republican Camp of high tariff fliers, they suddenly become friendly to Canada and talk reciprocity, when we, like Britain, have fought out our own destiny, becoming independent, and are on the high road to success and coming greatness.

"Whether we are to give away our forests and other raw material to be manufactured in the U.S. is a very grave question, but, to adopt free trade, or lower the tariff to admit American manufacturers or displace Canadian manufacturers would be disastrous not only to manufacturers but to very many of our workmen who have made and built their own homes expecting continuous employment. It would also injure many of our farmers who supply thousands of our workmen with vegetables, fruit and other produce which they could not ship to a foreign market.

Would it not be better for us to make Canada, with our wealth of water power and raw material, a great manufacturing country as well as a great agricultural country?

"Which of the following policies would free traders prefer – 1. To give us free trade or a lower tariff and allow American labor to work up our forests and vast raw materials, and the Americans to pocket the millions of cash made on the finished article, and for Canadians to send their money across the line and buy back the finished product and see an exodus of our workmen and population leave their birthplace and native shores.

"2. On manufacturing, leave the tariff as it is and make Canada a home of industry, continue to bring in more and more large American industries as we are now doing, keep our own workmen in Canada and add to their number, and also keep our millions of money and use it to develop our own country."

In his note to the editor of the *Globe*, Robert flexed his political muscle: "In a private way, I might call your attention to the fact that I have been a member of the Manufacturers' Executive Council for about fifteen years, and understand the feelings of both Liberal and Conservative manufacturers. So far, Liberal manufacturers as a whole have supported the Liberal Government, but, I am free to say that if in dealing with reciprocity with the U.S. Mr. Fielding would lower the tariff on manufactures, he would lose the support and influence of the said Liberal manufacturers."

He then added a barb of his own: "Previous to Mr. Taft's approach to Ottawa, re reciprocity, we were in touch with a very wealthy Auto Car Company who proposed to us that they would invest half-a-million dollars if we would form a Company and raise an equal amount. In order to be prepared for this, we purchased a twenty-acre lot, but, upon the announcement that Mr. Fielding would take up the matter of reciprocity in the autumn, and being in the dark as to what might be done with the tariff, for the present time the scheme is abandoned."

This was pure bluff, and it didn't work. The Liberals made a free-trade deal with the Americans, and Canadian manufacturers cried out: "No truck nor trade with the Yankees!" On September 10, 1911, Robert attacked the Laurier government's free-trade policy on the front page of the *Globe*. Ten days later the Liberals went down to crushing defeat, and McLaughlin, a renegade and apostate Liberal, found himself adrift in the land of his Conservative enemies.

His son Jack was dying. The daily management of the J. J. McLaughlin Company had passed into the capable hands of Jack's partner, A. L. Gourley, and Jack divided his time between Arizona and Muskoka. Canada Dry would leave his family well provided for, and Jack seems to have been more philosophical about his fate than were his younger brothers. The taboo of tuberculosis, linked with the premature death of Jack's son Allan, created a superstition that the McLaughlins' first-born sons were doomed to die young. Sam had no sons, although he called his fifth and last daughter, Eleanor, born in 1908, "Billie," but George and his wife, Annie, developed a pathological anxiety about the health of their eldest son, Ewart.

Jack McLaughlin was already too ill to walk, and during his last visits to his factory he was pushed in a wheelchair. Jack died at home on January 28, 1914, and was buried next to Allan in the Toronto Necropolis. He was forty-eight, and his children were still in their teens. Responsibility for Canada Dry fell on the shoulders of Jack's executors, his brothers George and Sam, and Jack's proud widow, Maud, was now dependent on her unsympathetic in-laws.

Death became a familiar visitor to Canadian homes during the four years of the Great War and the influenza epidemic that followed it. Prime Minister Sir Robert Borden was golfing in Muskoka on July 31, 1914, when he was told of the assassination of an obscure Austrian archduke in Sarajevo; Borden lingered on the golf course, not far from the McLaughlin cottage, before reluctantly returning to Ottawa to declare war on Germany. Canada's participation was never in question. "Ready, aye, ready!" was the Tory cry, and Ontario men were so eager for a fight Oshawa's new red-brick armoury filled up with recruits overnight. Robert McLaughlin was so angered to see that the men were not supplied with blankets he bought them out of his own pocket.

The McLaughlins were not pacifists, unlike Henry Ford, but they shared the American manufacturer's opinion that war was bad for the automobile business, especially when the British army insisted on fighting with horses, and the Canadian Corps bought its wagons through Conservative Party channels. The few orders for armoured trucks and staff cars that came to Canada went to the Russell Motor Car Company of Toronto, whose owner, Major Tommy Russell, had been appointed purchaser of military vehicles for the Canadian government. The McLaughlins had to be content with building Buick ambulances, and selling them at a 20 per cent discount to the Red

Cross. Production fell from 1,098 McLaughlin–Buicks in 1914 to 1,012 in 1915; Ford's Model T production rose from 15,675 to 18,739. Of all the cars licensed in Canada in 1914, 38 per cent (21,456) were Fords. In the United States, Ford, with an annual production of about 300,000 cars, had half the market, and in both countries Ford's share was growing.

The McLaughlins publicly dissociated themselves from Buick. The McLaughlin–Buick became a "McLaughlin." A McLaughlin Motor Car Company advertisement in an Ontario Motor League newsletter in 1915 praises the success of the "McLaughlin" car in an Ottawa Valley endurance test: "Nothing that has ever happened during our eight years connection with the Motor industry so thoroughly and completely demonstrates McLaughlin "Valve-in-Head" superiority as the recent phenomenal record established by Mr. G. B. McKay, of Ottawa, in his 55 horse power Six Cylinder 'McLaughlin.'" McKay's victory in a gruelling 140-mile race through "veritable seas of mud, up greasy hills, down treacherous valleys" was proof, claimed the ad, "of the sturdy and enduring value in the drop forged steel with which the 'McLaughlin' is strengthened against the stress and shocks of every-day use."

This was blatantly false advertising. Nothing had changed in the McLaughlins' close partnership with Buick. The valve-in-head engine had been invented by Buick, and its steel chassis, while it was built in Canada, was designed by Buick engineers in Flint. When Buick protested, Sam argued that the "McLaughlin" name sold much better in Canada, and he was right: his production more than doubled the next year, and it tripled again by the end of the war. Buick didn't press the issue, for the time being, and there were cosmetic differences – gumdrop colours, wooden spokes and dashboard, and nickel-plated fittings – that made the "McLaughlin" a "tastier" automobile than the Buick.

Sam did produce some custom McLaughlin "Specials." Sam loved flash, and the "McLaughlins" Sam and his engineer, Billy Moyse, designed were ancestors of the DeLorean: "In the very early days there had been a custom-built car with automatic folding steps that eliminated running boards, and a streamlined back incorporating a trunk – unheard of at the time," Hugh Durnford and Glen Baechler note in *Cars of Canada*. "Another custom model, of which three were produced in 1915, was built along the lines of a motorboat. It had a copper-rivetted mahogany body, marine lamps and upholstered wicker chairs." The "McLaughlin" C-55 driven by G. B. McKay was similar to the previous year's model B-55: "Much sleeker than its Buick counterpart, it featured an uncluttered hammered aluminum body, full-crown fenders, nickel-plated radiator shell and English Burbank top with wood bows and nickel-plated sockets. Inside were such deluxe items as a clock and a locked glove box."

Sam borrowed some of these features from English automobiles, and, to Buick's horror, he bought his engines from just about anywhere, including the junked Welch company. Sam either failed or neglected to persuade Buick to adopt his most important innovations, the enclosed trunk and aluminum body, yet for years he attempted to credit Moyse with the invention of the electric self-starter, a device Charles Kettering of the Delco company in Dayton, Ohio, had patented in 1912. Sam's assertion of independence was more than vanity, although there was plenty of that: the McLaughlins were secretly investing in Chevrolet.

On January 8, 1912, Sam had purchased 200 shares of Chevrolet stock from Billy Durant for $19,400. Sam had seen Louis Chevrolet's new Classic Six on display at the New York auto show, and it was the kind of car he loved: big, powerful, and expensive. The Americans, however, were expecting something sleek and speedy, and Chevrolet's car bombed. Durant, however, had other tricks up his sleeve. He had hired his former manager, Bill Little, to design a Little car, a four-cylinder runabout to sell for about $650, and Little had produced 3,000 cars in 1912. To give Little more factory space, Durant purchased James Whiting's Flint Wagon Works, the shop where David Buick had gone into production, as well as the rights to Whiting's own experimental car. Out of scrap and shoestrings, Durant was trying to put together another General Motors. Once again he was building a paper empire: the Little company was capitalized at $1.2 million, with a cash investment of $36,500.

To boost the flagging sales of the Chevrolet car, Durant announced that he was forming a corporation called Republic Motors, capitalized at $65 million, with eleven regional factories and headquarters in New York. He bought a tract of land outside Henry Ford's Detroit domain, Highland Park, and, across the road from the Ford works, he put up a billboard advertising the site as the future home of a Chevrolet plant. To prove that he owned more than a billboard, Durant opened a factory in downtown Manhattan where potential investors could see Chevrolets being built, although by the end of 1913 Louis Chevrolet had left the company.

"The real reason [for Chevrolet's departure], perhaps, was that Durant had decided not to continue the large, luxurious car of Louis Chevrolet's dreams," writes Lawrence Gustin in *Billy Durant*. "Instead he wanted to compete more directly with the low-priced Ford. But a more immediate reason was an ongoing, and petty, dispute over Chevrolet's cigarette-smoking habits. Louis Chevrolet's version is that Durant told him he wouldn't make any money until he became a gentleman, that he should smoke cigars, not cigarettes. Every time they talked, Durant would mention this. Finally Chevrolet could contain his irritation no longer: 'I sold you my car and I sold you my name, but I'm not going to sell myself to you. I'm going to smoke my cigarettes as much as I want. And I'm getting out.'"

"And so Louis Chevrolet departed, not too gently, into the peculiar night that enveloped David Buick," Bernard Weisberger comments in *The Dream Maker*. "Both men would have their names mentioned literally thousands of times a day throughout the United States and parts of the world, but those who spoke the names would rarely have any idea that they once belonged to men."

Like Buick, whom Durant had ignored until he left the company, Louis Chevrolet was of no further use. All Durant wanted was Chevrolet's fame, and a resonant European name he could pair with a bow-tie logo he copied from an illustration in a popular magazine. In 1914, the year Ford introduced the assembly line and a five-dollar daily wage, Durant produced two Chevrolets, a touring car and a roadster, priced at $875 and $750. This small, cheap Chevrolet was mostly a Little, with an engine supplied by the Mason Motor Company of Flint – Mason also sold engines to the McLaughlins – and this Chevrolet was an encouraging success. The following year Durant took aim at Ford with the Chevrolet 490, a car targeted to compete with Ford's $490 Model T. Equipped with electric lights and a self-starter, the Chevrolet 490 really cost $550, but by June, Durant had orders for 50,000 cars worth $24 million. In Toronto, Durant bought the Dominion Carriage Company to manufacture Chevrolets, and by the spring of 1915 he was organizing to buy back General Motors.

General Motors had trimmed the flab, written off millions in debts, hired a hardnosed manager at Buick, Walter Chrysler, and dug in with an 8 per cent share of the market. Although the bankers' trust expired in November, James Storrow showed no inclination to invite Durant to return as president. Storrow dismissed the Chevrolet company as a chimera, Durant as a burnt-out comet, yet GM was paying no dividends, and on Wall Street the company's shares were trading far below value. Durant saw his opportunity: he urged his Chevrolet investors to buy up General Motors stock.

In the first six months of 1915, Sam McLaughlin's personal holdings of GM stock increased from $76,995 to $208,479: GM's price per share rose from $86.50 to $159. The higher the price, the more stock Sam bought: 100 shares at $157 on June 29; another 100 shares at $159 on July 6. Exhorting his investors not to sell as the price inexorably rose, Durant bought all the GM stock he could persuade its owners to sell. He had no trouble getting proxies from old friends, and during the summer of 1915, GM stock certificates were reportedly carried into his office in bushel baskets.

Where was Durant getting the money? He was virtually penniless, and he was borrowing heavily to increase Chevrolet's production. GM's board of directors dismissed Durant's threatened coup as another prank until Pierre S. du Pont walked into the board's annual meeting on September 16, 1915. Heir to the gunpowder empire of the E. I. du Pont de Nemours company, Pierre du Pont was the only American financier powerful enough to challenge the New England bankers. Shy, balding, and slightly lame, du Pont could easily have been mistaken for a college professor or an Episcopalian deacon, and as a young man he had seemed the least likely of the large du Pont clan to rule the family dynasty. He had lived with his mother until she died, and in the spring of 1915 he had married, at age fifty, his first cousin, Alice Belin. Beneath Pierre's courtly, unassuming manner lay the mind of a corporate tactician, and the thwarted dreams of a Louis XIV. Du Pont seemed an unlikely associate for a brash little hustler like Durant, but in New York, where Jews were excluded from companies and professions, clubs, hotels, and "society," they shared a private bond.

Catherine Durant was Jewish, and du Pont had Jewish ancestors. The couples shared friends, and those friends included Louis Kaufman, president of the Chatham & Phenix Bank of New York. Du Pont was on the bank's board of directors, and in 1914 the bank underwrote a $5-million loan to enable Durant to get the Chevrolet 490 on the road. Durant had been introduced to Kaufman by Nathan Hofheimer, a young Wall Street player with a wide circle of contacts in the Jewish financial community.

In 1914, du Pont had been persuaded to buy two thousand shares of General Motors stock by his secretary and financial adviser, John J. Raskob. Like Durant, du Pont surrounded himself with ambitious young men, and Raskob, a Roman Catholic from Alsace, was a financial whiz. E. I. du Pont de Nemours was making enormous, embarrassing profits selling explosives to the Allies in the Great War, and Pierre was looking for obscure, undervalued American companies in which to sink his money.

Du Pont's presence at the annual meeting took the directors by surprise, but not as much as Durant's cool announcement: "I am in control of General Motors." In fact, Durant was short of a majority of the shares, and after six hours of bitter wrangling, chairman James Storrow asked du Pont to break the stalemate by nominating three new directors not allied with either faction. Du Pont nominated his brother-in-law, Lammot Belin, John J. Raskob, and a du Pont company executive, Amory Haskell. All were approved. Charles Nash remained as president of General Motors, Durant and the bankers as directors, but the du Ponts had gained a strong foothold. General Motors celebrated by announcing a dividend of fifty dollars a share.

Sam McLaughlin's two thousand GM shares paid out an instant $100,000, and within one week the price of GM shares rose from $250 to $340. On September 17, 1915 Sam hopped on the train for New York to claim the reward for his support: Chevrolet Canada.

"I went to the auto races at Sheepshead Bay, N.Y. but it rained so hard that the races were called off, so I went on to New York City," he told *Maclean's* in 1954. Sam never breathed a word of his gamble with Chevrolet – even the Governor may not have known – and he went to elaborate pains to describe a "chance" luncheon with Durant at Pabst on the Circle. "It was my custom whenever I was there to have lunch with Edwin Campbell. On this day, I found myself lunching not only with Dr. Campbell but with Mr. Durant and another Chevrolet stockholder, Nathan Hofheimer. I asked Durant casually how the Chevrolet project was coming in Canada. Before he could answer, Hofheimer shot at him: 'Why don't you give that to the McLaughlin boys, Billy?' Durant and I looked at each other and we both laughed. 'Well, Sam, do you want it?' he said.

"I certainly wanted it. But there were two obstacles that had to be overcome. First, how did we stand with our Buick contract if we took on another line of cars? More important, could we persuade the Governor to sell the carriage business? Certainly if we undertook to make a car with the volume Chevrolet promised in Canada we couldn't go on making carriages. And if the Governor decided against abandoning the business that was his life, we couldn't take on Chevrolet.

"George and I would abide by the Governor's decision. Apart from any considerations of filial loyalty, Robert McLaughlin was still the boss. Sam might be the president of the McLaughlin Motor Car Company, but the Governor was the president of the McLaughlin Carriage Company and the carriage company owned the motor car company. As a matter of fact, by buying up the stock of our outside shareholders I actually owned control of the McLaughlin Carriage Company but that fact was not considered for a moment as my father, George and I always worked as a team. There was no doubt that, from a business viewpoint, it would be a smart move to drop carriages and take on Chevrolet. By 1915 carriage sales were declining steadily, automobile sales were rocketing. I calculated that there would be only three or four more years in which carriage production would show a profit."

Sam asked for two days to make a decision, and telephoned George in Oshawa. GM lawyer J. T. Smith assured Sam that making the Chevrolet would not jeopardize the McLaughlins' Buick contract, and once again Billy and Sam sharpened their pencils. "Our experience arriving at the Buick contract eight years before made it not too difficult to reach terms," said Sam. "The Chevrolet contract wasn't quite as favourable as the Buick deal – but then both Durant and Smith thought the McLaughlins had got much the best of the Buick deal."

"My brother George travelled all day by train and got to the Vanderbilt Hotel on Sunday evening. Tired as he was, we talked into the early hours of Monday, mulling over the agreement. In the morning, we again went to see Durant, talked over the contract again, suggested a couple of changes, then we agreed to it all around. We got on the train that night and came home.

"George said to me on the way to the office in Oshawa: 'You will have to talk to the Governor.' I knew how he was feeling – I was feeling that way myself. I said: 'We'll both talk to him.' George looked unhappy at that. 'I know what a shock this will be to him,' he said, 'and I can't face him.' So I was elected. I walked into the Governor's office and told him all about my trip and what was in the wind. I said we couldn't run three businesses, and that the carriage business was dying. I quoted him our own figures to prove it.

"It hurt to have to do that. But to my surprise, he took it calmly. 'Sam,' he said, 'I'm about through. George is in accord with this?' 'Absolutely,' I assured him. We called George in and reviewed the whole matter briefly. We assured the Governor that if he said the word we would abandon the Chevrolet project; after all, he had started the business and felt a deep sentiment for it. We shared that sentiment too. The Governor shook his head. 'Do what you think best,' he said.

"As soon as I left his office I put in a call to Jim Tudhope, president of Carriage Factories Ltd., Orillia. That company had tried to buy McLaughlin many times. It had never been for sale. I said to Jim Tudhope right off: 'Do you want to get rid of your largest competition?' 'Do you want to sell the business now?' he asked in reply. I said 'Yes, she is for sale if we can get quick action.' We even agreed, in that one telephone call, on the basis of sale." Three days later, the McLaughlins' entire stock of carriages was cleared out of their factory.

Robert McLaughlin was more chipper about unloading his carriage business than he had let on. "It is not an easy thing to sever the tie that has bound us in the past so closely to our business associates," he wrote to his agents on November 4, 1915, "but 'time and tide wait for no man.' The invention of the gasoline engine and its adaption [sic] to vehicular travel is, in my judgment, at present working a revolution in the horse-drawn vehicle trade."

Robert sold his buggies but not his company: the McLaughlin Carriage Company continued as the holding company for the McLaughlin Motor Car Company, and Robert remained as its president. Durant retained majority ownership of Chevrolet Canada. There were inducements: he offered the McLaughlins the opportunity to buy Chevrolet shares for $75, and within days their shares were trading at $97. No wonder: Durant had organized a syndicate to boost the price of Chevrolet stock. The syndicate, to which Sam and George contributed $100,000 each, was made up of the same General Motors insiders who had catapulted Durant and the du Ponts into a position of power at GM. Since the McLaughlins were already producing both Chevrolets and Buicks, they may have inspired Durant's new scheme to use Chevrolet stock to buy back General Motors.

It was simple enough. With the support of Louis Kaufman and the

All the employees of the McLaughlin Carriage Company and motor works.
(*General Motors of Canada/Thomas Bouckley Collection, Robert McLaughlin Gallery*)

Chatham & Phenix Bank, Chevrolet was recapitalized at $80 million, a figure utterly unrelated to the company's real worth, and Durant offered to trade GM investors five shares of Chevrolet stock for one share of General Motors. With Chevrolet shares selling strongly at more than $100, GM shares soon inflated to $500 and stockholders stampeded to take their windfall profits. Durant controlled the majority of GM shares by the spring of 1916, and on June 1, he was reinstated as president of General Motors. The minnow had swallowed the whale.

Sam and George McLaughlin each received a cheque for $20,196.88, profit on their $100,000 investments in the Chevrolet syndicate. Their GM stock had reached dizzying heights, and the perky little Chevrolet was proving that it could take on the Model T. The McLaughlin Motor Car Company turned out 7,796 Chevrolets in 1916 and 13,898 the following year, four times their production of McLaughlin–Buicks. They were still not close to Ford, with annual Canadian sales of 50,000 cars and trucks, but in ten years their positions in the market would dramatically reverse.

The buggy business was dead, a casualty of the Great War. Carriage horses were sold or requisitioned for military service overseas, and even the police were forced to motorize. The Royal North-West Mounted Police in Saskatchewan bought eight McLaughlin–Buicks, but the Toronto police chose motorcycles and a Ford ambulance that doubled as a paddy wagon. "Detectives are at a great disadvantage in not having

a motor car," Toronto police commissioner H. J. Grasett complained in 1916. The reason: 277 cars had been stolen, and while all but four had been recovered, some were badly smashed up. By 1918, car thefts had increased to 1,106, and Grasett was fed up: "Owners of cars are increasingly indifferent as to what becomes of them, and the penalties imposed on the thieves have little effect in stopping the practice, which is confined chiefly to young men and boys."

Toronto didn't isolate motor-car fatalities until 1914, when eighteen people were killed. There were no drivers' licences and no traffic signals: vehicles travelling north and south had right of way over those going east and west until 1917, when priority was given to the vehicle on the right. Motorists signalled by honking their horns. Twenty-eight people were killed by cars in Toronto in 1918, seven fewer than casualties from inhaling illuminating gas. The police recorded 5,599 breaches of the Vehicles Act. Most of them seem to have been for illegal parking since Grasett commented: "The streets are becoming an open air garage. The places set aside for parking are being misused by cars being left there nearly all day."

The commuter had arrived, and Toronto was unprepared. Overnight, this city of church steeples and tree-lined boulevards had become noisy, smelly, and dangerous, and this "chaotic state of affairs," noticed by the police as early as 1907, got worse. The electric streetcars had encouraged people to build houses on the city's outskirts and in the neighbouring villages, but while the streetcars were cheap, they were cold, dirty, and overcrowded, and when the power failed, the passengers walked. The automobile infinitely expanded the possibilities of

Changing a flat on a McLaughlin–Buick, 1917. (*Bill Sherk*, The Way We Drove)

suburban life, and as the tracks became clogged with cars, travel by streetcar grew slower and less convenient: the idea of a right-of-way for public transit didn't catch on until the Toronto subway was built in 1954. The aggressive little automobile muscled its way in wherever it wanted to go, and after 1918 few houses were built without a garage, although the garage was commonly placed at the back of the yard, where the stable used to be.

The McLaughlins prospered during the war. "Business conditions are unusually bright this spring owing to the fact that we had a very

The Royal North-West Mounted Police with their first McLaughlin–Buicks, 1917. (*RCMP Museum, Regina*)

Filling 'er up in Winnipeg, 1916. *(Imperial Oil)*

fair crop last year, and the farmers are buying cars in a way hardly seen before," Ford dealer A. W. Bowman reported from Elrose, Saskatchewan, in the April 1917 issue of *Motor in Canada.* "Naturally the Ford is in the lead by about ten to one, and it is estimated that about forty will be sold out of here this spring." In Bow Island, Alberta, however, dealers Wilmot & Henderson claimed: "We have unloaded three carloads of McLaughlin cars and two carloads of Chevrolets in the past two weeks, and we are building a 25 × 50 addition to be used as a repair shop." R. J. Riddell iin Nokomis, Saskatchewan, boasted: "I have unloaded my second carload of Chevrolets this month, and have sold all of them to farmers of the district." Car salesmen had returned to prairie villages like swallows to Capistrano, and as C. F. Stevens wrote cheerfully from Deloraine, Manitoba: "The roads are very bad at present, but in a week or two we expect to hear the honk, honk and the squawk of the auto again."

There wasn't much to buy except a car. Food was rationed and liquor prohibited – sales of Canada Dry soared – and the production of "McLaughlins" and Chevrolets was not interrupted by military requirements. The small amount of British army business that came to Canada went to cronies of the imperial munitions commissioner, Sir Joseph Flavelle. Flavelle gave his old friend, Tommy Russell, a lucrative contract

Ford meets the new kid on the road, Chevrolet. *(National Archives of Canada, C 29454)*

to manufacture shells; the McLaughlins got nothing. The Canadian government could have requisitioned the McLaughlins' factory, as well as all their supplies of iron, steel, nickel, and rubber, but it saw no need to do so, and while the automobile was still taxed as a luxury, it was proving to be a necessity.

George McLaughlin gave generously to the Red Cross and sold Victory Bonds; Sam supported the National Patriotic Fund to assist the families of men overseas. The McLaughlins shied away from the hysterical Hun-hating of the imperialists for practical as well as personal reasons: thousands of their customers were immigrants from Germany and Eastern Europe, and, with several dealerships in Quebec, they were well aware of the French Canadians' hostility to British jingoism. By the autumn of 1917, with an election less than three months away, Sam seems to have reached a rapprochement with the Liberals. On September 15, under the headline "NEW SENATOR MOTOR MAGNATE," the Toronto *Globe* praised "Senator R. S. McLaughlin" as "a man of vision" and "a millionaire at age 46."

Sam was not a senator. Laurier, desperately seeking Liberals who would finance a campaign against conscription, appears to have offered Sam a Senate seat if he won the election, and Sam, as usual, jumped the gun. Sam compounded his *faux pas* by bragging about his killing on Wall Street: "It is a well-known fact," said the *Globe* reporter, "that no small part of his fortune is the result of sundry successful speculative ventures in the United States made possible by wide connections with industrial enterprises in that country." Laurier lost the election, and Senator Sam became a country squire.

In 1915, Sam had purchased Prospect Park, the Oshawa estate built by merchant John Warren. Following the financial ruin of its next owner, William Gibbs, Prospect Park had been operated as an amusement park. Sam renamed it "Parkwood" and tore down the old Warren house at the west end of the property. In 1916, Sam began to build the most expensive house in Canada. The architect, John Pearson, priced it at $100,000, double the $50,000 Sir Joseph Flavelle had paid for his Toronto mansion in 1904. For McLaughlin, Pearson designed a fifty-five-room Georgian-style country house with all the modern amenities: central hot-water heating, indirect electric lighting, a basement refrigerator, a pipe organ, an elevator, an indoor swimming pool, and reinforced concrete floors.

An army of workmen laboured to dig Parkwood's vast cellar, but Sam was too busy, or too obtuse, to notice that some men wore black armbands, and he attended church too seldom to hear the names of the dead, the sons of his friends, read aloud from the pulpit. Sam's cousin Arthur, Dr. James's only son, had been killed at the Somme, and Lorne, the son of his Uncle John, had been decorated for bravery, yet Sam seems to have been incapable of grief, unimpressed by heroism, and indifferent to the sacrifice of people who gave everything they had to the war effort. Did Sam not read the casualty lists in the *Globe*? Did he not hear the bells toll, or comprehend that on the eve of the battle of Passchendaele, his $100,000 might have been less selfishly and conspicuously spent?

Many people thought so, and one of them appears to have been Oliver Hezzelwood. Hezzelwood had been in England when war broke out, and on his way back to Canada he barely missed being torpedoed on the *Athenia*. He enlisted immediately in the Canadian Expeditionary Force, but, at age fifty-four, he was assigned to recruiting and home-guard duty. Hezzelwood had no sons, but he was emotionally stricken by the war, torn between his sense of duty and revulsion at the carnage. "He was very patriotic," says his grandson Norman Clark, "but he had a horror of war and anything that smacked of death."

Oliver had not lost his Methodist sense of sin, and the deadliest sins included vanity, avarice, and usury. Too principled to be part of Durant's syndicates and too modest to be a motor magnate, Hezzelwood left the McLaughlin Motor Car Company in 1915, sold his shares to Sam, and gave the money to charity.

"He was a loving person," says Clark, who remembers the boyhood joy of paddling with his grandfather in the clear water of Sturgeon Lake. Norman is an only child, as was his mother, Helen: "My mother was adopted," he says. "There was a family in Oshawa who sold their children. Her sister was adopted into a different family." Oliver and Letty Hezzelwood had no children of their own, and while the selling of unwanted infants was common practice in Ontario when Helen was adopted in 1899, everyone knew that Helen was not a "real" Hezzelwood, and she was not included among the young people Adelaide McLaughlin invited to her daughters' parties. Oliver's younger brother, George, remained with the company until his death, but Oliver drove his McLaughlin–Buick through the eye of a needle, and when he died in 1931 his $250,000 estate contained, to his family's astonishment, not one single share of General Motors stock.

On December 12, 1918, John J. Raskob, chairman of the General Motors finance committee, submitted to the directors a list of twenty-five parts-and-assembly plants he recommended General Motors buy for a total of $52.8 million. Fifth on Raskob's list was the "McLaughlin–Buick–Canadian company," and the committee approved its purchase for 50,000 shares of GM stock valued at $5 million.

Sam tells the story this way: "My wife and I had been blessed with five daughters, but we had no son to carry on. George was anxious to retire; he had never been strong and he had worked hard all his life. His sons had tried the business but had not taken to it. On the business side, there was the fact that if we decided to stay in the automobile business we almost certainly would have to make our own cars from the

Adelaide and Sam with their five daughters: Billie, in front, Mildred, Hilda, Eileen, Isabel. (*Ewart McLaughlin Collection*)

ground up. I had managed to make an agreement with Buick that was too favourable to us for them to renew on the same terms when the 15-year agreement was up in three or four years.

"Equally important was the fact that McLaughlin's had become by far the largest employer in Oshawa. My father had always felt, and George and I had come to feel, that the business was as much Oshawa's as it was ours. If Oshawa's motor industry became a General Motors operation, expansion and employment opportunities were assured. If we had to venture into making a car of our own in Canada, failure and unemployment might well result. Years before I had had to sell George on the idea of going into the automobile business. Now I had to sell him on the idea of going out of it by selling to General Motors. My argument took this form: 'We are through when the Buick contract expires. We could go on until then, but I wouldn't have anything to do with attempting to make a new car when that time came.'

"I didn't have to argue much with George before he agreed. So I went down to New York and saw the top men of General Motors: Mr. Durant, Pierre du Pont, of the great American industrial family, and John J. Raskob, the noted financier. I told them the basis on which we would sell. As had happened so often before in our major deals, this one was closed very quickly. It was no more than five minutes before Durant, du Pont and Raskob said 'Sold.'"

Sam, as usual, was putting his own spin on the story. The approach to buy the McLaughlin company had come from General Motors, and the sale had taken nearly a year to complete. George, in robust health, had needed no persuading: in a lengthy memo to Sam dated July 4, 1918, George judged the proposed merger to be "thoroughly sound." General Motors had bought out the McLaughlin's minority interest in Chevrolet earlier in the year, and GM already owned 49 per cent of the McLaughlin–Buick. The McLaughlins had sold only 6,300 Buicks in Canada in the past year, compared to 13,800 Chevrolets. They had forfeited their opportunity to develop their own low-priced Canadian car, and, their "McLaughlin" cars notwithstanding, their name was identified with Buick. Other Canadian manufacturers were going under – Russell was on the verge of bankruptcy – and GM's offer was five times the value of the McLaughlin company.

Sam didn't tell *Maclean's* about the rest of his deal, although it had been made public in 1953 as evidence in a United States government antitrust suit against E. I. du Pont de Nemours and Company. On December 14, 1918, two days after proposing the McLaughlin purchase to the GM finance committee, John J. Raskob, acting now in his capacity as a vice-president of E. I. du Pont de Nemours and Company, recommended to the du Pont company that it purchase the McLaughlins' 50,000 GM shares at their current market value of $6.5 million – approximately $94 million in today's dollars.

At the end of December 1918, nearly sixty years after Robert McLaughlin sold his first homemade cutters, his sons signed his company over to General Motors, and by February 1919 they had flipped the majority of their $5 million in GM shares to the du Ponts for $5,590,000. Sam and George retained 6,000 shares, valued at $780,000, as their investment in General Motors of Canada; the remaining 1,000 shares were likely held by General Motors. Sam carried on as president, and regained his position on GM's board of directors, but George, as vice-president, was not elected. The cash payout was divided among the McLaughlin Carriage Company's shareholders, which now included a dozen senior employees, and the McLaughlin family fortune was reinvested in a safe, diversified portfolio of stocks and bonds.

If the Governor, now over eighty, felt any sorrow or regret at the loss of his life's work, he never breathed a word in public. His granddaughter Dorothy, however, tells this story: "Then there was his dog, an Irish Terrier; he called it 'Joe.' How my grandfather loved that dog! As the years rolled by, my grandfather and his dog became more and more inseparable. I am sure Joe was there on that day 'Mr. Sam' insisted on taking the 'Governor' home from the office for his first ride in a brand new car that had glass windows. My grandfather, like so many respected citizens in those days, had the tobacco chewing habit. Indoors he had his spittoon. When motoring he had been accustomed to spitting out into the wide open spaces. This he did in the new car with the closed shiny glass windows. Of course the windows and beautiful upholstery were badly stained. My grandfather seemed quite unaware, and my uncle charitably ignored the whole matter."

The real value of General Motors of Canada was established after months of hard bargaining. George did not go down without a fight. "George was much more tight-fisted than his brother Sam," recalls bookkeeper Peter Hoskins. "When we were finishing the inventory,

GM executives inspect their latest acquisition, General Motors of Canada, c. 1921.
From right, Alfred P. Sloan, Sam McLaughlin, Pierre S. du Pont, George McLaughlin,
J. J. Raskob, two unidentified men. (*General Motors of Canada*)

George pointed to the water tank on top of the factory and asked,
'Have you included the water?'"

George had eventually been satisfied, and when he received a
cheque for $1.46 million on December 22, 1918, he wrote to Billy
Durant: "Allow me to express, on behalf of my brother and myself, our
very sincere appreciation of the confidence you have reposed in us from
the commencement, and the broad-gauged, fair and liberal minded
way in which you have always considered any representations we have
made touching our Canadian interests; and to the different members of
the American organization who have had to do with the detail of this
transfer, we entertain no feelings excepting those of friendship and the
utmost goodwill. In a deal of such dimensions, it would be natural and
only human that there were some points which probably had to be
debated with considerable vigor on each side, but all of these questions
have been amicably and satisfactorily threshed out and adjusted. All of
the Canadian units are in a very healthy condition and we are in a
position to assume leadership and command of all fields just as soon as
production facilities will permit of proper quantity production."

7

WEARIN' DIAMONDS

"We had a terrible accident last Sunday," Lucy Maud Montgomery confided to her journal on June 26, 1921. "It might have been a thousand-fold worse. I am thankful we escaped as we did. But it was horrible – horrible."

In the village of Zephyr, Ontario, where her husband, Ewan Macdonald, was a circuit preacher for the Presbyterian church, Maud's fame as the author of *Anne of Green Gables* didn't count for a pin, but the preacher's smash-up on main street after the Sunday service created a sensation.

"We stopped at the garage for gas," Maud wrote. "After we pulled out from the tank Ewan turned to cut the corner. Then I looked up and saw a car in the middle of the road and going very fast – Marshall Pickering's car, as it turned out. I said to Ewan 'Look out for that car' but it seems he did not hear me. Neither did he see the car, although it was right in front of us and only a few yards away. *He turned northwest across the road in front of the oncoming car.* Why he did such a thing without looking to see if the road was clear is inexplicable, unless – unless – oh, I fear that his mind was so fastened on the one gloomy idea of his melancholy dread that he was not thinking about anything else.

Too late he saw the other car. There was one awful moment when I saw that a collision was inevitable and felt that it was impossible to escape without someone being killed. Then the cars crashed together.

"The whole thing was like a nightmare. There was a tremendous crash, the sound of breaking glass – screams – then the cars were still. I said, 'Thank God nobody is killed.' Then I sat there in a curious numbness. Our new car was badly done-up – the Pickering car was worse – Mrs. Pickering was being taken out her face bleeding from a cut on the windshield – which looked very bad though it afterwards turned out to be very slight. The sight of the blood on Mrs. Pickering's face broke up this abnormal calm. I began to cry and shake. Mrs. Law took me up to her house and I stayed there an hour and cried all the time – just nervous crying that I could not stop. Mr. Law brought us home and I went to bed and stayed there for two days unable to eat or sleep."

Ewan had been driving *her* car, a classy Gray–Dort Maud had named "Lady Jane." Maud had splurged on the car out of her *Anne* royalties, and Lady Jane Gray–Dort was, like Anne, a beloved, if temperamental, friend. The damage was slight – it cost Maud fifty dollars for a new lamppost, fender, and a straightened axle – but Ewan bore the brunt of her wrath: "Oh, I thought he had gone violently insane at last and was taking us all to destruction with him." Ewan, convinced of his soul's eternal damnation, suffered bouts of depression that terrified his wife, but Maud was no slouch at "nerves" either, and Ewan may have been more afraid of Maud than God. Maud didn't drive, but motor trips with manic Ewan at the wheel were one of the real pleasures of her repressed, rural life:

"To put on a pretty evening dress and then spin down to town over the good roads in the clear evening air, under a cloudless silvery sky, was so exhilarating that it made me feel almost happy for the time being. Besides, riding in a car always cheers me up It is as if we went so fast that we *left worry behind*." Fast, it was. "We certainly smoked along," Maud confessed of a summer morning spin to Trenton. "I admit there *is* a witchery in speed."

As for Marshall Pickering, "he is notorious as a speeder and a road-hog. If he had been on his own side of the road as he should have been – since according to his own admission he saw our car in plenty of time to turn out – nothing would have happened. I am sick of the talk it has made. Everywhere we go we have to talk of it and explain. A hundred exaggerated reports have gone abroad concerning it. This is the third nasty automobile accident I have been in and I feel as if I had had enough."

So had Pickering, a prominent Zephyr farmer and an elder in the Methodist church. His wife was injured, his Chevrolet, a smaller cheaper car than the Gray–Dort, was badly damaged – repairs cost nearly one hundred dollars – and the morning after the accident he had been rushed to the hospital with severe abdominal pain. Reverend Macdonald had come by to express his sympathy, but made no offer to pay Pickering's costs. Maud was making it plain to everyone that Pickering, "a very conceited, arrogant, bumptious man," deserved most of the blame for "furious driving," and his wife, "an ignorant, insolent, vulgar woman, was very insulting to Ewan."

Pickering had surgery to remove his prostate gland, and in December he sent a letter to Ewan demanding that Ewan pay half his thousand-dollar medical bill. Ewan replied that they were both to blame for the accident, and it was well known that Pickering, who had suffered previous prostate attacks, was planning to have the operation anyway. In February 1922, Pickering again demanded five hundred dollars and threatened to settle it in the courts. Maud was not impressed by a letter that "raved on generally and abusively through several very badly written and badly spelled pages," but she got the message: "It is evident that he has talked to some lawyer about it. I suppose he imagines that Ewan, being a minister, will submit to blackmail rather than be dragged into the worry and notoriety of a law suit. If so he does not know either of us. This barefaced lie and demand is something neither of us can tolerate. We will not be frightened into paying his bills."

Ewan scrambled around Zephyr trying to find witnesses to testify against Pickering. Maud hired a lawyer. "Well, poor Ewan has paid bitterly for that carelessness of his on that fatal Sunday," she wrote, "and I have to pay, too." She could easily afford it, as she suspected Pickering had guessed, and his lawyer upped the ante to fifteen hundred dollars. "Marshall Pickering is like Ewan's melancholia," Maud wrote in June. "Just as soon as we begin to hope there is an end of him he comes back." Lady Jane was feeling blue too: "Of course she has never been really right since Pickering ran into us," Maud wrote on September 10. "Besides the smashing up she got, everything else was jarred and loosened so that something has been continually going wrong ever since." Lady Jane stopped seven times on a ten-mile drive to Uxbridge, and she stranded Maud overnight in Toronto after a screening of *The Prisoner of*

Zenda: "The Gray–Dort people had overhauled 'Lady Jane' and charged Ewan nine dollars – and she wouldn't even start. Next morning Ewan got Lady Jane overhauled again, paid some more cash and got away at ten. The brute stopped twice on the road home and we had four flat tires – or rather the same tire went flat four times. Tonight we started for Zephyr to attend a christening. Lady Jane stopped *eleven* times on the way over – a thunderstorm came up and torrents of rain poured down. I was worn out when we reached there and dreaded the return home. But that absurd car came home without a spark of trouble. Of course she is possessed – not a doubt of it. The Old Scratch himself is in her."

Ewan had another accident on September 20: "A car, *without lights* on the wrong side of the road had run right into him! Fortunately nobody was injured but Lady Jane was badly knocked up. It cost him seventy-five dollars, two days' delay and no end of worry to get her put into shape again. It is enough to make one suspicious. Ewan *has* dreadful luck in the matter of cars. I think it is because he is a man who is slow of thought and cannot think quickly enough what to do in a sudden emergency."

Ewan was seeking a new church, but on September 25, Maud wrote: "Ewan came home tonight feeling quite sure he had lost out in Hillsburg. And why? *Because he motored there* – or rather, because he has a car. It seems their last minister kept a car and by reason of it *spent too much time in Toronto.* So the people are prejudiced against a minister who has a car!"

Pickering was now demanding eight thousand dollars in damages: a thousand for his operation, five for "suffering," and two for injuries to his wife. "It is simply a conspiracy to get money out of us, nothing more or less," Maud fumed. "Two thousand dollars is quite a large sum for a

A fender-bender snarls traffic on the Toronto–Hamilton highway. (*Ontario Archives, 16856 - 15612*)

scratch that did not even leave a scar! Many people in Zephyr think that it is Mrs. Pickering that put Pickering up to this. She is a woman notorious for bad temper, tyranny and stubbornness. She looks it – her very face is obscene. She doesn't seem to have a friend. She is Pickering's second wife – by the way, he 'had to get married' as the country phrase goes, both times."

Maud knew what the Pickerings were saying about her, and her ears were burning: "It is hard that Ewan and I should be butchered to make a Roman holiday! I feel all raw and bleeding, mentally and physically." Slander fanned the flames of religious bigotry, and by the time Pickering's suit came to court in November, it had escalated to a Zephyr version of the Salem witch hunts. "From all reports the whole country side is going to the trial," Maud lamented. "It is true most of the onlookers are on our side and their curiosity friendly. It is curiosity just the same, and I will be mouthed over afterwards in a hundred assemblages of gossip, and my looks, bearing and evidence canvassed and detailed. It is indecent – indecent!"

Ewan, thoroughly persuaded of his innocence, rejoiced in his martyrdom, and he rejected the judge's suggestion that he settle out of court in a spirit of "Christian amity." There was no doubt in the judge's mind that Ewan was at fault, and after hours of exasperating testimony about Marshall Pickering's congested prostate, he awarded the Pickerings two thousand dollars and costs.

Outraged at the "horrible injustice of it all," Maud vowed: "I will do anything in my power to get the better of that pair of plotters and perjurers," and Ewan promised: "I shall never pay or let you pay a cent of money to Marshall Pickering." Ewan didn't have a penny. The church owned the manse, Maud had bought their furniture. She had even lent Ewan a thousand dollars to buy a Victory Bond. Ewan's only asset was his salary, and if his congregation could be persuaded to pay it monthly, he had nothing left that Pickering could seize.

"When we left the lawyer's office it was five o'clock and beginning to snow," Maud wrote. "I suppose the sensible thing would have been to stay in Toronto all night, but I had the instinctive and imperative desire of the wounded animal to crawl away and hide. So we started. About four or fives miles up town in a residential district Lady Jane, true to form, stopped. Ewan discovered that the little reservoir in front was empty of gas. We could not get any from our tank so there was nothing to do but go for gas. He had to go a long way. I stayed there, alone and cold – for it was turning very cold. It was snowing thickly. Cars of gay people streamed past. I felt so wretched and crushed that I was numb. After about an hour Ewan returned with gas and filled the reservoir. Even then Lady Jane wouldn't go. He had to work with her for over half an hour before she would start. I stood and held the flashlight with freezing hands and feet. The snow was getting thicker – I began to fear we would be stuck on the road home. And at that moment Marshall Pickering was probably spinning homeward in great spirits. Well, never mind Mr. Pickering. He laughs best who laughs last. You may find, dear Mr. Pickering, that getting a verdict is not quite the same thing as getting my money!"

In Zephyr, Pickering was pursued by boys shouting "Liar! Liar!" and when he telephoned a friend to say he had won, a woman's voice cut in with, "Yes, you have won the suit but *you've lost your soul*." On December 9, Maud wrote: "Last night I had my last ride in old Lady Jane. Today Ewan took her to Cannington and sold her. I saw her go with no regret. From first to last she has been a hoodooed car. But luckily she was registered in Ewan's name and so was legally his. If she had been in my name Pickering could have come after me for damages. I fancy his lawyers were a little disappointed." Maud bought a Dodge. Ewan's congregation rallied around, and three years later he was called to a more prestigious church west of Toronto. Marshall Pickering never collected a dime.

At least Pickering still had his Chevrolet. Billy Durant, on the other hand, had lost General Motors again, and in trying to hang on he had squandered a personal fortune estimated at $90 million. He had driven General Motors once more to the brink of bankruptcy, and this time the corporation had been bailed out by the Morgan bank. The new president of General Motors was Pierre S. du Pont, and du Pont's protégé was Alfred P. Sloan, Jr.

The McLaughlins, having sold their block of shares to the du Ponts, for a profit, now escaped taking terrible losses when the bottom fell out of the automobile market in the autumn of 1920. The North American economy had slipped into recession after the end of the war in 1918, but for cars the crash was sudden and devastating: sales dropped by 80 per cent in six months, and showrooms and factories were choked with millions of unsold cars. All manufacturers were hit hard: by December, even Henry Ford was forced to close his plant. General Motors suspended all production except Buick and Cadillac, and in Oshawa, for the first time in nearly fifty years, the McLaughlin works lay dark and silent in the snow.

Once, when asked how the Great Depression affected his business, Sam McLaughlin replied: "Oh, there were a lot of depressions!" This was one of the worst, and the ghost of William Gibbs must have been rattling its chains in Parkwood's cellar. During the war, pumped up by inflation, booming sales, and du Pont profits, General Motors had ballooned into a billion-dollar corporation, second only to United States Steel. Durant, like a Chinese emperor, became secretive, arbitrary, and cruel. Bernard Weisberger draws a compassionate but chilling portrait of a man, now nearly sixty, whose dreams were becoming delusions: "He delegated almost nothing. He would fuss endlessly with a letter or a piece of advertising copy, hounding it through a dozen drafts, staring at it, rearranging, excising, often throwing out an entire idea if it was not in perfect pitch to his ear. And he would fall into this paralysis over a trivial matter as readily as an important one. His chats with old friends while executives waited to see him were part of an oddly 'democratic' arrogance that inconvenienced the lordly and the commonplace associate impartially. But their end result was to pile unfinished business on his desk and bind him more firmly to it.

"He had always had moments of egocentric insensitivity to subordinates' needs. He would suddenly command an all-night or holiday session on some crash project, which would then be dropped. Or he would swoop into someone else's area of responsibility and undo weeks of work with a decision whose rationale lay hidden within him. Yet he was forgiven again and again because he was transparently without malice. But there were limits, and as the claims on his concentration multiplied, Durant began to exceed them. Those who came to him with problems found it a trial to get his ear for more than fleeting moments, as he broke off conversations to answer a battery of telephones – Chrysler counted ten, Sloan thought there were as many as twenty – linking him to plants, offices, and his brokers. There was scarcely a moment when a receiver was not in his hand. His voice stayed calm, his smile ready, but frenzy seemed disquietingly close.

"Forgiveness came harder and harder. He would summon people to his office on Sunday morning and talk to them while his barber, Jake, shaved him in the portable chair he kept there. Or worse still, he would call an executive meeting of ten or fifteen officials in Detroit. Some, like Sloan, would arrive overnight from New York. Walter Chrysler would have risen at dawn to drive the sixty-five miles from Flint. And they would wait and wait while Durant telephoned or fussed with minutiae, his mind away in some Emerald City of automotive wonders. The session might not start until four in the afternoon, and would drag on through short-tempered, dinnerless hours. Once Chrysler, on whose time Durant himself had set a price of nearly $10,000 a week, waited to see his boss for four days, then gave up and went back to the factory.

"He was going beyond the bounds of an important code. His lieutenants lived, as he did, for their work. It was their compass, their purpose in life, their true religion. By forcing them to stand idle, he was devising for them a torment worthy of a Caligula."

Chrysler quit in a rage; Sloan ordered a Rolls–Royce and went to Europe. Durant, however, had an accomplice: John J. Raskob. While Durant, on behalf of General Motors, was pumping millions into Frigidaire, Fisher Body, and a muscle-bound tractor named Samson, Raskob, representing E. I. du Pont de Nemours, was buying up American paint, rubber, and plastics companies. Raskob's dreams, however, did not include Durant. "Our interest in the General Motors Company will undoubtedly secure for us the entire Fabrikoid, Pyralin, paint and varnish business of those companies," Raskob gloated in an indiscreet memo to the du Pont board of directors in 1917. "It is the writer's belief that ultimately the Du Pont Company will absolutely control and dominate the whole General Motors situation with the entire approval of Mr. Durant, who, I think, will eventually place his holdings with us. . . ."

Raskob was exquisitely courteous and respectful to Durant. He never challenged Durant's authority, and he obligingly borrowed millions against GM's "prospective earnings" to pay for his own and Billy's "plunges." At the same time, Pierre du Pont was placing du Pont men in key positions within the General Motors executive, and he was paying close attention to Sloan's arguments in favour of an organized, accountable management structure.

General Motors was short $85 million in the spring of 1920, and Raskob persuaded the board to raise money by splitting five million GM common shares, each with a par value of $100, into fifty million "new common" shares at no par value. Raskob gambled that a stampede for the new GM stock would send the price soaring, but the market had soured, and the extravagance of the offer only confirmed investors' suspicions that General Motors was spending like a drunken sailor.

Brokers ignored the new shares; they contracted to buy old stock, speculating that the glut of new shares on the market would cause the price to drop by the time they had to pay up.

For Durant, the bear market was the opportunity of a lifetime. He sent telegrams to GM shareholders cautioning "don't sell until you get in touch with me," and urging "buy all you can afford." They heeded his advice: Sam McLaughlin bought 50,000 shares of the new stock, George, 11,000. With Durant buying furiously himself, the price of the old GM stock soared to $420 by the end of March. "The bears were faced with the ultimate disaster, for them, of a 'corner' – one buyer, or a group coordinated by one buyer, holding most or all of the shares they needed to fulfill their contracts," says Weisberger. "There was no alternative then but to pay the corner's price, however ruinous."

Durant had cornered the market and, in order to avert what the *New York Times* called a financial "catastrophe," the governing committee of the New York Stock Exchange permitted brokers to exchange ten shares of the new GM stock for one of the old. There were still plenty of new shares, and the old shares dropped seventeen points in half an hour. The price kept going down. Desperate for operating capital, Pierre du Pont unloaded almost two million shares at twenty dollars each to the Nobel explosives company, and in June he sold another 1.4 million shares to the Morgan bank in exchange for $28 million and six seats on the GM board.

"Durant accepted the Morgan intervention as a bitter exaction of necessity," claims Weisberger. "The Du Pont group went forth rejoicing and dancing to meet their new partners, as if they had achieved a longstanding intention. From the moment of their involvement, Durant was in jeopardy. The collective judgment at 23 Wall Street was still that he was an irresponsible speculator. The partners saw in him what they most despised, the egotist and anarchist, resistant to the indispensable claims of economic order. Their new position offered them a potential for acting on that judgment that could be aroused by any slip."

The Morgans were justly concerned about the legitimacy of Durant's methods. When Billy sold stock in one of his companies, he persuaded the buyers to let him keep the shares "in trust," as he had held the McLaughlins' shares in trust for Buick. He demanded blind faith, offered no guarantees, and treated the shares as his own. He spent their cash, traded their shares for shares in other companies, then used these companies as collateral to borrow more money to buy more shares in more companies. As long as Durant's shareholders received dividends – and in good times his payouts were spectacular – they were willing to trust the wizard's sleight-of-hand, but now people who had obeyed Durant's call to hang on to their GM stock when it was trading at $420, were stuck with stock worth $25 and sinking fast. Durant's telephones were ringing off the hook, and his office was full of people demanding payment for stock Durant had optioned at the peak of the market. He had only the vaguest idea how much money he owed, or to whom, and when Raskob jokingly asked him if it was $6 million or $26 million, Durant replied: "I will have to look it up."

Raskob may have anticipated that Durant would be grateful for an opportunity to sell his GM shares, but Billy kept buying. His motives were both honourable and selfish: he bought back stock from old friends and investors who were facing bankruptcy, and he gambled that he could, singlehandedly, create a resurgence in the stock market that would allow him to take General Motors back from the bankers once more. Wall Street, however, was disillusioned, and this time Billy Durant had no Chevrolet to pull out of his hat.

In October, Durant made the slip that justified the Morgans' concerns about his ethics: he offered to sell GM shares at $18 to investors in his personal company, the Durant Corporation. Du Pont and the Morgans were aghast. Not only was the president of General Motors independently speculating in his company's shares, he was dumping them at two dollars below the price set by syndicates controlled by members of the GM board of directors.

Smiling and relaxed as ever, Durant bluffed that he was only encouraging public investment in General Motors, and he blithely asked du Pont to lend him another 1.3 million GM shares. Du Pont complied. Du Pont had no inkling that Billy's own three million shares were gone, pledged to bankers as security for the money he had borrowed to buy them, and soon du Pont's shares were gone too. GM stock fell to $13, and during a panicky lunch meeting on November 11, Durant blurted out that he was "worried" about his personal accounts. The following Monday, Durant reluctantly confessed, to du Pont's horror, that he owed about $34 million to brokers and bankers, all of it secured by GM stock, but it wasn't until Thursday afternoon that he revealed that unless he came up with $1 million by Friday morning, his assets would be liquidated.

"The magnitude of Durant's revelation made it an earthquake," says Weisberger. "If he was about to be sold out, then up to four million shares of GM could be tearing the floor out of the market within days, ruining everyone who held GM stock or who relied on its value in any way." A modern Samson clutching the pillars of his crumbling temple of commerce, Durant was threatening the entire American economy with collapse, and the crisis wasn't averted until he surrendered his GM stock at 5:30 a.m. on Friday morning. On November 30, 1920, Durant resigned, for the second time, as president of General Motors.

As soon as the mare's nest of his finances was unravelled, Durant received a generous severance package of $1.5 million and 230,000 GM shares. His debts were quietly paid, and the grisly details of his departure were hushed up. Privately, the du Ponts and the Morgans made no bones about their anger, but Billy refused to admit, even to himself, that he had been irresponsible or dishonest, and on Wall Street his faithful claque put the word out that he had been "crucified."

The McLaughlins managed to emerge from this debacle on friendly terms with everyone. George and Sam apparently made money on their cheap GM stocks, or Durant redeemed them, and when Sam was in New York, he lunched with Durant, Dr. Campbell, and their circle of old friends. Within General Motors, the "McLaughlin boys," as George and Sam were known, cultivated friendships with Pierre du Pont, Raskob, and the Morgans. Their position on the northern fringe of the GM empire isolated them from dangerous palace intrigues, and their quaint "Canuck" mannerisms were reassuring to the Americans. When other Durant loyalists were purged from the GM board, Sam McLaughlin, with his repertoire of barnyard jokes, kept his seat.

Sam knew his intimate lunches with Durant would not go unnoticed at General Motors, and Sam was quick to snub anyone who endangered his reputation. But Durant was back in business by the spring of 1921, manufacturing "Durant" cars in plants abandoned by bankrupt automobile companies, including a factory in Muncie, Indiana, liquidated by General Motors. Raskob and the bankers on the General Motors board were terrified that "the wild man" was going to attempt another takeover, and the McLaughlins, while keeping an eye on Durant's activities, had their own interests to consider. Durant had opened a rival factory in Toronto in the summer, and at the end of August he mailed a seductive letter to George offering to sell him a thousand shares in Durant Motors. "Pardon me for the expression," Durant added in a

Shortly before his death in 1921, Robert McLaughlin was photographed painting at his easel. (*McLaughlin Public Library*)

postscript, "but I am so thoroughly pleased with the car and the accomplishments of our engineers that I predict a repetition of the Buick success."

Billy had baited the hook: would the McLaughlins bite? Their stake in General Motors was small, and their Oshawa works were as moribund as Muncie. The McLaughlins, however, had a trump card to play with General Motors: an English king. Tariff agreements among the countries of the British Empire permitted cars manufactured in Canada to be sold in Great Britain, India, and Australia at prices much lower than the same cars imported from the United States, and Canada also enjoyed trade advantages in South America and the Middle East. By using General Motors of Canada as GM's export division, GM would save money, and car production in Oshawa would increase far beyond the requirements of the weak, fragmented Canadian market. General Motors, spinning its wheels in a stagnant American economy, had nothing to lose, and awarding this plum to the McLaughlin boys would nip in the bud any danger that they might jump ship to Durant. In the autumn of 1921, Sam sailed for England to persuade the British to buy made-in-Canada American cars. Sam was in London when his father died on November 23, 1921.

Robert had celebrated his eighty-fifth birthday only five days before, and his last illness came as a shock to his family. He had complained of no pain, and apparently ignored the symptoms of cancer until his bowel had become completely obstructed. There was nothing Dr. Hoig could do, and Robert prepared himself for death with the same resolute self-assurance he had brought to his life. His will was written, his accounts were settled. Earlier in the year, he had donated twelve acres of lake-shore property to Oshawa for a public park; the street railway he had helped build twenty-five years before would provide his workmen's families with cheap transportation for picnics on the beach. Like Lear, he had divested himself of his patrimony, but if he ever felt an urge to rend his clothes and wander naked on the heath, he suppressed it. Robert had kept his old office in the factory, and had gone there almost daily to daub away at his peculiar paintings. The Old Man may well have been keeping an eye on things – he had run his business much more efficiently than General Motors seemed to be doing it – and the new American broom was sweeping away the trust and loyalties of fifty years.

"General Motors sent their people up here and cleaned the place out," recalls Peter Hoskins. "They fired people right and left." Hoskins had been promoted and had just bought a house. "I was scared to death. A man named Coates sat in the office and went through the list of employees. I was afraid it was going to hit me. I was getting ready for a nervous breakdown." Hoskins arranged a transfer to the Winnipeg branch office, headed by Richard Mackenzie. "The cost of living in Winnipeg was higher, but Mr. Mackenzie was a nice man. He had once loaned the McLaughlins some money, and he had been told that he would never lose his job. I had a guaranteed salary of $175 a month."

In his final years, Robert McLaughlin's relations with his sons were not as harmonious as Sam later suggested. "I remember about 1916 the sons tried to get Robert to stop buying the wood," says Hoskins. "They kept telling him he was too old. McLaughlin got angry. 'I own the McLaughlin Carriage Company,' he shouted, 'and the McLaughlin Carriage Company owns the McLaughlin Motor Car Company, and if I want to buy the wood, I will continue to buy the wood!'"

Hoskins was not allowed to pay an invoice unless Robert had initialled it, but the Old Man's enthusiasm for paperwork had not increased with time. "I would go into his office to pick up the invoices. There was a big partners' desk, and he'd be at the easel painting a picture. 'I'm busy painting,' he'd say. 'Put them on the desk.' 'I brought them in yesterday.' 'Well, they must be here somewhere.'" After rooting among his papers for the invoices, Robert would give Hoskins careful instructions about each one: "He'd say, 'You'll have to write and get credit for this tally that's a little under.' I'd say, 'But this other one is over.' 'Oh, don't worry about that, it's probably third grade.'" The Old Man's parsimony may have encouraged him to sell to GM. "They were just getting by in 1918," Hoskins recalls. "There were troubles with the first Chevrolets. They broke. The McLaughlins were buying their Chevrolet engines from Brampton, and I remember that the bill of lading had to be paid before the engines were delivered. You have to have a good cash flow, and work would be up and down. They tried to borrow from the Royal Bank, and they were turned down."

Robert's last gesture was to summon to his bedside, one by one, the old workmen who had built his first buggies in Enniskillen. These men, gnarled and bent like himself, were his true friends, his closest companions. Robert clasped their hands, and said goodbye. When his death was announced, Oshawa's factories shut down, stores closed, and flags were lowered to half-mast. On the day of his funeral, mourners choked the streets around St. Andrew's Church and hundreds more stood silently, heads bowed in the rain, as the cortege of McLaughlin–Buicks, laden with chrysanthemums, inched its way west on the Kingston Road to Union Cemetery. The Old Man would have been embarrassed by the fuss, but it was a sincere tribute to a prince of industry.

Robert's death marked the company's transformation from a semi-rural, family-owned shop with its roots in ancient crafts into a contemporary capitalist enterprise run by engineers and accountants according to rules of mechanics, systems, and numbers. By January 1922, automobile exports were booming and the value of the Oshawa plant was boosted to $20 million. Seventeen hundred workers, split into two eight-hour shifts, produced an average of two hundred cars a day. General Motors of Canada had added Overlands, Oldsmobiles, and trucks, and by the end of the year production reached a record 37,428 vehicles, more than double the 15,544 produced the year before. The expansion was phenomenal, and Sam was so thrilled he hired the Pathé motion-picture company to film the departure of a trainload of cars for England. As entertainment, a movie of sixty-three boxcars rumbling out of the Oshawa station couldn't compete with the Keystone Cops or Rudolph Valentino in *The Sheik*, but Sam's smiling face made the theatre newsreels, and he established a promising alliance with a young whiz in the Toronto advertising business, Jack MacLaren. Sam also threw down the gauntlet to his smaller Canadian rivals:

"The motor car industry will rapidly right itself," he said in an interview with the Toronto *Globe* on March 4, "and those firms manufacturing cars of enduring merit, who are capable of giving proper service and who are properly financed and properly run will survive and grow stronger than ever, while small assembly institutions whose only excuse for existence has been that during the last few years most anything built on four wheels and with an engine in it would sell are bound to disappear."

Although Sam was bragging about General Motors, he was still advertising his Buicks as "McLaughlin" cars manufactured by the McLaughlin Motor Car Company Ltd. of Oshawa. The old family company, however, was merely a repository for the McLaughlins' remaining shares of General Motors stock. The factory was a branch plant and the instruction manuals for McLaughlin cars had Buick illustrations. Sam was trying to have it both ways, and he continued to produce six-cylinder "Specials" that had a distinctive McLaughlin touch: bevelled-glass rear windows, mahogany dashboards with clocks and locking glove boxes, nickel trim, and extra tires.

"While the Specials were among Canada's favourite prestige cars, they also attained a certain notoriety – at least in western Alberta," Durnford and Baechler write in *Cars of Canada*. "An important citizen of Blairmore, Emilio Picariello, started an 'import' business catering to the prohibition thirst of his neighbours. Mr Pick, the Bottle King, as he came to be called, used Fords at first, but in 1918 graduated to the bigger, faster McLaughlins. In 1919 he bought two Specials, which proved so satisfactory and became so popular with all suppliers in the trade that they became known as Whiskey Sixes. Many an innocent owner of a McLaughlin Special got sly, knowing glances in those days."

The Roaring Twenties got its fast reputation from the automobile and the roadhouse, hideaways where homebrew or smuggled booze could be consumed far from the prying eyes of parents and police. "Automobiles have become a menace to the morality of boys and girls," the Women's Christian Temperance Union complained on October 10, 1922. Back-seat groping and drunk driving were becoming part of the Canadian teenager's coming-of-age, and police were too busy chasing bootleggers to pay attention to dangerous drivers. There was no hue and cry when a six-year-old Oshawa boy was run over by a car on October 9: the car had no brakes, but the child's death was ruled accidental.

Bathtub gin went down a little easier when mixed with flavoured syrups, and prohibition brought an unanticipated boom in American sales for Canada Dry. In 1919, the J. J. McLaughlin Company had begun shipping carloads of Canada Dry to New York, and two years later its phenomenal success provoked the United States to raise its tariff on imported ginger ale by 50 per cent. The McLaughlins established an American subsidiary, Canada Dry Ginger Ale Inc., on 38th Street in New York City. The plant was capable of turning out twenty-five thousand bottles of ginger ale a day, but demand soon exceeded capacity, and by 1923 the family was faced with a difficult decision: should they expand their American business or sell out to their New York promoter, P. D. Saylor?

"Down From Canada Came Tales of a Wonderful Beverage," Saylor proclaimed in his first American advertisement, exploiting Canada's reputation for fresh air, mountain lakes, and sparkling natural springs. Thirsty Americans knew that anything that came from Canada had to be cold, and if bottles of Canada Dry were stored in a new Frigidaire, they were. Saylor persuaded the McLaughlins that mass advertising would make Canada Dry a household word, and, as American sales grew, an immense investment would be needed to increase production.

"With control divided among the various members of the McLaughlin family, it was difficult to build up the necessary reserves to provide for such a major expansion," reported the *Financial Post*, hinting at a family squabble. Certainly the J. J. McLaughlin Company lacked the capital, but reserves were not necessary: American financiers were clamouring to invest in Canada Dry, and Sam and George McLaughlin, both members of the board of directors, would have had no difficulty borrowing the necessary capital. They were acting, however, as trustees: the company really belonged to Jack's widow, Maud. It was her sole source of income, and any risk would jeopardize her family's future. Her oldest son, Donald, now in his twenties, was the intended heir, but Donald seemed more interested in boats and girls than in running a multinational corporation. Donald's free and easy ways irritated his Uncle Sam, and Sam decided that Donald lacked the necessary "grey matter."

In later years, Sam virtually erased his brother Jack and Canada Dry from the McLaughlin myth. Was he jealous? As a young man, his own freedom had been harshly curtailed, while the Governor had given every privilege to his beloved "Johnny," and Jack had created a genuinely Canadian product, something Sam and George had failed to do. Why should they risk their fortune now for Johnny's lazy boy, or for haughty Maud? Roland, her youngest son, was the family favourite, Maud's "eye-apple," as she phrased it, but Roland was pursuing an academic career in science and engineering, and had no interest at all in fizzy water. Sam's failure to father a son itched like a ringworm, and he may have felt the need to justify the sale of the McLaughlin Motor Car Company to the Americans by advising the same course of action. On December 27, 1923, all of the assets of J. J. McLaughlin Company Ltd. were sold to P. D. Saylor for $1 million.

Saylor pinned the million-dollar cancelled cheque as a trophy on his office wall. He had snapped up one of the biggest bargains in the history of American industry: by 1930 Canada Dry would be worth $30 million. Maud and her children had kept twenty-five thousand shares, but, acting on the advice of the McLaughlins' cautious broker, J. C. Fraser, they sold their stock. Donald's last duty was to deliver to New York his father's secret recipe for Canada Dry.

Six months later, on June 1, 1924, George McLaughlin retired from General Motors of Canada. "It will be thirty-nine years as this month closes since I left school and started work in the carriage business," George wrote to Quebec City dealer J. H. Fortier. "I have had an uninterrupted connection with this enterprise ever since – five years in the factory or mechanical work, thirty-four years at the desk and on the road. From fourteen to fifty-four makes quite a steady pull at one set of oars, and for some time I have felt a desire for a little more freedom and out-door life."

In a personal letter to Durant written on September 26, George reveals more complex motives: "When I left the General Motors Corporation in June, the record of the Canadian operations since you consummated the deal most abundantly indicated your judgement and vision as not only had the entire purchase price paid by you been returned to the Corporation but a very handsome profit in addition. It was not a very easy job for me to take the plunge and say goodbye to an enterprise in which I had spent one-third of a century, and now that I have had two or three months of the outside vision I no wise regret my action. I still have quite a block of General Motors stock, although considerably less than I originally had, and strange to say, I expect to have a little ready cash by the first of October. I am wondering if I could not put these securities to work. I want to get

General Motors into something with a little more life. Could you suggest a switch that might be profitable for me? You have done so much for me in the past that I hesitate about writing you in this strain, but owing to my independent position, I feel there are no attendant circumstances to prevent me in any way from following any course I choose."

Durant, still playing the stock market like a virtuoso, recommended Cast Iron Pipe and American Safety Razor: "Our crowd controls this company, which is doing a very safe and profitable business." He couldn't resist adding: "The action on General Motors is very disappointing, and many of our old friends like yourself are getting out of it." George bought shares in Durant Motors and made an astute investment in a lively new automobile company founded by Walter Chrysler.

The McLaughlin boys still preferred to chew the fat with Billy than to shake the limp, clammy hand of the new president of General Motors, Alfred P. Sloan. Sloan, for his part, could not conceal his scorn for the old "cut and try" car-makers from the early days, or for Sam's gussied up "McLaughlin" Buick. "I remember once a General Motors executive visiting in Oshawa was particularly impressed with one model of Buick," Sam recalled. "He asked us to send one to the New York office to let the boys there see what we were doing in Canada. We sent it and before long it came back. Presently we learned why. Alfred Sloan had seen it parked in front of the New York showroom and ordered: 'Get that thing out of here, and quick. It's gathering crowds – and it's no more like one of our Buicks than a St. Bernard is like a dachshund!'"

Sloan, as president of the Hyatt Roller Bearing Company of New Jersey, had spent most of his career manufacturing ball bearings, and he intended to transform General Motors into a corporation where the gears meshed without friction. Durant had permitted his jostling multitude of companies a great deal of individual autonomy, but Sloan marshalled them into divisions – placing the Canadian plants firmly at the bottom of his organizational chart – and centralized control over policy and finances. As a result, General Motors of Canada had its own sales staff and dealer network, its own advertising, engineers, and production managers, but the company's treasurer was in New York, and Sloan held the purse strings.

Sloan had a single common denominator to measure the performance of General Motors' various components: profit. How that profit was obtained was up to the ingenuity, hustle, and ruthlessness of the competing divisions. Sloan bluntly stated this credo in his autobiography, *My Years with General Motors*: "The primary object of the corporation we declared was to make money, not just to make motor cars. The problem was to design a product line that would make money. The future of the corporation depended upon its ability to design and produce cars of maximum utility value in quantity at minimum cost."

George McLaughlin had been schooled in a different business ethic, and on January 24, 1924, he expressed his dismay in a letter to Charlie Nash: "The fancy systems of intensive advertising, schools of instruction and the hundred and one intensive methods that are now being employed through Sales Departments are in the main alright, but during the last few years of my association with General Motors Corporation I became more thoroughly grounded in the belief, and upon every occasion where I felt I had any influence, I did not hesitate to take the stand that all these things were as 'The Mist on the Mountain' unless the man at the head of the institution gave first and principal heed to the fact that no matter what class of product they were offering to the public it had to be built just as well and just as conscientiously, or even a little better than that of any competitor."

Sloan would not have appreciated George's criticism, or the insinuation that he was foisting shoddy products on the public, although his experts thought the Chevrolet was so cruddy they wanted to scrap it. Centralization had left George with little authority as manager of General Motors of Canada, and Sloan was promoting a young American, K. T. Keller. Charlie Nash had chosen independence, and his reply from Kenosha, Wisconsin, in July may have caused George a twinge of regret: "I came over here and started in a business bearing my name, and I can say to you, George, that I have now had almost eight years of the happiest years of my life. We have a family organization here that would remind you of your old organization before the days when you had expanded to the degree you have now. I think you have done the wise thing to retire from the General Motors Company. I was positive, when I visited you a year or so ago, and we had a little chat, that you were not at all happy in your position. As a matter of fact, it has been a quandary in my mind for some time how you and Sam could stand the proposition at all. When you permitted your controlling interest to pass from your hands, I said then that I was sure the McLaughlin boys would never be as happy again."

If Sam was unhappy, he expressed it in a lifelong determination to stamp his personality on the Canadian division of General Motors, as if by creating an illusion of control he could recapture the past. Sam began to revise the history of the motor-car company, placing himself front and centre as the sole founder and presiding genius. He claimed that his father refused to have anything to do with automobiles: "I couldn't sell the Governor," he said. "We never sold him." Sam depicted his father as a doddering old crank at a time when Robert was still running the business, and Sam developed a childish compulsion to be one-up on George. George built a big house; Sam built a bigger one across the road. George bought a cottage in Muskoka; Sam built a cottage on Lake Ontario. George gave five thousand dollars to the Oshawa hospital; Sam gave ten thousand. George donated a plot for veterans' graves in the Union Cemetery; Sam financed the Ontario Regiment and became its honorary lieutenant-colonel.

George accepted his younger brother's rivalry with patience: it is said that when the McLaughlin boys got into an argument in the shop, they put on boxing gloves and slugged it out until they cooled off. George gracefully yielded the limelight to Sam, and in Sam's recollection of events George was relegated to an inconsequential, ineffectual role. Sam's memories became more distorted as he grew older, and near the end of his life he boasted that he had fired George for hiring his two useless sons behind Sam's back.

This was malicious nonsense, but the fact that George's boys did not "take to" the business stuck in Sam's craw. The younger, Ray, preferred raising livestock, and Ewart was fond of golf and racing boats. Neither saw any compelling reason to toil in a factory for Uncle Sam. George set Ray up on a farm – Sam bought a farm across the road – and financed a partnership for Ewart in an Oldsmobile dealership, Moffat Motors. Ewart achieved modest fame on his own. He was one of the first dealers in Canada to experiment with a car radio, a wireless set he successfully installed in an Oldsmobile in 1923, and, at the wheel of his speedboats, *Whippet* and *Baby Olds*, he was the acknowledged champion of the Muskoka lakes.

Ewart's spending money, like everything else, came from his father; George managed Ewart's investments, bought his boats, gave him cars, and bailed out Moffat Motors when it faced bankruptcy. Ewart had little education, and years of imaginary invalidism made him autocratic and narcissistic. Bed, however, was his refuge and redoubt.

Champion of the Muskoka lakes, Ewart McLaughlin guns *Baby Olds*. *(Ewart McLaughlin Collection)*

In 1928, at age thirty-four, he had the confidence to marry a creative, attractive widow, Margaret Luke Smith, and adopt her infant son, Dick.

The family believed that Ewart had been "ruined," but his home movies of boat races, family weddings, and games at the cottage indicate that being spoiled rotten could be a lot of fun. Fun was something his mother did not approve of. Annie had grown up across the road from the old McLaughlin homestead at Tyrone, and she remained "country": plain, blunt, and antisocial to the point of rudeness. Annie shunned charities. When one brave soul phoned to ask her to donate a cake to a bazaar, Annie snapped, "I don't bake," and hung up. She was a good cook, and she was making a point: ladies bountiful didn't bake their own cakes, their cooks did, and Annie was saving her own cook extra work.

Her three younger children, Ray, Dorothy, and Kay, were healthy and happy-go-lucky. They went to local schools and played with the neighbours' kids, but their friends were rarely invited into their dark brick house. It was stuffed with expensive antiques and bric-a-brac Annie picked up at estate auctions in Toronto. "She cornered the market on Krieghoffs," sighs her granddaughter Mary Hare. "Unfortunately, half of them were fakes." Going to auctions was one of the two great passions in Annie's life: the other was Sam McLaughlin.

"Annie couldn't *stand* Sam," says her grandson Dick. "She hated him with a *passion*." It may have been Sam's irritating one-upmanship, his fondness for booze and cigars, his reputation as a ladies' man, his refusal to provide a sinecure in General Motors for Ewart, or some personal slight, but Annie's hatred of Sam caused an estrangement between the families. George and Sam tried to make the best of it, but one night, having been invited to stay for supper, Sam came home in a rage: "You'll never guess what she served!" he roared, "*Porridge!*" Dick recalls: "We were warned not to mention Sam's name in her home. Annie referred to him as 'across the road.'"

8

PARKWOOD

Across the road was Parkwood, and every time Annie went out her front door she had to confront the tall white Corinthian columns that framed the entrance to one of the most flamboyant, idiosyncratic houses in Canada. Architects Frank Darling and John Pearson had designed the Sun Life head office in Montreal, the Toronto General Hospital, the Royal Ontario Museum, Trinity College, the Winnipeg Grain Exchange, and, from coast to coast, innumerable branches of the Canadian Bank of Commerce, the Bank of Nova Scotia, the Bank of Montreal, the Dominion Bank, and the Standard Bank. Sam McLaughlin had joined the board of the Dominion Bank in 1917, and Darling and Pearson's temple-of-commerce style suited Sam's tastes to a T.

Sam's delight in being fabulously rich was so naive, so sunny and swaggering, everyone was grateful to bask in its glow. There was nothing mean or stingy about Sam McLaughlin, even if he spent almost all of his money on himself, and unlike other Canadian million-aires, Sam didn't adopt a phony air of pious rectitude, or wring his hands with guilt and remorse, and the ways he chose to unload his cash express his personality more accurately than the McLaughlin–Buick

Parkwood, c. 1918. *(Parkwood)*

car. Sam's pride in his success was a compliment to his workmen, and his decision to build his mansion near the old factory in Oshawa won their respect. Parkwood, expanded and refined over a period of more than twenty years, is Colonel Sam's real work of art, and, like a medieval pope, he hired the best artisans in the business.

The first was Pearson, who won the commission to design a new Centre Block for Canada's Parliament Buildings as he was beginning work on Parkwood in 1916. Parkwood contains, in miniature, several of the features that have made the Centre Block Canada's most famous architectural symbol. Both "houses" feature wide hallways, Romanesque arches, and domed glass skylights; the carved woodwork around Parkwood's fireplaces bears a striking resemblance to the ornamentation in the Commons and Senate chambers, and a long, glassed-in sunporch off the upstairs bedrooms is a small-scale version of the parliamentary press gallery. Pearson's buildings presented an austere and intimidating facade to the street – Parkwood's entrance is as unwelcoming as the door to a bank vault – but his interiors were bright and adorned with wood panelling, inlaid plank and stone floors, marble, tiles, embossed silk wall coverings, and decorative designs painted on plaster or woodwork. Pearson was particularly fond of murals, an art form associated with hotels, steamships, and theatres, and both Sam and Adelaide shared his enthusiasm. Parkwood was designed as a "public" building where the McLaughlins could display their wealth, taste, and hospitality.

Their taste was sentimental, and their choice of painter nostalgic. As an apprentice to a Toronto lithographer, Frederick S. Challener had illustrated McLaughlin Carriage Company catalogues. Challener was now a distinguished *salon* painter and a member of the Royal Canadian Academy, but he taught art at Central Technical School and did commercial work to make ends meet: some unsigned McLaughlin–Buick catalogue covers from the war years feature his characteristic birch trees and breezy, bucolic charm. Challener's most famous public work is a series of lush, erotic murals depicting such subjects as "The Meeting of Venus and Adonis" and "The Arab Sheik with His Many Wives" on the walls and ceiling of Toronto's Royal Alexandra Theatre.

For Parkwood's majestic south hall, Challener chose an Art Nouveau style reminiscent of his McLaughlin–Buick catalogue drawings. The "delicate charm" of Challener's Parkwood mural is praised by his fellow artist Stanley Moyer in a profile Moyer wrote for *The Canadian* magazine: "There is a freshness about the colour and a note of joy that amounts almost to ecstasy. This keynote is struck by the centre panel with the etherealized figure of the fairy spirit of the Enchanted Island hovering in rapt joy and watching over, with mystical benevolence, a group of children with a dog, in a lovely birch wood, and smiling upon them through the luminous, dreaming atmosphere. Scores of birds and their nests appear here and there as you watch the lovely scene; a humming bird and the nest of an oriole, swans floating with stately grace in a pool. The birch tree motif continues, and portraits of the McLaughlin children and grandchildren, in charmingly casual and unconventional groups, take their places naturally with the lace-like draperies of foliage for background, and form important and harmonious elements in a scheme that, in spite of being most successful as pure decoration, is portraiture and poetry as well; full of the song of the woodland and the shy winsomeness of wild flowers."

Robert McLaughlin had made the family fortune chopping down the woodland; Challener conjures up its ghost for Sam's plaster wall. There is an eerie stillness to his Enchanted Isle, and the figures are arranged in stilted poses as if playing the childhood game of statues. Challener's pre-pubescent nudes are reminiscent of Lewis Carroll's photographs of little girls, and their presence give his Parkwood mural a peculiar sexual tension. His "portraits" are chocolate-box caricatures, but the idea of idealizing his family pleased Sam so much he commissioned Challener to do a series of panels for the billiard room. This group, says Moyer, "contains what I am told is the only equestrian group of portraits in Canada. They are used in the Hunt Club scenes in this series of panels depicting the favourite outdoor sports engaged in by Mr. McLaughlin and his family, and include also yachting, fishing and hunting. This combining of portraiture with the pictorial and decorative is by no means without precedent in Art annals and many cases of the kind could be cited from Ancient to Modern times, but it is the sort of thing that only the greatest skill and the most unerring taste can save from hopeless inanity."

Sam's flirtation with inanity began with the bankruptcy of Canada's Colonel Blimp, Sir Henry Pellatt, and the auction of the contents of his *ersatz* Scottish castle perched on Toronto's western escarpment. Sir Henry had made a fortune selling electricity, and he had spent it all, and millions more, building and furnishing Casa Loma. The unfinished house was considered a worthless eyesore – who would buy it? – but the antiques and exotic treasures Sir Henry had collected attracted an excited crowd of bidders when they went under the hammer on June 23, 1924.

The five-day auction was held in Casa Loma's spacious conservatory, and most of the early bidders were fashionable ladies attracted by bric-a-brac and bargains. The propriety of taking part in this jackals' feast no doubt kept some away, but Pellatt himself, round and red as a ripe tomato, greeted people cheerily in the hall, and Sir William Mulock, kingpin of the Liberal Party in Ontario, gave his *imprimatur* to the auction by successfully bidding forty-four dollars for some French vases and fifty-four dollars for a tea set. "A Chinese bronze incense burner went for fifteen dollars," writes Pellatt's biographer Carlie Oreskovich in *The King of Casa Loma*. "A full suit of steel armour was sold at thirty-five dollars. A dainty Sheraton writing table in mahogany with five drawers and a brass rail netted only fifty-eight dollars, and the chair to match sold for eighteen." Auctioneer Charles Henderson bemoaned the "slaughter" prices, but the bewildering variety and vulgarity of Pellatt's swag – a 1,500-pound life-size bronze buffalo head was knocked down at fifty dollars – made buyers leery.

On June 26, the Toronto *Globe* reported: "Mrs. R. S. McLaughlin of Oshawa got a quantity of the lovely old table silver." Adelaide had caught the auction bug, and the next afternoon Sam was listed among those who bought paintings. He also paid $3,500 for a pair of Louis XVI vases in royal blue and bisque, $310 for a Sèvres jewel casket and $250 for a Louis XVI rosewood desk embellished in gilt ormolu. Their Casa Loma souvenirs encouraged Sam and Adelaide to furnish Parkwood in a more opulent style than the rather spare English Country manner John Pearson had anticipated, but they were not connoisseurs or collectors: much of their "antique" furniture came from Eaton's. Sam bought their cheap Oriental rugs at Eaton's too, and insisted on a hefty discount. He filled the floor-to-ceiling shelves in his library with leather-bound classics imported from New York, and lined his dining-room walls with cadaverous portraits of himself, Adelaide, and all five daughters. In 1925, Sam's accounts show: "Investments (Silver, China, Linens, Books, Pictures, Furniture, etc) – $56,586.42." He spent another $38,757.08 the following year and, in 1927, a staggering $96,493.21 – over $1 million in today's dollars.

The McLaughlins' eclectic style suited Parkwood's personality: its stucco, wooden shutters, striped awnings, and green tile roof give this sprawling house the insouciance of a Mediterranean villa. "Vincent Massey once referred to it as the 'perfect Hollywood house,'" writes architectural historian Robert Hunter. "As slighting as Massey likely intended this comment to be, he was inadvertently quite close to the mark in identifying American influence in its design. The design of Parkwood is clearly influenced by an interest in the grander, smoother and more boldly detailed American Beaux-Arts houses of the period."

Sam McLaughlin kept his American connections under wraps in Canada – his friends and colleagues from General Motors seldom visited Oshawa – but Sam spent a good deal of time in New York and Detroit, and he was influenced by the opulent country houses the American millionaires were building. William Randolph Hearst's San Simeon made Spanish tile roofs all the rage in Hollywood, and, in automobile circles, pipe organs were in fashion. Sam installed an Aeolian organ in Parkwood's front foyer, concealing its massive pipes behind the walls of a circular staircase. His, however, was a player organ, and once the appropriate roll was inserted, the organ thundered out everything from Bach to boogie all by itself.

The billiard room. (*Parkwood*)

Sam was also among the first to install an automated pin-setter in his bowling alley. He probably got the idea from GM director C. S. Mott, who put a bowling alley in the basement of his mansion in Flint, but Parkwood's cellar wasn't good enough for Sam: his bowling alley was placed in the front hall, just past the billiard room, and the wall alongside it provided an ideal place to hang his collection of paintings by Clarence Gagnon and the Group of Seven. At the end of the hall, a door led to Sam's private YMCA: an indoor swimming pool, a squash court, and a shower room equipped with a barber's chair. In middle age, Sam remained a fitness fanatic; his colleagues learned to fear his bone-crushing handshakes and evade his chest-thumping invitations to sock him in his steely solar plexus. The billiard room was Sam's lair, a sump-tuous clubroom with overstuffed chairs where Sam and "the boys" could smoke and tell tall tales in front of a blazing fire. At billiards, however, Sam wasn't a patch on Adelaide, who could beat him handily. Adelaide also played an energetic game of golf, and when she went fishing on the salmon stream Sam leased at Cap Chat in the Gaspé, she caught more and bigger fish.

Adelaide had grown stout, and a mastectomy had made her self-conscious about her appearance: she dressed in a conservative, high-necked style, and her ramrod posture accentuated her regal bearing. "Adelaide was a *lady*," her brother Ralph says emphatically. Adelaide knew her place, which was firmly at the pinnacle of Oshawa society, but she was gracious about it, and while she was extremely strict, her prickliness – Sam's nickname for her was "Cactus" – was softened by her big laugh and her *joie de vivre*. "Why doesn't anyone drop in on us any more?" Adelaide lamented after the family moved to Parkwood. Drop in? What woman in a housedress and pincurls would dare to venture uninvited through Parkwood's imposing wrought-iron gates? And if she did, would she rap on the front door, or the back? All the "right people" in Oshawa had hired help to cook meals and clean up, but Parkwood boasted a staff of forty, including two dozen gardeners, three chauffeurs, and a Scottish butler, James Telford Lindsay.

"The first thing my father did was to take the ketchup bottle off the dining-room table," recalls Lindsay's son Douglas. "Sam could be a pretty crude boy. He could be rough, and not much of the help had formal training. My father tried to introduce some hoity-toity things." Lindsay had been a footman in the household of the Duke of Buccleuch when he enlisted as an officer's batman with the King's Own Scottish Borderers during the Great War. After the war, he emigrated to Toronto with his future wife, and in 1920 answered an advertisement Sam had placed in the *Globe*. Slight and quick-stepping with a brisk, military air, Lindsay was efficient, tactful, and discreet. "He was very close-mouthed," Douglas remembers. "He never swore. The worst he would say was 'silly ass.' He could roll with the punches."

The Lindsay children saw little of their father: "When we were having dinner at home, he'd be serving dinner at Parkwood. He worked 24 hours a day, seven days a week until the day he died at seventy-eight. He had Tuesday afternoons off, and every second Sunday." Nattily attired in striped trousers and a black, swallowtail coat, Lindsay pressed and packed Sam's clothes, polished his shoes, and introduced the McLaughlins to the mysteries of oyster forks, finger bowls, and French wines.

"Drinking! Oh, dear no!" laughs Isabel McLaughlin about her mother's abhorrence of liquor. "Dad would have one cocktail before dinner. We thought them very dull. We would persuade Lindsay to make us stronger ones." Adelaide relented enough to drink an occasional pink lady, and she argued that cocktails with a lot of fruit in them were less wicked: "If the fruit takes up so much space, there can't be as much room for the liquor, don't you think?" Champagne, because of its medicinal reputation, occupied an ambiguous area on the moral scale, and Adelaide's frugality occasionally triumphed over her scruples. On a shopping trip to Paris during prohibition, a French count, smitten with one of her daughters, presented Adelaide with a case of vintage champagne. The gift did not encourage his suit, and Adelaide gave most of the champagne away before they sailed, but as their ship neared New York, a few incriminating bottles remained. Adelaide wrapped them in her corsets, and, to Sam's horror, smuggled them through customs.

Frugality was a habit that died hard. "My father was not overly well paid," Douglas Lindsay says dryly. His mother worked in the kitchen at Parkwood, and the Lindsays, like the family of Sam's chauffeur, Clarence Lowry, were housed in grace-and-favour cottages across the street: Sargent, the head gardener, lived in the gatehouse on the corner. The unmarried female staff lived in Parkwood's attic, the men above the garages. It was a feudal arrangement: room, board, and a little spending money in exchange for a lifetime "in service." Many of the British-born servants, accustomed to looking up to the gentry, took pride in their employment at Parkwood, and became devoted to the house and the family. Servants who didn't like it could leave – Lindsay considered a job on the line at GM – but if they could put up with low wages, punishing hours, and lack of privacy – staff would be summoned at all hours of the day and night – they were rewarded with affection and security, the chance to gossip about famous visitors and, for a fortunate few, regular trips to London, Paris, and New York.

"If you owed Adelaide a quarter, she made sure she collected it," says a fellow bridge player. "She would do it in the nicest possible way, but she never forgot." Adelaide played cards for money, but she was less concerned with the sum owed than with the moral obligation, and she was scrupulous about enforcing a social code derived from the rural, churchgoing community in which she had been raised. Adelaide patronized every Protestant charity in Oshawa – one reason, perhaps, why Annie did not – and she spent her days organizing bazaars, bake sales, raffles, and craft shows that, after months of toil and expense by the ladies' auxiliaries, raised pitifully small amounts. Working for charity was the only respectable way a wealthy married woman could spend her time – bridge parties were of dubious repute – and her public goodness compensated for her husband's private pursuit of profit. The charities allowed Adelaide to exercise her formidable organizational skills and share some of the public limelight with Sam. In 1910, she spearheaded a successful fund-raising drive to open an Oshawa hospital, and she became the first president of its ladies' auxiliary. Adelaide lost the presidency the next year, but regained it in 1912 and remained president, without interruption, until her death in 1958.

"Adelaide was a white-glove do-goody," scoffs a disenchanted relative. "Neither she nor Sam had time for their five children. They were raised by nannies. There was emotional neglect of those daughters." Others thought the girls indulged: "They had more money than they knew what to do with," grumps a cousin. The five McLaughlin girls, born about two years apart, were very different in appearance and personality. Eileen, a tall honey-blonde, was athletic and strong-willed; Mildred was tiny, dark, and self-effacing. Isabel – everyone called her Izzy – was fun-loving and artistic, Hilda was the beauty, and Eleanor, known as "Billie," was horse-crazy. The girls were emotionally very close, and Hilda once said she had the happiest childhood anyone could wish for. Eileen, on the other hand, felt "on the edge," split between her parents' Victorian attitudes and the luxurious reality of their lives.

Adelaide dressed her daughters like princesses. They had horses and riding lessons, debutante parties and summer vacations at posh St. Andrew's, New Brunswick, yet Adelaide insisted that they attend Oshawa public schools in order to grow up "democratic," and she equipped Parkwood with its own schoolroom. The five girls, in 1918 ranging in age from nine to nineteen, shared three bedrooms, as cramped and gloomy as monastery cells, on the second floor of Parkwood's north wing; in hot weather they slept on cots in the glassed-in sunporch. The girls' rooms appear to have been designed as servants' quarters: they had a narrow communal bathroom – one tub, one toilet, two sinks, and a tiny mirror – furnished in the white tile common to hospitals, hotels, and boarding schools. The contrast between the girls' rooms and the spaciousness of the guest bedrooms and their parents' suites is astonishing, as is their location, directly above the billiard room, connected to the front hall by a secret staircase concealed behind an oak panel.

"I had the girls all packed away in this section," Sam chortled. Sam was possessive, determined to use his daughters as projections of his personality, proof of his potency, and emblems of the McLaughlin

Eileen McLaughlin, right, and Josephine Hodgson perform *Dance Pastorale* at the Parkwood lawn fête, 1918. *(Diana Jackson)*

slogan, "One grade only, and that the best." Sam's daughters became players in their father's private *Fantasia*, an extravaganza produced, directed, and scripted by Sam, starring Sam in all the leading roles. Pearson had designed Parkwood with a broad terrace perfectly suited for the kind of spectaculars Sam had in mind. A breathless reporter from the Oshawa *Reformer* describes the first "Parkwood Lawn Fete" in the summer of 1918:

"About two hundred guests enjoyed a delightful afternoon at 'Parkwood,' the beautiful home of Mr. and Mrs. R. S. McLaughlin on Saturday last. The affair was given in the interest of the Navy League of Canada, the Oshawa branch of which has for its President Mr. R. S. McLaughlin, who promises to be most energetic and enthusiastic in his new office. The entertainment was in the form of a lawn fete and the beautiful green lawn to the south with the fine old trees for a background made a most artistic setting for the exhibition given by the fair young dancers who for almost two hours charmed the interested spectators who thronged the terrace and porch.

"The entire program was given under the direction of Miss Josephine Hodgson of Toronto, by her Oshawa dancing class, assisted by ten of her best pupils from Toronto. From the opening number, a dance of flowers, the taller girls, prettily costumed as narcissi, and the wee tots so sweet as daisies, to the end of the program, each feature was a revelation of grace and beauty and those watching were transported in imagination into Fairyland. Probably the most popular dances were "Butterflies," by Hilda McLaughlin and Margaret Bull; "Moment Musical" by four fairy-like little creatures, and Miss Hodgson, their clever teacher; the difficult and unique "Dance Archaic," by four Toronto girls, and the quaint "Gavotte Renaissance." But more captivating than all the others was the "Pastorale Dance" with Miss Eileen McLaughlin as the shepherd and Miss Hodgson the maid. Then came as a fitting climax to an entertainment given for the interest of the navy the hornpipe and other sailor dances, while the closing scene formed by these sailor girls and boys with 'Billie' McLaughlin in their midst, holding aloft an immense Union Jack, all singing 'Rule Britannia' will long remain a pleasing picture in the memories of those who saw it.

"About $175 was raised which will be handed over to the Navy League for relief work by the host and hostess, who afforded the opportunity to so many to witness this interesting exhibition. The affair was truly a happy conclusion to the year's work which the young ladies have engaged in. Not only were they able to give pleasure to their friends but also to raise a handsome sum for a worthy cause."

The spirit of the old Prospect Park amusement park lived on, but now guests arrived by invitation only, and three sides of the Parkwood grounds were surrounded by a solid wooden fence. The custom of a family's unmarried daughters entertaining guests by singing or playing instruments was an old one, and Adelaide's desire to show off her daughters' accomplishments triumphed over her prudishness. No wonder Eileen felt "on the edge": the spectacle of a beautiful nineteen-year-old girl cavorting about in pastoral drag would have been unthinkable five years earlier, and by the strait-laced standards of Oshawa the McLaughlins were being extremely avant-garde. The McLaughlins' artistic standards were set, however, by Pierre du Pont, and in du Pont's outdoor theatre at his Pennsylvania estate, Longwood, voluptuous nymphs in diaphanous dresses gambolled on the lawn before a backdrop of evergreens. In one snapshot the nymphs appear to be stark naked.

Sam McLaughlin visited Longwood several times after 1915, when du Pont became influential in General Motors. Like Parkwood, the du Pont farm contained some ancient spruces and a few exotic relics of an arboretum the original owners had planted. The Sun King of Delaware was using these as the framework for his Versailles, a series of monumental formal gardens featuring fountains, marble statuary, and exotic plants. As his *orangerie*, du Pont constructed a glass conservatory the size of Grand Central Station, and filled it with tropical vegetation imported from Central and South America. Lowry, Sam's chauffeur, remembers the conservatory as a swamp full of crocodiles. Du Pont's gardeners must have been pulling his leg – there were no crocodiles, and the swamp was a carefully manicured rain forest where visitors could listen to chamber music and take afternoon tea.

Solariums and conservatories were common to grand Canadian hotels and houses, but they were either chilly places with marble floors and a few potted palms, or earthy greenhouses where the groundskeepers raised houseplants and seedlings for the summer garden. The du Pont conservatory was hot and humid, and in the winter it glowed like a mirage of Tahiti in a snow-covered landscape. Sensual, irrational, and magnificent, the conservatory also cost a fortune to heat: du Pont had discovered a quintessentially American way to spend money.

Sam could pay du Pont no greater compliment than to seek his advice on how to improve his grounds. Landscaping was virtually unknown in Canada. Gardens were for vegetables, with some berry bushes and raspberry canes, sunflowers, and wild roses. Until the arrival of running water and sewage, the chief ornaments in the back yard were the pump and the privy, and coal left an ugly patch of black dust by the basement chute. Even in the cities, families kept chickens, and as long as rural yards had a stable for horses and cows, the stench and the flies discouraged aristocratic fancies, although at Kingsmere in the Gatineau Hills, Canada's prime minister, Mackenzie King, was conjuring up his woodland version of Woburn Abbey.

The McLaughlins still kept chickens and a cow at Parkwood, and at the western edge of the property, Sam built a stable for thoroughbred riding horses and an arena where his equestrian daughters, Eileen and Billie, put them through their paces. Owning horses was, and is, the only way an upstart industrialist can crack Toronto's anglophile aristocracy, and the stables gave Parkwood an English tone. The horses, however, were upwind from the house, and the stables made an unsightly backdrop for that other important English institution, the garden party. Du Pont provided the answer: hedges.

Pearson designed a small glass palm-house for Parkwood's north wing, directly across from the bowling alley, and behind it built green-houses for growing orchids, chrysanthemums, and potted plants. A circular rose garden was laid out behind the house, and, in the back corner, a large vegetable garden was hidden behind cedar hedges and wooden trellises. Perhaps because Sam felt a little embarrassed about the grandeur of his house – he said later that he had built it to provide work for men ineligible for military service – the grounds remained very rural until 1925, when an enclosed Italian garden was added beside the library.

The Italian garden bears the charming, artistic, and very English imprint of its creators, Lorrie and Howard Dunington-Grubb. The Dunington-Grubbs had arrived in Toronto as newlyweds in 1911, enticed by a contract to landscape the new Toronto suburb of Lawrence Park. The developers went bankrupt, leaving the young landscape architects dependent on the largesse of Ontario philistines whose knowledge of horticulture ranged from aspidistra to geranium. The Dunington-Grubbs were, however, one of those weird couples who hit it off in Rosedale: Lorrie Dunington had a sharp tongue and a superior tone that sent shivers of inferiority down colonial spines, and Howard Grubb – "Grubbie" to his friends – was an extraverted *bon vivant* famous for his parties, theatricals, and his striking physical resemblance to the Caterpillar in *Alice in Wonderland*. Grubb, an American, had worked in England for the distinguished landscape architect Thomas Mawson, and both were disciples of William Morris's Arts and Crafts movement. In Toronto, their "natural" aesthetic – already *passé* in Britain – found allies in the Algoma school of the Group of Seven.

In 1925, one of the Group, Arthur Lismer, was teaching at the Ontario College of Art, and among his enthusiastic students was twenty-two-year-old Isabel McLaughlin. Isabel had studied botany at McGill, and her interest in botanical drawing led her to France to study painting. Isabel was the only member of the family to inherit her grand-father's "knack with the brush," and while her talent was indulged, it was not encouraged. Isabel had a studio in Toronto, and she refused to divulge the phone number to her father for fear Sam would criticize her and boss her around. Sam's nickname for Isabel was "Bawly," and he seems to have taken a cruel delight in hurting her feelings. When she brought her paintings to Parkwood, he would hang them upside down – "If a work is any good it shouldn't matter," joked Isabel – or give them away to casual visitors. "Isabel's father was a cross she carried," says a fellow student, artist Doris McCarthy. "He was a pain in the neck."

Isabel's parents regarded her bohemian friends with horrified fasci-
nation. When Isabel went to France, accompanied by a chaperone,
Adelaide's greatest fear wasn't seduction, absinthe, or the sight of nude
male models; it was smoking. "Smoking was worse than drinking," says
Isabel. "She was more upset by us smoking than having a cocktail. I
didn't smoke until I was twenty-one. I thought, 'I'd better start practising.' Mother came to France to bring me back. I told her this. She burst
out crying. It was a deadly sin."

Sam didn't mind a little sin, and it may have been his admiration for
Lorrie Dunington-Grubb's marble nudes that clinched the garden deal.
"Far back in antiquity, as far back indeed as records take us, we find that
architectural features and sculpture were regarded not merely as casual
embellishments but necessary parts of any well ordered garden," she
wrote in *Canadian Homes and Gardens*. Lorrie didn't mean flagpoles,
"ruins," and the other bits of rural kitsch Mackenzie King was strewing
around Kingsmere, but a return to the traditions of Plato: "Greece at
this time was steeped in philosophy and therefore it seems appropriate
that her most famous gardens should have belonged to her philoso-
phers who used them as outdoor academies where their students gathered together for intellectual instruction. Sculptural art had reached a
high state of perfection and statuary was lavishly used for ornamenting
their gardens. Pavilions, fountains and colonnades were also important
architectural features of the period."

Sam nixed a colonnade, but if gardening could make him a
philosopher-king, he was for it, and, for all Sam cared, that little creeping charlie, Vincent Massey, could corner the market on the Group of
Seven. The Canadian bush was anathema to the Dunington-Grubbs,
whose idea of "informal" included stone walls, urns, niches, fountains,
and "an imposing piece of statuary placed in the centre of a wide inter-
section." Wrote Lorrie: "Statues never looked as well as when placed
against a background of formally clipped evergreens or a group of
stately pyramidal cedars."

Sam's household accounts for 1925 include "Building Expenses
(Italian garden, Fountain, Pool, Trellis work, alterations to house, etc.):
$25,091.43," and an additional "Outside Expense (including stables,
gardens, conservatory, etc.)" of $30,366.48. The expense was worth it:
the Italian garden, adjoining Sam's library on the north side of the
house, was a serene private sanctuary shielded from the kitchen and

The sunken garden. (*Parkwood*)

garages by thick hedges and a high white trellis covered with climbing roses, wisteria, and morning glories. Stone paths surrounded a rectangular lily pond, and the small, formal flowerbeds were densely planted with bright flowers in symmetrical patterns. The focal point of the garden was a classical marble fountain of the Three Graces, and the illusion of antiquity was enhanced by urns and marble benches along the sunny walls.

The Dunington-Grubbs laboured over Parkwood for four years, adding a balustrade and sundial garden to the terrace, a pavilion here, a gazebo there, and they framed it all in dense borders of shrubs and flowers developed by their Swedish gardener, Herman Stensson, at their experimental nursery in Sheridan, Ontario. By adapting plants imported – or smuggled – from England and the United States to Canadian conditions, the Dunington-Grubbs introduced to Ontario gardens begonias, cannas, lindens, and the ubiquitous, indestructible Japanese yew.

The Dunington-Grubbs understood landscape architecture as a form of performance art – they were particularly concerned how the garden would look in winter – and they encouraged participation by providing pathways, shady nooks, and stone benches. The sunken garden was the Dunington-Grubbs's specialty, and Parkwood's has a peculiarly Canadian eclecticism: "In the foreground are wide steps,

Hilda's wedding to John Pangman, 1926. Hilda smiles at the guests, Adelaide dabs at her tears. Isabel turns toward the three other bridesmaids, one of whom (not the tall one) is Margaret Bull. (*Parkwood*)

marked with marble pedestals at either side, and leading down to a broad flagged walk," writes M. E. Macpherson in *Canadian Homes and Gardens*. "In the centre, on a dais, stands the figure of a woman, in flowing draperies, a lovely translation of Grecian grace in Carrara marble. The figure, which is more than life-size, shimmers white and translucent against the dark greens of the spruces in the background, while, for colour, there are flat, neat beds of each side, packed with the delicate fibrous begonias, with little star ageratum and with foliage plants. The retaining walls are of rough-hewn stone, and to complete the seclusion there is a fine growth of Japanese yew hedge topping the wall.

"At the farther end, shaded by the spruces, is a little pillared tea-house, open on all sides to the summer breeze, with gay red roof and red tiled floor. Comfortable rustic furniture invites the guest to rest and relaxation, and, if he is a wise guest, he will discover that what appears to be a walled cupboard at one end is in reality a tiny kitchenette, equipped with electric plates and a refrigerator, china and all the paraphernalia necessary to a happy tea hour. On either side of the tea-house are small circular pools centred with pedestal bird baths. A guest in his hickory chair may sip his tea and gaze upon the luminous features of the Grecian figure, or, approaching the garden from across the wide lawn, he will suddenly find himself in a grove of Arcady, with goddess, flowers, trees, pavilion and shadowy pools. His enchantment is complete."

Sam and Adelaide were seldom far from food and drink: even the riding arena featured an upstairs lounge with kitchen facilities. The Parkwood kitchen was immense, and so were the meals: "They ate everything in sight," recalls a former housekeeper. Sam was usually home for lunch, followed by tea at 4 p.m., and dinner could be an intimidating ritual. "My brother Derek and I, still quite young, were asked to a special evening dinner party at Parkwood," granddaughter Diana Jackson recalls. "Dressed in our evening best, we joined the adults for dinner. However, there was a difference! Derek and I shared our own small two-seater mahogany dining table. Our table was set like the adults' – the difference was only in size. All grandchildren shared this table for two, graduating to the 'big' table when 'of age,' and when our manners warranted it!"

Diana preferred climbing trees, but when Hilda married John Pangman at Parkwood on June 16, 1926, she was a flowergirl. Pangman was a blueblood from Westmount, and Hilda's was the McLaughlins' first big, formal wedding: Eileen had eloped at nineteen with a local war hero, Eric Phillips, and in 1924 Mildred had married a handsome American playboy, Coard Taylor, in New York City's Little Church Around the Corner. Hilda was less rebellious, and Parkwood provided, in the words of the *Reformer*, "a scene of resplendent beauty, the decorations within the palatial residence and without being carried out on a most elaborate scale." Hilda's wedding set Sam back more than $15,000. Many years later, Margaret Bull gave her treasured portrait of the wedding party to her son, novelist Timothy Findley.

"My mother was a bridesmaid, and in the picture, there she is in the bridal party – this is taken outside by the terrace in the garden, the terrace rising up with the balustrades, etc. The bridal party was on the lower part of the terrace – the girls all in satin shoes with pointy toes, and dresses with uneven hemlines. My mother, just before she gave me the photograph, was looking at it to see who was there in the background, and suddenly she said: 'My god, there's your father!' And sure enough, there is Dad with his friend, Dick Babbitt, looking over the balustrade towards the wedding party – and he had not yet met my

Eileen and Billie put McLaughlin show horses through their paces. (*Diana Jackson*)

mother! It's charming to discover my parents in the context of a wedding, before they knew one another."

Sam's expenses hardly made a dent in his million-dollar income, and all except his $62,000 General Motors salary and a $1,000 Dominion Bank director's fee came from dividends and interest on his investments. His income taxes, including arrears, were only $17,611. Sam spent $522,431.94 in 1926, nearly as much as his entire income for 1925. He gave Adelaide $14,207 for her personal expenses, paid himself $8,000, and distributed $100,000 among his five daughters: $57,299 went to Mildred, likely for a new house. Parkwood's household expenses cost him $34,097, the arena $19,424, and his automobiles $7,534. He paid $47,727 for "amusements, donations, presents, etc.," and another $25,000 to winter with the family at a rented estate in Aiken, South Carolina. His salmon stream at Cap Chat cost a modest $2,600, and he paid another $1,000 to dam a stream in the hills north of Oshawa and stock the pond with brook trout.

"Go catch yourself a fish," Sam would bark at a guest he was too busy to see for a while. It wasn't hard: a fish would jump on a hook almost as soon as it hit the water. Sam's pond was freshly stocked in the spring and drained every fall, when the remaining trout were gutted for the Parkwood freezer. Sam's mass-production approach to fishing was typical. George had transformed himself into a convincing version of a tweedy Scottish laird the day after he left General Motors, but Sam never got it quite right. His cigars were too long, his suits were too snappy, and his bantamweight posture gave him a style more suitable to the Capone gang. George raised prize-winning apples at his Red Wing orchards, imported purebred cattle, and won ribbons with his Clydesdale horses at the Royal Winter Fair; Sam joined the Toronto and North York Hunt Club, and Eileen and Billie, both excellent horsewomen, won more than fourteen hundred trophies and ribbons at horse shows throughout North America. Sam rode almost daily, and attended the annual Hunt Club ball, but Toronto's fox-hunting set was dominated by the formidable Flora, Lady Eaton, a department-store aristocrat only too delighted to put a country squire in his place.

"Sam felt that with some of the Toronto group he was a bit of an outsider," says Allan Lambert, president of the Toronto–Dominion Bank in the 1950s while Sam was still on the board. "The Old Toronto establishment would look down their noses at him. He was a farm boy. He wasn't part of the bluebloods here. It was a cliquish group. I am not sure even the Eatons were part of it. Some people would say, 'Oh, they're in *trade*.'"

Sailing provided an entree into both Old Toronto and New Detroit, and Sam, with his outsider's sensitivity for subtle shifts in power, ran with the wind. "You were speaking to me at the meeting about yachts," he wrote to John J. Raskob on October 2, 1925. "I gave you the names of Tams and King, John H. Wells and Cox and Stevens. There are, of course, many Brokers, and boats for sale are usually listed with all of them. I bought my present yacht through Cox and Stevens. If I were you, I think I would charter a larger yacht, in order to get some practical knowledge as to how you and your family are going to like it.

"The Consolidated Ship Building Company showed me a very fine yacht, called the Thetis I believe. It is owned by one of your well-known families, and was the prettiest one I came in contact with during the months when I was looking for a sailing vessel. The Thetis was in perfect condition, very roomy, beautifully furnished, and kept right up to the minute. She eats up quite a lot of gasoline, however, but it is the only thing against her. She carries a crew of eleven. If I had not had the opportunity of buying my present craft, I would probably have bought the Thetis on sight. If you want to take the boat South for the winter, you will have to get a fairly shallow draught, but otherwise, do not consider anything but a deep draught boat."

Sailor Sam McLaughlin with lady friends, c. 1926. (*McLaughlin Public Library*)

Sam was speaking from experience: his yacht, *Azara*, sailed like a soap dish. Sam had bought *Azara*, a 113-foot schooner, for $25,688, and spent another $30,000 to refit her, but as the *Annals* of the Royal Canadian Yacht Club tactfully put it, her five foot, ten inch shallow draught "made her performance in windward work unimpressive." *Azara* had been built in New England in 1904; Toronto distiller George Gooderham bought her five years later and renamed her *Oriole III*. Gooderham, commodore of the RCYC for years, sold her to a New York company in 1921, and she was *Lady Mary* when Sam brought her back, with her original name, to Lake Ontario. Sam was no sailor – *Azara* came with her own crew – but his purchase of the commodore's old boat gave him privileged access to the inner sanctum of the RCYC, and he may have been swayed by the fact that Edward, Prince of Wales, had been Gooderham's guest on board in 1919. The prince, a sentimental symbol of British imperialism, played an important role in Sam's personal iconography; he is portrayed in hunting pinks, riding to hounds, on the wall of Sam's billiard room.

Sam, resplendent in new yachting whites from Abercrombie & Fitch, paced *Azara*'s deck like Admiral Nelson and dreamed of conquest: he had the biggest boat on the lake, now he wanted the fastest. Gooderham boats, skippered with dazzling skill by RCYC Rear-Commodore Norman Gooderham, had dominated Lake Ontario

Sam's yacht, *Azara*. On the right is Commodore George Gooderham's flagship ketch, *Oriole IV*. (*York University Archives*)

racing for years. His *Nayada* had won the Richardson Cup, emblematic of the Great Lakes championship, in 1924, but *Nayada* was now out-classed by the new American R boats, long, narrow "slinks" that were faster than the boats designed and built in Oakville by T. H. "Bing" Benson. Commodore Gooderham washed his hands of the Yankee trai-tors – the War of 1812 was still being hard fought in the island club-rooms - but Sam bellowed: *"I'll* build an R boat!" He told Benson to build the fastest racing yacht he dared, and to hell with the cost. Astonished, Commodore Gooderham picked up the gauntlet: he com-missioned a rival R boat, *Acadia*, to be built in Nova Scotia.

Sam's named his boat *Eleanor* after his youngest daughter "Billie," and *Eleanor* was everything Sam could have wished: strong and stoutly built, forty feet long and a lean six feet, seven inches across the beam. "It was an absolute and radical departure from all that Bingley Benson and those who, with him, admired a good boat, held sacred," wrote C. H. J. Snider in the Toronto *Evening Telegram*. "This new one had a mast that curled back at the top like a forefinger curled to summon a bellhop. And such a mast! So light that a man could lift it with one arm."

Raked and raffish, Benson's *Eleanor* beat out all comers, including *Acadia*, for the honour of representing Canada in the Richardson Cup races at Toledo, Ohio. *Eleanor*, however, would be skippered for the cup races by *Acadia*'s captain, Norman Gooderham. Gooderham, as the *Evening Telegram* pointed out, "is also one of the owners of the plant which built her," while R. S. McLaughlin "pays the bills." Sam welcomed Gooderham aboard, but *Eleanor* was now identified as Gooderham's boat, and while Sam watched through binoculars from the shore, Gooderham skippered *Eleanor* to two victories in three races against American challengers *Fantome* and *Elyria*. "SKIPPER NORMAN GOODERHAM — HOW DOES HE DO IT?" crowed the *Evening Telegram*. "Norman Gooderham, with about five hours actual sailing experience in *Eleanor*, toddles off to Toledo, and the Richardson Cup comes back to Toronto with him."

Sam claimed he was "delighted" with the victory, and received his share of praise as *Eleanor*'s owner, but he sold both *Eleanor* and *Azara* the next year. Sam retained his membership in the RCYC, but he never bought another yacht, and after Norman Gooderham's death, he presented to the RCYC the handcarved model of *Eleanor* Gooderham had given him.

Sam had envisioned *Azara* as a floating saloon where he and his cronies could drink and do a little horsetrading, but while prohibition had ended in Canada in 1926, it remained in force in the United States. The U.S. border ran right down the middle of Lake Ontario, and *Azara* could be seized by the U.S. coast guard if she was caught in American waters with liquor on board. It put a crimp in Sam's style, and, as he hinted later to *Maclean's*, he had to bail his yacht out on at least one occasion.

Before he sold *Azara* to a Detroit businessman in the autumn of 1927, Sam had enticed on board General Motors' director of research, Charles Kettering, to enlist his support for an industrial research centre in Ontario. "What I had in mind," Sam wrote Kettering later, "was a modest sort of institution for the province, and it was my intention to make a contribution from my personal funds." The proposed research centre reflected Sam's frustration at being excluded from GM's experimental work in Detroit, as well as his desire to keep the McLaughlin name in the forefront of Canadian industry. Kettering's achievements — quick-drying Duco paint was his latest sensation – had helped establish General Motors as a leader in automobile technology, and Ontario businessmen were becoming alarmed that Canadians would be "hewers of wood and drawers of water" for the Americans.

Mackenzie King's "Suburban" station car, 1929. (*National Archives of Canada*, PA 134790)

In May, Ontario's Conservative government had set up an industrial research council chaired by the McLaughlins' old nemesis, Sir Joseph Flavelle. Sam had not forgiven Flavelle for cutting the McLaughlins out of wartime munitions contracts, and Flavelle's reputation was tarnished by allegations he had sold "tainted meat" to Canadian soldiers overseas. General Motors of Canada had been invited to invest $20,000 a year in the research council. "Personally I cannot see that we could justify a request for an appropriation of this kind," Sam wrote to Kettering. "My own idea is that the Federal Government should follow the lines which your government has been pursuing – throw everything into a corking good institution, and let the government pay the expense. I think, as we are large taxpayers to the Government, that we should not be called upon in this way."

General Motors of Canada could afford to set up its own research institute, and this seems to have been the proposal Sam broached to Kettering. The American's response was blunt: "In regard to our own business over there, I do not feel that the research you would do in Canada would contribute very much to the motor industry." Kettering effectively squelched Sam's attempts to expand Canada's influence in General Motors, and his tone reflects the attitude of GM executives

American tourists on Parliament Hill, 1929. (*National Archives of Canada, C 30786*)

that the Canadian operation was a rustic backwater in constant need of American hustle and know-how.

When it came to styling, however, Sam McLaughlin could show General Motors a thing or two. Alfred P. Sloan had just hired a Hollywood car designer, Harley Earl, as General Motors' new art director, but it would be years before Earl produced anything as glamorous as the custom-built McLaughlin–Buicks Sam built for Canada's governor general, Lord Byng of Vimy, and for the Prince of Wales, two celebrities who did more than any movie star to make the Canadian Buick synonymous with class. Byng's limousine, presented as a gift by the troops he had commanded at Vimy Ridge, was Stafford blue with a silver beaver mounted on the hood. The interior was panelled in walnut and carpeted in grey. The passenger compartment, equipped with silk curtains and pillows, featured a reading light, clock, telephone, smoking set, and vanity case; the upholstery was grey twill and Spanish leather. The prince's car, a vanilla-coloured convertible with turquoise trim and snakeskin upholstery, reflected the popular influence of European sports cars. Prime Minister Mackenzie King, however, desired something more practical, and in the summer of 1928 General Motors of Canada built the first Buick station wagon.

"Since my return from England," King wrote to Sam on December 14, 1928, "one of the real surprises and greatest pleasures I have had has been the new Suburban Car. The car, in every particular, is what I most wished it would be, and I shall take a special pride in exhibiting it to my friends as a product of General Motors."

The Suburban was modelled on the "woodies" King had seen in England: closed wooden cars with varnished bodies designed to haul weekend guests and their baggage to country estates from railway stations. The prime minister needed a vehicle to transport his furniture, papers, and visitors back and forth between Ottawa and Kingsmere, and an English station car would make Mackenzie King, at least in his own mind, every bit as much a gentleman as his archenemy, Lord Byng of Vimy.

King's car was really a truck, and it was made at the GM truck division in Walkerville, Ontario. A Buick chassis was fitted with a body made of varnished oak covered by an imitation leather roof; the chassis, roof, and dashboard were painted beige, and the interior was finished in cocoa-coloured leather. Instead of windows, the station wagon had roll-up blinds, and its rear door folded down into a tailgate. The wagon carried six passengers with a large space for luggage in the rear; on the highway it could hit eighty miles per hour.

"My purpose in writing," King went on, "is not only to express my delight in the car itself, but to express to you personally my very sincere thanks for the generous consideration shown me in connection with the charge in the invoice, and which, I understand, has been fixed at what it is by your personal direction. Needless to say, I am very grateful to you, and I should like you to know that the car will ever be associated in my thoughts with this expression of your own kindness and good-will."

Sam knew the way to the prime minister's heart. He had donated $100,000 to the Liberal Party during the last election campaign, including $25,000 for King's own personal fund, and no doubt he sold the prime minister his Suburban at little more than cost. Sam delivered it in time for King's birthday on December 17 – a date of mystical significance in the prime minister's life – and, together with a telegram of congratulation, he replied to King's note by letter on December 17:

"I wish to assure you, Sir, that the many employees who were responsible for the construction of this car were, like myself, delighted to be of service to the Premier. We felt honored that you should have entrusted your requirements to us, and it will be a pleasure indeed to pass on to the Engineers and the others responsible your kind words of commendation. I hope the car will give you every satisfaction, and that you will live long to enjoy its use." Mackenzie King had met his match in Sam McLaughlin: no one reading this unctuous correspondence would ever guess the depths of their mutual mistrust.

PART TWO

9

STRIKE

The Hampton cemetery is a shady grove on the east side of Bowmanville Creek about three miles south of the old McLaughlin burying ground at Enniskillen. The village of Hampton is more English in its traditions than the neighbouring Irish enclaves of Enniskillen and Tyrone, and the tranquillity of the cemetery, which also fronts the road, is a sharp contrast to the severe arrangement of the McLaughlin graves. Four generations of Howard Knapp's family are buried here; Howard is the sixth generation descended from English immigrants who settled here in 1831, a year before the McLaughlins sailed for Canada. The patriarch, Daniel B. Knapp, is buried in the northwest corner of the yard, and his weathered white stone tilts at a severe angle. Daniel died on March 26, 1875, at the age of seventy-five, and beside him rests his son, Daniel S. Knapp, who died on the same day at thirty-three.

Did their wagon fall through the soft spring ice on Bowmanville Creek? Or did they die of influenza or smallpox, plagues that came so often with the first days of warm weather? The story has been lost, and until this spring day in 1993, Howard had never investigated these mossy old headstones set apart from the others. Howard's family tree is

as venerable and robust as the McLaughlins', and their roots are inter-
twined – a "C. Knapp" in Robert McLaughlin's old account book is
likely Charles, buried here in 1896 at the age of fifty-four – but Oshawa's
schools, streets, and libraries are not named in honour of auto workers.
The Knapp family story has become woven into the McLaughlin
legend: Howard, his father, Douglas, and his younger son, Joseph, have
been making cars and trucks for General Motors since 1928. Howard
and I have stopped to visit the Hampton cemetery during a tour of
McLaughlin landmarks, including Sam's trout ponds, an innovation
much appreciated by the fishermen among his employees; more than
one plump, poached trout has made its way into a GM lunch pail.

Howard drives along the back concession roads, pointing out scrubby
fields and gullies where he used to shoot pheasants, foxes, and rabbits. "I
was born at the right time for hunting and fishing around here," he says.
Now monster houses with manicured lawns are springing up like toad-
stools – we pass a Spanish villa once owned by Lorne Greene – and rows
of hydro towers from the Darlington nuclear plant at Bowmanville
bestride the hills. Nothing remains of Robert McLaughlin's first carriage
works at Enniskillen, and the site is not marked. The family homestead
at Tyrone has been sold, and John McLaughlin's house torn down,
although the mill next door remains in business, selling apple cider. The
approximate location where Robert built his first cutters is marked by a
heritage plaque by the roadside and a shed with a glass window displaying some old McLaughlin carriages. The shed is locked, and the glass so
obscured by dust and cobwebs it is impossible to make out any details of
the carriages' design or workmanship. The village of Tyrone has
changed very little in the years since Robert left: the white Methodist
church where Sam courted Adelaide still stands, and across the road is
the handsome red-brick school where she taught.

"I hunted pheasant on the farm where the GM plant stands now,"
Howard says, sounding like Rip van Winkle. As a teenager he also did
summer jobs for the families who lived in Oshawa's big Tudor houses,
including mowing the grass at their lake-shore cottages near Whitby.
Sam McLaughlin owned one of these rambling, clapboard cottages,
and, after our visit with the Knapp ancestors, Howard and I head for
the lake, passing on the way an automobile graveyard far larger and
gloomier than the grove of granite stones at Hampton. The lots where
the cottages once stood is now a Kiwanis park; all that remains are a

few broken concrete steps leading down to a pebbly beach. Sam hated his cottage, for reasons which remain obscure – he may have resented mingling with the *hoi polloi* on the beach – and rather than sell it to a man he despised he tore it down not long before he died. His neighbours followed suit.

Scorched earth. In downtown Oshawa, acres of dusty vacant lots mark the spot where Robert McLaughlin built the biggest buggy works in the British Empire, and where the first McLaughlin–Buicks were pushed out the door in 1908. The railway line Robert built in 1895 is choked with weeds, and the "gander pasture," where new cars were stored for shipment, looks like a junkyard. Deserted and derelict now, the Art Deco office building Sam put up in 1927 is slated for demolition. Its enormous "General Motors of Canada Limited" neon sign has long since hit the scrap heap. Hailed as "the largest in the Dominion," the sign stretched 320 feet across the top of the building and rose seventeen feet in the air. The eight-foot letters were painted white with a red border and mounted with neon tubing that was supposed to glow with a deep blue light; at night, however, reflection from the red border gave the sign a pinkish tinge, and when the temperature dropped, the blue glow changed to red, or to a mottled purplish hue. Everyone in Oshawa woke up and went to bed in the sign's lurid glow, and during daylight hours they used it as a thermometer.

Douglas Knapp was hired at GM about the time the sign went up, and Howard's tour ends, appropriately, at his father's neat bungalow on the northern edge of town. Douglas, eighty-three now, has been tidying up the back yard. It is a small, sunny space bordered by a cedar hedge, and the raspberry patch is immaculate. The cedar hedge reminds me of Parkwood, and when Howard opens a gate, my God, it *is* Parkwood: a mown lawn bordered by cedars, a white trellis, and, in place of Sam's reflecting pool, a perfect rectangle of freshly turned earth. Parkwood's vegetable garden has disappeared underneath a concrete parking garage, but Douglas Knapp's garden produces enough vegetables to supply his children and grandchildren, friends and neighbours.

"During the Depression," he says, "a lot of city lots went back for unpaid taxes. If you were on relief, you got free land from the city to grow your own garden. We got a peck of potatoes a week on relief, so I cut out the eyes and planted 'em. I got thirty-five bags of potatoes. I sold 'em, or I gave 'em away – some people had nothing to eat."

Douglas has only a few years of school, but he is a resourceful man, and he was standing at the General Motors gate on Mary Street in the winter of 1927 when the company was hiring hundreds of new employees to meet a phenomenal and unprecedented demand for GM cars. The jobs didn't require any particular skill or education. "If we can get the type of man we want and he is willing to work and do what is right he can get on in the plant and we'll train him," employee manager Norman McIlveen told the press. "We break in nearly all our men. If a man wants to learn the automobile business it is better for him to go to a good garage than to an automobile factory."

Douglas recalls: "It was quite a job to get hired then. Twenty-five to a hundred men would be standing outside waiting for the guy to come out and pick who they wanted. Usually it was somebody who just got off the train. My father was told he was too old to be hired. 'I've got a son,' he said. 'He's about seventeen.' 'Send him in,' they said. You had to go in the side door by the hospital where all the people went who got hurt. There were two guys who had been at the door several days. A man comes out with some security guards, gets on a chair, points and says 'You, you,' and takes two or three. These guys are angry. 'What's wrong with us?' 'I've a choice to pick out who I want,' the man says. They both hit him at the same time. He landed back in the office."

Douglas started in the Chevrolet paint department prepping bodies for the paint sprayers, and all the preliminary sanding, filling, priming, and buffing had to be done by hand. There wasn't much colour variety: Chevrolet coupes were Brewster green, sedans green or brown, and all the tops were black – the buggy wasn't going down without a fight. Car tops were Fabrikoid, a rubber-like du Pont synthetic, and the Fisher Body frames were hardwood. Steel plates were nailed or welded to the wood, but once the car had run a few hundred miles on dirt roads, water would seep in under the seams. Mouldy cars were common, and if the car was stored in a damp garage, mushrooms grew in the hot, unventilated corners behind the back seat. Nobody seemed to mind: Chevrolet sales were booming, thanks to the sudden disappearance of the Model T.

Tin Lizzie had become more than a joke: she was antiquated, uncomfortable, unreliable, and slow. Henry Ford had stubbornly refused to introduce the basic improvements – a three-speed transmission, floor accelerator, springs, and a six-cylinder engine – that were now standard equipment on Chevrolet, and Lizzie was still the angular black box she had been for nearly twenty years. Chevrolet was

The trim shop, General Motors of Canada, late 1920s. (*Thomas Bouckley Collection, Robert McLaughlin Gallery*)

competitive in price – in Canada both cars sold for between $650 and $950 – and Chevrolet had acquired the longer, low-slung lines that characterized the higher-priced Buick and Cadillac. In May 1927, Ford reluctantly discontinued the Model T. Ford Canada sold only 37,395 cars and trucks that year; GM Canada sold 46,309 Chevrolets and 15,841 trucks.

GM workers were paid on a piecework basis at a rate that worked out to about two cents a car: Douglas Knapp prepped seventeen or eighteen cars an hour for thirty-five cents. With the plant going full blast, his days were long and holidays few. "The first year I made a little over a thousand dollars," he says. "I thought I made a lot of money, so I bought a 1923 Star touring car for a hundred dollars." In departments such as trim and hardware, where jobs could be done more quickly, experienced workers earned seventy-five cents to a dollar an hour, a banker's wage for men who had never put in a day's apprenticeship.

At peak production in the spring of 1928, Oshawa was producing a car a minute. General Motors of Canada was paying $8 million in wages to five thousand employees, a sum that included Sam McLaughlin's $62,000 salary and $20,000 for his general manager,

H. A. Brown. The workers were satisfied with their ten-hour days and the big paycheques, but Brown, a bumptious young accountant from Detroit, thought GM should be getting more value for its wages. In March, Brown speeded up the assembly line and cut piecework rates by 45 per cent, forcing workers to do nearly twice as much work for the same wage. "They tightened the screws," says Harry Benson, then a trimmer still in his teens. "These 'efficiency' experts would sneak up and hide behind the cement pillars. They timed the fastest guy. I tried to take one guy's head off. I was tacking and I let the hammer go. He ducked, but he got the message." Brown cut the trimmers' rates by another 30 per cent. The workers had had enough. "We'd sit down, have a slowdown," says Benson. "We were the fightingest gang." The older hands formed the Trimmers' Social Club, and when Brown refused their demand for a compromise, they went on strike.

"Three hundred trimmers, employees of General Motors' Oshawa plants, walked out this morning in protest against a wage reduction particularly affecting Pontiac and Chevrolet trimmers," the Oshawa *Daily Times* reported on Monday, March 26. "The trimmers on Oldsmobile, Buick, Oakland, LaSalle, and Cadillac lines struck out of sympathy, and according to a decision arrived at following a mass meeting in the skating rink this afternoon, will remain out until the former scale has been put into effect."

Brown took a hard line: "The present difficulty with the trimmers has been given consideration by the Employees' Association, and the action of the management has been upheld. Consequently the action taken on the part of the trimmers today caused the management of General Motors of Canada to consider each and every one as released from our employ. Instead of dealing collectively with the trimmers, each case will be dealt with individually."

He went on: "The management of General Motors of Canada has always shown a very keen interest in the welfare of the employees, and has in all cases paid a fair wage. In fact, prices paid to trimmers in this division have in the past been much in excess of the rates in the U.S. divisions of this corporation. We also appreciate that many of these men are permanent citizens of Oshawa and own their own homes, and have been unduly influenced by a small group who have rather radical ideas. For that reason, our personal service section will be as equitable as possible with individual cases. Due to the present condition of the labour market, we will have little, if any, difficulty in filling the positions vacated, and if none of the trimmers return our production for the current month will be little affected."

On Tuesday morning, the Chevrolet and Pontiac assembly lines came to a standstill when the men walked off in sympathy with the trimmers, and the strike spread to the Buick plant. The paint shop shut down for lack of work, and Doug Knapp joined the noisy mob of strike supporters milling about outside the gates. Brown's statement, read to a mass meeting of fifteen hundred strikers in the local movie theatre, did not improve the men's tempers, and they became more incensed when they calculated their losses in wages. Reported the *Daily Times*: "The schedule for this month, although at its peak of nearly 250 cars per day, does not assure the workers of more than 52 cents an hour. The men expressed the feeling that if the trimmers took the cut offered, their wage might be further reduced in the future. With the great profits of General Motors, stated to be $210,000,000 last year, the men thought they should be entitled to better wages than they were at present receiving."

The men elected a strike committee, headed by a skinny, towheaded firebrand, "Slim" Phillips, summoned union organizers from Toronto, and marched through the streets of Oshawa in mass parades that brought traffic to a halt. On Wednesday, workers in the GM stockroom, export division, and stamping plant joined the strikers. "Girls are now taking a prominent part in the strike proceedings," the *Daily Times* reported. "This afternoon about two o'clock another parade filed down King Street and into the New Martin theatre for this afternoon's meeting led by the girls. These girls are from the trimming room, and it is now stated that 100 of them have walked out. With flags and banners, they formed in fours, and it was estimated that there were over 2,000 in the march."

The workers' spontaneous revolt paralyzed the city. Brown met with the strike committee, but while he claimed to be "impressed by the quiet demeanour of the delegation," he refused to negotiate. Said the *Daily Times*: "Mr. Brown said that either a new staff would be engaged or the men must soon decide to return. The men taken on in the last two days would be retained. Mr. Brown said he realized that the 'scabbers' were one of the principal items of dispute now, but they had been hired and would not be fired."

Brown's tone was aggrieved: "We are confident that there is not a plant in Canada which surrounds its employees with more ideal working conditions than exist in our institution. Everything possible is done to make the plant absolutely ideal from the standpoint of safety, and the plants are all well-lighted, sanitary and comfortable. Every employee is insured for the sum of $1,000 at a cost to the employee of $6 per year, regardless of age and physical condition. Every employee also, who has been in our employ for three months, is eligible to participate in the Corporation's Savings Plan which permits any man to deposit an amount equal to 20 per cent of his earnings, providing such an amount is not in excess of $300 a year. The Corporation has other plans for encouraging thrift, such as our Preferred Stock Purchase Plan and our Modern Dwelling House Plan which encourages the employees along the line of owning their own homes."

The labour expert who had persuaded American capitalists to adopt this kind of benevolent despotism was Mackenzie King. King fancied himself a masterful conciliator, and although, as prime minister, he had no jurisdiction in this strike, his labour minister, Peter Heenan, arrived in Oshawa Thursday afternoon. So did two Communists, L. R. Menzies and Jack MacDonald, who harangued the crowd at the New Martin theatre, sold copies of *The Worker*, and handed out pamphlets denouncing General Motors in language the Oshawa press described as "of the most violent and 'Red' nature."

The strike committee chose special constables from among the men to keep the demonstrations orderly, and pickets were placed at the plant gates. On Friday morning, another six hundred workers from the Cadillac and LaSalle lines, the mill room, and the wiring department joined the strike. The *Daily Times* reported that "production at the plants was practically negligible in the last two days." The crowds in the New Martin theatre grew so large the meetings were moved to the armoury, and on Friday afternoon three thousand strikers voted to "pledge ourselves to establish a trade union organization."

The roar from the armoury could be heard in H. A. Brown's oak-panelled office, and, as the union vote was taken, Brown dictated a letter of capitulation to Peter Heenan: "I will be not only willing, but glad, to have these employees all return to their former positions without prejudice, which of course involves the removal of the men temporarily employed in the Trimming Department to other positions in our plant.

"I am surprised to find that some of the grievances of our employees seem to be attributable to the lack of understanding between employees and certain Superintendents and Foremen, and this misunderstanding I feel sure can be adjusted to our mutual satisfaction. I agree to your suggestion that a Board of Conciliation be formed and function with regard to the disputed reduction in piece rates established in the Trimming Department on March 22 and on Chevrolet and Pontiac assembly lines on March 15. I agree, pending the findings of the Board of Conciliation, to re-establish the rates applicable immediately prior to the above-mentioned dates."

"What about our union? The union first!" some men cried out when Slim Phillips read Brown's letter aloud in the armoury that afternoon. Phillips pointed out that James Simpson of the American Federation of Labour would be on the three-man conciliation board, and the AFL was already organizing the GM workers into what the *Daily Times* called "the largest group of employees ever assembled in Canada as an organized body."

"We have the union – absolutely," Phillips said. "General Motors has given us everything we asked for. The terms are the best obtainable and every employee should return to work." The *Daily Times* had an extra on the street before the meeting ended: "STRIKE OVER: All GM Employees Back at Work Monday."

Sam McLaughlin took no public part in negotiations. He was vacationing on his rented horse farm in Aiken, South Carolina, when news of the walkout reached him. He ordered Lowry, his chauffeur, to drive hellbent sixty miles through the mud to catch an express train for Oshawa. "I don't blame the men," he told Lowry when he returned to Aiken several days later. "Agitators came over from the States. I promised the men I would look into it and they all went back to work."

Brown's *volte face* appears to have come at Sam's insistence, and by making his general manager back down, Sam reinforced his personal authority at the plant. As president, Sam's relationship with his American managers was adversarial. His office faced theirs, separated by a common reception room, and when Sam was displeased, he stormed past the secretaries to bellow expletives in a voice that could be clearly heard in offices down the hall. Sam saw to it that the young pups from Detroit were surrounded by Canadian watchdogs loyal to him: his sales manager, Jack Beaton, his factory manager, Bill Coad, and his senior engineer, "Daddy" Moyse, had all been hired in the early years of the McLaughlin Motor Car Company, and Brown's right-hand man, Frank Chappell, was a lieutenant-colonel in the Ontario Regiment. When Sam was away, his private secretary,

George Hezzelwood, observed everyone who came and went from the manager's office, and Sam kept in daily contact by phone and cable. Nothing happened in the plant that Sam didn't know about, and he didn't like being pushed around.

Brown had cut the workers' pay because he claimed that they were less efficient than the Americans. This was an insult to Sam, as well as to his employees. The walkout gave General Motors a further excuse to disparage the Canadian operation. "So far as General Motors is concerned," president Sloan pontificated to the press, "operations in Canada have been largely of an assembling character and it is well equipped to operate on either side of the line to any degree that the economies of the situation require." It may have been Sloan's thinly veiled threat to close the Canadian operation that sent Sam high-tailing it for home. His company was at stake, and so was his reputation.

Sam conducted his labour relations on the same principle as had his father: be straight with your employees and they will reward you with good work. Sam still walked through the plant regularly, stopping to joke with old-timers he remembered from the carriage business, and many an apprentice quaked at the prospect of an unexpected encounter with the Boss. Sam had his journeyman's papers as a trimmer, and he was proud of his trade. The McLaughlins had promised that General Motors would guarantee jobs and prosperity for the working people of Oshawa, and Sam was a man of his word. "The town's interests are the interests of General Motors, and the interests of General Motors are the town's interests," Sam said. Sam's army of workers was defending his Canadian garrison.

The report of the conciliation board, published on May 7, supported the strikers' demands and established the principle of collective bargaining. GM agreed to rescind the pay cuts until the new 1929 models were introduced, "when a new rating will be established and submitted to the employees." The company also agreed that "in the employment, dismissal and treatment of their employees they will not discriminate between such as are members of a labour union and such as are not."

Sam was polite, but he wasn't yielding any ground: "I cannot tell you how pleased I am that the misunderstanding we had here in March is now a matter of history," he told the *Daily Times*. "During the past 27 years, our relationship with our employees has been happy and satisfactory and I am looking for an uninterrupted and lengthy period of pleasant and cordial association with what I believe to be the finest lot of employees in the country. The award speaks for itself. We shall continue, as in the past, to run our plant on the principle of the Open Shop, which is, after a great deal of experience and study, the only practical method under which our particular business can operate."

Sam was obliquely referring to a brief strike at the carriage company in 1902. The Carriage and Wagon Workers of North America had organized a local in the McLaughlin works, and on February 18, 263 men went out on strike for union recognition and higher wages. The strike lasted a month. In his interview with Floyd Chalmers of the *Financial Post*, Robert McLaughlin said that the men had the sympathy of the townspeople until he had "opened up the company's books and showed that the men on strike had been drawing the highest wages in the town. Sufficient loyal employees remained at work to keep the plant going and not a day was lost because of the strike. The strike failed because it was ill-advised and absolutely unnecessary."

Sam McLaughlin had taught his workers everything they needed to know about organizing strikes. In the spring of 1926, Sam had instigated the largest labour demonstration in Ontario labour history, a protest against the Liberal government's new cheap-car policy. For twenty years, General Motors of Canada had sheltered behind the 35-per-cent tariff on imported cars, but Canadian consumers, increasingly dependent on motor-vehicle transportation, resented paying hundreds of dollars more than Americans for the same product. A campaign for free trade in automobiles had been taken up by the farmers' political arm, the Progressive Party, and following the election of 1925 the Progressives held the balance of power in the House of Commons. Mackenzie King, clinging to office, was sympathetic – he owned a Pierce Arrow – and King was hostile to Ontario's Conservative industrialists.

Relations between the McLaughlins and the Liberals had been chilly since Robert had turned against Laurier over free trade in 1911, and they worsened when George McLaughlin shared an election platform with King's despised rival, Conservative Party leader Arthur Meighen. Rumours that the government intended to lower the tariff on automobiles were rife, and when Sam read a speculative story in the Toronto *Globe*, he fired off a peremptory letter to Finance Minister J. A. Robb on December 30, 1925.

"This article has had the effect of producing much disquiet in the minds of our dealers and prospective customers," Sam wrote. "A number of our largest dealers have cancelled their specifications and shipping instructions unless we place ourselves in the position of guaranteeing our prices against decline. This premature announcement, if it is officially inspired, will unquestionably have the effect of causing us to reduce the production of cars required for domestic trade during the months of January, February and March to such an extent that thousands of workmen will be thrown out of employment. This, of course, would work a great hardship not only on the thousands of people we are employing here in Oshawa, but on workmen in other cities who are furnishing us with a tremendous volume of parts."

Robb brushed Sam off with an evasive reply, but Sam had made it clear that he would hold his workers hostage in any confrontation with the government. Sam's ego, as well as his social status, depended on his role as president of General Motors of Canada, and Sam privately owned four upscale Toronto dealerships, McLaughlin Motors, making him one of the "largest dealers" he refers to in his letter. Sam followed his threatening letter with a personal confrontation at a Toronto meeting early in March 1926. Robb recalled: "Mr. McLaughlin came to me at once and declared: 'If you change the duty on automobiles I will lock the doors of my plant.' My reply was: 'That is no good, and you can't bluff me. If that is your attitude, then our interview is off.'"

Robb immediately slashed the tariff to 20 per cent on imported cars worth up to $1,200 U.S. ($1,800 in Canada) and to 27 per cent on cars worth more. Robb's stick, however, was accompanied by a carrot: if 50 per cent of the cost of a car sold in Canada was manufactured in Canada, the automobile companies would be allowed a 25-per-cent refund on material used in the manufacturing process. Robb's strategy was to lower the price of cars, stimulate Canadian industry, reward the auto manufacturers with a bonus equivalent to a 45-per-cent tariff, and create more jobs for Liberal voters.

"GENERAL MOTORS CLOSES PLANT," the Oshawa *Daily Times* headlined on Friday, April 16, the day after Robb's legislation was presented to the House. "This morning," the paper reported, "2,500 employees of General Motors were thrown out of work for an indefinite period. Arriving at the plant, they were greeted with the following official notice posted on all entrances: 'On account of tariff changes the entire plant is closed indefinitely until the company is able to arrive at an intelligent conclusion as to what future course may be deemed advisable.'" The workers went without their pay, and their anxiety was increased by Sam's statement: "We will continue our operations here until we have liquidated our immense inventories and discharged our obligations to suppliers at a heavy loss to ourselves. By the end of that time – probably two months – we will be in a position to arrive at a conclusion as to what the future of our operation here in Oshawa will amount to. I would hesitate to make a forecast, but my belief would be that there would be a very heavy curtailment."

The *Daily Times* reported that the auto industry had been dealt a "death blow." "Grass will grow in the streets, and the honk of the motor car will no longer be heard," proclaimed GM factory manager Frank Chappell. On Saturday, Sam announced: "We will resume on Monday in order to liquidate the stocks of cars on hand. We have definitely decided to discontinue the manufacturing and assembly of the Oakland, the Cadillac, the Oldsmobile and the GMC truck immediately. We were preparing to manufacture the Pontiac in July, but have cancelled all arrangements to do so. All the above mentioned cars will now be imported complete from the United States." Sam held out no hope for the Chevrolet or the McLaughlin–Buick: "If the tariff goes into effect, the future of the industry is doomed."

In New York, Sloan added: "The effect of the Canadian tariff regulation will evidently mean the transfer of production from the Canadian factories to the United States factories, or in other words, employing a greater amount of United States labor and the elimination of a corresponding amount of Canadian labor. Due to the fact that prices in Canada will be reduced, it is fair to assume that consumption will be increased, with correspondingly increased profit to United States manufacturers. From the standpoint of the corporation as a whole, we are not particularly affected one way or the other."

Sloan had seized the opportunity to rid General Motors of Sam McLaughlin's irritating little Canadian fiefdom. Sam was a relic from the past, one of Durant's old cronies. Sloan had not invited Sam to join GM's prestigious finance and executive committees, and Sam had to rely on his friendships with influential directors C. S. Mott and John Lee Pratt to find out what was going on inside GM. Sloan was also systematically eroding the Canadian export business, 40 per cent of the company's production, by building branch plants in countries that imported Canadian-made cars. By closing the Canadian plant himself, McLaughlin had saved Sloan a good deal of trouble, and the Canadian government could take the blame.

Sam had no wish to join the unemployed. He had denounced Robb's Canadian-content rebate as an "impractical delusion," but now he began to see the point: by buying his parts in Canada, Sam could cut his own deals and stick it to Sloan. On Monday, the Oshawa plant was up and running. The job of rousing the rabble was handed over to the war veterans, who knew how to march, and Conservative politicians. Oshawa mayor Robert Preston, supported by delegations from Toronto and Leaside, where the Dodge and Durant plants had closed, as well as the mayors of the industrial towns of Ford City, Windsor, St. Catharines, Hamilton, and Gananoque, arranged a meeting with Prime Minister King and his cabinet for Friday.

"This is no pilgrimage to ask for a favour," wrote the Daily Times. "It is the voice of the people calling for justice. Our workingmen are asking for the security of their positions, for a chance to pay for their homes, for the right to live in Canada. First, this is a workingman's deputation; secondly, it is a citizens' deputation. All are in accord. All ask a chance to live. Oshawa cannot live as a city if this tariff reduction is adopted."

The workers had no official representation on the delegation, but all the factories gave their employees Friday off, and signed up almost two thousand men to take part in a mass demonstration on Parliament Hill. "Evidence that the ladies of this city are backing the 'On to Ottawa' movement was evidenced this morning by two enthusiastic meetings in the General Motors plant," said the April 22 Daily Times. "The first meeting was for members of the office staff, when the girls were addressed on the latest details of the pilgrimage to the capital. The second meeting was held in the trimming room and was equally enthusiastic."

The "girls" booked five sleeping cars for the overnight trip; the men travelled coach in six trains that left Oshawa between 11:40 p.m. and 1 a.m. They were given a rousing send-off at a mass meeting in the armoury, probably the first labour rally held under the auspices of Canada's armed forces. Sam McLaughlin praised the delegation as "the finest men God ever produced," but he carefully distanced himself from the pilgrimage. "I am not making a political speech, or criticizing the government," he said, "but am only making a few remarks on the tariff which I believe is not fair and just to anybody."

The *Daily Times* pointed out: "General Motors of Canada, Limited, with the aid of the parent organization, General Motors Corporation, is well able to take care of itself, come what may. Our concern is for the home owners, the work people, the school supporters and general taxpayers, the bondholders and every other person who is in any way dependent on this city."

The paper reported the railway stations were "black with people" as the trains pulled out: "Never since the time when Oshawa turned out to see the troops away to lay down their lives for their country has there been witnessed such crowds. Hundreds of automobiles lined the streets near the station and congested traffic around the platform, and thousands of people crowded the station platform. Although some of the younger men seemed light-hearted, and among them occasional songs were heard led by a mouth organ, for the most part a spirit of quiet prevailed, embodying deep thoughts and moroseness, with groups here and there talking in low tones while others walked the platform in nervous suspense at what the morrow might bring, each wearing a badge with the slogan 'On to Ottawa' and 'Save Our Homes.'"

Three thousand auto workers from across southern Ontario gathered at the Keith Theatre in Ottawa on Friday morning, and marched quietly from there to the Parliament Buildings. Five hundred men were admitted to the Centre Block committee room to meet with the prime minister and his cabinet. The meeting was polite, but King was noncommittal and Robb declared: "I intend to stand by my guns." The women from General Motors met separately with Canada's only female member of Parliament, Agnes Macphail, a former teacher who sat as an Independent. Miss Macphail was a farmer's daughter, and she wasn't intimidated by Sam McLaughlin, or anyone else. She was sympathetic to the plight of the women, some of whom had been terrified into believing they would have to move to the United States, but she gave them a stern lesson in economics.

"The Canadian people since 1904 have paid $200 million as a tax in order that the automobile industry might be protected," she said, "but the increased price of the automobile does not go into the homes of the workers – into your homes – or into the treasury of Canada: the increased price of the motor car goes into the bank account of the manufacturer of the automobile. Now, if you girls who are facing me today got this 35 per cent I would feel very differently about this whole problem. The workers do not get the benefit. According to the automobile industries' own booklet for 1925, total salaries and wages paid amounted to $14,219,136. The value of production was $88 million. The workers got only 16.1 percent of the cost of production. Yet the manufacturers were protected all that time to the extent of 35 per cent, so that your wages could have been twice what they were and the industry would have had 1 per cent to go on."

General Motors paid "girls" less than half a man's wage for equivalent work. Agnes knew that these women were lucky to make four dollars for a ten-hour day, and after she spoke they blurted out their resentment toward the company. Agnes then explained the point of cheaper cars. "By lowering the price, we increase the number of automobiles bought by the people of Canada; and when we do that it takes more people to manufacture the automobiles. And that is not all: it takes more gasoline stations, more garages, it takes more accessories, more of everything. So you will have a vast increase. I honestly believe that you will find in one year, two years, or three years that the automobile industry will have grown tremendously."

Her optimism was shared by the prime minister. "This has been a gala day," King gloated in his diary. "The Tories have been staging a huge demonstration from Oshawa against reductions in the duties on automobiles, all kinds of dire prophecies as to storming the city etc. I really think I succeeded in turning the whole business to our advantage."

The "On to Ottawa" pilgrimage – the phrase is an eerie premonition of the hunger marches of the unemployed less than a decade later – may have thrown a scare into the Liberals, or perhaps Sam's $100,000 donation toward King's election expenses sweetened the pot. Robb cut the Canadian content requirement from 50 to 40 per cent for the first year, and removed the duty entirely from dozens of components imported from the United States. Sam still grumbled that he had no plans to keep his factory open past July 31, but in mid-May he sang a new tune. "FULL STEAM AHEAD," the Daily Times rejoiced in a banner headline. "GM Plants to Be Enlarged and Speeded Up. Company to Give New Policy a Fair Trial for Twelve Month Period."

General Motors of Canada had been manufacturing cars at top speed all through the weeks when, according to Sam, the company had been "practically ruined." Production for the first six months of 1926 set a new record of 35,000 vehicles; it totalled 56,683 by the end of December, 12,000 more than the previous year's record high. Sam

Bay Street, Toronto, on Saturday morning, December 6, 1924. The police had no authority over parking, and downtown streets had already become "an open air garage." (*Toronto Transit Commission*)

announced, however, that "if the Company is to continue operations in Canada on a sound and permanent basis, it is of the utmost importance that the volume of business be increased, and that the greatest possible degree of efficiency be attained so that manufacturing costs can be reduced to a minimum. The entire plant at Oshawa will be thoroughly gone over and new methods and some new equipment introduced." Sam thanked the mayor and citizens of Oshawa, saying that "the loyalty and deep concern of all members of the organization from the youngest apprentice to the general manager have been the one bright spot even when the situation looked the bleakest."

Sam did not reward his workers with a raise; he made them work harder. The line moved faster, hours increased by 17 per cent, and every month GM set new production targets from 40- to 70-per-cent higher than the year before. "This is the sad thing," Agnes Macphail had warned the GM girls. "A decrease in the tariff injures the workman, because the manufacturer seizes that opportunity to cut the

Sam McLaughlin is made an honorary chief to celebrate the opening of a General Motors of Canada car assembly plant in Regina, Saskatchewan, 1929. (*McLaughlin Public Library*)

wages of his employees, not because he should or needs to, but because that is one thing he wants to do."

The price of the 1927 Chevrolet was reduced a modest fifty dollars – at $865, a sedan still cost two hundred dollars more than in the United States – but as Macphail had predicted, sales soared. Cars could now be financed through the General Motors Acceptance Corporation, and a buyer with credit could put a dollar down and drive away in a car he didn't have to pay for until he was ready to trade it in for a new model. Sales of Canadian Chevrolets doubled to more than 51,000 by 1928, and for customers who wanted something a little racier, GM introduced the Pontiac, a clone of the Chevrolet with fancier trim and a price tag one hundred dollars higher. Chiefs in feather headdresses from the Six Nations reserve at Brantford took part in the Pontiac's official unveiling. They created such a sensation GM invited a band of Crees to take part in the opening ceremonies for their new assembly plant in Regina in December 1928. Chief Red Dog presented Sam with an eagle-feather headdress and christened him "Kitchie-Kahso-Kin-Esko," Chief Strong Arm.

Sam wasn't afraid of the union. The American Federation of Labour was conservative and old-fashioned. It split the workers into a multitude

Two men from the Six Nations reserve near Brantford, Ontario, show off the roomy rumble seat in General Motors' new Pontiac. General Motors of Canada dressed up several Six Nations chiefs in Wild West Indian costumes to promote the first Pontiacs off the Oshawa assembly line. (*Harry Schoon*)

of craft guilds and destroyed their solidarity. Slim Phillips was promoted to foreman, then let go. Disillusioned, disorganized, and unsophisticated, the workers were easy prey for con men. "I joined the union," Doug Knapp says. "It cost one dollar. The treasurer took off with all the money. The union went broke. That was the end of it."

Sam McLaughlin's income in 1928 was $1.5 million, and there were a million cars in Canada. In Hollywood, movie stars posed beside their Buicks, and behind the wheel of a red Chevy roadster, any kid could be King of the Road. Drivers' licences were now required, but no one who had already been driving more than six months had to be tested, and in Ontario the speed limit of thirty-five miles per hour was so routinely ignored that some politicians said it should be abolished. Fast cars made life easier for both cops and robbers, and shoot-'em-up car chases were almost commonplace.

Main thoroughfares were paved with asphalt, concrete, or wooden blocks, but most residential streets were narrow and dimly lit, and in the country signs were so scarce motorists drove off piers, or into trains. Hundreds of motorists were killed at railway crossings every year – Ontario averaged two deaths a week – and more died when poorly built

Noon-hour traffic at the corner of Yonge and Queen streets, Toronto, August 31, 1929. (*Toronto Transit Commission*)

roads and bridges collapsed. "Combined forces of the Oshawa fire department and citizens are still searching for the body of Helen Wright of Peterboro, who was drowned early this morning when the McLaughlin touring car in which she was driving with three others crashed into the Harmony Creek following a washout of the Harmony bridge on the Kingston highway," the *Daily Times* reported on April 6, 1929.

Women were routinely knocked down crossing the street, and children killed when runaway cars mounted the sidewalks. Drivers made the highways dangerous for rural people who were still accustomed to walking. On February 20, 1929, not far from the Harmony bridge, thirteen-year-old Nathaniel Etcher was struck and killed while coming home from his paper route. The hit-and-run driver, who shrugged "to hell with him," was convicted of negligence and sentenced to two and a half years in prison. It was a stiff sentence. Coroner's juries usually brought in a verdict of accidental death, and in the rare instances when drivers were charged, most were acquitted, even if they had been drunk and their cars defective. Five hundred people were killed in traffic accidents in Ontario in 1928, half the total for Canada, but while the public was anxious about the danger, the finger of blame invariably pointed at the weather, visibility, the roads, and the victim.

A McLaughlin–Buick gets the worst of an encounter with a Franklin limousine near North Bay, Ontario. (*Ontario Archives, 13131 S 17210*)

Pedestrians were cautioned to be more alert, carry lights at night, and walk facing the traffic. Only Ontario Premier George Henry raised the possibility that flaws in the design and construction of automobiles might contribute to the carnage. Commenting on the numerous cars on the road at night with burned-out headlights, Henry said: "I blame the manufacturer more than anyone."

An automobile was built to last about six years. Its life span was no secret – Sam McLaughlin talked enthusiastically about the sales of new models as his old cars rusted out – and planned obsolescence brought a degree of predictability to a fickle and cyclical industry. For all its shiny paint, a car was still a bucket of bolts, and if it was driven hard over gravel roads, it rattled to death. The *Daily Times* pointed out how often cars "turned turtle" on the Kingston Road, crushing their occupants underneath, and grisly photographs show twisted parts strewn over the fields, with nothing at all left of the car. There were no quality inspections or safety standards, and anyone with a few dollars could buy a jalopy; dealers were so swamped with used cars the manufacturers bought them up for twenty-five dollars each and destroyed them.

General Motors had no trouble meeting its Canadian content quota, and Sam coined a new slogan: "It's better because it's Canadian." By

The *Superiors*, a
General Motors of
Canada women's
baseball team, c.
1925. (*Win Wilcox
Conlin*)

1929, GM had invested more than $1.5 million in expanding the old
McLaughlin works until the plant sprawled over several city blocks.
Sam bought Mackinnon Industries of St. Catharines, his supplier of
engines and axles, and his operation grew to eight thousand employees
with an annual production of 104,000 vehicles. Wages were no higher,
but almost every employee belonged to the GM savings plan and paid
fifty cents a month into a life-insurance fund that guaranteed $51.04 a
month for twenty months to any worker permanently disabled before
reaching the age of sixty. The plant looked after sick and injured
workers in its own hospital: three doctors treated one hundred workers
every day. These modest benefits – very generous by the standards of
the time – were shared by GM workers in the United States, but
Canadian employees had an extra incentive: patriotism.

"The American girls' work does not come up to ours," a member of
the ladies' trimmers' delegation told Agnes Macphail. "The gentlemen
in the General Motors have told us so. If they want any experimental
work done, it comes to the Canadian girls, or if they want any
exhibition work it comes to the Canadian girls. Last summer myself I
saw some of the work done by American girls and it was nothing to
ours; it was not fit to be seen. If we were to turn the work out as the
Americans do we would get fired."

There is no evidence that the Canadian-made car was better or
worse, but the mystique of superiority boosted morale and created an
illusion of independence. Using an American car to inspire Canadian
nationalism was no more incongruous than a Liberal economic strategy

of developing Canadian industries around American corporations, and in 1929 *Canadian* still meant *British*. Sam liked to boast that 94 per cent of his employees were British, although there were several thousand immigrants from Eastern and Central Europe living in town who could make cars as handily as anyone else. The majority of the "foreigners," as they were called, were ardent anti-communists, while many of the British immigrants, as it turned out, were Marxists.

This ambivalent definition of "Canadian" allowed Sam McLaughlin to shape his company in his own image, and he projected onto it his muscular Christian belief in the moral, physical, and political virtues of athletic activity. House leagues were organized for hockey, soccer, lacrosse, and baseball, pitting Buick workers against Chevrolet, Stampers against Mill Room, and General Motors of Canada teams were fielded in provincial and national competitions; the most famous was the Oshawa Generals hockey team, subsidized by the company until Sam decided that fighting on the ice was bad for GM's image. Team rivalries created enthusiasm, and winning trophies brought General Motors a bonanza in free publicity. For workers more artistically or intellectually inclined, the Oshawa plant sponsored a mixed choir of seventy-five voices, a thirty-piece symphony orchestra, a dance band, a male quartet, a literary and dramatic society, and adult-education classes. Employees were allowed to use the company's convention hall, with a revolving platform designed to show off new cars, and the chief function of the Employees' Association was organizing dances and socials, culminating in a company picnic every August that drew as many as twenty thousand people to Lakeshore Park.

Sam was also a firm believer in the paramilitary structures of British imperialism, and working at General Motors was a lot like joining the army. Recruits were given a physical exam and divided into A, B, and C categories: C was reject. Discipline was strict: workers who talked back to the foreman were fired and political activists soon found themselves out on the street. On paydays, workers' wages were deposited directly into their bank accounts "for the stimulation of thrift." The company credo, printed on the back of membership cards in the Employees' Association, read: "To develop and maintain on a definite and permanent basis a spirit of mutual confidence and good will between those charged with the responsibility of directing the affairs of the Company and employees generally; also by friendly and sympathetic cooperation one with the other to bring added happiness and prosperity to all members of the General Motors family."

Doug Knapp was laid off in the summer of 1929. "We realize that the seasonal slump in production has hit some families pretty hard," the company apologized, "and we are trying to give the married men as steady jobs as possible. The wheat harvest going bad in the west has hit business, and this, coupled with the fact that our anticipations were a little too high in the spring, when we built too many cars, has forced us to curtail production."

Said Sam: "I blame the wild speculation that occurred on the stock market this spring. Many of our prospective customers lost a large portion of all their surplus money and were unable to purchase automobiles." An early tremor of the coming crash had shaken the market, and on March 6 a brief obituary had appeared on the front page of the *Daily Times*: in Detroit, at the age of seventy-five, David Buick had died "in comparative poverty."

10

THE THIRTIES

David Buick had been earning a meagre living teaching at a technical school, but he bore no grudge and begged no favours from General
Motors. Durant had shared Buick's fate, but he was not content to
share Buick's humble obscurity; by the spring of 1929, he had become
the only financier on Wall Street powerful enough to challenge U.S.
President Herbert Hoover. Earl Sparling describes Durant's comeback
in his 1930 book, *Mystery Men of Wall Street*: "He helped begin the long
bull market in 1923 and 1924, bolstering a new-found shoe-string
fortune under stocks still convalescent from the post-war crash that
had left him flat. He helped introduce Wall Street into an era of cosmic
speculation that was to throw that seasoned thoroughfare successively
into bewilderment, hysteria, dementia praecox, and finally paralysis
and complete mechanical collapse."

Durant raised money by selling shares in Durant Motors on the
instalment plan – three dollars down and three dollars a month at 6 per
cent interest – while inflating the price of the stock by the methods he
had used to boom Chevrolet and General Motors. "The little people
were getting in now," writes biographer Lawrence Gustin, "the shop
workers, the school mistresses, the widows. Durant said his stock

program was inducing thousands of families who had never saved a dollar to start paying for securities 'bit by bit out of weekly earnings.' This, he said, was one of the most important thrift campaigns ever undertaken." Durant, as usual, paid scant attention to bookkeeping or engineering: his Durant and Star cars were expensive and old-fashioned, his plants obsolete, and his market too small to compete with Ford or General Motors. He wasn't investing in automobile production, he was using his shareholders' money to gamble on the stock market.

Sparling writes: "He rode the 'greatest bull market' by means of a bull consortium so gigantic in aggregate wealth and power that there is nothing in Wall Street's 140 years of Arabian Nights to furnish even a contrast. He used not only his own new millions but the millions of many associates, of at least twenty-five multimillionaires who had confidence in him and his judgment. He handled in 1928 more than 11 million shares of stock, representing an investment of more than $1.25 billion. In addition, at least two or three billions more were invested individually on his advice by members of the clique, three or four billions in all, marshalled under the command of one man. He was the bull of bulls."

The McLaughlin boys knew the wild man well enough not to trust him with their money, but George still profited from his advice, and Sam, a member of the board of International Nickel, may have put Billy on to one of his hottest prospects. Nickel-plated steel had replaced brass as trim for automobiles, and the INCO mine in Sudbury was a major source of supply for the North American industry. INCO was a more secure and reputable investment than most Canadian mining stocks, but Sam also had an interest in the McIntyre–Porcupine gold mine. The company's president, J. P. Bickell, belonged to Toronto's coterie of flashy young stockbrokers who had made millions speculating in the gold and silver mines of northern Ontario. The Toronto mining exchange had an odious reputation, but the mining men were the high-living, hard-drinking diamonds in the rough Sam liked to chum with, and although Jack Bickell was a generation younger, he and Sam became fast friends. They shared an interest in objets d'art – Bickell had been an avid bidder at the Casa Loma auction – and Parkwood paled in comparison with Bickell's estate in Mississauga, where the wine cellar was worthy of a Rothschild and the indoor swimming pool was illuminated by coloured underwater lights.

The floors of Bickell's mansion were marble, but his nudes were not.

"He used to import girls by the carload from New York," says one retired financier. "He had a private railway car, and a spur line ran near his house. He could bring the girls in at night and nobody would be the wiser." Bickell was a bachelor with epicurean tastes and the money to indulge them, and, like Sam McLaughlin, he loved to impress and delight his friends. Girls, like cars, could be bought, shown off, enjoyed, then dumped for new models, and sex with a young woman was the best deal an aging Presbyterian could get for his dollar. As long as he didn't desert his wife, or flaunt his mistresses, a wealthy man could do very much as he pleased in the privacy of his office, railway car, yacht, country house, fishing lodge, hotel suite, or limousine, although a reputation for immorality could prevent him from being appointed to public office or received by his friends' wives. Jack Bickell was not welcome at Parkwood. Adelaide played bridge with the wives of some of Toronto's leading financiers, and stories of Bickell's bacchanalian orgies had certainly come to her ears. As well, Sam and Bickell went on a monthly junket to New York City which would include a night on the town and a visit to Billy Durant's favourite spot, the Cotton Club in Harlem.

In his old age, Sam liked to boast about his "lady friends." In the early years, an Oshawa garage owner was summoned with his tow truck in the middle of the night to pull Sam's car out of a country ditch; Sam was out with a woman who was definitely not his wife. He was rumoured to have a mistress in Brooklin, and he may have fathered an illegitimate son in Uxbridge: every Father's Day Sam received a flowery card addressed to "father" with expressions of affection and effusive thanks for his generous financial support. Sam had hideaways dotted around the countryside, including a snug furnished cottage in the woods behind his trout pond, and as a director of the CPR he was entitled to a suite at Toronto's Royal York Hotel. A mysterious entry in his private account book for 1924 reads: "Highland Park Hotel, $6,310.24." Highland Park, a suburb of Detroit, was Ford territory, a peculiar place for a GM man to hang out, and for six thousand dollars somebody could be kept in considerable style.

"One thing you have to give Sam credit for," says an old acquaintance, "any of that kind of nonsense had nothing to do with Oshawa. Sam may have dallied with the ladies, but at least he didn't do his dallying around here." Unlike his lecherous friend, GM director C. S.

Mott, who married four times, Sam not only remained married to Adelaide, but took a censorious attitude toward other peoples' moral lapses. "He didn't like people who were too 'prunes and prisms,'" says his former household secretary, Elizabeth McMullen, "but then he could be pretty 'prunes and prisms' himself." Sam was highly conscious of Chevrolet's image as a "family car," and while he loved the high life, he had a horror of behaviour that might embroil his company in scandal. He was at heart a "man's man," comfortable in a smoke-filled world that excluded women or relegated them to subservient roles. Sam was rarely without a pipe in his mouth. "He made a great show of smoking," recalls his nephew Dick McLaughlin. "It was a ritual. He never inhaled. His brand of tobacco was Barking Dog, 'Barking Dog, It Never Bites.'"

Sam earned $1.725 million in 1929. His expenses were $1.1 million, including nearly $400,000 in unpaid income tax dating back to 1926. His assets were over $28 million, on paper. All kinds of people were paper plutocrats; they had paid as little as 10 per cent down for their stock, and their stock was the only asset they had. Some had invested their wages, others had borrowed from the bank or mortgaged their houses. Early in 1929, President Hoover, worried that stock prices did not reflect real assets, raised interest rates and restricted credit. Foolish investors were pushed out, the cautious sold out, and brokers sold stocks they hadn't bought yet, gambling the price would go down.

Everyone was selling except Durant, who, true to form, was buying. After the bottom fell out of the market in October 1929, Durant kept buying up millions of worthless stocks, believing that he could single-handedly turn the tide. He threw away his own money, and when that ran out he borrowed from the banks, pledging everything he owned, including shares he held in trust for the people who had invested in his syndicates. He had already allowed Durant Motors to fail, taking with it the faith and goodwill of his old friends in Flint, and now he pauperized his wife. In 1930, Billy persuaded Catherine to lend him the 187,000 shares of General Motors stock – $18.7 million par value – that he had placed in trust for her; she never saw the stock, or the money, again.

Sam's assets shrank by almost $10 million in 1930, but still, $18 million was a comfortable fortune, and he earned more than $1.5 million in dividends and interest. "Basic conditions in Canada are good," Sam told the Toronto *Globe* on January 3, 1930. "Highway development is proceeding rapidly, building operations are going on apace; manufacturing generally is in a healthy condition. It is extremely unlikely that 1930 production will show any appreciable decrease." A reporter noted that Sam carried a wad of bills "the size of a soccer ball."

Sam spent more than $1 million in the first year of the Great Depression. His taxes and business expenses took $350,000; $157,000 went toward a new house for Eileen and Eric Phillips. He gave another $150,000 to Adelaide and his daughters, spent $23,475 in Miami, and paid $12,527.73 for Billie's August wedding to Churchill Mann, a career officer with the Canadian army. He also purchased, for an undisclosed sum, the famous painting "After the Bath," by Paul Peel. Far from being anxious or down in the dumps, Sam set his sights on winning a new prize: the King's Plate. Horseracing did not enjoy the prestige in Canada that it did in England or the United States; it smacked of cruelty and cheating, and racetracks encouraged gambling, a sin that ranked with lust and greed. Sam was a moderate gambler, but he enjoyed the camaraderie of the racetrack crowd, and the Ontario Jockey Club offered him the society of other self-made men who were not ashamed of their origins.

In the summer of 1930, Sam had his stables and arena dismantled and reassembled on a farm he had purchased on the northern outskirts of Oshawa. The farm, also named Parkwood, supplied the house with beef, milk, eggs, and poultry, and now Sam added pasture, an exercise track, and living quarters for his horse trainers. He spent $94,000 on the facilities, and another $45,500 buying brood mares and stallions. Sam was now truly a country gentleman, engaged in the sport of kings, and with the election of a Conservative prime minister, R. B. Bennett, Sam's appointment as Ontario's next lieutenant-governor, with a knighthood, was not entirely out of the question.

Sam's interest in racing led him to the architect who designed the Jockey Club's new headquarters at the Woodbine racetrack, John Lyle. Celebrated for his recent collaboration on Toronto's Union Station, as well as his first commission, the Royal Alexandra Theatre, Lyle, like John Pearson, had made his money building banks. He was Sam's contemporary, a Presbyterian from Belfast who had been raised in Hamilton and trained at the École de Beaux Arts in Paris. Like Sam, Lyle was small, balding and opinionated, and he shared Sam's taste for luxury; the interiors of Lyle's austere, classical buildings were finished with gilt and patterned marble, murals, bas-reliefs, polished steel, and wood panelling painted jewelbox shades of jade and robin's-egg blue. Lyle called himself a Modernist, but unlike Frank Lloyd Wright, who thought furniture a sacrilege, Lyle prided himself on his skills as an interior designer. He introduced Canadian flora and fauna into his stylized decoration – he was instrumental in getting the beaver, maple leaf, and caribou on Canadian coins – and he commissioned Ontario craftsmen to reproduce classic designs by Sheraton, Adam, and Chippendale.

Sam hired Lyle to design an addition to Parkwood's south wing, and Lyle came up with a sun room of classical grandeur. Tall arched windows overlook the lawn and the terrace, and the old screened porch was transformed into a loggia that served at night as a screening room. Home movie theatres were the rage, and Sam was on the Canadian board of Famous Players theatres. Lyle used Challener's mural as his inspiration for the sun room's decor, creating in the furnishings an impression of sunlight filtered through water and leaves. Once Sam hung "After the Bath," over the dining-room fireplace, Neverland was complete.

John Lyle never cited Parkwood's sun room among his achievements. The McLaughlins squabbled with the designers, White Allom & Co. of New York, over the furniture, and the final choice, Chinese Chippendale, may not have been Lyle's preference. Sam and Adelaide's taste ran to drab green, and Lyle decorated both her bedroom and their drawing room in the ornate, overstuffed style of the French bourgeoisie. The sun-room addition wrecked the lines of the house, destroyed the second-floor balcony, and blocked the view from the bedroom windows. The Dunington-Grubbs had also departed, apparently on bad terms. "Howard never spoke of Parkwood," says landscape architect Janina Stensson, who worked with him until his death in 1965. Sam, for his part, never publicly praised Lyle or the Dunington-Grubbs, giving all the credit to himself and his own gardeners.

Automobile production was cut in half at General Motors in 1930, but Sam argued that the Depression was largely psychological. "Confidence in business and financial circles was much below normal," he announced in January 1931, "and this was not justified by any actual crisis in the country's buying power." In order to boost consumer morale, General Motors of Canada produced a series of patriotic radio broadcasts, "Canada Carries On," featuring rousing music by the company's orchestra and insufferable speeches by prominent public figures, including Sam, who chipped in at the end of each program with a few platitudes delivered in a rasping, high-pitched voice. "Canada Carries On" soon got the hook, and, as GM's radio star, Sam was replaced by Foster Hewitt.

The inspiration for "Hockey Night in Canada" came from Jack MacLaren, the Toronto advertising executive who handled General Motors' Canadian account. Hewitt's excited play-by-play commentary from the rafters of Maple Leaf Gardens – "He shoots! He *scores!*" – attracted an audience of more than a million by 1933, and made the General Motors hockey broadcasts the highlight of Canada's Saturday night. "More than 57 percent of all listeners on the night of a hockey broadcast were listening to the General Motors program," the Toronto *Mail and Empire* reported on September 16, 1933. "On a Saturday evening, 72 percent of all sets turned on were tuned in to General Motors hockey. In every Canadian city surveyed, General Motors hockey had a larger number of listeners than any other program on at the same time. In a contest conducted by a Canadian radio weekly last winter, General Motors hockey broadcasts placed fourth among all programs on the continent, being exceeded in popularity by only Eddie Cantor, The Baron and Amos 'n' Andy."

Hockey wasn't selling cars – GM stopped sponsoring the broadcasts in 1935 – and GM dealers were going broke. Ford slashed his prices, but GM had a new idea: Why not ask the customers what they wanted? Canada was chosen as the testing ground for this experiment in consumer research, and about 200,000 questionnaires were distributed from coast to coast. Responses showed why GM's highly touted "free-wheeling" transmission had bombed – drivers hated it – and nobody was begging for a sixteen-cylinder Cadillac. Speed and appearance ranked last among the things Canadians were looking for in a car. Consumers wanted, in descending order, dependability, operating economy, safety, convenience, ease of control, and low prices. They also requested less chrome, rubber floor mats, a single key for all locks, and more ashtrays. Quebec drivers objected to green cars – they liked maroon – and women complained about filthy service stations. Everybody disliked car salesmen.

Consumer research alerted GM to the possibilities of customizing cars to suit individual tastes, but research didn't sell cars either. The market was glutted with unwanted 1929 models, and used cars could be picked up for a song from dealers who had repossessed them, or from owners who could no longer afford the gas. On the Prairies, destitute farmers removed the engines from their automobiles and harnessed their horses to the steering columns, remodelling their Chevs and Fords into "Bennett buggies" in honour of the plutocrat prime minister they blamed for the Depression. The McLaughlins had relied on the western market since the 1890s, and the collapse of the farm economy contributed to a catastrophic drop of 80 per cent in GM's Canadian sales in the first three years of the Depression.

The impact on their workers was devastating. As early as December 1929, the Oshawa *Daily Times* reported that four hundred families were in need of food and fuel, and mothers with children were begging at the offices of the Women's Welfare League: "These cold and bitter winter days have caused untold suffering to many children of the needy families of the city whose parents, handicapped by the lack of employment, have been unable to provide them with clothes. Every day, investigators are finding fresh cases of destitution and poverty amounting almost to starvation." General Motors kept running, but hours were short and sporadic and wages were slashed. When the plant shut down for weeks or months at a stretch, the employees scrambled for part-time jobs or relied on Oshawa's skimpy charity: in December 1930, with three thousand men and women unemployed, the welfare fund's annual appeal raised only $30,000. Sam considered $1,000 a fair contribution, and he paid more for his racehorses that year than he spent on "amusements, donations, presents, etc." At Christmas, he gave fifteen hundred needy families each a turkey, not realizing that many of them had no oven to cook it in.

Sam cruised off the Florida coast that winter, but George was at

A Bennett buggy, near Brandon, Manitoba. (*Western Canada Pictorial Index, Winnipeg*)

home with a troubled conscience. After leaving GM, George had opened a small private office above the Dominion Bank at the corner of King and Simcoe streets where he supervised his investments and lent a sympathetic ear to anyone who wished to bend it, although he didn't have much time for the anarchists and communists who accused him of being a fascist. George, however, was the only man in town who could pick up the phone and get the mayor, the premier of Ontario, or the prime minister of Canada on the line in a matter of minutes, not to mention a who's who of influential people in Canada, the United States, Great Britain, Europe, and Japan. A sparrow did not fall in Oshawa without George having some say in it; he belonged to every organization that wasn't specifically Ukrainian or Catholic, chaired every charitable fund-raising campaign in succession, and was in popular demand as an after-dinner speaker at the testimonial banquets Oshawa businessmen continually held in each other's honour. Although George no longer had any formal association with General Motors, he had many old friends in the office, and he didn't hesitate to intervene if a GM employee in trouble asked for his advice or assistance.

Automobile sales collapsed as dramatically in the United States as they did in Canada, and between 1928 and 1932 General Motors Corporation's total net profit plummeted from $296 million to less than $8.5 million, a figure that included a $7-million loss on its automobile divisions. Henry Ford slashed the price of his cars; GM slashed cars. The Oakland, Marquette, and LaSalle disappeared, a new Viking V-8 never saw a Canadian showroom, and model changes for Buick, Chevrolet, and Pontiac were cancelled. In Canada, GM closed its Regina plant, discontinued the Cadillac, and laid off senior executives. Men like Jack Beaton, who had been with the McLaughlins since 1907, were suddenly "retired," and Sam set the example for drastic salary cuts by reducing his own paycheque from $62,000 to $20,000. GM repossessed the company houses of employees who could not make their payments, then rented the houses out or let them stand empty; if an employee allowed GM to use his company savings fund to pay his mortgage, he stood to lose both his savings and his house.

General Motors of Canada stopped boasting about its happy corporate family, but in the midst of the carnage, company advertising projected an almost surreal public image of comfort and prosperity. In April 1931, glamorous colour advertisements in *Mayfair, Canadian Homes and Gardens,* and *Bridle and Golfer* touted "20 luxurious models" of McLaughlin–Buick Straight Eights "directed to the highest type of motor car purchaser" at prices ranging between $1,200 and $2,900. Only 3,582 McLaughlin–Buicks were built that year, slightly more than one-tenth of Oshawa's entire production, an output that hardly justified the expensive advertising, and in 1932 sales of McLaughlin–Buicks fell to 2,026. As foremen in Oshawa were handing out pink slips and telling their men, "I'll let you know when to come back," General Motors of Canada published a fifty-page illustrated booklet, "Canada as a Builder of Motor Cars," showing clean and cheerful young workers assembling a steady stream of cars and parts in Oshawa and in the plants of the company's major suppliers.

"CHILDREN SEEKING FOOD IN REFUSE AT CITY DUMP," the Oshawa *Daily Times* headlined on September 2, 1932. "Men, Women and Small Children Swarm Like Flies Around Garbage Wagon as Each Load Arrives." Following a complaint to the city's board of health, Mayor Thomas Hawkes had investigated the dump that morning. "When a load of refuse arrived," reported the *Daily Times*, "everybody immediately got into the action and followed behind the cart. Little children of tender age, young women, men, and older women, some armed with sticks and the majority carrying either bags, baskets or buckets, literally pounced on the newly arrived refuse to see what they could find. Particles of food rapidly found their way into the baskets and buckets, while old rags and other salvage were placed in the bags." The supervisor of the dump said: "I saw one woman the other day find a crust of bread. She wiped it off with her hands and skirt and ate it right there with the remark that it was the best breakfast she had eaten for some time." Mayor Hawkes agreed that "conditions are certainly terrible. Like you read about them in Moscow or some place like that. We shall have to put up a fence, or something, make some effort to keep these people off."

George McLaughlin was a close reader of the *Daily Times* – the McLaughlins were among the paper's principal shareholders – and his office gave him a bird's-eye view of the thousands of unemployed men who marched through the streets behind their popular spokesman, Eddie McDonald. Oshawa was close to bankruptcy, and although George was over sixty, and his own future secure, he volunteered to run both the city's finance and welfare committees, two thankless jobs that earned him the bitter enmity of the taxpayers, who hated to part with their money, and the poor, who resented having to take it. The

McLaughlin name and George's reputation kept the creditors at bay, and his Conservative connections enabled him to get $200,000 in road work for the unemployed. George was determined that the people of Oshawa would not go hungry, and he arranged for a relief store to be opened in the showroom of a bankrupt Chevrolet dealer. Among the thousands who lined up every week for their $1.67 worth of rations were Douglas and Edith Knapp.

They had married in Toronto in 1930, where Doug had worked for Ford. He'd made seventy-five cents an hour, but the conditions were humiliating: "If you had a pair of mitts in your pocket, you had to pull them out. You had to open your lunch pail. You put your coat, hat, and lunch pail on a rack. It went up to the ceiling. It came down at noon. At one o'clock it went up again." A bout of pneumonia laid him up for a year, and he moved his family to the outskirts of Oshawa, where, now a married man, he had priority when a job opened up at GM. Edith usually walked the two miles to the relief store; recipients of relief were not allowed to drive cars, and the welfare office confiscated their licence plates. In winter she pulled the flour and oatmeal home on a sleigh, and in summer a neighbour who owned a horse and wagon hauled supplies for everyone on the street. "I could have ridden in the wagon," Edith says, "but I could walk faster than that horse could walk." She was given vouchers for milk and meat – she could buy three pounds of hamburger for twenty-five cents – and the city supplied firewood or coal.

"I was pretty handy on the sewing machine," Edith says. "If you wanted clothes, you had to show them you really needed it. If you'd get something new, one of the neighbours would report you. My mother gave me some flannelette sheets. I washed them and hung them on the line, and an inspector came and asked me where I got the sheets. I said, 'It's none of your business.' They gave you a rough time. There was one man, he was the meanest man that walked. Some people got everything for nothing, and another poor person would get nothing."

The Knapps got by with their garden, a cow, and chickens, and after an unemployed worker released a jar full of cockroaches in the relief store, they were allowed to get their groceries where they pleased. In 1934 Doug was hired back on the GM paint line. A sudden surge in car sales signalled that the 1928 models were wearing out right on schedule, and customers had not been entirely lost to horsepower or public transit. More than a hundred thousand Canadians felt they could

"All in the Family" was the name of this General Motors of Canada advertising brochure for 1934. (*Ron Bouckley*)

afford a new car or truck in 1934, and GM got its customary 40 per cent of the sales. A new car was the badge of the middle class; it proclaimed that its owner, through prudence, effort, or God's will, had managed to hang on to his job and his bank account, and he didn't mind setting an example for the less fortunate. Automobile designs mirrored the conservative, rather fearful tastes of the buyers. The broad, tank-shaped bodies had tiny windows, drab upholstery, and their bulbous fenders gave the driver the appearance of a tortoise peering from its carapace. The colours were limited.

"If it was green or blue, you gave it two coats," says Doug, "red, three coats." He was equipped with cans of paint and a primitive spray gun. Painting the body was simple enough – the trick was to avoid drips and bubbles – but that was only part of the job: "When you finished, you put your initials under the hood, then you put your fingers in two little holes and shoved it in the bake oven. It would bake for about three-quarters of an hour at 240 degrees. There was a canvas curtain in front of the oven, and it was so hot you'd walk in with your eyes shut. You'd hold your head sideways so the sweat would drip on the floor. You always put Vaseline on your face. I put it on every morning." The sharp metal edges of unfinished bodies cut the men's fingers. "There was always somebody getting hurt," Doug says. "We had facemasks, but at the end of the day, you'd cough up the colour of paint you'd been using. If it was green, you'd cough green, if it was blue, you'd cough blue."

The men bought their own overalls and wore them "until they were past wearing," but Doug could sign his initial "D" on a Chevy truck as confidently as "Vincent" van Gogh on a piece of canvas. "I always took a quick glance to see how it was," he says. "I took a kind of pride in my painting." His skill and care didn't count for much. "They were fussy. If the foreman didn't like it, he'd give you a rough time. They could give you whatever job they wanted. One foreman was a drinker. Some of the guys bought him a lot of drink. They got the better jobs. It depended a lot on religion. If the foreman was a Catholic, Catholics got preference. Seniority didn't matter. It all depended on how much 'brown' you had on your nose." The worst was the uncertainty of work: "Layoffs would last three, four, six months. You'd be off in the summer, and lucky to get back by Christmas." Doug drove a truck, and bought a horse so he could plough gardens for his neighbours. He missed out, however, on the garden built in the summer of 1935 by his boss, Sam McLaughlin.

Sam always claimed that Parkwood's last, most perfect garden, like the house itself, was an employment scheme, but he was really copying du Pont, who had recently moved tons of earth to create an immense, wet, and inhospitable Italian fountain garden. Realizing that spray was perhaps best enjoyed from a distance, du Pont set his fountains to music and illuminated them at night with coloured lights controlled from an electric keyboard. The kitsch appealed to Sam – he may have been thinking of Bickell's swimming pool – but John Lyle's taste ran less to Disney, and for Parkwood he created an Art Deco garden of such unique beauty he was awarded a bronze medal from the Royal Canadian Institute of Architecture.

To create a "monumental effect" in a space only four hundred feet square, Lyle designed "a pool 21 ft. wide by 161 ft. long, leading to a larger central pool 61 ft. square, giving a total length of 222 ft. At the westerly end, as the central architectural feature, is placed the tea house. There are five minor fountains and one major fountain. A carpet bedding of begonias edged with Japanese yew hedge forms a surround to the pool areas. Spaced at intervals are pyramidal cedars alternating with standard hydrangeas, these latter acting as vertical accents. The tea house is brought close to the edge of the pool so as to obtain reflections in the water. The fountains are controlled electrically from control boxes in the tea house and on the upper terrace, both as to water and light. There are three lights in each of the minor

John Lyle's Parkwood
water garden, c. 1939.
(Parkwood/
McLaughlin Public
Library)

fountains – white, blue and green – and six in the major fountain."

Popularly known in Oshawa as the Taj Mahal, the garden is estimated to have cost as much as $1 million, but $100,000 – $1 million in
today's dollars – is more realistic. It was nothing, however, compared to
the money Sam was losing on his horses. In 1931, his farm and stables
cost $118,171.14, including $23,397 for horses, but he earned only
$10,000 in winnings and prize money for a net loss of just over
$108,000. During the next two years, his losses averaged $93,000 a
year, and by 1933 his annual income had shrunk to less than $900,000.
Sam was undeterred; his eye was on the American Triple Crown as well
as the King's Plate, and his chauffeur, Lowry, spent months on the road
driving his horses to Toronto, Belmont, Lexington, and Miami.

Sam wasn't in racing to make money. Spending money was more
important, and the racetrack provided him with a new stage, script,
and costume: a pearl-grey top hat, striped trousers, and a cutaway coat.
Sam had closets full of costumes – his role as honorary colonel of the
Ontario Regiment called for a dozen different uniforms – and dressing
up played an important part in the daily drama that gave meaning
to his life. Sam used his clothes as disguises. He had a brand-new,
perfectly tailored outfit for everything, and his clothes were always
so impeccable, so free from wrinkles or creases, he looked like a
department-store dummy. This stagey effect was enhanced by Sam's
round, balding head and toothbrush moustache, a combination that,
with his stiff posture and short legs, gave him a disconcerting resemblance to Charlie Chaplin.

Sam was almost as well known to the Canadian public as Chaplin,
and he was photographed more often than England's little princesses,
Elizabeth and Margaret Rose, although not as often as the Dionne quin-
tuplets. His fame wasn't vanity; it was public relations. Sam was General

Motors of Canada's greatest salesman, and he wasn't selling cars, he was selling himself. Sam liked to kibitz with newspaper reporters, although he could get frosty if they kibitzed back, and he was always the hero of his own story. Like Henry Ford, Sam identified himself with his products, and he saw to it that General Motors deluged the media with pictures, press releases, and itineraries featuring the doings of "Mr. R. S. McLaughlin, president of General Motors of Canada." Unlike Ford, Sam never said or did anything original or controversial, but the press ran almost weekly reports on his opinions, travels, charitable gifts, and sporting activities, and Adelaide's teas, meetings, and speeches to the home and school association were covered with equal obsequiousness in the women's pages. Eileen's golf tournaments made the sports section – she was a frequent finalist but never a national champion – and both Eileen and Billie dominated the show-jumping news. Isabel organized the Canadian Group of Painters, and Mildred, following a quiet divorce, married another American tycoon, E. S. Turner.

The McLaughlin family soap opera was perfectly in tune with the radio age, and at the racetrack Sam had a large and sympathetic audience: any bum could bet a dollar on a McLaughlin horse and dream of glory. It would be easy to criticize Sam for being a blowhard and a show-off, but he saw it as part of his job, and during the Depression, Sam's princely life style gave General Motors of Canada a golden gloss that boosted customer confidence at a time when the company depended on it.

Among those customers was the King of England. In the summer of 1935, while still Prince of Wales, Edward VIII had strolled into the London showroom of Buick's British agents, Lendrum & Hartman, and ordered two Buicks, a Limited limousine for himself, and a Roadmaster for his friend, Wallis Warfield Simpson. The prince was notorious for his infatuation with all things American, particularly Mrs. Simpson. Mrs. Simpson favoured Buicks, perhaps because her royal lover remembered the McLaughlin–Buick Sam had provided for him in 1927. All of Lendrum & Hartman's Buicks were made in Canada, and the Commonwealth connection would let the prince off the hook in case the press challenged his loyalty to British cars. Edward gave careful instructions about specific features for his custom limousine, and in Oshawa an elite crew of thirty men worked on it for nearly six months. The car arrived in England in February 1936, a month after the prince became king on the death of his father, George V.

Sam had achieved a coveted ambition: purveyor of fine automobiles to the Royal Household. He was so proud of his coup he had photographs of the king's car mounted in albums bound with red leather and inscribed: "A McLaughlin Canadian Built Buick Car." Sam as yet had no inkling that the king's affair with his "sweetie," as Sam called Mrs. Simpson, would erupt in scandal, but the car Edward designed reveals a man bent on evading public scrutiny. The rear window was reduced to a peephole and covered with a silk blind, and the quarter windows on either side of the passenger compartment were replaced with mirrored lights. A glass partition separated Edward from his driver, and below it a cabinet, inlaid with the McLaughlin trademark burled walnut, contained the essentials of his life:

"A sandwich box of nickel silver was hand fabricated to match the canteen equipment, which was completed in every detail, and included a silver cocktail shaker, vacuum ice jar, large and small silver cups, silver topped cordial bottles, silver cigarette and tobacco boxes, which were all neatly tucked away in holders and recesses, to be readily accessible upon opening the cabinet lids. The upper lids were arranged to fold down and form luncheon trays, and consisted of black glass surrounded by a one-piece casting of chrome plated brass supported by heavy chrome quadrants on each side. Two sliding drawers fitted into the bottom of the cabinet, of special size to accommodate two London telephone directories. A partition in one drawer permitted carrying a washable linen holdall, in which [there was] a long spoon, a silver lemon knife, a combination measure, corkscrew and crown top opener, and a pair of ice cube tongs."

The King of England didn't plan to party alone; he intended to marry Mrs. Simpson. Divorce was forbidden by the Church of England, and the prospect of a twice-divorced American becoming their queen so infuriated the British public that the prime minister offered Edward an ultimatum: his kingdom or his wife. Mrs. Simpson fled to Cannes in her Roadmaster, and on the night of December 6, 1936, having relinquished his crown for "the woman I love," Edward drove into exile in his McLaughlin–Buick. The king's abdication was an ill omen for General Motors of Canada: by the following April, the workers were in revolt.

II

UNION

In the spring of 1936, C. E. McTavish, sales manager for General Motors of Canada, received a letter from corporation president Alfred P. Sloan asking for McTavish's views on how General Motors might achieve "Progress with Stability." Sloan delighted in slogans and memoranda. Consultation preserved the illusion of a democratic, decentralized corporation, encouraged competition, and inspired terror in GM's junior executives, who knew that a correct response led to promotion, while a gaffe meant eternal banishment. Sam McLaughlin hated this kind of bafflegab. He knew as well as Sloan that while GM's Canadian and export sales had increased to sixty thousand from a low of twenty thousand in 1932, the company had lost both dealers and customers to Ford, whose cheap, dependable new Model A's were outselling McLaughlin's products by as many as twenty thousand cars and trucks a year. Sloan was hinting to the Canadians that they had better pull up their socks.

McTavish passed this hot potato on to his distribution manager, W. R. Carnwith, a man cast in the sturdy mould of Oliver Hezzelwood, and Carnwith's reply throws a beam of light on the problems facing General Motors. "It seems to us," Carnwith wrote, using the royal we, "that the Products designed by the Company during the depression were not as they should have been to suit the conditions. At a time when money was scarce in the hands of the multitude, we introduced Knee Action, which added to the cost of production, and followed along with Turret Tops, which also increased the cost. In our opinion, any so-called improvements which will increase the price of our Products should be made when money is easy, rather than when we are in the midst of a serious depression. The fact that McLaughlin–Buicks were permitted to fall from 5.4 percent of the Industry in 1931, which was a bad depression year, to 2 percent in 1935, when signs of recovery were very evident, is no indication that we are making progress with stability. The fact that Pontiac in 1931 was so designed and priced that it could secure 7.4 percent of the Industry in Canada and this year 3 percent, is certainly no indication of progress with stability."

Carnwith's acid criticism was understandable: for nearly three years he had been cajoling and encouraging a thousand angry GM dealers who couldn't sell cars, or, because of screw-ups from GM suppliers, couldn't get enough cars to sell. The source of trouble, Carnwith decided, was close to home: "Over a period of years with the Company, the writer has seen more changes in personnel and more changes of practices than should have perhaps been necessary. These changes are a result of a lack of foresight combined with poor choosing of personnel. The result has been that all employees have been inclined to be nervous and worried about their positions. As Mr. Highfield [plant manager] recently remarked, 'jittery employees produce a jittery Product and operation.' We believe employees should be paid on the basis of their worth to the Company, and our set-up should be such that an employee should feel that as their experience makes them more valuable to the Company, their pay will be increased and that as long as they are faithful and loyal employees, their positions will be secure."

It's unlikely that McTavish passed Carnwith's opinions on to Sloan. Sloan was not noted for self-criticism, and since the election of Democrat Franklin D. Roosevelt as president of the United States in 1933, Sloan, a Republican, had become convinced that the only serious threat to GM's progress and stability came from communists and labour unions, specifically the great bogeyman of American capitalism, John L. Lewis, president of the Congress of Industrial Organization. The hulking, beetle-browed son of a Welsh coal miner, Lewis had made his reputation as the militant leader of the United Mine Workers of America and, while he wasn't a Communist, he had been converted to Marxist principles of class war and labour solidarity. "So we're supposed to be your partners, are we?" Lewis bellowed at American industrialists. "Well, we're not. We are your enemies!" In 1935, the CIO had broken with the conservative American Federation of Labour, and Lewis had initiated a wave of sit-down strikes in the rubber, glass, and textile industries that won union recognition and wage increases for nearly two million workers. Among the CIO's membership was the small, struggling United Automobile Workers of America.

The UAW was run by Communists, largely because no one else had the motivation to organize an amorphous, fluctuating mass of workers who were spied on and threatened by company goons. The Ford plants were notorious for violence and terrorism, but GM had its own methods. "The extent to which GM resorted to labour espionage was bewildering in its complexity and frightening in its implications," Sidney Fine writes in *Sit-Down: The General Motors Strike of 1936-1937*. "The corporation employed at least fourteen detective agencies for espionage services between 1933 and 1936, and it spent approximately $1 million for this purpose. GM was Pinkerton's National Detective Agency's largest industrial client. At times, as many as two hundred spies were reporting on union activities in GM plants." Plant managers hired private detective services, and GM's department of industrial relations used spies to spy on the other spies in what Fine calls "a weird framework that bewildered even the Pinkerton officials."

General Motors of Canada does not appear to have used professional detectives; it wasn't necessary. Every line had a stool pigeon or two who would tip off a manager or a foreman in return for a promotion or a secret bonus in his pay. "We had to be secret about the union for awhile," says Doug Knapp. "Guys got fired. Some of them got back in again." The McLaughlins' paternalism and Sam's indifference to political ideology allowed hotheads and radicals like Harry Benson to keep their jobs, even though they instigated slowdowns and work stoppages when they had a grievance. The Oshawa plant was full of agitators of all kinds of political stripes, but the most bitter feuds pitted Protestants against Catholics. To get on at GM wasn't a matter of what you knew, it was who you knew, and Sam's insistence on giving priority to local residents meant that everyone in the plant knew everyone else. Relatives of GM workers were hired almost automatically, creating a network of extended families that encompassed several generations and extended from the shop floor to upper levels of management. Friends hired friends, and while workers and foremen gave each other hell, arguing was an expression of intimacy: they had grown up together and gone to school together, they belonged to the same clubs, attended the same churches, and bumped into each other at the bootleggers' on Saturday nights. Talk was cheap, and if a foreman got along with the guys, they would do a good job for him. Allowances were made for an employee's personal circumstances: Benson supported his widowed mother and several younger brothers and sisters.

The Communist Party, operating as the Workers' Unity League, was making little headway in Oshawa. In spite of the earnest efforts of organizers Joe Salsberg and Becky Buhay, their little band of sympathizers numbered about two dozen. The Russian Revolution didn't cut much ice with Canadians of British ancestry who still regarded Jews and Europeans as "foreigners," and as far as Canadian socialists were concerned, the freedom to organize and bargain collectively was a fundamental right of British democracy. In the United States, Roosevelt's National Industrial Recovery Act had enshrined this principle in law, but no comparable law existed in Canada, and the Liberal government, returned to power in 1935, still insisted that striking workers return to their jobs while a conciliation board resolved the dispute.

The Communists, for all their lack of converts, gave the auto workers a view of the capitalist system that made sense of their lives, and taught them a revolutionary language that articulated their anger. They lectured, organized, and inspired, and they showed a personal courage that won the respect of tough guys like Benson. "Some of those fellows were damn good strategists," he says. "They were realistic, and they were damn good fighters." In the summer of 1936, Joe Salsberg was asked to speak at a rally against war and fascism in Lakeview Park, and he arrived in Oshawa with a young colleague named Dorothy.

"She and I reported to a certain little food store and I inquired how the preparations went," Salsberg recalled. "I was told, 'Things are very bad. There is talk in the town. The local paper has been agitating and we know it is coming from the offices of GM. They decided to break up the meeting and if possible give you a bit of a dump in the lake.' There was a GM baseball club financed by the company with sweaters and so on, and these boys would come with baseball bats in case it got into a pitched battle. 'Well,' I said, 'we'll go ahead with the meeting.' Then the chap says, 'Well, you see, Joe, I'm very sorry but none of us can act as chairman because not only is it as much as our jobs are worth, but because the stories in town are very, very bad. They're mobilizing all sorts of riffraff to come and bust the meeting.'

"So I said, 'Okay, we'll have no chairman.' So I said to the little girl [Dorothy], 'You get up and just speak for a minute.' The young woman was so frightened. I said, 'Just say this is a meeting against war and fascism and I now want to introduce the speaker. Don't worry, I'll be standing there.' It was clear there would be just the two of us out there on the bandstand. The others said, 'Don't worry, Joe, we'll be there in the bushes. We'll jump out and try to break it up and drag you away.' I said okay. To my surprise, there was an enormous crowd. There were these guys in baseball sweaters. I no sooner walked up to the microphone than there was a thundering boo and catcalls. I decided we were not going to give up so easily. They were just senseless cries so I tried again and again. There were hundreds of people around. A woman tried to stop them and the hoodlums yelled at her to keep quiet. I said, 'I resent this. This lady has the right to say what she likes as much as you have.' The crowd was divided.

"I finished shorter than I had anticipated and the question became, 'How do I get out of here?' We walked down the stairs and began to go towards the pop stand. The mob moved behind us. When we'd bought the pop, Dorothy stood with her back to the crowd and I facing them, and there they all stood ominously not saying anything. So we began walking with the crowd to the exit. The people who had come to hear began to get in their cars and head for home, but the mob stayed. We got to the bus stop and a car pulled up. [A man] said 'Get in,' and the girl began running. Somebody grabbed me by the arm and said, 'Don't get into that car,' so I yanked her back. It was one of their ringleaders.

"We waited for the right car to come and the mob waited too. The guy that warned me said, 'This is it.' They took us to Whitby by the country road. We had a car following us all the way, and when we pulled up to the bus station in Whitby, the car pulled up. They were two policemen. I was never so thankful for police behind me than I was at this time!"

Among the curious crowd of onlookers was a young torch welder on the Chevrolet body line, Vince Jewison. Vince came from Baillieboro in Cavan township, a village just down the road from where Robert

McLaughlin had been born. His mother ran a boarding house in Oshawa. Almost every family boarded as many single men and women as they could squeeze into attics and cellars. Mabel Jewison usually had six. "She ran two shifts in the same bed," Vince remembers. "She worked night and day. I can remember her cooking skillets full of potatoes and carrots. My dad helped. He was the scullery maid." Hector Jewison also worked as a shaper in the mill room at GM, feeding two-by-twelve boards into electric saws fitted with razor-sharp knives. "My dad told me, 'Never come in the mill room,'" says Vince. "From time to time one of the knives would come loose. The operators could hear the change in the tone of the saw. The men would drop on the floor and shout 'Push the button!' to shut the machine down. One foreman came out while the saw was still running. A knife flew across the room and cut his tie right off, then embedded itself in a post. Once a guy didn't duck in time. The knife hit him on the head and he fell backwards. His head was turned right around. His throat was cut right through."

Vince apprenticed to a plumber, but in 1930 his boss went broke. "I road the freights," he says. "That was terrible. A Mountie caught me in North Bay. I'd bought a blanket. Lucky I still had the sales slip. The Mountie said, 'You see that road? That goes east. Get on it and get outa here.' I hitchhiked back to Oshawa." Vince sold eggs door to door, then worked for a confectioner who ran a lunch-hour tea wagon at the GM plant; he earned five dollars a week selling meat pies for five cents apiece. The pies smelled so good he decided to expand his business: "I took a basket of pies and went into the head office at 11 a.m. I saw the personnel manager. 'I'll have no more of it!' he said. 'The boys are wasting their time running after that wagon.' He didn't take one pie. 'How about me getting a job in here?' I asked. I saw the employment manager and he put my name down." Vince's plumbing job had given him some welding experience, and he had a friend on the body line, George Burt.

"I went in there, the line was running strong, the smoke was hanging down. The guys all shouted, 'We need more help!' When the foreman asked if I could do the job, they yelled, 'Sure he can!' I didn't know a thing. I had an hour to learn. It was a hectic spot. Everything was profanity." The bodies were welded on the wooden frame up the line, but the welds left a bump that had to be smoothed: "You'd put acid on, then tin and solder. It was like putty, then you'd torch it down over the weld." Vince had four or five spots to torch, and he had to work up the line, dragging the air hose as far as it would reach: "You had to stretch the hose to get your job done. There was always somebody yelling, 'Hurry up with that torch!' The line was poppin'. We had to change torches, and the torches were always on. You got burned. You got acid in your eyes and you'd run to dunk your head in the fountain. I got acid on my glasses. There were no goggles. I still have scars from acid burns on my nose. It was hot. The ceilings were low, and the sun would beat in the windows. I got an ulcer, and I worked with this terrible pain in my stomach."

Vince was earning 53 cents an hour, and by the autumn of 1936 he was working a fifty-nine-hour week: five ten-hour days and nine hours on Saturdays. In rush weeks, GM added another six hours. There was no extra pay for overtime. The top rate for a skilled production worker was 73 cents an hour; the bottom rate was 48 cents, and both depended on a 133-per-cent efficiency ratio – the company's calculation of the speed and motion required for each job. Anything less meant that pay would be cut. More than half the 4,000 workers earned less than $1,200 a year; 1,500 made under $1,000. General Motors Corporation was making a mint; in 1936, net profits rebound to more than $283 million, close to the peak of the 1929 boom, and GM couldn't turn out cars fast enough.

The frantic pace was caused by the automobile manufacturers' joint decision to introduce their 1937 models in the fall of 1936, rather than at the beginning of the new year. Customers were expected to order their cars early in the winter for delivery in the spring, guaranteeing the industry work during the lean months, but buyers, not surprisingly, wanted their new cars *now*. General Motors of Canada was poorly equipped to meet the demand. Unlike GM plants in the United States, each of which produced a single make of car or truck, Oshawa turned out multiple models of Buicks, Chevrolets, Pontiacs, and Oldsmobiles. The selection demanded an almost infinite variety of parts, many of which were provided by American suppliers, and because of Canada's relatively small production – one car for every fifty sold in the U.S. – Oshawa was a low priority. Inefficiency didn't improve tempers on the line.

"A lot of the time we couldn't get our jobs done on time," Vince recalls. "People were getting hot. Somebody would push the button. The line would stop. 'We want management to come,' we'd say. 'It's too hot. There aren't enough men. We're not getting enough money.' Highfield would come and promise everything. 'I'll look after that right away,' he'd say, and he'd forget about it as soon as he left."

Spontaneous sit-downs and slowdowns happened throughout the plant as the exhausted workers reached the limit of their endurance. Afraid to talk openly on the job, or to be seen together on the street, the men and their families began to get together at each other's homes for euchre or "hard-time" parties where they could blow off steam without fear of being interrogated at the plant gate the next morning. "The men made homebrew," recalls Ethel Thomson, who, with her husband, George, was a left-wing militant. "We'd chip in a quarter or fifty cents, and they'd get the stuff to make the brew. Of course it had to be aged so we had to know in advance who was going to have the party. We had one of those record players, you know, with the horn on the top, a gramophone, and someone would take a salad and someone would make sandwiches and the men would have their beer and we had a ball Saturday night. You see, Saturday night the whole thing was listening to Foster Hewitt on the hockey game."

One group got together regularly in a back room at Mike's pool hall – the door was marked with a red sticker when a meeting was in progress – another met in a room at the CCF hall: the socialists were fighting the Communists tooth and claw for control of the workers. A cell of the radical Unity group huddled in the basement of Bill Gelech's unfinished house. The men arrived from different directions under cover of darkness, and this little cloak-and-dagger drama added a touch of Bolshevik mystique to the workers' dissatisfaction with General Motors.

The founding meeting of what would become the first Canadian local of the UAW was held on Remembrance Day, 1936, at the home of Malcolm Smith. Smith, a Scot, had lost his job in the British coal mines after the failure of the General Strike in 1926, and like many other British immigrants, he and his brother Jimmy were uncompromising trade unionists with a long and honourable tradition of Labour Party politics behind them. Only two other men attended the meeting – their names remain unknown – and the four agreed to recruit fifteen men to apply for a UAW charter. The identities of most of those fifteen remain secret, but they appear to have been a curious assortment of Stalinists, Marxists, trade unionists, and two Orangemen who probably voted Conservative.

"In the plant, they got one guy in each bunch to talk about it," recalls Doug Knapp. "Most were ready to join up." What angered the workers more than their physical hardships was being pushed around by insulting foremen. Says Knapp: "The foreman would come up to you at quitting time and want you to work another twelve hours. They didn't mind telling you there was someone outside the gate waiting for your job."

Weeks passed; nothing happened. Nobody arrived from CIO headquarters in Washington, although rumours were rife that the UAW was signing up workers by the thousands at GM plants in the United States. Canadian workers were suspicious of American agitators, and many still felt betrayed by the failure of the union in 1928. GM paid better wages than anybody else in town and long weeks meant good money. Christmas was coming, and worries about the civil war in Spain, Hitler, and Edward VIII's abdication took people's minds off their own troubles. Nobody had a beef with Sam McLaughlin.

"Sam was liked," says Harry Benson. "Some guys knew him personally. The thing about Sam, for every dollar, he'd get a thousand dollars in publicity." On every important anniversary, and none was ignored, Sam threw a formal banquet honouring the oldest employees, many of them aged veterans, who had served the company for more than twenty-five years: there were no company or old-age pensions, and men and women worked as long as they were able. In his rambling, off-the-cuff speeches, Sam singled out individuals for special praise, and he reminisced for hours about the good old days when the McLaughlins still owned the works. The honoured guests were presented with engraved souvenir programs featuring their photographs, with brief biographies, and every worker's name listed according to years of service. The programs would mark the first time these assembly workers had ever seen their names in print just like Mr. Sam in *Mayfair* magazine – and Sam could not have come up with a more appropriate souvenir for them to cherish.

"Every time I took something into his office, he'd bark, 'How are ya t'day, my boy?'" recalls Clarence Greentree, then a young clerk in the product engineering department. "R. S. wielded a pretty big stick. He talked tough and ran his operation the way he wanted to. I admired that man. I loved that man." Sam called every man younger than himself "boy," and he affected a slurred, southern drawl that made him sound like a character on "Amos 'n' Andy." Sam always had a quip or a wink for the people he encountered, and he liked to walk around the plant in a battered old hat so he could be "one of the boys." Every Hallowe'en, he would stand outside Parkwood's front door handing out shiny new pennies to the children: the early birds might get a five-dollar bill. Although Sam was personally responsible for the Dickensian working conditions at his Canadian plants, he deflected criticism by building a bandshell in the park and buying instruments for the band, supplying the Ontario Regiment with uniforms, and writing cheques to boost every worthy fund-raising campaign over the top. Sam was not the target of threats or violence, and apart from Lowry, who accompanied him everywhere, he had no bodyguard. A few pebbles were thrown at Parkwood's windows, but local legend records only one act of guerrilla resistance:

"McLaughlin had his farm and it straddled Oshawa Creek," recalls George Burt, "so he dammed up the creek and had a fish hatchery built right in the creek. I'd been through the two ponds. He had the very small fish in the first pond, then he'd put the big ones in the other pond. When his friends came down to fish, they caught all the big ones. A big tinsmith by the name of Bill Slott comes to me one day and says, 'George, I was thinking, geez, I haven't had a mess of trout for a long time,' and I says, 'No, I haven't either.' 'Look at that goddarned McLaughlin up there with all those trout in those ponds.' I says, 'Yeah.' He says, 'Well, I been talking to Fat Robinson and a couple of other boys and we decided to go up and cut the dam out. We'll put a piece of seine net across the creek and catch ourselves some fish. What do you think of that?' I says, 'I think it would be a damn good idea.' Well, they didn't wait for me. Bill got some of his friends together and they were drinkin' wine. They'd put a quart of gin in it to spruce it up – it'd kill ya. So they went up and cut the dam out and they had nets all the way down the creek and they got bags of trout. Oh, I got some lovely trout. McLaughlin never found out who did it."

At the end of 1936, Sam was so nonchalant about the threat of a strike he was golfing in Bermuda. He had just purchased Cedar Lodge, a spacious old house overlooking Hamilton Harbour – George had rented it for his family the year before – and had persuaded himself that a winter in Bermuda was vital to his health. At sixty-six, Sam was as strong as an ox, and while Bermuda's climate was invigorating, the winter winds from the north Atlantic could make the island's houses damp and miserable. Sam was more likely thinking about his financial

Cedar Lodge, Bermuda. (*Parkwood/McLaughlin Public Library*)

health: Bermuda was a tax haven. The Canadian government was taking a bigger and bigger bite out of rich men's pockets, and Sam, who hated paying taxes, moaned as loudly as Sir Harry Oakes, the mining millionaire from Kirkland Lake who had taken all his gold to the Bahamas.

Bermuda was also Sam's last chance to become "Sir Sam." In 1934, Prime Minister R. B. Bennett had revived the discredited practice of awarding knighthoods, but while Sam had publicly pronounced himself in favour of the idea, Bennett had ignored businessmen in favour of artists, philanthropists, and scientists. (George may have been offered a title and turned it down, knowing that Sam would have to have one too.) With Mackenzie King back in power, there was no more talk of titles, but in colonial Bermuda knighthoods were distributed like shiny pennies to rich men who caught the governor's eye. Sam had dealt with his own "Governor" until Robert had died, and he felt at ease among island aristocrats who entertained their guests with bloodcurdling stories about their pirate ancestors. Bermuda's quaint society was reminiscent of his childhood – automobiles were forbidden – and in the winter, after the American tourists had gone home, wealthy Bermudians settled into a decorous ritual of teas and banquets alternating between Government House and the Admiralty, where Sam could alternately play Mr. Sam and Colonel Sam.

At 8 a.m. on Wednesday, December 30, 1936, Sam was likely doing his callisthenics. In Flint, where it was 7 a.m., a metal finisher on the line at the Fisher Body Plant #2 pulled the switch. The line stopped. The men looked at each other in silence, then rushed to barricade the doors. Their sit-down was spontaneous, but that night union organizers, eager to back them up, provoked a second sit-down in Fisher Body Plant #1. Plant #1 made all the bodies for Buicks, and it employed about seven thousand men; Plant #2 made Chevrolets with a workforce of almost three thousand. The Flint plants were old and decrepit, and their immense size, coupled with the speeded-up rate of production, added psychological stress to the workers' daily burden of exhaustion and pain. "Something about the monotonous routine breaks down all restraint," a Buick worker told Sidney Fine. "Suddenly a man breaks forth with a mighty howl. Others follow. We set up a howling all over the shop. It is a relief, this howling."

The UAW had signed up only a few hundred of the Flint workers, and General Motors took the position that the occupation of company property was an illegal act of trespass inspired by a handful of malcontents. Hunger and discomfort would soon make them surrender, the company reasoned, and if the men had any grievances, they could take them up with the plant managers. General Motors had no intention of bargaining with the UAW. Company policy had been clearly stated by Alfred P. Sloan in a 1934 speech distributed throughout the organization.

"We believe in the principle of collective bargaining. On the other hand, we will under no circumstances permit any group, be it a majority or minority group, to prevent other groups from dealing with us. Under no circumstances will we recognize any union as that term is interpreted by the American Federation of Labor – that means the closed shop. American industry would be dominated by an organization in no sense interested in the real problems between the individual employer and the individual employee, but concerned solely with the enhancement of its own selfish interests. The greatest monopoly the world has yet seen would be created, and all outside the law. There need be no misunderstanding as to the position of General Motors on that point, and there is no compromise."

Sloan did not reckon, however, with Michigan's feisty governor, Frank Murphy, a populist Democrat who owed his job to the votes of the state's industrial workers. Murphy ruled that needy strikers' families could get relief, and that food could be taken in to the men through the main gate. Murphy wasn't about to starve people into submission, and he allowed the strikers to come and go from the plants via ladders from the windows without interference from company guards. These concessions, designed to force GM to the bargaining table, infuriated Sloan, and as the strikes spread, crippling plants in other cities, Sloan dug in for a hard siege.

General Motors, for all its Pinkerton agents, had underestimated the UAW's organizing expertise. Far from being an unruly mob, the strikers were a tightly knit, disciplined unit with elected leaders and committees to look after everything from sanitation to sing-songs — "Solidarity Forever" was a favourite — and they had their own police patrol to prevent the company from retaking the empty parts of the plants. The buildings were warm, the car bodies made cosy beds, and piles of door hinges gave the strikers a handy arsenal of missiles. Buoyed by visits with their families and daily meetings with the UAW executive, the strikers were as chipper and cheerful as Davy Crockett at the Alamo.

Then GM turned off the heat. On January 11, 1937, when the temperature in Flint was sixteen degrees Fahrenheit, twenty-two company policemen armed with clubs marched through the main gate of Plant #2 shortly after noon and joined the eight guards already stationed at the door. The guards removed the workers' access ladder and barred the gate to union stewards delivering food. By 8:30 p.m., when UAW organizer Victor Reuther drove up in a sound car, the men in the plant were cold and hungry, and a surly crowd of about two hundred pickets and spectators had gathered outside the gate. When the guards refused to open up, the pickets stormed the gate and barricaded themselves inside the plant's main door. The guards took refuge in the washroom.

Flint police charged the building, breaking windows and pumping tear gas into the plant, but the strikers, directed by Reuther's voice booming from the sound car, drove the police back with fire hoses and a barrage of scrap metal. The crowd, which had grown to about three thousand, hurled cans, frozen snow, milk bottles, and pieces of pavement at the police, who drew their revolvers and fired blindly into the darkness before retreating to a bridge.

Cars full of strikers roared up and barricaded the street. Headlights pierced the dark, and Reuther's amplified voice boomed over the battlefield "on one steady, unswerving note like an inexhaustible, furious flood pouring courage into the men." Bonfires were lit, and from time to time a young woman's voice came over the loudspeaker, shouting "Cowards! Cowards!" at the distant police, who continued to fire tear gas into the crowd from the bridge. In the plant, the strikers prepared for an armed assault. Fire hoses and extinguishers were placed near the windows, and the men armed themselves with homemade blackjacks and truncheons taken from the guards. By midnight, however, the police had run out of tear gas, and when a cold grey dawn lightened the sky, the bridge was deserted. The workers had won the Battle of the Running Bulls.

"We were not involved in that riot," said General Motors executive vice-president William Knudsen. "Our people were not in it." Riots and bloodshed were commonplace in U.S. labour disputes, and while the skirmish in Flint boosted union morale, GM still refused to meet with the UAW until the Flint plants were evacuated, by force if necessary. Thousands of GM workers were laid off as production ground to a halt, and Governor Murphy called out the National Guard to keep the peace between union supporters and angry workers who wanted their paycheques.

On February 1, when the strikers' resolve was beginning to waver, the UAW launched an offensive. Writes Sidney Fine: "At 3:55 p.m. the horn was sounded on the overhead crane at Chevrolet No. 6, whereupon Ed Cronk took out a small American flag from his pocket, picked up a piece of lead pipe, and called for the workers to follow him. About thirty-five men, armed with hammers and pieces of sheet metal and pipe, followed Cronk from the plant. When they emerged, they were directed to proceed to the Chevrolet No. 4 plant. Cronk burst into the No. 4 plant, 'his hairy chest bare to the belly,' and leading 'the most ferocious band of men' Kermit Johnson had ever seen but not the army of three hundred he had expected.

"Cronk returned to the No. 6 plant and gathered another hundred or so men. The new force surged into No. 4 and aided by perhaps two hundred unionists on the inside, sought to take over the plant. The unionists marched up and down the aisles, pleading for support and 'threatening' workers who would not join the strike. Many workers left the plant while the battle raged, some of them climbing over the fence since the strikers were guarding the gates. Some company police tried to enter the plant but were driven off by strikers armed with pistons, connecting rods and fire hoses. The supervisory personnel were rounded up, instructed to leave the plant, and told, in the words so familiar to the frequently laid-off auto workers, 'We'll let you know when to come back.' The strikers won complete control of the plant shortly after 5:30 p.m., and during the next few hours, aided by hundreds of outsiders from Detroit and Toledo, barricaded the entrances with a variety of heavy objects moved into place by cranes and electric trucks."

Michigan judge Paul Gadola ordered the strikers to evacuate the Fisher Body buildings by 3 p.m. on February 3. The men in Fisher Body #2 replied with a telegram to Governor Murphy: "We have decided to stay in the plant. We have no illusions about the sacrifices which this decision will entail. We fully expect that if a violent effort is made to oust us many of us will be killed and we take this means of making it known to our wives, to our children, to the people of the state of Michigan and of the country that if this result follows from the attempt to eject us you are the one who must be held responsible for our deaths."

As the deadline approached, an armed mob of ten thousand union supporters converged on Plant #2. Fine describes the scene as "one of the most amazing labor demonstrations ever seen in America. Singing pickets, six abreast, circled the plant for an hour while the sit-downers leaned out the factory windows to join in the singing and cheering. The pickets carried 'clubs, pieces of pipe, claw hammers, iron bars, sod cutters, spades,' clothes trees, and body parts. As the pickets marched, the sound car 'bombarded all ears' and exhorted the unionists to keep up their courage. There was not a policeman in sight, and such traffic as could get through the crowd was directed by the strikers themselves. Chief of Police Wills drove up to the plant but was chased out of the area – 'running for his life,' one observer thought – by thirty or forty strikers. Had he stopped his car and fired, Wills said, 'The war would have been on,' and he may have been correct."

At 3 p.m., the sheriff announced that no attempt would be made to evict the strikers until court procedures had been exhausted. An exuberant crowd paraded through the streets, cheering and honking their horns. Flint had fallen to the workers, but a quieter revolution had taken place in the boardroom at General Motors: sequestered in a Detroit courthouse, William Knudsen was negotiating an end to the strike with John L. Lewis. "Big Bill" Knudsen, a rough-hewn Danish immigrant who had worked his way up from the shop floor, could match Lewis in bulk and profanities, and Knudsen wanted to get his machinery rolling. Sloan's war of attrition had cost General Motors about 280,000 cars valued at $175 million. Violence had tarnished the company's image, and public sympathy, influenced by Chaplin's recent movie, *Modern Times*, was solidly behind the besieged strikers. Knudsen could remember as vividly as Sam McLaughlin the panics caused by Durant's obsessions, and Knudsen had no problem with recognizing the union. The sticking point was the closed shop.

With Governor Murphy acting as mediator and President Roosevelt on the telephone to everybody, the talks went on around the clock until a deal was signed on the morning of February 11, 1937. General Motors agreed to recognize the UAW as bargaining agent for the union membership, but it granted the union exclusive bargaining rights for only six months, and only in the plants on strike. The UAW, however, had complete freedom to sign up new members, and GM promised not to intimidate unionized workers or "inspire" rival organizations. The strikers were allowed to return to their jobs without penalty, and the company celebrated the end to the strike by announcing a five-cent hourly raise, a benefit most workers believed had been won by the union.

"The strike was like measles, it spread," jokes Harry Benson. The five-cent hourly raise in the United States galvanized the Canadian workers into action: they wanted their five cents too. The first skirmish with General Motors of Canada began on Thursday, February 18, in the metal-finishing shop. "We'd started to organize openly then," recalled George Burt. "We used to sit down. We'd just sit down and they'd have to shut the line down. We had sit-downs all over the place then. We had a deal at noon hour. I was at the top of the line and I was at the button, and they said to me, 'Well, George, we have to have a signal.' I said, 'All right, when it's time to go out, we'll go across the road on the loading dock and we'll have our meeting right on the dock.' They had some great big timbers over there and it was just a nice tier where the guys could sit down. The signal was for me to take my overalls off. I took my overalls off and, boy, they couldn't get to the door fast enough. So we sat on the loading dock and formed a committee which I was on to see the company."

Vice-president and general manager Harry Carmichael told the committee that Canadian workers would have to increase their productivity by 30 per cent to American levels before they got the raise. Since American productivity for the past six weeks had been nil, and shortages caused by the strikes had hindered Canadian workers, Carmichael's argument intensified the workers' hostility. They contacted Ontario's minister of labour, David Croll, and George Burt went off to a meeting with federal conciliator, Louis Fine.

The Communists, meanwhile, had been phoning the UAW pleading for an organizer to come to Oshawa, and on the morning of February 19, Hugh Thompson arrived from Buffalo with his wife and young daughter. Thompson was thirty-four, Irish-born, and his handsome, neatly dressed family looked as if they had stepped out of a Buick advertisement: the *Toronto Star* compared Thompson's style to a "polo-playing broker." A British citizen, Thompson had worked in Windsor before moving to the United States, and his conservative manner reassured the Canadians that the UAW was not a bunch of scruffs and thugs. After Thompson spoke in the CCF hall that morning, he was mobbed by men asking where they could sign up.

"There were meetings all through the plant," says Vince Jewison. "Every night, there were little meetings with different spokesmen. Everybody was for it. Then there was a big meeting with Thompson and his wife. The whole plant shut down. There was so much commotion! 'Let's get it going!' 'We've got to have a union!' 'As long as we all walk out we'll be all right!' Thompson says, 'We got to get some names. Put your name on a piece of paper.' Mrs. Thompson took the names." Vince still carries the receipt for his two-dollar membership tucked away in his wallet: the tiny slip of paper shows that he is member 713 of Local 222.

The local's charter was issued on March 2, and with almost unanimous support from the plant's four thousand workers, it appeared that recognition of the UAW would be almost a formality. The union was in a much stronger position in Oshawa than it had been in Flint, and following their brief walkout on February 18, the workers had been dutifully back on the job. The Communists kept out of sight, and the president of Local 222, Charles Millard, was a well-mannered Ontario farm boy who had gone to school with Ontario's Liberal premier, Mitch

Hepburn. Local 222 drew up a list of four demands – union recognition, a forty-hour week with time-and-a-half for overtime, seniority,
and a grievance committee – and set a strike date of April 1, 1937.

During February, however, the sensational newspaper accounts of
CIO-inspired violence in Flint had scared Ontario businessmen into
imagining that hordes of armed terrorists were about to overrun their
factories, and now Hepburn exploited the CIO bogey to enhance his
own authority. "Those who participate in sit-downs are trespassers and
trespassing is illegal in this province," the premier warned. "There
will be no sit-down strikes in Ontario. This government is going to
maintain law and order at all costs." When Local 222 workers walked
out at the Coulter plant, a supplier of parts for GM, Oshawa mayor
Alec Hall used a scuffle on the picket line to warn: "We are instructing
the police to apprehend all cases of law breaking, and we promise that
they will be prosecuted and punished *promptly, severely and inexorably.*"
Hall secretly requested Attorney General Arthur Roebuck to send
reinforcements from the Ontario Provincial Police; Roebuck
declined, but, on orders from Hepburn, OPP constable Alec Wilson
was assigned to infiltrate union meetings and report unlawful activity.

On March 25, Wilson checked into Oshawa's Genosha Hotel,
where Hugh Thompson had established the UAW headquarters, and,
in the evening, accompanied by a shorthand reporter, he attended a
union rally addressed by CIO vice-president Edward Hall. Hall
announced that GM vice-president Charles E. Wilson had instructed
General Motors of Canada to meet with UAW representatives, and
praised GM as "one of the finest people to deal with since the strike."
Hall promised: "It is not our desire to start any kind of revolution. It is
not our desire to cause strife and trouble." Constable Wilson reported:
"The meeting was very orderly."

General Motors of Canada was prepared for a strike. The company
had been stockpiling cars since January, and now it shipped them out
by rail or drove them to Toronto and parked them on the grounds of
the Canadian National Exhibition. Plant manager J. B. Highfield
adopted a conciliatory attitude when negotiations began on March
18. He acquiesced without argument to the union's demands for
seniority, a grievance committee, and time-and-a-half overtime – a
benefit the corporation had granted to its U.S. workers six months
before – but he refused to meet with Thompson or recognize the UAW,

UAW Oshawa strike organizers, left to right: Charles Millard, Homer Martin, Hugh Thompson. (*Globe and Mail Collection, City of Toronto Archives*)

which he called the "spearhead of the CIO in Canada." Highfield emphasized that General Motors of Canada was "completely self-supporting" and therefore not bound by the American contract with the UAW.

Highfield seems to have hoped to settle the grievances without a contract, and after he stubbornly refused to acknowledge Local 222 president Charles Millard as a representative of the UAW, bargaining became impossible. On March 31, the eve of the strike date, David Croll, whose Windsor constituency included thousands of unorganized Ford workers, jumped in as a self-appointed mediator, but Croll created only distrust and misunderstanding. At 7:05 on the morning of April 8, the Oshawa workers walked out.

"We knew we were going out when we went into work," says Doug Knapp. "So we went in, then went out. One guys says, 'Nobody's big enough to take me out!' He wasn't standing on his feet before he was lying down. Two guys hit him. He come out later. All the guys booed him. He had to go home – he had no place else to go. We'd carry some guys out on chairs, sit them down outside. The foreman got pushed around a bit." Four hundred pickets circled the locked gates, and a

J. L. Cohen. (*Globe and Mail Collection, City of Toronto Archives*)

hundred union stewards, led by George Burt and Harry Benson, made sure that the strikers were sober and well-behaved.

"A city more peaceful than Oshawa cannot be imagined," reported the *Toronto Star* on April 9. "It is neither grim nor gay but placidly ordinary." The *Star* was incredulous; Hepburn had led the press to expect riots.

"This is the first open attempt on the part of Lewis and his CIO to assume the position of dominating and dictating to Canadian industry," Hepburn announced hours after the strike began. "The time for a show-down is at the start. There will be no illegal sit-down strike or illegal picketing. We know what these agitators are up to. They are working their way into the lumber camps, the pulp mills and our mines. Well, this has got to stop – and we are going to stop it. If necessary, we'll raise an army to do it."

Early that morning, Hepburn had ordered the OPP to mobilize a hundred officers for possible duty in Oshawa, and had sent a telegram to the federal justice minister, Ernest Lapointe: "Situation becoming very acute and violence anticipated every minute also impairment heating plants and fire protection service." Lapointe authorized a detachment of one hundred RCMP officers to take the train from Ottawa to Toronto, and when the trainload of "redcoats" passed through Oshawa, news of Hepburn's army spread like wildfire on the picket lines.

"We were fighting mad," says Doug Knapp. "We would take on anything. If Hepburn wanted to fetch 'em, go fetch 'em. We had a lot of Scotchmen, Irishmen. They were strong when they made up their minds. 'Bring 'em on,' the fellows said. I felt the same way. It was a threat. We were ready to fight. There wasn't too many houses around that didn't have a gun. Some fellows might have took it."

Hepburn relished the kind of shoot-'em-up politics that got his big grin plastered all over the front pages of the newspapers. "Mitch," as he liked to be called, was a boisterous young onion farmer with the political convictions of a weathervane, and his riotous private life evoked comparisons to Louisiana's lascivious governor, Huey Long. Elected as the champion of the "little guy," Hepburn had surrounded himself with a coterie of hard-drinking mining millionaires that included George McCullagh, publisher of the *Globe and Mail*, and Sam McLaughlin's friend, Jack Bickell, president of the McIntyre–Porcupine gold mine. Rumour had it that Hepburn had invested heavily in mining stocks, and that his attack on the CIO was orchestrated by the mine owners' fear of union organization.

Sam McLaughlin didn't hang out with Hepburn's rowdy crowd at the King Edward Hotel, but he was part of the "body of gangsters," as Mackenzie King later called them, who used Hepburn as a puppet to promote their own interests. Sam sat on the board of McIntyre–Porcupine as well as on that of INCO, and ten days before the GM strike date, Hepburn flew to Florida in Bickell's private plane. Mitch said he was just off for an Easter vacation, but with insurrection brewing in Oshawa, and Sam a quick hop away in Bermuda, Bickell's purpose seems to have been to arrange a private meeting between McLaughlin and the premier of Ontario. Hepburn had already had one secret meeting with General Motors of Canada executives: in a letter dated March 9, 1937, an OPP staff inspector noted that the previous day, Hepburn, George McCullagh, and "two representatives of GM St. Catharines" had discussed instructing the OPP to infiltrate union meetings.

Sam wasn't going to give up his "open shop" without a fight, and General Motors may have hoped that if the corporation beat the UAW in Canada it could weaken the union's bargaining power in the United States. Sam was sly enough, however, not to stick his own head into a hornets' nest, and by persuading Hepburn to lead the crusade against the CIO, Sam got off the hook for the consequences.

Picket line. *(Globe and Mail Collection, City of Toronto Archives)*

On his return to Ontario, Hepburn announced that General Motors had insisted that he participate in negotiations with the UAW, and he and J. B. Highfield used identical insinuations of "intimidation" and "coercion" to denigrate the CIO. The secret "evidence" Mitch claimed to have as proof of illegal activity seems to have been passed to him by General Motors; the OPP could find nothing dangerous or subversive in the union's behaviour. Mitch tried to have Hugh Thompson deported, and when that failed, he denounced Thompson as a foreign agitator. The tactic only called attention to the fact that General Motors of Canada was a subsidiary of a foreign company, and at a strikers' rally on April 8, Thompson shouted his defiant reply: "I say to the premier of the province of Ontario, you can send 50,000 of your militia in, but you still can't build automobiles because we are the ones that build them, and General Motors can't make ten cents until they sign with this international union, and they 'will do it before they make another car in Canada!"

GM salaried employees cross the line. (*Globe and Mail Collection, City of Toronto Archives*)

Mitch had made himself the issue, and the focus of the fight now moved to the premier's office, where Mitch played the role of anxious midwife, bouncing back and forth between Local 222 negotiators in his outer office and General Motors executives in his inner office, with Hugh Thompson cooling his heels in the hall because Mitch refused to speak to a UAW representative. When the talks stalled, Mitch put out the word that communists, by the thousands, were preparing to descend on Oshawa. The Communist Party huffily replied that it had no interest in Oshawa, while in Oshawa, the union was trying to get the communists out of town. "I saw Joe Salsberg over on the William Street picket line," says Harry Benson, "so I fell into step beside him. 'You're going to get us branded as being run by the Communists,' I said. 'If the *Globe and Mail* saw me talking to you, I'd be branded. If you want to do us a good turn, fade out of the picture.' 'I just want to help,' he said, and he walked away."

Mayor Hall, wearing his Conservative politics on his sleeve,

Pickets yell, "Yellow scab! Dirty scab!" (*Globe and Mail Collection, City of Toronto Archives*)

declared that Hepburn had no right to send in the provincial police until Hall asked for them, and he had no intention of asking for them. He ordered all liquor stores and beer parlours closed for the duration of the strike, and with the union stewards keeping homebrew off the picket line, the *Toronto Star* reported that except for crowds of sight-seers, Oshawa was "as quiet as if every day were the Sabbath." Picketers paraded in their Sunday best, singing "The Music Goes Round and Round" and other popular tunes, and when he wasn't on picket duty, Doug Knapp was seeding his lawn. The only excitement came when General Motors' managers, grudgingly permitted access to their offices, entered or left the building: hundreds of picketers converged from all directions, booing, hissing, and chanting: "Yellow rat, dirty rat; dirty scab, yellow scab." The gauntlet of sulphurous profanity was an ordeal, but General Motors made no attempt to hire strikebreakers or harm the pickets. "A few of us were positioned on the railroad tracks where they came into the yard," says Vince Jewison. "This train was coming towards us. I was afraid I was going to get run over. I was getting ready to jump. Then just as it got to us, it stopped."

Vice-president and General Manager Harry Carmichael took no part in the public controversy. A hard-headed production man like Knudsen, Carmichael spoke a language that Jacob Cohen, the lawyer for the union, understood: jobs. Cohen, famous for defending Tim Buck and other Communists charged with sedition, had taken Hugh Thompson's place at the bargaining table, and while Carmichael and Cohen looked like Mutt and Jeff, they shared practical common sense and a working-class background: Carmichael, a former semi-pro baseball player in Detroit, had started his career at Mackinnon Industries as a tool-and-die maker. While Hepburn preened for the flashbulbs, Carmichael and Cohen got down to the work of making a deal.

The coolest man on the scene was Oshawa's chief of police, Owen Friend, who expressed complete confidence in the good character of the strikers and the ability of his small force to keep order. "Our old cops were pretty good guys," Vince smiles.

Every evening, the union held monster pep rallies in the collegiate auditorium, right across the street from Parkwood, and the speakers gave a crash course in labour history, industrial economics, and strike tactics. On April 10, Homer Martin, the American president of the UAW, arrived in Oshawa to a hero's welcome. Speaking at a rally in the armouries, Martin, a former Baptist preacher, made short work of "Herr Hepburn," and then, his mellifluous voice rising to a crescendo, he promised: "The thing we want to say to you, without equivocation, is that the International is squarely behind you with every bit of resource and strength we have, and if they don't make cars in Canada under union conditions, they won't make them at all in the United States!"

On April 14, as the strike entered its second week, Hepburn dumped David Croll and Arthur Roebuck from his cabinet for failing to support his anti-CIO crusade. Croll replied: "There are today, and have been for many months, some ten thousand workers in the province of Ontario who are members of unions affiliated with the CIO, and most enjoy the protection afforded by our own Industrial Standards Act. In my official capacity, I have travelled the middle of

A settlement is reached. Left to right: Harry J. Carmichael, J. B. Highfield, Premier Mitch Hepburn, J. L. Cohen, Charles Millard. (*Globe and Mail Collection, City of Toronto Archives*)

the road, but now that you have put the extreme alternative to me, my place is marching with the workers rather than riding with General Motors."

When Mackenzie King refused to order the RCMP to Oshawa, Hepburn ordered the OPP to recruit two hundred special constables. Volunteers for "Hepburn's Hussars" were mostly university students looking for summer jobs, and the "Sons of Mitches," as they were dubbed in Oshawa, gave Hepburn's attempts to mediate the strike the quality of a "Katzenjammer Kids" comic strip.

"One afternoon two carloads of us went into Toronto to see Mitch and his army," Vince chuckles. "We went into a hotel. The beer parlour was full of these guys in uniform. We said, 'Are you the guys that are going to turn their machine guns on us? Are you Hepburn's army?' They looked at us. We were noisy. We all had our union buttons on. They said, 'Gee, we hope nothing like that ever happens.' They weren't so tough."

General Motors was allowing the strikers to draw their back pay, and after ten days their commitment to the union was beginning to waver.

Thousands of workers line up outside the Oshawa armoury to ratify the agreement. (*Globe and Mail Collection, City of Toronto Archives*)

Thompson had promised a $65,000 strike fund from the UAW Detroit headquarters, but when the money didn't arrive, calls to Detroit revealed that no such fund existed. Mayor Hall warned the strikers that they had been "hookwinked" by Homer Martin's promise of a sympathetic strike in the U.S. Hall was booed off the stage, but he was telling the truth: the Detroit UAW executive had no intention of calling a U.S. walkout that would wreck their own negotiations and jeopardize the union. "Homer Martin," says Vince, "was a big bag of wind." Hall urged the strikers to go back to work without a contract, and General Motors assured Hepburn that more than a thousand men were eager to return.

On Tuesday, April 20, Mitch wired Sam McLaughlin, who was steaming toward New York on the *Queen of Bermuda*: "Would urgently request that you advise Carmichael to suspend any negotiations with strikers until your return Thursday morning. Would also ask you to give no statements regarding situation until I have had a chance to confer with you. Confidential reports indicate total collapse of strike imminent."

Sam left no trace of what he said or did when he arrived in Toronto, but six hours later, the strike was settled. Hepburn announced the agreement just before 6 p.m. on Thursday, April 22, and it was ratified in Oshawa early the next morning by a vote of 2,205 to 36. While the workers agreed to a forty-four-hour week, compared to forty in the U.S., they won time-and-a-half for overtime, two daily five-minute rest periods, a reduction in their efficiency ratio, and an increase in the number of workers. There was a wage hike of five cents an hour for all women, and for men earning more than fifty-five cents; men earning fifty-five cents or less received a seven-cent raise. Seniority and grievance procedures were equivalent to those in the U.S. The sticky point of UAW recognition had been avoided by the following circumlocution: "The agreement covering the Oshawa factory of the company is signed by the union employees who signed on behalf of themselves and their successors in office representing the employees of the company who are members of the local union." Since they were virtually all members of the UAW, recognition was tacitly admitted, and the agreement was to run concurrently with the agreement between the UAW and General Motors Corporation in the United States.

"I am overjoyed for the workers, their families, the citizens of Oshawa and the Company," a relieved Harry Carmichael told the Oshawa *Daily Times*. Sam, however, was full of sour grapes. "I was grievously disappointed that they went on strike," he told the press. "I didn't think they would do it. We have always tried to be fair and generous in our treatment of our workers and I didn't think they would go on strike. I guess they were promised the moon." Commenting on the ratification vote, Sam went on: "Where were the rest of the 3,000 or more members the union claimed? I don't think they ever had them. We have a list of 1,200 signatures here of men who did not want to go on strike. We have letters from dozens and dozens who were threatened into joining the union and of others who did so because they didn't want to be bothered any more." Sam praised "the attitude shown during the strike by Premier Mitchell F. Hepburn and Hon. Ernest Lapointe, Minister of Justice. I'm glad they would not tolerate the iniquitous condition that exists in the United States where they step right in and take possession of your property and will not move out even at the request of State police. If such a condition ever developed here I'd move right out of the country, but I don't think it ever can happen in Canada."

Sam, celebrating the fiftieth anniversary of his apprenticeship with the McLaughlin Carriage Company, found sharing power with "the boys" more painful than selling out to General Motors, and in his old trim shop, Sam now had to make peace with the union steward, Harry Benson.

"We were afraid," Benson says. "Don't ever think we weren't. We thought, 'We're down as far as we can go, so what's the point of going through the bottom of the barrel?' We had to go up, and that was a fight. The only thought we had in mind was to make things better so we could stand on our own two feet with a little dignity and have some say in what was done."

12

PEACE AND WAR

Alfred P. Sloan resigned as president of General Motors in April 1937, immediately after GM signed its first contract with the UAW. He remained as chairman and chief executive officer, but his confrontation with the UAW had demonstrated that he was too doctrinaire, stiff-necked, and isolated from the shop floor to run an international conglomerate with nearly two hundred thousand employees. He had infuriated President Roosevelt and embroiled General Motors in political controversy, an error that GM's *éminence grise*, Pierre du Pont, did not tolerate.

Du Pont, through Christiana Securities, a holding company owned by numerous relatives, controlled 25 per cent of General Motors' shares, and the du Ponts, along with two of their appointees, Donaldson Brown and John Lee Pratt, dominated GM's executive and finance committees. Pierre du Pont's primary interest was his own chemical company – he had distanced himself from General Motors when Sloan took over – and the various subsidiaries of E. I. du Pont de Nemours and Company had found in General Motors a huge and very profitable market for their paint, rubber, plastics, and synthetic fabrics. The last thing du Pont wanted to do was to attract the attention of muckraking journalists and antitrust crusaders in Washington. The previous President Roosevelt, Teddy, had made his political reputation as a "trust-buster," and Franklin Roosevelt was regarded by America's corporate elite as a dangerous socialist, if not a Bolshevik. In 1928, du Pont had forced John J. Raskob to resign from the General Motors board when Raskob had joined the presidential campaign of Democratic candidate Alfred Smith, and du Pont may, in his quiet way, have suggested to Sloan that by stepping aside as president of General Motors he would be able to devote more time to developing his theories of management.

Sloan didn't go quietly. He wrote the first edition of his memoirs, *Adventures of a White-Collar Man*, a chatty, egotistical, and highly imaginative account of his career in which Sloan identifies himself with all the corporation's achievements, ignores its failures, and slights everybody else. Sam McLaughlin, who joined General Motors ten years before Sloan, doesn't rate a mention, yet Sloan had the effrontery to send Sam an autographed copy "with my personal appreciation for your contribution which has helped make this story possible." Sloan describes General Motors very much in his own image: austere, efficient, dedicated, and profitable.

"I am proud of General Motors' figures," Sloan writes, and he had reason to be. General Motors had grown from a ragtag bunch of small-town factories to a $2-billion multinational corporation, and even in the worst of the Depression GM had never failed to pay a dividend or make a profit. In the first six months of 1937, General Motors of Canada, in spite of the strike, made a net profit of $3 million, nearly 10 per cent of its $32 million in sales. Sloan attributed GM's success to his "scientific management," and the promulgation of his ideology signalled the arrival of a new icon on the American scene: the Corporation Man.

"The profit motive is an essential component in the capitalist system," Sloan writes, "but it is far from the sole influence as an actuating force as applied to the individual in contributing to the world's great accomplishments. Beyond a certain point, the sole urge is for still greater success, a recognition of one's ability to accomplish, and the satisfaction that results from it all. The anxieties, the responsibilities, the necessity of living the life of the cause rather than one's own life could not possibly be compensated for in any material way."

Sloan's "life of the cause" gave a quasi-religious tone to the pursuit of profit that over the next five decades transformed not only General

Motors but every large North American corporation into a secular monastery of white-collar men. Sloan's puritanical and obsessive personality defined the corporate identity, and corporate rituals took on the secrecy and complexity of a Masonic rite. In *Adventures of a White-Collar Man*, Sloan portrays himself as the anointed successor to the patron saint of General Motors, the lovable, if somewhat befuddled, Billy Durant, and long after Sloan had retired from General Motors his word, however foolish or awkwardly expressed, was gospel. The essence of "Sloanism," as it came to be called, was his credo: "The only true answer to the great question of more things for more people everywhere is more work more efficiently performed."

Sloan was the guru of capitalist modernism, but his techniques went back to the Caesars. "I developed a General Staff similar in name and purpose to what exists in the army," he says. Sloan didn't police his divisions in person, but his headquarters staff of "co-ordinators" provided him with regular, detailed reports on every aspect of the corporation. Sloan's staff, however, had no authority – division executives reported through other channels – and, to keep all his officers from getting in each other's hair, Sloan created a buffer zone of interlocking committees. Bigness, a cult inherited from Durant and Ford, was essential to Sloan's concept of capitalist imperialism, and, ironically, one of the strongest spurs to Sloan's passion for bureaucracy was the UAW.

Signed in haste and under duress, GM's agreement with the union, as sacred to auto workers as Moses' tablets from the Mount, entrenched a lengthy and cumbersome grievance procedure that mired both sides in tedious arguments until one side said: "Oh, to hell with it!" Their right to grieve provided workers with an effective tool to harass management, rewarded activists with jobs as union stewards and committeemen – a protocol of obscene language effectively excluded women – and within the corporation it created a thriving new division of "industrial relations."

Grieving – such an apt and evocative word – created a personal bond between white- and blue-collar employees who otherwise would not have exchanged a nod. For more than a year, Jacob Cohen acted as chief negotiator for Local 222, and his verbatim minutes reveal that, while tempers flared, both sides worked hard to establish common ground. "It seems that we can only have animosity and dissension instead of being happy in our dealings during our daily toils," J. B. Highfield barked during one particularly acrimonious session. "I may be in a different place than the rest of you, but I would like us to be able to meet problems and get over them and do a good job of it." While the company was finding it hard to adjust to the fact that it could no longer manipulate wage rates or dismiss workers without consulting the union, workers were learning that a union card didn't allow them to be lazy, late, or drunk on the job.

The union and the company were so friendly, in fact, that on September 28, 1937, Cohen wrote a "Dear Harry" letter to general manager H. J. Carmichael praising the "esteem and good will which has marked the relations between the company officials and myself, a relationship which I have somewhat appreciated." Cohen then asked Carmichael, "as a friend" and in view of "a mutual high regard between us," to intervene in a dispute he was having with J. B. Highfield. Highfield had arbitrarily laid off sixty-eight women workers, many with years of seniority, and replaced them with teenage boys, intimating to the union bargaining committee that Cohen had approved. Cohen, however, vehemently objected in a letter to Highfield on October 7, 1937: "It appears to me to be most improper for the company, in effect, to summarily discharge a group of employees, without cause, so far as their own qualifications or behavior is concerned and without immediate and adequate substituted employment."

Cohen's note to Carmichael was temporarily effective – thirty of the women were rehired on October 9, the remainder by the end of the month – but discrimination was entrenched in the union agreement, which stated: "In any department in which both men and women are employed, they should be divided into separate non-interchangeable occupational groups." Although women worked at the same jobs as men making wiring harnesses, cushions, seats, and radiators, they were segregated by sex and paid half the wage; boys to the age of twenty were paid a cent or two more. The women had no seniority beyond their group; GM could get rid of them simply by reclassifying their job as unsuitable for women. "The management did not favour mixing male and female help in a department, and would rather hire the sons of employees on these jobs," Highfield told the union. "This would help the boys out so that after a few years they can further their ambitions."

A year later, when Cohen was no longer involved in negotiations, the company simply eliminated the women's jobs. When Local 222 complained, Highfield replied: "Their job is gone. Their job is done away with. There is no work on bucket seats anymore. Three girls on the key cutting machine were told a year ago that these jobs would be eliminated. I wouldn't want my daughter to work around the filth of the things that are said around there. From a moral standpoint it would be better to put the girls by themselves in a department by themselves. Even in the girls' department they are bothered by male workers. That is the reason we have taken the girls and put them together so that they would not have to take anything in the way of abuse. Ever since last year they were told that this job is going to be turned over to the boys. They agreed. I am not discriminating against any of these people. I am a friend of labour rather than an aggressor against it." Highfield adamantly refused to acknowledge that the women had seniority anywhere else in the plant, but after several sobbing women appeared at his home begging for work, he grudgingly rehired them in cutting and sewing. Women were ghettoized in the plant and patronized by their union, and hiring boys guaranteed the company a supply of young workers no better educated than their parents.

Jacob Cohen apparently acquiesced in the discriminatory wages paid to the women workers, and he supported the company's paternalism. "We must arrange our affairs within the corners of this room, and within the corners of the meeting-place of the union committee and members," he told the management bargaining committee. "We do not want our union business made a subject of press publications, any government interference or any party politics. The public is not to put its nose in. We don't want our arrangements and interests used as a football by the public. This is a family affair as long as we are a family."

Cohen likely had Hepburn's witch hunt in mind, but the code of silence worked to the advantage of the company. GM didn't have to tell the public anything, and when it did, it had a public-relations department and an advertising agency to get its message across. Local 222 had a small monthly newsletter, the *Oshaworker*, distributed to forty-three hundred plant workers, and the *Oshaworker*, published by the executive, toed the official union line. Secrecy encouraged suspicion of the press, including the pro-labour *Toronto Star*, and isolated the union from the thousands of sympathetic Canadians who had been stirred by the strike.

Political feuds within the union appear to have been the reason for the fearfulness. The trouble originated in the Detroit headquarters of the UAW, where Homer Martin launched an attack on the Communists that matched Hepburn's rhetoric for venom and paranoia. Martin

enlisted Local 222 president Charles Millard as his Canadian extermi-
nator, and Millard, encouraged by the CCF, attempted to flush out the
Reds. Who was a Red? Apart from the two dozen Communist Party
members who were well-known union stalwarts, a Red could be a
fellow-traveller, a sympathizer, a dupe, or a do-gooder, and since the
men Millard suspected denied any connection with the Communist
Party, and no subversion was proven, his futile efforts left a legacy of
poisonous mistrust.

Local 222 split into two caucuses – the "Unity" (communist)
caucus on the left, the "Democratic" [CCF] caucus on the right –
while ornery independents like George Burt and Harry Benson
formed the "Young Turks." Bill Gelech, who, with Joe Salsberg, had
brought the UAW to Oshawa, was sacrificed. Gelech had been fired
from GM in March 1937, a few weeks before the strike began. Gelech
had asked for a half-day off, saying that he didn't feel well, but then
he had driven to St. Catharines and delivered a rousing union speech
to Ukrainian workers at the GM engine plant. Speaking in Ukrainian
was enough to get anyone fired, and General Motors had acquired a
thick file of RCMP surveillance reports on Gelech. Highfield claimed
that Gelech had broken a solemn promise to him to stay clear of "any
agitation or radical activities," and while he praised Gelech as a
"good worker, and quiet," he refused, in spite of persistent union
requests, to reinstate him. The final word came on June 4, 1937,
when, as Millard wrote to Jacob Cohen, "Mr. Carmichael and Mr.
McLaughlin gave report that Galech [sic] was not to be re-hired in
any part of the plant."

Sam should probably have retired with Sloan. He was over sixty-five
and General Motors was only one of his many business interests.
Sam's financial stake in GM, about 150,000 shares, was small compared to the holdings of other directors, and although he never
missed a monthly board meeting, his long absences from his office
rubbed the Americans the wrong way. "All your vacations run into
each other!" Charles Kettering once twitted Sam. "When do you get
any work done?"

Sam didn't have much to do. The automobile industry was already
pulling out of the Depression, and although only one Canadian in
nine owned a car, compared to one in five Americans, this discrepancy
meant plenty of room for growth. Provincial governments had become

so dependent on revenue from gasoline taxes, motor-vehicle licences, permits, and fines that the manufacturers could now rely on the politicians to take on the job of promoting highway construction, tourism, and bus transport. Completing the Trans-Canada Highway through the Rockies had been a federal public-works project, and in 1936 American tourists had spent in Canada an estimated $160 million; total revenues from licences and gasoline taxes amounted to $60 million. Motor buses were muscling in on the streetcar lines, and in Oshawa Sam McLaughlin had the honour of tearing up the first rail of the now defunct Oshawa Street Railway.

With the invention of the automatic transmission in 1937, automobile technology had reached its peak. Emphasis now switched from engineering to appearance. Cars, like railway carriages before them, became "parlour cars" with padded, sofa-style plush seats, broadloom, radios, cigarette lighters, and ashtrays. GM boasted that its vehicles offered "a million possible options." Said Sloan: "You can have an Oldsmobile with or without Hydra-Matic drive, with six or eight cylinders, any one of a dozen body styles, choice of fifteen kinds of interior trim, any one of twenty colors over-all, or different on the wheels, with or without radio, heater and so on." Advertising "a car for every purse and purpose," General Motors began to develop the sales strategy designer Harley Earl called "dynamic obsolescence."

Sam kept himself busy quarrelling with his family. He picked a fight with George that he nagged at for years after George's death in 1942. George had bought up all of the McLaughlin family farms around Tyrone, and he had torn down many of the old buildings, including their grandparents' log homestead by the mill. "To tell the truth," Sam wrote to George's son Ewart in 1952, "I was terribly upset when your father bought the property and without ever saying a word to me, he had the old original homestead torn down. Quite true, it wasn't much of a house but there was a lot of sentiment connected with it. He did not speak to me about it at all – in fact he never took me into his confidence about anything."

George must have been taken aback by Sam's emotion. Sam had taken no interest at all in the family homestead, nor in the villages of Tyrone and Enniskillen. The shed where Robert had built his first wagons and cutters, as well as his factory in Enniskillen, had been allowed to collapse from old age, and while Sam would cruise through the villages on Sunday afternoons in his big Cadillac limousine, it was

George and Annie who gave money to the local charities, restored the graveyard, and built a community hall. People in Tyrone said that if they ever built a monument to a McLaughlin, it would be to George.

Sam and George remained, if somewhat formally, on friendly terms. Sam treated his daughter Eileen more harshly. "You might say my mother was 'put out' of the family," says her daughter Diana. Peter C. Newman tells the story this way in a footnote in *The Canadian Establishment*: "Eric Phillips' first wife, Eileen, one of Sam McLaughlin's daughters, ran away on Christmas Eve with the father of Frank McEachren (who is a Flavelle and who married John David Eaton's sister)." Eileen married Frank McEachren, Sr., briefly, after her divorce from Phillips, but Eileen wasn't running away with McEachren; she was running away from Phillips. Newman sums up his personality in a quote from a Toronto lawyer: "If you cut Eric up into little pieces, you'd have a thousand razor blades."

Phillips had inherited his father's business manufacturing wooden mouldings and picture frames, but Sam had set him up as the president of Duplate Glass, with a contract to make windows and windshields for General Motors of Canada. Big, beefy, his florid face sliced by a razor-thin moustache, Phillips was rude and abusive to his wife. "Eileen had organized the Sea Rangers," recalls Nora Herd. "We were part of the Girl Guides. She would take the girls swimming at the pool in Parkwood, and we would meet at her house. Phillips would come barging in and interrupt the meetings. He was just showing off. Nobody liked him. Even Eileen's dog was afraid of Eric. The dog would crawl under the chesterfield and growl at him."

Nora worked in the office at General Motors, and Eileen would often phone her at 8:30 a.m. just for a talk. The hour was late for Eileen: she would have been out riding since 6 a.m. Nora was puzzled by these calls from an older, sophisticated, and wealthy woman she scarcely knew, and she was embarrassed at being singled out by the boss's daughter. "Sometimes Eileen would meet me at lunchtime. She would park out front and we'd sit and talk in her car. We didn't talk about much. I felt that she was a very lonely person."

Diana makes her hands into fists and bangs them against each other: "My parents were like *this*." Eric Phillips' only friend in Oshawa was Eileen's father, and Sam liked his son-in-law's hard-edged, arrogant style. Sam introduced Eric to powerful Toronto financiers, indulged his weakness for Ditchburn motorboats, and gave him the money to build a $400,000 brick mansion. Sam, however, kept title to the property, and if Eric had married Eileen for her money, he had leisure to repent. Sam saw to it that his generous allowances went to his daughters, not to their husbands, and Eileen was financially independent. She spent her winters competing in horse shows, her summers playing tournament golf. The Phillips children were teenagers when their parents divorced, and they remained with their father: Eileen had virtually no chance of getting custody even if she had tried. Eric destroyed any reference to her in his personal papers and scissored her out of photograph albums. He remarried almost immediately, and added three stepchildren to his family. Diana was philosophical. "I felt, if they had to do it, it had to be done," she says. "My mother was always constant in my affection. I remember defending her; if somebody snubbed her, I would snub them. I loved her."

When Eileen walked away from the marriage, Sam ripped her portrait off the dining-room wall and, in language that must have made Parkwood tremble to its concrete foundations, forbade the family to communicate with her. They disobeyed him, of course. Her children visited her; Adelaide sent her surreptitious notes, and the loyalty and affection of her sisters never wavered. Eileen, exiled to a solitary life in Todmorden, on the northern fringe of Toronto, developed an independent career as a breeder of champion Kerry Blue terriers. Her father's wrath gradually abated, her portrait reappeared and, with both daughter and father feeling prickly, Eileen returned to Parkwood for family celebrations.

At General Motors of Canada, "Young Harry" Carmichael, as Sam always called him, was relegated to the role of the son Sam never had. "I spent a great deal of time at his home, playing billiards and cards," Carmichael recalled later. "They sort of adopted me there. I used to go out mornings with him and watch his horses work out. We had common interests there – we both had racing stables. He was always very helpful as far as the business was concerned. There was never, in any manner, shape or form, any interference. It was delightful to work with Mr. Sam."

Harry ran the company, but Mr. Sam took the credit. Sam refused to relinquish his title as president, or his perks, including his $70,000 salary and his seat on the General Motors board of directors. He denied "Young Harry" the status in the industry that was his due, and hindered his chances for advancement. Carmichael, for his part, refused to move to Oshawa, and commuted every day from St. Catharines. Sam had

King George VI and Queen Elizabeth ride in style in one of two dark-red McLaughlin–Buicks custom made for their Royal tour of Canada in the spring of 1939. (*McLaughlin Public Library*)

interfered in the strike, and he may have considered Carmichael too friendly with the workers. Carmichael had made peace, however, not because he was soft on unions, but because he knew, and Sam knew too, that their maximum effort would be required to win the coming war against Germany and Japan.

When Germany invaded Poland and Canada went to war on September 10, 1939, critics charged that the Canadian armed forces were caught flatfooted and unprepared for combat. It is true that Prime Minister Mackenzie King admired Hitler and had strongly supported the British policy of appeasement, but Canada's chief of defence staff, Lieutenant-General H. D. G. Crerar, had for several years been secretly experimenting with armoured vehicles. Crerar had no illusions about Hitler's intentions. "The zero hour will come when Germany is militarily prepared," Crerar wrote to a friend on April 11, 1936, "although action by Japan might influence Germany to move a bit earlier than she otherwise desires." Crerar predicted that Hitler would move first against Austria, later against France and Russia, and that the British would try to "steer clear" of a war between France and Germany.

In 1936, the British War Office belatedly began to convert its horse-drawn transport to motor vehicles. The British assumed that Canadian transport would conform to their specifications, and on April 20, 1936, a Canadian artillery colonel aptly named N. O. Carr returned from London with photographs of trucks and tractors being developed by British manufacturers, including General Motors' English subsidiary, Vauxhall.

The Vauxhall connection provided a golden opportunity for General Motors of Canada. Colonel Sam's honorary rank had not gained GM any business from the Defence department; the Canadian army was equipped with Fords. Now, however, GM engineers were included in an invitation to Camp Petawawa to discuss military vehicles, and Harry Carmichael followed up the meeting with a letter to the minister of defence, Ian McKenzie, offering the services of his "entire engineering and manufacturing divisions to assist your Government in any way that we can, should you care to use them."

Colonel Carr met with Carmichael and Sam McLaughlin on December 10, 1936, to discuss production of two British model armoured vehicles, a three-quarter-ton delivery truck with a short, 98-inch wheelbase and a six-wheel, 115-inch chassis for a 1.5-ton all-terrain vehicle. Both units would be equipped with Ford or Chevrolet engines, and production would be divided equally between Ford and GM. Both McLaughlin and Carmichael assured Carr of their willingness to co-operate with Ford, and Carmichael promised to sell the army his vehicles at cost.

GM delivered a prototype of a Chevrolet delivery truck to Petawawa in August 1937. It was pronounced satisfactory, and the army ordered seventy. Ford, however, had run into snags, and the army's order was reduced to fifty-one. GM could make them all, but the master of ordnance, Clive Caldwell, remained loyal to Ford. "In spite of the probability that one make of vehicle might be quoted at a lower price, it appears desirable that orders be distributed equally between the General Motors and Ford companies," he wrote in a memorandum. "This will ensure that a protected source of supply for these special vehicles will be conserved at each company."

Once the soldiers drove the Chevy truck, they discovered serious defects. It had no rearview mirror or tool box, the gas tank leaked, the engine overheated, the springs were too light, the seats were uncomfortable, and the celluloid windows in the side curtains cracked. The cab was too small for soldiers over five-foot-seven, and there was no room for a heater underneath the glove compartment. Ford gave up trying to make the truck at all, and while GM made major improvements, the company became mired in endless bickering with the army about who was responsible for broken axles and faulty steering. The six-wheel chassis experiment was a complete failure. The British insisted that extra wheels be attached with a heavy, English-made "bogie" that doubled the weight of the chassis. The vehicle was slow, the brakes didn't grab, and the extra weight burned out the bearings. "It has been decided not to pursue the question of conversion of lorries," the Canadian army's director of mechanization, E. F. Lynch, wrote tartly to the Canadian High Commissioner on October 8, 1938. "Should a more suitable design be evolved and tested the results will be forwarded to you."

The experiments effectively ended Canada's dependency on British military technology. On June 1, 1939, Harry Carmichael drove Colonel Carr around the back roads of Durham county in a new four-wheel-drive Pontiac truck that was about to be shipped to the Malay States. "This is very interesting," Carr reported to headquarters. "The whole design was evolved in Pontiac and all parts are at present being imported from the United States." Equipped with American army headlights, the Pontiac had eight speeds forward, two in reverse, and it easily hit forty-three miles per hour on the country roads. "The vehicle was most unstable," Carr reported, "but it was pointed out that the front end geometry had not been finally determined."

Carmichael offered to build two trucks for testing by the Canadian army, and asked Carr to give him specifications. "No mention of purchase was made," Carr reassured his superiors. "We should produce what we thought was the best vehicle and leave it to them to try to sell the idea abroad. I am of the opinion that it is advisable to go ahead on our own design based on our knowledge of British trends. Anything we produce on these lines which is satisfactory to us is likely to be at least equally satisfactory to other Empire countries."

General Motors engineers were hard at work on a Canadian Chevrolet truck when the war came, and Carmichael promised the Defence department total co-operation in the war effort. All military vehicles were standardized and their production split between GM and Ford (Chrysler was included later). Parts and bodies made by the rival companies were interchangeable, and everything was painted Service Green #22.

Initially, GM and Ford were in a peculiar position. The United States was not at war, and in Canada the two giant companies were fighting it out in the automobile market: General Motors of Canada sold 54,000 vehicles in 1939, Ford, 61,000. Conversion of their facilities to war production would dramatically curtail their automobile sales just as consumer demand was increasing, and both companies produced a relatively small number of military vehicles on contract during the first two years of the war. It wasn't until August 1941 that they finally signed a master agreement with the Canadian government, and the 1942 models were the last cars to be produced until the end of the war.

The agreement stipulated that the companies "should not be entitled to a profit in excess of five per cent (5%) on cost," a requirement that virtually guaranteed that company profits would never be less than 5 per cent. It set a minimum wage of thirty-five cents an hour for men over the age of eighteen, twenty-five cents for women. "Beginners" could be paid twenty cents a hour for the first four weeks, working up to the minimum after three months. These wages were higher than the Ontario minimum, and a "time is of the essence" clause opened the door to unlimited overtime.

For the first time since 1918, General Motors of Canada was acting independently: the United States did not go to war until the Japanese attack on Pearl Harbor in December 1941. Carmichael, having got Sam McLaughlin his war contract, left GM to join C. D. Howe's

Mosquito bombers ready for take off.
(*McLaughlin Public Library*)

Department of Munitions and Supply as director of wartime production. He sold all his GM shares, but he didn't forget his old company: in addition to trucks, tractors, ambulances, armoured cars, and tank bodies, General Motors of Canada was awarded contracts to build gun mounts and, in a throwback to the carriage days, wooden fuselages for de Havilland Mosquito aircraft.

"It took a war to put Oshawa on its feet," says Walter Kirby, a machinist hired as an apprentice in 1943 at the age of fifteen. "I was making twenty-nine cents an hour and I thought it was fantastic. We all wanted to go overseas. We said, 'The big guys are gone, we'll go next.' It was a great time for romance. The town was full of girls of eighteen and twenty with no fellas, so the older girls would date younger boys. It was real ego-building. We'd go down to the dance pavilion for thirty-five cents. It was the big-band era, Count Basie, Stan Kenton, Glenn Miller. The music was fabulous. A lot of things catapulted young people into being adults. We're little boys that got old."

Kirby created homemade explosive devices out of Pepsodent toothpowder cans, and he and his friends liked to blow holes in the bluffs near the lake. "Later, we'd hear about 'mysterious explosions at Camp X,'" he laughs. Camp X, a secret spy school and commando training centre set up by Intrepid, Sir William Stephenson, was located on the lake shore near Whitby. Local residents were threatened by armed guards if they ventured too close, and they grew used to hearing strange noises from the direction of the lake. Officers from Camp X occasionally came to Parkwood to use the swimming pool and squash court; they arrived at the back door in a van with blackout curtains, and departed as secretly as they came.

The Ontario Regiment was mobilized as a tank unit with its headquarters in the old Williams piano factory in Oshawa. "The men wanted tanks," writes regimental historian Len Schragg. "None was forthcoming. As a substitute, the officers improvised 'tank' demonstrations and tactics at the Oshawa country club with civilian automobiles. In desperation, the instructors gave their tank crews logs, and urged the crews to imagine that these wooden battering rams were tanks. The crews, of course, were incapable of such stretches of fancy, but the exercise did them no harm." In summer of 1943, equipped with American Sherman tanks, the Ontario Tank Regiment took part in the invasion of Sicily and fought with great courage in the long, bloody battle up the boot of Italy.

Hundreds of GM line workers enlisted in the armed forces and the company rehired women as welders, riveters, and aircraft builders. "There was no bitching about women working," says Kirby. "God, they were good. They were fantastic. Everybody knew the job and got on with it. There was no such thing as a shirker." Married women were hired: the company had no choice. Eileen Manning made armrests for trucks. The khaki fabric was thick, coarse, and saturated with non-flammable chemicals. "We earned our money," she says dryly. After Hitler invaded the Soviet Union in 1941, the Communists in the UAW supported the Liberal government's no-strike policy, at the same time recruiting all the new workers into the union, and when the Red Army defeated the Germans at the battle of Stalingrad in 1943, Premier Hepburn and Canadian Communist Party leader Tim Buck shook hands at a pro-Soviet rally in Maple Leaf Gardens.

Ninety General Motors of Canada employees were killed in action, and their brief, poignant obituaries were published in the company's monthly magazine, *War-Craftsman*: "Pte. George F. C. Lindsay died of wounds received while fighting in France, August 4. He worked in the Body Tool Department and was a member of the General Motors Choir." Wing Commander Lloyd Chadburn, son of the local Ford dealer, toured the Oshawa plant during a Victory Bond drive in April 1944. Nicknamed "Angel" because of his good looks and curly blond hair, Chadburn had led his "City of Oshawa" Spitfire squadron on more than one hundred sorties over occupied France, accounting for one hundred downed enemy aircraft, and he had been awarded the Distinguished Flying Cross and the Distinguished Service Order and bar. Chadburn modestly told the *War-Craftsman*: "It is swell to have the chance to do something while you are still young, when such an opportunity does not come to most men in a life time." On June 13, 1944, Chadburn's body was found in the wreckage of his Spitfire in Allied-occupied Normandy. He was twenty-four.

Sam relished the excitement of the war effort and delighted in showing off his plant to a stream of celebrities, including King George VI's younger brother, the Duke of Kent. Entertaining visitors gave Sam a chance to have his picture taken, and so many photographers and journalists traipsed through his plant that Nazi spies must have had details of Canada's armoured trucks down to the last screw. The British Eighth Army, however, credited Canada's Chevrolet truck as a major factor in their victory over General Rommel in North Africa, quoting an intercepted German reconnaissance order: "For this reconnaissance, as indeed for *every* desert reconnaissance, only captured English [Canadian] trucks are to be employed since German trucks stick in the sand too often." By the time the five-hundred-thousandth piece of military equipment rolled off the line on June 19, 1943, General Motors of Canada had produced $291-million worth of war matériel. The target for 1944 was $400 million, more than double the company's $150-million motor-vehicle output in a good peacetime year. With a 5-per-cent profit margin, General Motors of Canada stood to make $20 million. Sam, to show his support for gasoline rationing, hitched a horse to an old McLaughlin buggy and drove himself to work.

Sam and Adelaide relinquished their Bermuda house for use as a convalescent hospital during the war and remained at Parkwood for the winter. In January 1943, Sam's private secretary, J. J. English, phoned the Whitby Business College looking for an assistant. Ruth Bowman was despatched to Parkwood. "I was overwhelmed," she says. "I had just turned eighteen and I hadn't been in the college four months." Ruth was to work 9-to-5 and four hours on Saturday for ninety-five dollars a month, but many evenings she would be there until 8 p.m. "Mr. McLaughlin loved people around," she says. "He took a very proprietary interest in his staff. They were *his*. Mr. English was run off his feet all the time."

Sam called Ruth "Cutie" and conscripted her for croquet when all the letters had been typed: "He was a demon on the croquet pitch. He *hated* to lose. Oh, he was a very competitive man! I was frightened to death of him at first. He would let out a roar and everybody would jump. He would come banging in the door shouting *'Adelaide!*

The Canadian-built truck that won the Germans' respect in Africa. (*McLaughlin Public Library*)

Adelaide!' and take the stairs two or three at a time. He was volatile. He had the black Irish temperament. He would fall into the depths of a depression you wouldn't believe. He would sit bent over in a chair and not speak. We would try to cajole him out of it, but the mood would last for days. Christmas was usually the worst."

Sam could be the jolliest of companions when out with the boys, and a tyrant at home. "Mrs. McLaughlin was always covering up so Mr. McLaughlin wouldn't find out," says Ruth. "She was always saying: 'Don't tell Mr. McLaughlin!'" Sam and Adelaide occupied the same house, but "they seemed to be on different wavelengths," says Ruth. "They went their separate ways." Adelaide's silk-and-satinwood *boudoir* was at the front of the south wing, Sam's modernist Art Deco suite at the far end of the hall beside the back stairs. "It was the *coldest* room," says Ruth, who nearly froze taking dictation when Sam was in bed. Sam's bedroom was air-conditioned, and he kept it at an arctic temperature even when the fireplace was lit. The bedroom, with an adjoining dressing room and bathroom, had been decorated in 1940 by John Lyle in a minimalist style, and everything except the chestnut furniture was a uniform shade of apple green. A painting of three polar bears on an ice floe hung over Sam's bed.

Adelaide put Sam in his place by responding, "Oh, piffle!" to his more outrageous remarks. "She could beat him at chess and billiards," says Ruth. "*Then* he was angry! He frowned on the things she did. She could only have her Home and School friends to the house when he was not there. She never saw her old friends." Adelaide had taken a keen interest in the Home and School movement since 1920, and she served terms as national president of the Canadian Federation of Home and School Associations during the 1930s. It is tempting to cast Adelaide as an Eleanor Roosevelt, but far from being controversial or radical, Adelaide's views reflected her conservative, conventional Christian faith: the role of the school, like the church, was to uplift and inspire as well as instruct. She succeeded, however, in having music included in the curriculum.

Adelaide's charitable activities gave her access to a feminine world that excluded and irritated her husband, and she kept up a voluminous correspondence with women friends across the country. When Sam was away, Adelaide would steal out to the Mowbray farm at Kinsale to visit her unmarried sister, Louella. Sam disliked Louella, who highly disapproved of him, and his Methodist Mowbray kin were infrequent visitors to Parkwood. Adelaide, however, kept track of them all, and she sent her nieces and nephews well-chosen gifts on appropriate occasions.

Adelaide sat in Sam's box at Woodbine for the annual running of the King's Plate, but she rarely went near the stables or visited the plant. At home, she had no privacy and no freedom: Sam gave her money, Hayes drove her car, Lindsay ran her house, English paid her staff, and Sargent ruled the garden. Turner, her loyal and beloved personal maid, cleaned her clothes and, in the basement, Lee King washed and ironed her Egyptian cotton sheets and Irish linen tablecloths.

"Mrs. McLaughlin didn't have a chance to touch anything," Ruth says. "When I was married, she came to visit us in our little bungalow. I remember her standing in my tiny kitchen saying, 'I've always wanted a kitchen like this.' She loved their cottage by the lake. There she could play 'house.' Sam hated it. She didn't really want to entertain, and there was someone for dinner every night. She would have been perfectly happy to putter along, write letters, do her needlepoint and knitting."

Adelaide tried her best to get out of the dinner parties: she served war-ration recipes. "They were awful," says Ruth. "Just *awful*." Adelaide drew a family tree that went back to her mother's United Empire Loyalist ancestors – she pointedly ignored the McLaughlins – and she became an active member of Canada's U.E.L. Association. At seventy, Adelaide looked like what she was, a kindly, strict grandmother, and her nest was empty. All the McLaughlin daughters had left Oshawa, taking their children with them. Isabel and Eileen were in Toronto; Hilda and John Pangman had settled in Montreal, Billie was in England where Churchill Mann had become a staff officer with the Canadian army, and Mildred, unhappily married for the second time, lived in Florida. Mildred's three surviving sons were American citizens; John, the eldest, had been killed by a car at the age of nine.

If she felt sad or lonely, Adelaide put on a happy face and suppressed her emotions. She was very conscious of her role as the lady of the manor – she arrived at church basement meetings in her chauffeured car – and she clung to the presidency of the hospital auxiliary as fiercely as Sam clung to General Motors. She was ambivalent about her wealth: she loved clothes and jewellery and all the beautiful things that money could buy, but she would hire a dressmaker to patch an old, torn blouse.

Adelaide called Sam, in public at least, "my dear husband," and, to Sam, Adelaide was always "the best wife a man could have." For better or worse, they put up with each other. Sam's sister, Mary Jane, had divorced her husband, J. B. McCulloch, in 1919, and she was so humiliated by the experience she became a virtual recluse. Adelaide was not a woman to ruin her reputation, and she had no patience with self-pity. In a 1933 letter to a friend, Mrs. L. A. Vanskiver, Adelaide writes: "Mother is better than she was a year ago. Of course each week she thinks will be her last. Each time I go out she thinks when I leave it is the last good-bye. I told her yesterday she was not to say that to me again, that I had heard it too often and was tired of it. Sometimes I think they feel that I am rather hard hearted." Adelaide was made of stern stuff. She took pride in doing her duty, and found solace in reading the Bible. Any idea of freedom had vanished in her youth, when she was denied the opportunity to go to university. "I felt sorry for Mrs. McLaughlin," Ruth says. "She was squashed." By the end of the war, Adelaide had a new rival for Sam's attentions, a capable and attractive young nurse, Margaret Nelson.

13

NURSIE

In 1945 the McLaughlins gave the now-vacant Phillips mansion to the YWCA, and while Adelaide was inspecting the renovations, she fell down the back stairs. Her leg was broken in several places, and she spent weeks in the Oshawa General Hospital. Margaret Nelson, the supervisor on her wing, was one of the few young nurses tall and strong enough to lift Adelaide, who had become enormous. Adelaide grew very fond of her, and Margaret soon found herself at Adelaide's beck and call. She was on vacation back home in Wyoming, Ontario, when Adelaide was due to leave the hospital, but Adelaide said, "I'll just wait until Miss Nelson gets back," and she did. The wish of the hospital's founder and benefactor was a command, and when Adelaide insisted that Miss Nelson to come to Parkwood as her private nurse, she could hardly refuse.

"I was very apprehensive," Marg says. "I didn't want to get pinned down. Not that I disliked her. I thought, 'I'll get stuck with the night shift.' What could I do?"

Adelaide told her: "I don't really need a nurse. I am just so used to having you around." Miss Nelson refused to work nights, and made it clear that she would come and go through the front door. Her dignity, intelligence, and Irish sense of humour won Adelaide's respect, and she quickly became indispensable: before Adelaide was back on her feet, Sam suffered an embolism, a serious blockage to the pulmonary artery. He was carried away on a stretcher, calling out "Goodbye, Mama!" as he passed Adelaide's bedroom door, and he underwent emergency surgery in the Toronto General Hospital.

"He was very ill," Marg says. "He was frightened." She was standing by Sam's bed when he came out of the anaesthetic. "He just beamed all over! He was so glad to realize he was alive. Two arms came out, and I got a big bear hug. My cap came flying off. There was the supervisor standing in the doorway. I felt like a nickel."

There were as many as five nurses on duty at Parkwood when Sam came home, but he monopolized Miss Nelson. "Mama, I've stolen your nurse!" he crowed to Adelaide. Having a nurse in attendance was a new perk for Sam, and he loved to show Miss Nelson off to his visitors. Introducing her one day he forgot her name, and in exasperation blurted out "Nursie." She laughed, although Adelaide thought Sam was being too familiar, and "Nursie" she remained until Sam died nearly thirty years later.

"Mr. McLaughlin was a tease," she says. "He was full of fun. He told the most awful, off-colour stories. You never knew what he was apt to do. Mrs. McLaughlin thought she was keeping him on the straight and narrow. She would say, 'Oh, Sam!' in the most disgusted voice." Sam's sense of humour could be gross. He strode into one General Motors board of directors' meeting wearing a black lace brassiere stuffed with huge foam-rubber "falsies" strapped over his suit jacket, and he infuriated a stuffy GM president at a reception by bellowing, on being introduced to the man's obese wife, "It looks like you've been feeding her too many oats!"

Nursie's acid test came on her first trip to Bermuda. "I was 'elected' to go," she says. "I had never been farther away from home than Oshawa. Mrs. McLaughlin was on crutches, Mr. McLaughlin on medication. We took a private railway car to Montreal, then to Baltimore, where we were to catch the flying boat. There was a new maid with us. She was very nervous, and on the way to Baltimore she went completely off her rocker." The maid locked herself in the bathroom, and while Nursie, in her nightgown and hair curlers, was trying to coax her out, Sam pointed out the window toward two specks in the harbour. "You see that plane?" he said. "You see that rowboat there? That's how we get to the plane." Says Nursie: "I knew he was pulling my leg. 'Your face didn't change expression at all!' he said. He didn't get any fun out of it."

Sam had met his match. Nursie held over him the power of life and death, and she wouldn't be bullied. "He'd come home from the office," she says, "and the front door would bang so it would practically shake the house. 'Come on, girls, time for a game before lunch!' We played cards, dominoes; there were rousing games of croquet that went on after dusk. He wanted me to learn to play bridge. I flatly refused. I was glad I hadn't given in to that. Bridge evenings were the only free time I had. Once on the plane to Bermuda, Mrs. McLaughlin said: 'I knew we should have brought Scrabble.' I thought: 'Oh God, that's all I need!' We had *altogether too many games*."

Nursie was absorbed into the McLaughlin menage as a surrogate daughter, a vivacious companion who helped keep everyone entertained. "You didn't leave at 4 o'clock," she says. "It was tea time. Then it was game time. Then you stayed for dinner. It was easier to go to bed there." She was given Sam's old Spanish-style bedroom adjoining Adelaide's suite. Nursie liked to read in the evenings; Adelaide loved crossword puzzles. "Mrs. McLaughlin was a real night owl. She believed that time spent in bed was wasted time. I was tired. I was dying to get into bed. She would call: 'Come and sit beside me and we'll have a look at this crossword puzzle.' Oh, dear! She was already snug in bed!"

Nursie woke Sam in time for the 8 a.m. radio news, and tucked him into bed in time for the 11 p.m. news. She accompanied him everywhere: to board meetings in Toronto and New York, to his office, to the jockey club at Woodbine, and to his Cap Chat fishing lodge. "Mrs. McLaughlin *was* jealous," Nursie says. "I knew she was. She soon got over it." Sam's health was more fragile than he liked people to know. He suffered from fevers and bouts of pneumonia, and he had developed a rectal abscess that had to be cleaned and dressed. Nursie took his temperature, administered his antibiotics, and helped him evacuate his bowels. "He had a perfect horror of cancer," she says. "If any of his friends had it, he thought of them as already gone." George McLaughlin had died of bowel cancer, and during the last year of his life, George had employed a private nurse.

Nursie was the only person who could boss Sam around, and her strictness allowed him to indulge in the infantile pleasures of being both scolded and coddled. In her white shoes and cap, Nursie was the physical embodiment of the white-robed "Spirit of the Enchanted Island" Frederick Challener had painted in Sam's hallway mural, and while their relationship was not a love affair in the sexual sense, it was affectionate, intense, and enduring. Sam enjoyed the salacious gossip Nursie caused; Nursie ignored it, and made Sam take his pills.

Every October, Sam dragged Nursie off for a week of duck shooting at the exclusive Long Point Club on the marshy north shore of Lake Erie. Membership was restricted to about a dozen elderly, millionaire members – Henry and Junius Morgan were among the most prominent – and living conditions were Spartan. Each member was assigned to a red frame cottage perched on stilts over the marsh; the cottages were not insulated and on stormy days the wind whistled up through the floorboards. Sam went off into the marsh with his punter at dawn, and Nursie spent the day keeping the fireplace going:

"I was supposed to listen to the World Series and tell them the score when they came in. I am not sports-minded. I would be reading or sewing, having a snooze, and I'd suddenly come to and think, 'Oh! I don't know what's going on at all!'" None of the other members thought to bring a nurse, and if anyone needed a hot compress or a cough remedy, Sam breezily promised: "Nursie will fix you up in no time." She cured an American financier of the hiccups by placing a paper bag over his head, taking care that he didn't suffocate, and spent an uncomfortable night sleeping on his couch. She was the only woman among the guests – wives and mistresses were restricted to one week in the summer – and while she got along well with Junius Morgan, she was not invited to the evening cocktail hour at Morgan's cabin, the "Sin Center."

Nursie was unfazed by money or social status. When she bumped into Canada's governor general, Lord Alexander of Tunis, on the Long Point boardwalk, she smiled and said hello. "Didn't you curtsey?" Adelaide's English maid, Turner, asked later. Says Marg: "I couldn't think of anything more ridiculous than curtseying in the middle of the boardwalk in the marsh. I was all dressed up in my woollies."

Nursie was paid the standard nurse's wage, with one day off a week, and Sam tested her patience. "One day it was very stormy, and by the time it was getting dark all the men were in except Mr. McLaughlin. Soon it was pitch dark. No Mr. McLaughlin. The manager said: 'I don't know where to start looking for him.' We waited, and soon, in the dark, we heard a man's voice out on the lake singing. It was Mr. McLaughlin.

He was singing 'Bringing in the Sheaves' at the top of his lungs and bailing the boat. His punter, Wilf Snooks, was scared stiff. They had decided to stay out to get some more ducks, and they had been caught in the storm. Well, they made it. I was so mad at Mr. McLaughlin I could have given him a shake. That was one time he didn't get pneumonia when he should have."

Every November, Nursie went pheasant shooting with Sam on his private game preserve in Georgian Bay, Griffith Island. The largest of three offshore islands north of Owen Sound, Griffith had been logged, farmed, and mined for gravel; in 1943 Sam and Jack Bickell bought the twenty-six-hundred-acre island through a syndicate they formed with stockbroker Ben "Bet a Million" Smith, a Texas oil millionaire, a Seagram, and Frank Farwell, president of Canada Coach Lines. The syndicate imported a championship Hereford bull and forty cows, but the cattle operation was a screen for their real intent: breeding deer and pheasants for private shooting parties.

Pheasant chicks were raised in incubators from imported eggs then shooed out into the bush; prime golden pheasants were kept in pens. Gordon Macauley, a reporter with the Owen Sound *Daily Sun-Times* who visited the island in 1945, estimated the pheasant population at twenty thousand: "The sky seemed to darken and a sound like thunder smote our ears as a flock of the birds rose from the ground directly in front of us," he wrote. "It would be impossible to be long on the island without seeing deer. The herd numbers in the neighbourhood of two hundred and it is not unusual to see forty to fifty of the graceful animals together at a time. Smaller groups are quite common and roam at will about the island. The deer are fairly tame, though perhaps it is due more to their natural inquisitiveness that keeps them silently watching from the bushes until one is almost on top of them before suddenly dashing away at full speed causing pheasant to scatter in every direction."

Macauley described Griffith as "a hunter's paradise." A staff of gamekeepers patrolled the island to scare off poachers; they shot the wolves and foxes and trapped the hawks. A road circled the island, and near the wharf an old farmhouse had been transformed into a comfortable lodge with electric light, hot running water, a propane stove and refrigerator, and a radio telephone. Sam's guests were ferried over from Big Bay in an open motor launch, along with a chef Sam hired from the CPR and a load of liquor Lowry picked up in Wiarton. "The fella in the store asked me if I were a bootlegger!" Lowry laughs.

"Every year I shot a deer for the boss and one for myself," Lowry says. "He'd have company up there, and some of them, hell, they couldn't hit a barn door. The boss used to lend me to Lord Alexander to be his guide up there. He'd come to Owen Sound with three coaches on a train. We'd go by boat about four and a half miles from the mainland. By cracky, it would get rough sometimes. I remember the last year he went up. The day he was to come away it was wet snow, and we went out and we got the deer. Of course you had to bleed the deer, and put it on a rack on the side of the tractor, guns on the other side, and so we were all wet, mud, and blood, and we brought it down to the camp. He said, 'How soon can we leave?' I said, 'As soon as I get cleaned up.' He said, 'Ah, don't get cleaned up. Nobody knows us. Let's go as we are.'

"We got to Owen Sound and he said, 'I got some of the nicest apples here I've ever had in my life. Do you know where they got them?' I said yeah, and we walked around the corner to the store. Then he said, 'Do you know of a good magazine store?' I said yeah, so we went there, another block, and he said, 'We had some lovely trout,' so we went and got the last two trout in this store, about ten pounds apiece, and he bought them too. And here is him and I carrying apples and trout and magazines and stuff coming back down to the car and nobody had any idea he was the governor general. So we went to the train and he said, 'Well, come on in, Lowry, and have a farewell drink. I'm out of a job. I have to go back to England and I'll miss this next year.' So we had a couple of drinks. He was just the nicest guy that ever was."

Lord Alexander drank Irish whiskey neat, out of a tumbler, as if it were a glass of milk, and he went for a swim in the bay every morning, his pyjamas flapping in the freezing wind. Marg Nelson remembers his first trip to Griffith Island: "It was rough. We picked up a man with two bird dogs. The dogs were sick. The CPR chef got sick. When we arrived, the house staff had all gone. The CPR chef decided that I would wait on table. I said, 'No I won't! I'll peel potatoes, I'll hand you the food but I will not wait on table.' Mr. Bickell went into Owen Sound and came back with a linen tablecloth and a dozen unhemmed napkins. He tossed them to me, 'Here, Nursie can hem these up.' I hemmed six napkins before dinner. I could have killed him."

During the daytime, she tramped through the bush. "I was the bird dog," she says. "I went out and picked up the birds and wrung their necks, just gave them a flip. The poor things weren't quite dead. I was amazed at myself; I wouldn't chop the head off a chicken. I carried the shells. I carried an extra gun. Mr. McLaughlin said that in England a bearer always carried an extra gun, loaded, and handed it over, and he was getting me primed to do this too. At one time, the gun went off. It's a wonder I didn't shoot Mr. McLaughlin."

Sam's hunting companions were all old men, and one of them, his heart surgeon, Dr. John Oille, was blind in one eye. "You are never supposed to shoot at low-flying birds," Nursie says, "but he was a determined man and I could just imagine him thinking, 'I'm not going to let that bird get away from me!' I got hit in the behind. It almost knocked me flat on my face. It was the strangest feeling. It burned so much I sat right down in the snow." A blast of buckshot had torn through her leather jacket and peppered her back from her shoulders to her calves. Her wounds were only skin-deep, and Dr. Oille comforted her with the words: "Those little pellets are red hot. You don't have to worry about infection." Sam had received a pellet in the leg, and Nursie's pain was soon forgotten in the firestorm of his rage. "Oh my, Mr McLaughlin was mad!" she says. "We left for home the next day." For many years, as she undressed, she would hear a 'ping' as a pellet fell out, and as soon as Sam cooled off, he joked about her as "the nurse with lead in her ass."

Sam resigned as president of General Motors of Canada in 1945 at the age of seventy-five, but he retained his office and his staff, and he mercilessly pestered his successor, William Wecker, a pale product of GM's executive assembly line. General Motors had begun turning out automobiles as soon as the war ended in 1945, and by 1949 GM's Canadian production had climbed back to ninety-three thousand vehicles, the highest sales volume since the 1929 Crash. Canada had

Sam McLaughlin and Margaret Nelson hunting on Griffith Island. (*Parkwood*)

emerged from the war a mechanized nation. Wages were rising, and the auto workers had negotiated a one-week paid vacation. "I remember the first time we raised it with Carmichael," says Harry Benson. "He just laughed, a big guffaw. Like, how crazy can you get?"

On June 30, 1949, in a U.S. District Court in Chicago, lawyers for the United States of America filed a civil action against E. I. du Pont de Nemours and Company, Christiana Securities, General Motors Corporation, and United States Rubber, charging them with conspiracy "to restrain trade" in certain of their products and "to monopolize a substantial part of such trade" in violation of the Sherman Act. The suit also claimed that the du Pont company had acquired an illegal controlling interest in General Motors.

The antitrust suit was the culmination of an exhaustive investigation into Pierre du Pont's financial interests in General Motors dating back to his original purchase of shares in 1915. U.S. prosecutors charged that du Pont's investment had been deliberately calculated to secure for his company the "green pastures" of General Motors, and that he subsequently bought up paint, plastic, and chemical companies that serviced GM to provide himself with a "closed market." The voluminous evidence revealed a network of syndicates, holding companies, and interlocking directorships dominated by members of the du Pont family and du Pont executives – Alfred P. Sloan had been elected to the du Pont board twelve days after he became president of General Motors – and it appeared that du Pont companies were using insider information and sweetheart deals to cut out cheaper competition.

The most incriminating document was the 1917 memo to Pierre du Pont from J. J. Raskob stating that du Pont people would "assume charge and be responsible for the financial operation" of General Motors. It continued: "Our interest in the General Motors Company will undoubtedly secure for us the entire Fabrikoid, Pyralin, paint and varnish business of those companies, which is a substantial factor." Raskob's files revealed his incestuous role in the McLaughlins' sale of their General Motors shares to du Pont in 1918, and investigators turned up a revealing letter from R. S. McLaughlin to A. B. Purvis, Canadian president of Canadian Industries Limited, that suggested that General Motors of Canada was taking orders from a du Pont subsidiary, U.S. Rubber.

Du Pont held a substantial interest in CIL, and CIL owned 35 per cent of the Dunlop Tire Company. In a "personal and confidential" letter dated March 25, 1929, Sam explained to Purvis why Dunlop was getting a relatively small share of his tire business. "It was only through solicitation from New York, from Sir Harry McGowan, and from Mr. McMaster [directors of General Motors] that we consented to give the Dunlop Company the percentage of the business which they have been getting from us for some years. Their product was not satisfactory a number of years ago."

Sam went on to say that "a new situation has arisen, namely that the DuPont Corporation has taken a very large interest in the United States Tire Company, which owns and controls the Dominion Rubber Company. The DuPont interest, I have been told, amounted to nearly $200,000,000, and, of course, they naturally would like to see us do some business with the Dominion Rubber Company." Within weeks, Sam's Dunlop business had been transferred to Dominion Rubber.

Purvis was furious. He wrote to the president of the du Pont company, Lammot du Pont, and enclosed Sam's letter. "Insofar as the investment the DuPont Company has in Canadian Dunlop through Canadian Industries is a company investment, as distinct from our understanding that the investment in United States Rubber Company (the parent company of Dominion Rubber) is held by DuPont individuals, I am hoping it will be possible for you to do something for us to relieve General Motors at Oshawa from the evident pressure to which Mr. McLaughlin refers. At the present state of Dunlop Canada's affairs, the taking away of this business may be vital."

Lammot du Pont passed the letters on to the president of U.S. Rubber, F. B. Davis. "Now it is, of course, all right for United States Rubber to 'go after' the General Motors of Canada business through the Dominion Rubber Company," du Pont wrote, "but I do not believe it is either fair or proper, under the circumstances, to use as an argument the interests of the U.S. Rubber stockholders or their connection with General Motors. Could you not get the business on the basis of quality, services and prices?"

Davis' reply to Lammot's letter incriminated Sam even further. "Early in 1929," he wrote, "Mr. Eden, president of our Dominion Rubber Company, told me that he had been working to get a portion of General Motors of Canada business and had been told by Mr. McLaughlin that he would be very glad to give him a portion of his business but that his hands were tied as he had a letter of instructions from Mr. John L. Pratt of the General Motors Company requiring him to favour Dunlop. Mr. McLaughlin further stated that if Mr. Eden were able to get this letter rescinded he would then be able to give the Dominion Rubber Company some of his tire business, that he recognized the quality and service he could receive and that he felt this was better than he was getting from the Dunlop Company, with whom his relations were not particularly pleasant. Mr Pratt arranged to have the instructions, whatever they might have been, rescinded."

Pratt's letter was never produced, and Pratt claimed under oath: "I don't see under any condition that I could have given any such instructions." In fact, while Dunlop's General Motors business had dwindled from $716,000 to $44,000 between 1928 and 1930, and Dominion Rubber's had increased from $6,000 to $57,000, General Motors of Canada had been buying the bulk of its tires from Goodyear. The U.S. government eventually dropped its case against U.S. Rubber and Sam was exonerated of any complicity: the judge decided he had been merely making up excuses to deny his business to both Dunlop and Dominion Rubber.

Sam emerged as either a knave or fool, and the antitrust suit, which dragged through the courts for years, cast a pall over General Motors. In 1951, a combination of personal embarrassment and financial worry may have prompted Sam to sell 100,000 GM shares for $2.5 million and embark, at the age of eighty, on a new career as a philanthropist.

The R. Samuel McLaughlin Foundation was incorporated on August 8, 1951, and the trustees were instructed to "expend the net income of the foundation for a period of fifty years in such a manner as shall constitute a charitable object of learning, teaching and education, primarily in the medical and health and physical and mental therapy fields." The medical slant reflected Sam's own concern about his health, and his motives were not entirely selfless; recent changes in Canadian law made charitable foundations attractive tax shelters.

Sam was a latecomer to the idea of giving his money away, and he liked to have his name on his monuments. Adelaide Hall and the McLaughlin engineering building at Queen's University in Kingston, Ontario, had been Sam's first major forays into public benefaction, and Queen's had rewarded him with an honorary Doctor of Laws degree in 1946. The inspiration for the McLaughlin Foundation came from Dr. W. E. Gallie, retired chief of surgery at the Toronto General Hospital, through Sam's stockbroker, J. C. Fraser. Fraser had been investing the McLaughlins' money for forty years, and he had gradually assumed the role of chancellor of the exchequer in Sam's little court. Sam's first phone call of the day was to the dusty old Bay Street offices of Fraser & Dingman, and he expected Fraser to do as he was told. "If Sam were sitting here and said, 'Get down on the floor and crawl to me like a snake,' I would have done it," Fraser once told his junior partner, Jack Lewis. "And he did," Lewis adds. Fraser travelled with Sam, placing stock orders by telegraph from railway stations; he fished with him at Cap Chat, and he and his wife spent weeks as the McLaughlins' guests at Cedar Lodge in Bermuda. His McLaughlin account made Fraser wealthy, and he was able to use Sam's insider tips to make money for his other clients.

Among them was Dr. Gallie. A big, warm-hearted man with great personal magnetism, he had retired after an outstanding career as a physician and a teacher of surgery – his devoted students called themselves the "Gallie slaves" – and he was concerned that young doctors graduating from the University of Toronto could not afford to continue their research overseas. He approached Fraser with the idea of establishing annual travelling fellowships for outstanding graduate students from across Canada. Dr. Gallie asked: "How are we going to pay for this, Jack?"

They both knew exactly how, but separating Sam from his money

J. C. Fraser hoisting a trophy salmon at Cap Chat. (*Ewart McLaughlin Collection*)

was a task to be approached with great caution; if Sam thought they were gouging him, they would both find their heads on pikes at Parkwood's gates. Fraser had introduced Dr. Gallie to Sam in July 1944 when he had accompanied Fraser and Dr. Oille to Cap Chat for a week's fishing. Dr. Gallie could fish – he killed seven salmon, two more than Sam – play bridge, hold his whisky, and tell ribald medical stories that kept Sam in stitches. The two of them hit it off, and the fishing foursome became an annual event. It was likely in late June 1950, when heavy rains and a turbulent river kept them confined to the lodge, that Dr. Gallie and Fraser successfully broached the idea of the medical fellowships.

The idea appealed to Sam's nostalgia for his own youth, and he always called the McLaughlin fellows his "boys," even though they included women. Dr. Gallie stipulated that every fellow return to Canada to take a teaching position at a university, a more imaginative approach than pouring money into concrete, and since 1952 nearly nine hundred Canadian medical students have been awarded McLaughlin Fellowships totalling almost $18 million. When Dr. Gallie died of cancer in 1959, Sam endowed the Dr. W. E. Gallie Visiting Professorship at the Royal College of Physicians and Surgeons in Ottawa, and before Sam's death in 1972, the McLaughlin Foundation contributed $8 million toward medical research and education at Ontario universities.

Mr. Sam, the squire of Parkwood, was rehearsing his new role as Colonel Sam, the benevolent, white-haired old patriarch. In 1950, Sam sold his farm and racing stable to Toronto brewery tycoon E. P. Taylor; Taylor renamed the farm Windfields and sold off all Sam's horses. Sam's horses had never won a race in the coveted Triple Crown of North American racing, and while three Parkwood horses had won the King's Plate – Horometer in 1934, Kingarvie in 1944, and Mouldy in 1947 – Sam's failures had been exasperating and expensive. He had grown too old to go for his daily canters along the banks of the Oshawa Creek, and his horses had won the Orpen Cup, a gold cup and saucer, so often that the Orpens presented him with an entire gold tea service.

"Actually, Eddie Taylor had no intention of buying Colonel McLaughlin's farm," Muriel Lennox writes in *E. P. Taylor: A Horseman and His Horses*. "Over the past few years he had spent a tidy sum obtaining property adjacent to his acreage on Bayview Avenue and developing, if not the largest, certainly the most impressive and elaborate breeding farm in the country." Taylor's Bayview farm, however, was rapidly being surrounded by housing developments, and after moving his horses and stables out to Parkwood, Taylor developed the southern part of his property into a suburb he called Don Mills.

Don Mills perfected the symbiosis between the country and the car. It was an isolated enclosure of interlocking crescents miles from down-town, surrounded on all sides by freeways, and its heart was a shopping mall. There were no sidewalks, and the houses were spaced far enough apart to make walking a chore. Each house was reached by a wide private driveway ending in an open carport by the side door. The carport was impractical for the Canadian climate – it was replaced in other suburbs by an attached garage which moved around to the front of the house as the automobile's domestic dominance increased – but the carport's real purpose was to display the family car, or cars.

Don Mills residents drove to work, and if Dad had the car all day at the office, Mum needed another car, preferably a station wagon, to do the shopping and drive the kids around. The number of cars in the driveway, their age, make, and price, telegraphed a family's material status, while the colour combinations gave a hint of their taste. Washing the car, along with mowing the lawn, became a weekend ritual; a dirty car, like an unkempt yard, offended the mystique that suburban living was clean, healthy, and morally superior to living downtown. Cars were huge and heavy; their Cold War design owed a good deal to the armoured truck and the airplane, and if the tail fins on the 1953 Cadillac seemed a little decadent, well, Canadians were ready to have some fun.

"Money sells cars," says Bill Austin, hired as assistant to the presi-dent and director of public relations for General Motors of Canada in 1954. Consumer spending was up after twenty years of war and depres-sion, and so was the birth rate. The "baby boom" created a demand for automobiles the industry hadn't experienced since the Roaring Twenties. In 1950, production at General Motors of Canada soared to 160,000 vehicles, 56,000 more than the previous peak in 1929, and during the next three years production increased by 20,000 vehicles a year to a record of 220,000 in 1953.

"How can you have overproduction?" scoffed GM president Charles E. Wilson when he opened a new Frigidaire plant in Scarborough on October 16, 1952. "People always want and need more and more of everything. The most satisfactory thing for a country is to produce

more and more and so have more and more for everyone." A
refrigerator was a necessity, and modern new homes were equipped
with automatic washers and dryers, although some housewives still
stubbornly hung their washing on the line. Houses built for two-car
families usually had two bathrooms, and the bathrooms grew in size
and luxury in tandem with the cars. Bathroom and kitchen appliances
came in pastel shades of pink, green, and yellow, and walls were
covered with matching plastic tile; the kitchen table was chrome, the
chairs vinyl, and the floor linoleum tile. The house was being remade
in the image of the car.

Earlier that fall, at the Canadian National Exhibition's annual automobile show, Sam McLaughlin would have noticed a peculiar, bug-
shaped little runabout with the engine in the rear. Six Volkswagen
Beetles had been driven up from the U.S. for the show, and with them
came a tall, charismatic German salesman, Werner Jansen. "People
snickered and smiled," says Bill Dalglish, one of Volkswagen's original
dealers. "They thought it was a funny little car that wouldn't sell." At
the CNE, Volkswagen was assigned to the Cow Palace; the Big Three
American manufacturers had monopolized the Automotive Building.

Canada was Volkswagen's test market in North America because
Canadians were familiar with small, cheap British imports: Hillman,
Austin, Morris, and Sunbeam. British cars were imported duty-free,
and they were the cheapest new cars on the market; they were also
cramped, cold, underpowered, and prone to break down. They had,
however, a certain quaint charm, and the sports models were fun.

"I bought a little red MG after university," says Ewart's son, Dick,
who was hired as a junior engineer at the GM Oshawa plant in 1948.
Dick's English car was a gesture of independence: his Uncle Sam was
notorious for banning all Fords and foreign cars he spotted in the office
parking lot. Dick had carefully avoided using family pull to get a job
with GM; he had been accepted by the National Research Council in
Chalk River, and it was only after his NRC job was abruptly cancelled
that he applied for an opening at GM. "The chief engineer was against
hiring me," he laughs. "He asked: 'Who will fire him?'"

Dick stayed out of Sam's way, but one morning he was sent to the
president's office with some papers. "I had never been there before. I
had to go through this big, oak-panelled door with the brass signs on it,
'President,' 'Chairman,' very impressive. I wanted out of there as
quickly as I could. I gave the package to Mr. Wecker's secretary and I

had just come out the door when who do I see coming towards me down this long hallway but Colonel Sam and his entourage, Nursie, Lowry, I don't know who all else. Colonel Sam was a very impressive man, he always had a double-breasted suit, hat on, and he swung his arms as he marched, so I sort of got off to the side to let him pass. As soon as he saw me he stopped dead in his tracks and he said: 'Dick! Are you still driving that little MG?' I said, 'No sir, I've got a new Chevrolet convertible.' 'Good!' he said. 'Don't ever let me see you driving a foreign car again!' And then he took off, with everybody trooping behind him. I didn't tell him that I had sold my MG to my dad."

Volkswagen had sold only eight cars in Canada by Christmas 1952. The Beetle was "rather primitive" says Dalglish, but Volkswagen dealers stocked plenty of spare parts and offered efficient, friendly service. A sophisticated advertising campaign endowed the car with a cute "personality," and older drivers fondly compared it to the Model T. By 1955, Volkswagen's Canadian sales had climbed to 7,390, and a gleaming new chrome and glass service centre had been built on Scarborough's Golden Mile, right across the road from Frigidaire.

The Bug was more than a speck on the windshield for General Motors of Canada; imports of all foreign cars had grown to 12 per cent of the Canadian market, and by 1955 GM's sales were in a serious slump. Part of the reason was bad publicity: the U.S. antitrust suit had been making headlines across North America since it had gone to trial in 1953. In December 1954, Illinois judge Walter La Buy acquitted the corporations, but his verdict was eventually overturned by the United States Supreme Court, which found E. I. du Pont de Nemours and Company and General Motors Corporation guilty of behaviour likely to result in restraint of trade. Du Pont ultimately divested itself of its shares in General Motors.

In September 1955, only a year after it had built a sprawling modern assembly plant near Lake Ontario, GM's Oshawa operation was shut down by a five-month strike. Local 222 remained one of the most militant in the UAW. The membership was still split between the radicals and the moderates, or between those who opposed international UAW president Walter Reuther and those who supported him. Cliff Pilkey, then president of Local 222, describes Reuther as "a man with a halo around his head," and UAW policy and strategy were determined in an atmosphere of backbiting, name-calling, and purges. Homer Martin had been the first to be dumped, and, soon after, Charlie Millard had been defeated as Canadian director by Vince Jewison's old friend, George Burt. Vince wryly describes Burt as "the Mackenzie King of union politics," and Burt needed all King's skills of equivocation to keep peace between the Canadian factions and make friends with the Americans.

Walter Reuther, with the help of his brothers, Ray and Victor, used the union's internal turmoil to establish himself firmly in the centre and absolutely in control. Reuther used his personal friendship with GM president Charles E. Wilson to explore the idea of a "partnership" between workers and management that would stabilize the automobile industry. The initiative had come from GM. "General Motors believes in high wages," the corporation baldly stated in a supplement to its 1937 agreement with the UAW, "and will continue to pay high wages in the future as it has in the past." The corporation wasn't being entirely altruistic: high wages tightened the screws on smaller manufacturers such as Nash and Studebaker, who did not enjoy the Big Three's economies of scale, and they were a mixed blessing for the workers, who were laid off without pay for weeks every year while the manufacturers retooled the plants for the new models. As Harry Benson puts it: "You got rich by the hour and starved by the year."

Alfred P. Sloan had explored the possibility of smoothing out the annual production cycles by advancing workers part of their wages during slow months, but he had rejected the idea of a guaranteed annual wage. Instead, Reuther and Wilson worked out a *modus operandi* whereby General Motors would give its workers security through old-age pensions, vacations, health care, and other benefits in addition to their hourly wage; in return, the workers would give the corporation complete freedom to make engineering and production decisions.

In 1949, the UAW had signed a five-year contract with General Motors of Canada in return for a wage of a dollar an hour, a pension plan, medical benefits, and a reduction in the work week to forty hours. A shorter work week, however, meant a smaller paycheque, and the contract didn't stop auto workers being laid off when the economy slid into recession. Wages were falling behind inflation, and the workers were not sharing proportionally in the Big Three's enormous profits.

GM agreed to reopen the contract in 1953, and an acrimonious battle broke out between Local 222 and the international over the company's offer: an increase of five cents an hour, and, in the event of a layoff, a supplementary benefit to make up the difference between unemployment insurance and the worker's weekly wage. The SUB, as it came to be called, legitimized the company's right to lay workers off, and nothing in the contract addressed the workers' perennial bone of contention: the speed-up. GM was also offering a master agreement that gave the locals greater solidarity in the event of a strike, but concentrated negotiating power in the hands of the union executive. Reuther was shaping the UAW in the image of General Motors: a strong president, a powerful bureaucracy, an authoritarian structure, and a big bank account.

Local 222 tried to go it alone. It was frozen out by the UAW and stonewalled by General Motors of Canada. "They were not an easy company to negotiate with," says Pilkey. "They were no pushover. They were tough." Company and union fought bitterly over wage increases of a penny or two an hour, and it took a five-month strike, which ended on Valentine's Day, 1956, for Local 222 to gain parity with other locals in wages and benefits. The strike failed to gain for the workers any control over production, and for the next thirty years the Canadian region was treated as a branch plant in the UAW.

Canadians bought British and German cars because they were cheap, and there were no competitive American models. European imports were negligible in the U.S., but by 1956 they had captured 20 per cent of Canada's new-car market. There was a Canadian sensibility that said: if you must have a golden calf in your driveway, then choose a small calf, or a serviceable donkey.

Americans also felt ambiguous. Cars had been used as slapstick props in early silent movies, and then they became seductive, sinister presences associated with Hollywood: *Casablanca* features a Buick. In the movie *Rebel Without a Cause*, released in 1955 after its star, James Dean, had been killed at the wheel of his Porsche, the car becomes an instrument of death. In 1957, Jack Kerouac published *On the Road*, a hymn for the beat generation that parodies Walt Whitman's odes to America. To Kerouac, "speed" meant amphetamines, and he portrays a freaked-out America as seen through car windows, a blurry retreating landscape of dirt roads, hick towns, and gas stations. His favourite car is a 1947 Cadillac, "a big, beautiful car, the last of the old-style limousines, black, with a big elongated body and whitewall tires and probably bulletproof

At the Don Mills shopping centre, local models in the latest sports fashions pose with a 1957 Corvette. From left, Jackie Chapman, Linda Shreve, Marg Jewitt, Leslie Sniderman, and Dorothy Atkinson. (*York University Archives/Bill Sherk*)

windows." Kerouac is less interested in the Cadillac than in the terrific trip it delivers.

On the Road was an elegy for a vanished age: by 1957 the Cadillac symbolized everything vulgar, and the Buick everything ugly, about the Age of Chrome. Buick historians Terry Dunham and Lawrence Gustin call the 1957 Buick "a nightmare." A Buick executive admitted: "The styling was awful in 1957, particularly those split rear windows. Plymouth looked at them and said, 'Suddenly, it's 1949.' A dealer came in from California to see the new cars, then went back to the coast and told the other dealers to buy all the used cars they could get, because that would be all they'd sell." Buick sales in the U.S. dropped by 150,000 to 405,000; in Canada they fell by 5,000 to 14,870 and kept falling until they bottomed at 7,480 in 1961.

The reason, according to Dunham and Gustin, was that Buick "decided to try to overwhelm the public with gingerbread, resulting in what became known as the 'chromiest' Buick ever built: gaudy louvres and chrome on the rear fenders, twin gunsight ornaments on each front fender and 'the most dazzling grille design in the history of Buick.' It consisted of small chrome squares, 160 of them, each with four triangular surfaces to reflect light. It was called a Fashion-Aire Dynastar Grille, and was topped by new Vista Vision dual headlamps. A garish ribbed aluminum, chrome-trimmed rear quarter panel rerouted the sweepspear again, but it was still there. The VentiPorts were not. With all the other geegaws on the car, there was no room for them anyway."

The bloated Buick was everything a car should not be: cumbersome, sluggish, and overpriced. The Buick Limited was the worst. "A joke making the rounds," write Dunham and Gustin, "noted that the car was appropriately named because 'limited' was what parking places would be if too many of them were sold."

Fortunately for Buick, public derision was directed toward Ford's clunky new Edsel, although Plymouth's tailfins and Chevrolet's gull-winged rear end didn't escape ridicule: Chevrolet Canada's sales dropped by 6,000 to fewer than 70,000 cars a year between 1957 and 1959. Imports continued to rise steadily, and by the end of the decade they had captured nearly 30 per cent of the Canadian market. Squeezed between two competing concepts of foreign car, European and American, the Canadian automobile industry was faced with extinction. The answer, at least to the auto workers, was obvious: Why not build a Canadian car?

14

THE AUTOPACT

For Sam McLaughlin, it was *déjà vu*. Had he not tried, and failed, to build a Canadian car fifty years before? Had he not, as president of General Motors of Canada, argued that only big, international corporations would survive? Sam had done his damnedest to drive his Canadian competition out of business, and his prophecy had fulfilled itself: all of the Canadian-owned companies had failed, and so had all the small U.S. companies except American Motors (Nash) and Studebaker. Apart from foreign imports, the Big Three – General Motors, Ford, and Chrysler – enjoyed a virtual monopoly over the remainder, and GM had the lion's share of that. There was no incentive for them to compete with themselves with a new "foreign" car, and this attitude of complacency fuelled the controversy.

The idea of a Canadian car, and a Canadian union, had always been dear to the hearts of the radicals among the auto workers. Independence, they believed, would mean cheaper cars, more jobs, and freedom from American domination. A Canadian car could be designed to be driven in Winnipeg instead of Los Angeles, profits would remain in Canada and, as the Japanese were soon to demonstrate, there was a strong, unsatisfied demand for a simple, economical, and dependable car; British models tended to spend as much time in the service station as they did on the road, and Canada's craze for the cramped little Beetle was fading. Other nations were developing indigenous automobile industries, and the collaboration between General Motors of Canada and Ford of Canada during the war had established a successful precedent for mass, co-operative production of a single, standard vehicle. With annual sales of about four hundred thousand new vehicles, the Canadian market was far from saturated; in fact it was stagnant.

Canadians were cooler toward the car than Americans, partly because car prices were higher and wages lower. Fewer Canadians per capita owned cars, and outside of Ontario automobile production did not dominate the economy as it did in the United States. Public transit remained strong in the cities; Toronto had just built two subway lines, hailed as the last word in transportation technology, and rapid transit sparked the development of downtown office towers and highrise apartments. Dinah Shore belting out "See the U.S.A. in your Chevrolet" didn't strike a patriotic chord, and, in Canada, the glamorous girls who posed with GM cars at auto shows were fully clothed. In 1958 Canadians elected a Conservative prime minister, John Diefenbaker, a monarchist and "un-hyphenated" Canadian who exemplified a popular swell of nationalist sentiment. Critics were voicing concerns about American ownership of the Canadian economy, and thousands of auto workers were losing their jobs to automation. In this political climate the rhetoric of American imperialism struck a false and threatening note.

"We believe that free men, free labour, free management, working together within a free government in a free economic system, have the glorious opportunity of co-operating in the creating and sharing of economic abundance," proclaimed UAW president Walter Reuther in 1958. Reuther was proposing a union profit-sharing scheme with the Big Three automobile manufacturers, and since all the companies' profits went to the United States, there would be nothing for Canadian workers to share. His scheme raised hackles in Canada, and Canadian negotiators already resented Reuther's heavy-handed interventions to ensure that Canadian contracts were patterned after contracts signed earlier in the U.S. A group of young radicals accused Canada's UAW director, George Burt, of allowing the UAW to "blackjack" Canada into submission.

Sensing a political storm that could blow him out of his job, Burt responded with a letter to the presidents of the Big Three Canadian companies: "The workers in your plant are growing more and more apprehensive about the possibility of losing job opportunities as a result of the manufacturing of a small car, which may or may not be manufactured in Canada," Burt wrote on February 18, 1959. "I believe they have the right to know the policy of the company in this regard."

Burt knew that the American companies were on the verge of introducing compact cars, but they had made no commitment to manufacture any of them in Canada. "We are particularly concerned," Burt wrote in a covering letter to Prime Minister Diefenbaker, "about the possibility of being in competition not only against the workers of Europe for job opportunities, but against the workers of the United States. In the interests of the workers of Canada, and particularly the automobile workers who have suffered such wide-spread unemployment, I believe it is your responsibility to give some comfort to these workers by requesting these companies to divulge their plans for the future."

Diefenbaker loved a tussle with the Yanks, and Burt's letter, copiously copied to cabinet ministers and the media, found a sympathetic audience. In a whirlwind of publicity, Burt subtly transmuted the radical idea of a Canadian car into a conventional made-in-Canada American car whose only distinguishing feature would be its small size. It was easy to do. Creating a Canadian car would, like the CPR and the CBC, require an audacious investment of money, imagination, and courage by the Canadian government; Diefenbaker was narrow-minded and parsimonious, and he had just cancelled Canada's experimental aircraft, the Avro Arrow. He was in favour of Crown corporations, but he had a horror of socialism, and he had inherited a civil service committed to Liberal free-trade policies. Diefenbaker did the Canadian thing: he appointed a royal commission to investigate the Canadian automobile industry. General Motors of Canada enlarged its Oshawa plant to manufacture a new small car, the Corvair.

General Motors engineers had developed a small car, the Cadet, immediately after the Second World War, but plans to produce it were scrapped when the accountants pointed out that small cars made small profits. The Corvair, introduced in the fall of 1959, was a compromise: a six-passenger sedan with a sporty name, futuristic styling, and a rear engine copied from Volkswagen. In Canada, a Corvair cost $2,550,

$1,000 more than a Volkswagen and between $500 and $800 more than the British imports, including GM's own Vauxhall. Price wasn't the only problem.

"The Corvair was unsafe as it was originally designed," former GM executive John DeLorean revealed in a 1979 autobiography, *On a Clear Day You Can See General Motors.* "There are several bad engineering characteristics inherent in rear-engine cars which use a swing-axle suspension.

CORVAIR'S
REAR ENGINE MEANS...

far better traction — a practically flat floor — remarkable braking ability — feather-soft steering.

Corvair's rear engine sets off a chain reaction of benefits that no other compact car in Canada can offer.

You'll feel the effects just as soon as you pull away from the curb. With engine weight in the rear — where it belongs in a *compact* car — Corvair has the kind of traction that really takes a toehold. It can spring and corner like a cow pony, cruise

over ice, mud or snow with sure-footedness that will amaze you. With the engine, transmission and drive gears packaged together, you also get the 6-passenger comfort of a virtually flat floor. There's room for everyone, front and rear, including the passengers in the middle. And when it comes to stopping, Corvair's balanced four-wheel

braking brings you to a halt as smartly as a drill team — with none of the nose-heaviness you find in front-engine compact cars.

You'll also notice the advantages of Corvair's weight distribution in the effortless way it steers. It's a joy to jockey through traffic, a pleasure to park. And with independent suspension at all four wheels — an advance as

significant as the independent suspension of front wheels on full-size cars years ago — you get a poised, unruffled ride that rivals even the most expensive makes.

These are all things that would never have been possible if Chevrolet engineers had been content to make the Corvair merely a sawed-off version of a big car. And your dealer's waiting now with all the short, sweet details.

corvair
by CHEVROLET

There's nothing like a new car—and no compact car like a Corvair. This is the deluxe 700.

(Ted Enright)

In turns at high speeds they tend to become directionally unstable and, therefore, difficult to control. The rear of the car lifts or 'jacks' and the rear wheels tend to tuck under the car, which encourages the car to flip over. The car conveyed a false sense of control to the driver when in fact he may have been very close to losing control of the vehicle. The results of these characteristics can be fatal. These problems with the Corvair were well documented inside GM's Engineering Staff long before the Corvair ever was offered for sale. Frank Winchell, then an engineer at Chevy, flipped over one of the first prototypes on the GM test track. Others followed."

The Corvair had been built over the vehement protests of many GM engineers, but the new swing-axle suspension was cheaper than a conventional design and Chevrolet's general manager, Ed Cole, was keen on the Corvair's innovative technology. Corvair dealers were kept in the dark about possible faults, and drivers who complained were told that the problems stemmed from the car's peppy performance, imbalanced air pressure in the tires, road hazards, or their own incompetence. Says DeLorean: "The results were disastrous. I don't think any one car before or since produced as gruesome a record on the highway as the Corvair."

In Canada, the Corvair performed well in snow, but it flopped with consumers: it was competing with a new Ford Falcon and Plymouth Valiant as well as a Nash Rambler with reclining seats. George Burt swung the UAW in Canada solidly behind the Big Three compact cars and ordered his second-in-command, Paul Siren, to purge the Canadian executive of radical nationalists. Siren refused, and resigned. Siren, an experienced negotiator and able organizer, had been at Burt's side for seventeen years and his resignation brought the political feud within the UAW into the open.

At a membership meeting of Local 222 on January 7, 1960, Nelson Wilson, chairman of the shop committee, claimed that he "had personally attended several meetings during the long UAW strike against General Motors in 1955–56 at which known Communists were present and had participated." Wilson named a number of union leaders, most of them holding influential positions on the bargaining committee, who had been at the meetings. Among them was Paul Siren. UAW contact with Communists was nothing new – Burt himself had met more than once with Communist Party leader William Kashtan – and if Moscow was, as Wilson implied, trying to manipulate the UAW, why had he waited more than four years to sound the alarm?

Article 10, section 8 of the UAW's constitution precluded from any office in the union a member who was also a "member of, or subservient to, any political organization, such as the Communist, Fascist or Nazi organization which owes its allegiance to a government other than the United States or Canada, directly or indirectly." This clause, which could be interpreted to include Her Majesty the Queen, was merely another way of labelling people "un-American," and it allowed the Old Guard in the UAW, in the name of democracy, to eliminate anyone to the left or right of their conservative position. Burt fired Paul Siren before his resignation became effective.

The UAW international summoned the half-dozen men accused by Wilson to appear before an investigative committee at Toronto's Royal York Hotel on February 2 and 3, 1960. Each man would be questioned individually, and the proceedings would be held in secret, allegedly to protect the men's identities. Their identities, however, were well-known within the union – Cliff Pilkey was chairman of Local 222, Charles Brooks of Local 444 in St. Catharines, Jack Kane of Frigidaire Local 303 – and while the UAW was operating on nothing more than a "strong inference of Communist Party influence," the implicated men were given no chance to defend themselves before the union membership.

Accusing the UAW of a method of interrogation that "resembles the Star Chamber methods of the ill-famed McCarthy Committee," Siren publicly denounced the inquiry as a smear, a witch hunt, and American interference in Canadian affairs. The men defied the kangaroo court. When the first witness was called, they all trooped into the room together and Siren read aloud a joint statement condemning the investigation as "a desperate move to stigmatize and malign members of the UAW who have dared to oppose Brother Burt." All of the men except Siren flatly denied attending any meetings with Communists, and knew of no one who had. Siren said he had accompanied two or three union leaders to one meeting with Kashtan; he would not divulge their names.

With no evidence to corroborate Wilson's innuendoes, and a public image as a bunch of goons, the UAW committee reluctantly concluded: "These charges are, perhaps, insofar as the serious nature of the crimes against the union are concerned, analogous to treason, which in many common law jurisdictions requires, because of its severity, at least two actual witnesses to support a conviction. Unless further evidence were forthcoming, the democratic constitution and traditions of this union would preclude any action against this group."

The men were not convicted. Nor were they acquitted, and rather than retracting or apologizing for Wilson's "inferences," the committee reiterated them in a report circulated to all Canadian locals and praised Wilson's testimony as "most convincing and credible." Wilson had produced no evidence that Communists had subverted or even influenced the union – the 1955–56 strike ended with a settlement virtually identical to the one in the United States – but as far as the Americans were concerned, admitting to being in the same room with a Communist was enough to cost Paul Siren his job.

The UAW took away Siren's union card, and in the murk of fear and malevolence that the report created, Canadian auto workers lined up solidly behind the Americans. Sputnik, the satellite that had given the Soviet Union dominance in space since 1957, had created an atmosphere bordering on paranoia in the United States and Canada: Russian invasion seemed imminent, and while Canadian schoolchildren did not cower under their desks during nuclear-defence drills, Diefenbaker, who refused to have American nuclear weapons on Canadian soil, ordered a bomb shelter to be built deep in the granite rock outside Ottawa. Paul Siren appealed his blacklisting to a Canadian review board, won, and went on to a distinguished career as the executive director of the Association of Canadian Radio and Television Artists, but, within the UAW, radicals and activists were voted out of office and consigned to twenty years in purgatory.

The Americans knocked the Canadian car on the head, and Vincent Bladen, Canada's one-man royal commission into the automobile industry, buried it. Bladen, dean of economics at the University of Toronto, did not own or drive a car, but he had very fixed ideas about the automobile industry. During public hearings held during the last week of October 1960, Bladen dubbed the speculative Canadian car the "Beaver," conjuring up an image of an ugly, squat, brown, "utility, austerity" vehicle. He then suggested to Alf Gleave, president of the Farm Union Council, that this horrible little car would have to be built at taxpayers' expense by a public utility. He told Gleave: "Are you going to not only discipline the industry, but discipline the consumers as well and say: 'This is the kind of car you shall have. We, the Government, have decided what kind of car the people of Canada should have, and you have got to have it.' Is this the line? This is essentially what Hitler did when he introduced the Volkswagen."

Bladen believed in free enterprise and free trade, and he raised the possibility of free entry for American automobiles into Canada if the manufacturers purchased here an amount equivalent to their Canadian sales. Ford was intrigued, but the other manufacturers were dubious and, for the moment, the idea went nowhere. The industry, including the auto-parts manufacturers and the UAW, argued in favour of a tariff on British imports – GM claimed it could then make the Vauxhall in Canada – and for the elimination of the government's 7.5-per-cent excise tax on Canadian-made cars.

Bladen, and the Conservative government, gave the industry everything it asked for. On Bladen's recommendation, the excise tax was cancelled, a loss to the Canadian treasury of $66 million, and in 1962 a 10-per-cent tariff was slapped on British imports. Imports predictably plummeted, but sales of American models were already on the rise. Older cars were wearing out, the dollar was falling, the economy was picking up, and the job market was improving. General Motors of Canada sold 210,000 cars and trucks in 1960, 267,000 in 1962, and a record 308,000 in 1963; the company was also making more money on every car.

Financial records supplied to the Bladen commission by General Motors of Canada reveal that, in 1950, the company sold 159,000 Canadian-made cars and trucks worth $238 million for a net profit of $21.8 million – $137 per unit. In 1959, the company sold 180,000 vehicles worth $431.5 million for a net profit of $27.8 million – $154 per unit. The customer was paying more and getting less, but Bladen ignored or ridiculed numerous letters and formal submissions, including one from the Ontario premier, Leslie Frost, condemning the industry as wasteful and inefficient. One outraged economist called the Big Three "troglodytes."

A United States Senate committee had already excoriated the Big Three for monopolistic pricing practices that were stifling the industry. General Motors had made a sensational $1-billion profit in 1955, but in 1959 the corporation's annual report revealed that while GM had earned a net profit of $873 million on international sales of $11.2 billion – a margin of 7.8 per cent – sales, profits, and dividends were flat, and in the past year the value of GM's real estate, plants, and equipment had diminished by $1 million to $2.8 billion. GM, however, paid out $575 million in shareholders' dividends – $2 per share – and retained only $298 million – $1.06 per share – to reinvest in the business. Not that the corporation was broke: it had a surplus of $553 million and working capital of $2.5 billion. It was, moreover, making a profit of $229 a car, an increase of $20 since 1950.

In Canada, GM's profit was $75 per car below the corporation's international average, which included plants in the United States, Australia, Brazil, Britain, and Western Europe, and while the total value of Canadian sales had risen dramatically, profit on sales had shrunk from 9 to 5.5 per cent, more than two points below the corporate average. General Motors had invested $100 million in its Canadian operations, but the costs of production still gobbled up more than 80 per cent of revenue, and the company's profits as a percentage of assets had dropped from 30 to 8 per cent. High costs of production were, however, a bonus for Canada, as long as the money was spent here. The Canadian government took a $25-million tax bite out of GM's profits in 1959, and it was a token amount compared to the more than $300 million the company spent for material and wages. There was no incentive for the Canadian government to build a "Beaver," or tell GM how to cut its costs. As long as GM was making more money manufacturing cars in Canada than by importing them, it was easy to blame the Canadian company's relatively poor performance on cheap foreign imports.

Had the royal commission summoned Dr. Edwards Deming from Japan, where he was advising Nissan and Toyota, he might have had something enlightening to say about quality, waste, and management, but nobody in Canada had heard of Deming, much less Toyota, and when another unknown prophet, Marshall McLuhan, a communications scholar at the University of Toronto, expressed his views on automobiles, Bladen buried McLuhan's letter deep in his files.

"The French have a saying," McLuhan wrote to Bladen on January 21, 1961, "'that in an American car, you are not on the road, you are in the car.' That is to say, they are quite aware that the human senses are involved in a very different way in an American vehicle, as compared with European vehicles. Young French novelist Françoise Sagan was accustomed to drive her car in her bare feet, in order to feel more completely at one with the vehicle. To sum it up very briefly, the European tends to regard the vehicle as an immediate extension of himself. By comparison, North Americans have tended to use the motor car as a container, an enclosed space. The factors which have for the past decade or so been transforming the North American attitude towards space have pushed us steadily into the European direction of stress on the tactile and kinetic for vehicles, and away from stress on enclosed space and visual and pictorial values abstracted from the other senses. The most potent single factor in this change rises from the quality of the television image, which favours much interplay of the senses and departs from stress on the merely visual values.

"So far as the motor car is concerned, it is not therefore so much the size of the car, as those qualities of design which permit a high degree of participation of the driver. Even the sound of the mechanism now tends to enter into the other spatial and textural qualities of the vehicle. In this regard, the compact car does not meet the challenge of the new preferences, except in the most tangential and peripheral way. The designers of the compact car still have the occupant merely *in* the car, and not *on* the road. The compact car is built on the assumption of convenience and economy, but retains all the old abstract, enclosed space features of its predecessor. It will therefore fail to meet the real changes that are continuing very rapidly in the North American sensibility since television."

Bladen, who missed the point completely, assured McLuhan that Americans were about to return to the concept of "convenience and efficiency" after "an unfortunate venture into designing cars as 'extensions of oneself' not by giving the pleasure of driving but rather the pleasure of being seen." At the same time Bladen admonished Canadian drivers: "It should be remembered that multiplicity of models, frequent model changes and other such 'evils' are basically a function of demand and do not, as has been suggested, depend primarily on the whims of the automobile designer."

Bladen had never encountered whimsical Harley Earl, who liked to say: "I'd put smokestacks right in the middle of the sons of bitches if I thought I could sell more cars." The Cellini of Chrome, as Earl was jokingly called in the trade, had established GM's design department as the corporation's autocratic *politburo*: a new model was created in such strict secrecy that even the president of the corporation saw it only when the mock-up was finished, and if he didn't like it, tough. GM engineers were faced with the daunting task of bringing Earl's "dream cars" to life, and the cost was passed on to the consumer. For more than thirty years Earl had been designing GM cars to look longer and lower, and he concealed the automobile's functional parts beneath layers of flowing steel draperies. The draperies were rearranged every model year to persuade the buyer that the cars were new, and, like the portrait of Dorian Gray, they aged overnight.

"We design a car, and the minute it's done, we hate it – we've got to do another one," the chief of design at Ford told American writer David Halberstam. "We design a car to make a man unhappy with his 1957 Ford 'long about the end of 1958." Halberstam calls Harley Earl the prince of "Gorp," the only word to describe the Kewpie Doll look that enticed buyers into dealers' showrooms. "There really was nothing essentially new," said John DeLorean in his autobiography, "but year in and year out we were urging Americans to sell their cars and buy new ones because the styling had changed. It struck me that not only was this management dereliction, but also an unfair, even immoral practice, because the heart of the system was to take some American wage earner who was working his fanny off trying to pay for a car and, just about the day he got it paid off, convince him that he should start the payment process all over again. His 36 months were up."

It worked. Sales soared in the 1960s, spurred by the first wave of North America's postwar babies who were turning sixteen and learning to drive. Any kid who could start, stop, and park the family car could get a driver's licence, and passing the test was a coming-of-age ritual. City and provincial governments spent billions building, paving, and widening highways to accommodate millions of cars, and as camping became a craze, traffic was snarled by huge, ungainly house trailers lumbering down the road at a stately fifty miles per hour. The automobile had become a "utility" vehicle, and although cars cost 10 per cent more in Canada than in the United States, and the Canadian standard of living was 30 per cent lower, the gap between Canadian and American ownership narrowed to one car for every three Canadians, one for every two Americans.

General Motors of Canada had 56 per cent of the market, but the company's sales manager, E. J. Umphrey, lashed the dealers to get 60 per cent. "The sales department had an absolute free hand," says Bill Graham, who handled the GM account for MacLaren advertising. "'Don't tell me what it costs!' Umphrey would shout at me. 'We're a sales department, we're not a bookkeeping department!'" Umphrey, a native of Miami, Manitoba, had worked his way up through GM's regional offices to a position of virtual tyranny. Says Graham: "He was a man of limited education, unlimited energy and vanity, a vitriolic punisher." The dealers, however, were inspired by Umphrey's unstinting enthusiasm for GM's big, powerful, flashy cars. "We were selling style," Toronto GM dealer John Addison says a little wistfully. "People were car-crazy. We were selling way more cars for a lot less money, but it was a thrilling, exciting business. It was a way of life. The last four or five years, we've been selling iron."

General Motors of Canada spent $12 million a year on advertising, and the GM account was so important to MacLaren that it became a separate department in the agency. "All the advertising was created in Canada," says Graham. "We were not handed anything from Detroit. Umphrey never wanted any American stuff. The American stuff was too sophisticated for him. I don't think he thought of the audience. He had the absolute belief that everybody shared his views. Our advertising was not designed to seduce the public, but to seduce Mr. Umphrey."

Graham describes the Canadian advertising as "absolutely direct, full of statistics and graphs showing how far ahead Chevrolet was of everyone else. It was 'Read this and compare' stuff. There was no image. I asked Umphrey once, 'Who are we trying to get to buy the Buick custom?' He said: 'Everybody!' He never gave us any guidance. We'd go through an immense pile of layouts and he'd say, 'Well, you haven't got it.' That was the end. There was no idea of what 'it' was. He was absolutely dictatorial."

Graham drove a Chevrolet; he had no choice. Sam McLaughlin

1961: General Motors of Canada sales manager E. J. Umphrey, left, with president William Wecker, R. S. McLaughlin, and an unidentified man. (*Parkwood*)

insisted that agency president Jack MacLaren drive a Cadillac, although MacLaren hated to show off, and when the *Toronto Star* ran a story slightly disparaging to Sam, MacLaren pulled GM advertising from the *Star* for months. Graham would drive back and forth to Oshawa three and four times a day to get Umphrey's approval on something as trivial as a staff Christmas card, and for formal presentations, Umphrey held court in the GM boardroom surrounded by subordinates who sat there, says Graham, "mute and resentful." MacLaren executive H. M. Turner, Jr., gives his account of an encounter with Umphrey in an unpublished memoir:

"Many broke their picks on the Oshawa rock. The penalty for offending or disagreeing with GM was permanent banishment. Hugh Horler [MacLaren's director of radio and television] had run afoul of the Great One and was not allowed past the gates of the plant, evermore. Consequently, I was enlisted to assist Hugh Pryce-Jones, one of our PR men, in selling a BBC special prepared to commemorate the coronation of Elizabeth II."

MacLaren schemed to circumvent Umphrey by showing the film privately to president William Wecker. Writes Turner: "The film had almost run its course when the door burst open and Mr. Umphrey strode in and plopped into a chair and stuck his feet on the table. After a pregnant moment, he turned to the president and barked: 'What the hell is this crap, Bill?' Hugh made an unruffled explanation. The president said nothing. 'I can tell you one thing,' E. J. said to nobody in particular and without turning around, 'if you want to run this garbage, it ain't coming out of my goddamn budget!' At which point, the president rose, still without comment, and walked out of the room." The special was broadcast as a public-relations exercise.

MacLaren produced all GM's radio and television commercials, plus a CBC drama series, "General Motors Presents," that Bill Graham found "an endless aggravation." GM had to approve the scripts. "We'd have a batch of scripts and GM would see them. We had weekly hassles with the PR department. One script had a man being hanged when a horse was driven out from under him. No way would GM be associated with a lynching. In another one, the daughter of a wealthy family elopes with a postman. That was an absolute veto. The daughter of someone high up in GM had eloped with the milkman." Nonetheless, the dramas provided a wonderful opportunity for Canadian actors and writers – the thriller "Flight Into Danger" launched Arthur Hailey on an international career – and GM's advertising indirectly supported a cultural industry that had nothing to do with automobiles.

"We provided enough work for singers and dancers they could make a living, together with their CBC work," says Graham. "It was a big community." Bandleader Howard Cable arranged the music and Alan Lund the choreography for GM's glitzy annual "Motorama," a stage show that hyped the new models to GM dealers and customers across the country. Says Graham: "We'd have eight dancers, a pit chorus of eight singers, ten in the orchestra, three or four feature performers, a 'stylist' or pitchman, stage crew. It cost $300,000 for Toronto and Montreal, multiply that by six in today's dollars. There were no big stars, not like Dinah Shore in the U.S. The performers would be conspicuous for their lack of personality. The cars were the stars." Girls in evening gowns stroked and fondled the cars, but, says Graham, "the shows were never raunchy, *no*. If anybody got laid, it wasn't set up by the agency."

Graham put up with General Motors. "The money just flowed in," he says. The agency charged a 15-per-cent commission on its millions of dollars in General Motors billings, and once a creative decision was approved, cost was no object. "There were people lined up for cars," says Graham, "and we were spending all that money just to sell more cars than the competition." One day, Umphrey shoved a dramatic Volkswagen advertisement under Graham's nose. "Why can't you do that?" he demanded. Graham replied: "Give us a car like that and we can." "Oh," said Umphrey, "is there something wrong with the GM product?" Umphrey was outraged that Volkswagen had seized 10 per cent of the market, says Graham, but Umphrey decided that since "kooks and oddballs make up 10 per cent of the population, we'll have to live with that. GM never understood the small car." Sam McLaughlin confidently predicted that the small car would go the way of the horse and buggy.

In 1963, a new Liberal government cast a cold and calculating eye on the Canadian automobile industry. In spite of a 17.5-per-cent tariff on American imports and a Canadian-content quota, Canadian manufacturers were importing $580 million more in automobiles and parts from the United States than they were exporting to the U.S. This trade deficit worried the finance minister, Walter Gordon, who saw Canada's economy shrinking to the status of a Third World colony, and while Gordon was critical of the high level of American investment in

Canada, he accepted the integration of the automobile industry as a *fait accompli*. Expropriating the Big Three's Canadian plants was not "practical," as he put it later, and proposals to regulate increased Canadian content by manipulating the tariff provoked charges of illegal "incentives" from American manufacturers. The alternative was to "rationalize" the industry on a continental basis.

The poor productivity of the Canadian plants was assumed to be an inevitable consequence of their relatively small output of a multiplicity of products for a limited market. If production volume could be increased and variety reduced, it was argued, the economies of scale would equal those of the American factories. Continental free trade had an aggressive advocate in Simon Reisman, Canada's deputy minister of industry, and strong support in Washington from Robert McNeill, assistant to the secretary of commerce. Free trade, while opening the American market to Canadian-made products, would make it cheaper to sell American cars in Canada; it would stimulate Canadian industry and create jobs, and production economies would increase profits for the American corporations. It seemed like such a good idea all around that the Automotive Trade Agreement, known familiarly as the Autopact, was drafted speedily in the autumn of 1964 and announced in the House of Commons on January 15, 1965; the next day it was signed in Texas by Prime Minister Lester Pearson and U.S. President Lyndon Johnson.

It was the soul of simplicity. The American corporations were allowed to import vehicles duty-free into Canada as long as they manufactured in Canada vehicles valued at no less than 75 per cent of their Canadian sales, or the percentage in effect during the 1964 model year if that was higher. The dollar value of the Canadian content in their vehicles was also not to fall below the 1964 level. The real meat of the agreement, however, lay in the attached "letters of undertaking." By 1968, the corporations committed themselves to increase their Canadian content by 60 per cent of the value of their growth in Canadian car sales, 50 per cent of their sales growth in trucks and buses, plus make a cash investment of $260 million.

It was estimated that by 1968 Canadian automobile production would expand by one third, in addition to normal growth, and that most of the excess would be absorbed by higher Canadian demand. The Canadian public had to take the government's word for it: the trade agreement had been negotiated in secret and passed by order-in-council without a breath of debate in Parliament: it wasn't formally ratified until 1966. As economist Carl Beigie wrote in a 1970 analysis for the Canadian–American committee: "It was an *ad hoc* measure worked out to allay specific pressures, while questions of possible long-term complications – when asked – were rationalized away."

Sovereignty was a major concern for Canadians, as were relocation, layoffs, and other unpleasant side effects of an industry-wide shakeout. Canadian doubts, however, were eased by the intense opposition the Autopact encountered in the United States Congress, where it was condemned as a sell-out that would wipe out American jobs and cripple small business. After months of debate and delay, the bill narrowly passed Congress on October 16, 1965. By then, however, a young Washington lawyer, Ralph Nader, had published a book that blew the lid off the automobile industry.

"For over half a century the automobile has brought death, injury, and the most inestimable sorrow and deprivation to millions of people," Nader began the preface to *Unsafe at Any Speed*. "With Medea-like intensity, this mass trauma began rising sharply four years ago, reflecting new and unexpected ravages by the motor vehicle. A 1959 Department of Commerce report projected that 51,000 persons would be killed in 1975. That figure will probably be reached in 1965, a decade ahead of schedule."

Nader was articulating in concise, passionate prose the fear and resentment that North Americans had been struggling to define for years. Automobiles, unlike airplanes, ships, and railway trains, did not have to meet public safety standards. "The rule of law should extend to the safety of any product that carries such high risks to the lives of users and bystanders," Nader wrote. "The automobile is the only product in America which continues to be sold year after year even though it kills thousands of people and injures millions more. While old diseases such as tuberculosis, pneumonia and rheumatic fever are diminished as causes of death, the prominence of death by automobile rises." Nader quoted President John F. Kennedy, who in 1960 had called traffic accidents "perhaps *the* greatest of the nation's public health problems." Kennedy was fatally shot three years later driving through Dallas, Texas, in a Lincoln convertible, and the ghostly image of his shattered body slumped in the back seat was replayed on television until it was imprinted on the imagination.

Nader argued that the multi-billion dollar medical/police/repair/ insurance/funeral service industry that profited by cleaning up after automobile accidents should instead direct its energies toward demanding safer automobile design. Nader tore the Corvair apart, and was harsh on the new Ford Mustang, but he was really after big, expensive cars with no seatbelts, shoddy door locks, clumsy instrument panels, sharp projections, flimsy interior padding, and windshield glare that blinded the driver. If a corporation like GM was earning $2 billion a year, Nader asked, why were seatbelts "optional extras," as headlights and bumpers had been in 1910? Nader's basic message, documented with legal and scientific evidence, was that Americans were getting poor value for their money.

Canadian accident statistics paralleled the American. In 1965, 4,894 Canadians were killed in traffic accidents, and 150,156 were injured. Fatalities had increased by 200 over 1964, injuries by 10,000. *Unsafe at Any Speed* did not point out, however, that fatalities had decreased as a percentage of vehicles on the road. During the 1930s, when Canada had one million registered vehicles, fatalities averaged between 1,200 and 1,600 a year, while by 1965, with fewer than 5,000 fatalities, the number of registered vehicles had increased to 6.7 million. Five thousand deaths was still a terrible toll, and Nader was correct in pointing out the increase in injuries. In 1958, the first year that all Canadian provinces submitted complete traffic statistics, Canada had 4.7 million registered vehicles and 80,000 injured victims; in 1965, with an increase of 50 per cent in the number of vehicles, accident injuries had almost doubled to 150,000. The overwhelming majority of victims were between the ages of thirty-five and forty-four, mature, responsible people who were buying new cars.

General Motors had replaced the Corvair's rear-end suspension in 1964, and U.S. legislation would soon make seatbelts mandatory, but instead of seizing the safety initiative, GM hired a Washington private eye to dig up dirt on Nader. Unusual phone calls and sexual advances from strange women alerted Nader that he was being watched, and when two inept gumshoes mistakenly followed a reporter for the *Washington Post*, the scandal became front-page news. General Motors, horribly embarrassed, eventually paid Nader $425,000 in damages for invasion of privacy. GM never publicly admitted that the Corvair was faulty. The corporation defended, and won, lawsuits brought by Corvair owners, and after *Unsafe at Any Speed*, false complaints were prompted by hysteria. Canadian Corvair production wound down, and the Corvair was discontinued in 1969, the year Canadian-made cars broke open the U.S. market.

Canadian plants exported to the U.S. $1.5 billion more in automobiles and parts than they imported that year. In three years, the trade deficit had completely reversed itself, and not only did the Big Three fulfil all their Canadian quotas, they far surpassed them. Plants were expanded and new ones built – GM opened a big Chevrolet/Pontiac assembly plant at Ste-Thérèse in Quebec – and 20,000 more auto workers were hired, bringing the Canadian total to a record 80,000 blue-collar employees. Cars and trucks were built in numbers Canadian workers had never dreamed of – GM hit a production record of 498,000 units in 1969 – and most of them were sold in the United States.

Congress screamed blue murder, and analysts puzzled over the phenomenon. "It seems that the car companies actually prefer Canada as a place to expand," wrote the Washington correspondent for *The Economist* in February 1970, "largely because Canadian labor, while no longer cheaper than U.S. labor, is proving more available and reliable."

Canadian labour *was* cheaper: auto workers did not achieve wage parity with the Americans for another six months and the Canadian dollar was worth about ninety cents in American currency. There were other economies: health insurance and the Canada Pension Plan, both products of the Pearson government, saved the corporations substantial costs in workers' benefits. Most of the Canadian plants had once been family firms, and their roots went deep into their communities, whereas U.S. plants relied heavily on immigrant labour, and new factories were built in areas where unskilled workers had no experience with automated production or union organization. Canadian factories were also not disturbed by the racial strife that was tearing the U.S. apart. In 1967, the year a cheerful, prosperous Canada celebrated its centennial, Motown was gutted by incendiary race riots.

GM's Canadian plants, which had traditionally built low-priced, medium-sized cars, were well positioned to move into a growing segment of the U.S. market. General Motors of Canada closed its uncompetitive Frigidaire plant and consolidated its other operations.

GM transferred Canada from its "overseas" division and tagged it on to "Chevrolet–Pontiac–GM Canada," another weird anomaly since Canada still made Buicks, Oldsmobiles, GMC trucks, engines, axles, and body parts. General Motors of Canada acquired an American president, who got on everybody's nerves, and the company remained loyal to Colonel Sam.

For the Americans, the astonishing competitive success of McLaughlin's operation raised a troubling question: Could it be that the rinky-dink Canadian plants were *more* efficient? It seemed unthinkable. Efficiency *was* American; the word was repeated like a mantra and the dogma worshipped as revealed truth. In *Understanding Media*, published in 1964, Marshall McLuhan dismissed the motor car as a relic of the mechanical age, yet no Canadian economist, including Vincent Bladen, had seriously questioned the efficiency of the American automobile industry. The performance of General Motors of Canada's plants was not compared in detail to American plants of equivalent size and sales volume, and while the Canadian profit margin looked poor in comparison to the General Motors average, the corporation's total income was boosted by strong foreign sales and enormous profits from investments and loans; GM was as much a bank as an automobile manufacturer. General Motors of Canada has never been required to justify its financial performance to Canadian authorities, and its accounts could not be independently verified.

In his autobiography, John DeLorean gives a scathing critique of the state of GM's Chevrolet division when he took over as general manager in February 1969. Chevrolet was losing ground to Ford in sales and quality, and since 1964 its return on investment had declined precipitously from 55.4 per cent to 10.3 per cent. "It was obvious," DeLorean said, "that Chevrolet was headed for a big loss in the 1970 model year. Every department was outspending its budget every year. The Engineering Department hadn't met a budget in something like 15 to 20 years. Typically, in 1966 it was $13 million over its budget, $11 million over in 1968 and $15 million over in 1969. When problems developed in Chevy departments, the simple solution seemed to be to pour more money in."

In Canada, GM engineers had to read, correct, and interpret Detroit's specifications for fifteen thousand different Chevrolet parts, and assembly workers memorized pages of instructions in order to install the parts in an infinite variety of combinations. "The sales department would take an order for anything on wheels," says Clarence Greentree. If anyone goofed, the car was fixed at the end of the line, or not, and the reject rate was estimated to be as high as 50 per cent. "By 1969," says DeLorean, "Chevrolet was offering 179 different engine combinations for cars and 299 for trucks. There were 142 different axle combinations for cars and an astounding 440 possibilities for trucks. There were 165,000 different material order specifications for cars and trucks. The Chevrolet parts manual was over a foot-and-a-half thick."

Car buyers joked that it was wise not to buy a car built on a Friday night or a Monday morning, and while boozing workers could wreak havoc, DeLorean says: "Chevrolet's quality problems were due as much to the use of cheaper parts and material as they were to outright product defects. Under pressure from the corporation to increase or stabilize its falling profit margins, Chevrolet management from about the mid-1960s on had taken quality out of its products as a cost-cutting measure. Some of this cost-cutting was in highly visible areas such as the interior appointments, exterior trim, and size of tires. This directly affected the customer's perception of Chevrolet, how he felt inside the car, or how it rode."

General Motors of Canada enjoyed the benefit of being able to buy its most expensive components from its U.S. parent without having to bear the initial costs of tooling and design, and it had its own ingenious way of cutting costs. "The Canadian Pontiac was a Chevrolet with Pontiac trim," says retired GM executive Fred Popham. "Mechanically it was a Chev, the body was a Chev, but it was a little more expensive." Canadian buyers were blithely unaware of what they were driving unless they had an accident or engine trouble in the United States. *Unsafe at Any Speed* had made consumers suspicious and cynical, and Canadians took McLuhan's advice to shop for a barefoot, four-on-the-floor Zen experience.

Nissan and Toyota began to export cars and trucks to Canada in 1965; Nissan sold 1,194, Toyota 755. Not much bigger than sardine cans, the four-cylinder Datsuns and Toyotas had stiff springs, low bucket seats, floor shifts, and cockpit interiors that gave drivers an illusion of power. They were economical to run and repair, mechanically reliable, and they cost half as much as an American alternative. They were Spartan, and prone to rust, but their simple lines and plain colours recalled the American automobile's original personality, and they restored the feeling of being "on the road." By 1970, Nissan sales had rocketed to 38,000, Toyota's to 29,000.

For the Japanese, economy was prescribed by the high cost of importing raw materials, and the easiest way to achieve efficiency was by eliminating waste before it occurred. A better car was a cheaper car, and continuous improvement was achieved by a process of self-criticism, analysis, and experimentation. The worker, not the shareholder, was the heart of the Japanese system, and the emphasis was not on the strength of his hands – robots were stronger and better at repetitive tasks – but on his knowledge and creativity. Competition was keen – Japanese plants were not unionized – hours long, and the stress level high. Robert McLaughlin would have been quite at home in a Toyota plant, but Billy Durant had formed General Motors in his own image, and for all Alfred Sloan's talk of scientific management, GM remained a profligate creature of the stock market. GM's success as a manufacturer of motor cars had been based on Durant's uncanny ability to seek out inventors as gifted as Albert Champion and Charles Kettering, who, in turn, attracted America's best engineering talent to the corporation. In spite of management layered as thick as foam rubber in a Cadillac, GM's ideology was individualistic and competitive, and there was always room somewhere in the giant enterprise for unconventional personalities: DeLorean, who quit General Motors in 1973, was a clone of Billy Durant. Even Sloan and his successors had taken on aspects of Durant's isolated, autocratic persona and adopted his capricious, laissez-faire attitude toward the multitude of competing divisions under their control. General Motors was still the King of the Bulls.

15

CITIZEN SAM

"It seems to me there is a great and outstanding threat to all of us here in America in connection with the constantly rising costs as demanded by the labour unions," Sam McLaughlin wrote to GM director C. S. Mott on September 2, 1960. "What I cannot get through my head is that the unions know as much about this feature as anybody else because they hire as good economists as they can get and they must be able to show them what is coming to pass in the way of foreign competition. With English wages about 34% of what ours are here – German approximately 31% – French and Italian much lower than that and the Japanese away down in the cellar, what can possibly happen in the future? Now that they are actually manufacturing more cars abroad than they are manufacturing in the U.S., the whole picture is changed as with quantity production some of the big companies abroad can undoubtedly, with their cheap labour, outsell us very severely. This is the question that worries me."

As he reached his nineties, Sam had lost none of his business sense, but this private letter to Mott was as close as he ever came to a critique of the industry he had helped to build. In public, Sam always praised General Motors as "the greatest corporation in the world," and he never spoke a critical word about the competition, the workers, or the cars. "He didn't butt in," says Bill Austin, whose job it was to brief Colonel Sam on company affairs every morning. "He was very careful about that. He didn't try to run the business. He wanted to know how it was going. He knew his business very well, he knew what he wanted very well. We'd shoot the breeze. He would have heard rumours, Toronto gossip. We'd talk about personalities. He had good information. He didn't go into the plant; he was concerned that people would stop work to look at him."

Sam was told only what company brass wanted him to hear, and while he remained an intimidating presence in the corner office, his influence was minimal. "In terms of advertising, I never heard the phrase 'Mr. McLaughlin would like . . .,'" recalls Bill Graham. "One day I heard him pounding on Wecker's desk and shouting: "Young man, you're not telling me the truth!" Sam had his own devices for finding out what was going on.

"In the 1960s we were opening a new plant in Ste-Thérèse," says Dick McLaughlin. "The cars were not good. They had leaks, lots of problems. Colonel Sam ordered a new station wagon from Ste-Thérèse, so when it arrived I routed it through our experimental division for inspection. 'It's a disaster,' said the engineers. 'We can't fix it.' The only thing to do was to take the car into the plant and rebuild it. After a few days, Sam called Lowry: 'What's happened to my car?' I was summoned up to Parkwood. Sam blew his top! 'Why did you think I ordered that car?' he roared. 'I wanted to check on the quality and now you've spoiled it!' I've never had such a calling down. 'What was wrong with it? What are you doing about it?' We went through pages of defects. My ears were stinging. 'Young man,' he said, 'you don't realize how important this is! And I want my car!'"

As the director of quality control for General Motors of Canada, Dick was responsible for upholding the family motto: "One Grade Only, and That the Best." "Those were bad days," he sighs. "All the departments were fighting each other. Nobody was prepared to say, 'It's our problem, not theirs.' The president, Roland Withers, thought I wasn't doing a good job because I wasn't fighting all the time. If an inspector rejected a vehicle, and it was a grey area, production won out: they put the car out anyway."

GM relied on the British-made Vauxhall to compete in the Canadian small-car market. "Vauxhall had a poor reputation so Withers changed its name to Firenza," Dick says. "When the shipment arrived I was ordered to check them out. They always got me to do the dirty jobs. This was my worst nightmare. I thought, 'These cars can't be allowed to go on the road!' We fixed them in the plant. One Sunday, about 10 a.m., I see this Cadillac pull up to the gate. There are a couple of ladies in the back seat. Sam leans out and barks: 'Dick! What are all these Vauxhalls doing here? Quality problem? You're *fixing* all these Vauxhalls? I'll call Jim Roche [U.S. president of General Motors] in the morning.'"

Sam forgot, or Roche paid no attention. GM sold Vauxhall Firenzas in Canada until late 1972, when they no longer met Canadian safety and emission standards. In March 1973 an Association of Dissatisfied Firenza Owners was formed in Ottawa. In a telegram to the president of General Motors of Canada, forty owners complained of electrical and transmission problems, faulty lights, starting difficulties, and severe depreciation because of the car's obsolescence. They demanded reimbursement, and GM agreed to "review the service history of each of these vehicles to ensure that our obligations are being fulfilled." In December, however, four more Ontario owners filed a $5-million class action suit on behalf of themselves and forty-six hundred others. Helen Naken, who had hired Toronto lawyer Jeffrey Lyons, claimed that her Firenza had needed a new transmission after one thousand miles, a new engine at four thousand miles. GM had replaced the car, but this Firenza had required five new drive shafts. "The only thing it didn't do was rust," she said.

The angry Firenza owners received a wave of sympathetic publicity, and although independent investigations by the federal Department of Transport discovered no safety defects in the design or construction of the Firenza, the report added: "The quality of workmanship at the production level appeared to be inferior to that to which Canadian motorists have become accustomed. Vehicle servicing by some dealers may have been of questionable quality causing owner aggravation and annoyance."

GM blamed the Firenzas' problems on driver abuse and lack of maintenance, and in 1983 the Supreme Court of Canada dismissed the class action suit on legal grounds. In the meantime, however, GM had been fined $20,000 for a misleading advertisement: a 1972 ad had given the impression that four Firenzas had been driven from Halifax to Vancouver in February with no problems apart from three burned-out lightbulbs; in fact one of the cars had suffered a minor fire and two had failed to start at minus twenty-seven Fahrenheit. Poor publicity for the Firenza, however, did not hurt the popularity of Canadian-made GM products: sales rose to an all-time high of 580,400 in 1973, and to 645,400 the following year. The truck market, the country cousin of the GM family, was beginning to boom, and Chevrolet cars and trucks now accounted for four-fifths of Canadian production.

Sam sold 154,147 of his 157,722 General Motors shares in 1966 for $15 million. "I almost cried," he told the press, "but with U.S. succession duties running up to 78 per cent, what would you do?" Sam was ninety-five, but he had no intention of dying before the age of one hundred, and, as it turned out, he cashed in his GM stock at the peak of the market. The following year he regretfully resigned from the General Motors board of directors, keeping an honorary role as chairman of the board of General Motors of Canada. "So long as they are sweet enough to think that I am of use to them here I am at their service," Sam wrote to John Lee Pratt, who had also retired from the GM board. "I wanted to work for $1 but they would have no part of it and now I have the 'stupendous' salary of approximately $15,000." Sam's place was taken by a cousin, W. Earle McLaughlin, a great-grandson of Robert McLaughlin's brother, William, and president of the Royal Bank of Canada.

General Motors of Canada had become a rung in the ladder for aggressive young American executives on their way up to the fourteenth floor of the company headquarters in Detroit, and Sam was sensitive to perceived slights. "Our new President and General Manager is not much of a letter writer," he wrote to Dick from Bermuda on December 14, 1968, "as I have had only an acknowledgement of the letter I left behind me welcoming him. However, time will work changes no doubt. And if it doesn't, it looks to me as if I could very nicely and gracefully 'hang up the fiddle and the bow, and lay down the shovel and the hoe.' Of course, I have offered to do this many times but New York doesn't seem to want me to do it so I still have my good old office which I have occupied since I put up the building so many years ago. I guess the new boss wishes Jack English would get the H. . . out of his office. Will look into this when I get home."

Sam had been using "New York" as an excuse for fifty years, but Sam's silence on General Motors' affairs was in part the result of a sharp rebuke he had received from New York in June 1956. *Life*

Sam and Adelaide with their five daughters. Left to right, standing: Eileen, Isabel, Billie, Mildred. Seated: Hilda. *(McLaughlin Public Library)*

magazine was preparing a feature on Alfred P. Sloan, and, unable to resist getting his own oar in, Sam sent Pratt a copy of his three-part interview with Eric Hutton published by *Maclean's* in 1954. "It is a short story," Sam wrote in a covering letter, "very concise, and contained a lot of facts not generally known by the public. Would it be worthwhile writing the editor of 'Life,' who is preparing the article on Mr. Sloan and who has asked you for criticism, sending him a copy? I think that Eric Hutton has a master touch for telling the story and he might just get a few ideas from Mr. Hutton's article. In passing I might say that we have had a sufficient number of copies bound in heavy plastic to send to all the libraries in Canada."

"I do not feel like writing to the editor of 'Life' and sending him this copy of your article in 'Maclean's,'" Pratt bluntly replied. "The situation in connection with Mr. Sloan is that he has hired, as I understand it, a writer from 'Life,' I am told at $50,000 a year, to write this book for him. This book is to be entitled 'The General Motors Story.' The first chapters which I have seen make it more or less a personal story of Mr. Sloan, and I don't think it would be advisable for us to divert his line of approach to the problem. All I am trying to do, at his request, is to tell him that I think he has strayed a little from the facts."

Sam brooded, then gave in: "All right, John, let it go at that," he wrote from Cap Chat in July. "All these so-called histories of GM I have seen to date have been, as you suggest in your letter, full of inaccuracies with a lot of crucial points left out of them. However, here's hoping for the best." Sam remained an incorrigible self-promoter; on September 25, 1968, he sent Pratt a copy of a photograph of "two tough looking 'mugs,'" himself and Governor General Roland Michener taken when Michener visited Oshawa. Sam wrote: "He hung around my neck the ribbon and medal creating me a 'Companion of the Order of Canada.' This is the highest honour our good government can give to any Canadian and, of course, I have been blushing ever since."

Sam got his "knighthood" at last, and he was tickled pink. At his venerable age, still bright and full of beans, Sam's naive, infectious pleasure in parties transformed every milestone birthday into a saint's day celebration. His voice as strong and gruff as ever, "Colonel Sam" presided over lively family reunions and formal banquets; he made speeches and responded to toasts of congratulation, told stories, posed for photographs, and opened presents: Parkwood was chock-a-block with plaques and illuminated scrolls, medals, silver plate, cigar boxes, framed testimonials, gift books, souvenir albums, and engraved knick-knacks. Sam McLaughlin was still the boy on the bicycle racing for pickle dishes to impress his bride, but Adelaide was dead.

On January 9, 1958, less than a month before their sixtieth wedding anniversary, Adelaide died of cancer in the Toronto General Hospital. The official announcement said that Mrs. McLaughlin had been "taken ill suddenly" in Bermuda and returned to Toronto, but Sam's letter to Pratt on January 16 is more frank: "When I returned to Bermuda from New York, I found that Adelaide had taken a turn for the worse. Those cobalt bomb treatments apparently raise Cain with the internal workings of the body. The initial cancer was retarded indefinitely, but X-rays taken when Adelaide was flown to Toronto on Thursday, showed that she was in a most impossible condition. The doctors told me that her case was hopeless and they gave her about a week to live unless she had a relatively minor operation. Even with an operation she could only live for a month or so and that in misery. They gave my wife that option and she was brave enough to have the operation but about an hour later her heart gave out and she passed quietly away.

"I have lost a grand wife, John, as you know, and it will make my life much different. With the help of my children, grandchildren and great-grandchildren, I will try to get along. I will not be at the next meeting of General Motors as I do not feel like going but will probably be present in March. The doctors want me to get out of this climate as soon as possible and I am flying to Bermuda on Wednesday next."

Adelaide's body was laid out at Parkwood before the funeral, and one of the first mourners to call was the social columnist for the Oshawa *Times*, Jo Aldwinkle: "In the sanctuary of her own drawing room she lies in a bower of flowers, while the big grandfather clock in the hall ticks away her last night at home. A regiment of roses keeps watch, and a blanket of white roses and orchids lies like a drift of fresh snow. The quiet dignity of her days is about her; the softly curled grey hair, the firmly moulded features. Somehow, one waits for the welcoming smile. The beautiful, pale rose gown she wears was designed for a joyous occasion. It was fashioned in readiness for her diamond wedding anniversary, early in February. Of filmy chiffon, its fluid grace would float with every turn. No stop will show its flowing line. No breath comes now to stir its listless folds. Its silken beauty carries no caress.

"A diamond necklace, the gift of the bridegroom of nearly 60 years ago, gleams in the pale light, and a favourite brooch, a maple leaf in diamonds, was pinned in place by the trembling hands of a loving daughter. Hands tell so much in life; in death, what do they say? These are the hands that held books and precious things, that soothed a child's hurt, that smoothed a velvet gown; but hands that also kneaded dough and potted plants, that waved a greeting and clasped firmly in friendship. Now, they rest, pallid and still, and around one wrist is a treasured grandmother's bracelet bearing the names of all the grandchildren and great-grandchildren."

Jo Aldwinkle remembers the scene vividly. "All these people coming to pay their respects, it was like a show," she shudders. "I came in and Sam said something like: 'Go take a look if you want, she's in the next room.' He was very spry in view of the fact that he had lost his wife. I think he felt a sense of being released. He made some offhand joke. I don't remember what it was, but I thought that was very cruel."

Sam may simply have been incapable of expressing his love. "A grand wife," was his highest compliment, and in old age Sam still cast Adelaide as the remote angel of his youthful dreams. He did not mention her or include her greetings in his letters to friends, and of all the hundreds of surviving photographs of Sam and Adelaide, only two show him, somewhat tentatively, holding her arm. At a family dinner in 1956 honouring Sam's eighty-fifth birthday, Eileen proposed an eloquent toast to her mother, seated at her father's side. The children raised their glasses, and in the long silence that followed Sam spoke one word: "Adelaide." Adelaide said nothing.

Adelaide bequeathed her jewellery and personal treasures to her daughters, and left small donations to her favourite charities. She had never been part of the McLaughlin Foundation, but over her lifetime she had privately given away many thousands of dollars to church and educational organizations. She was awarded honorary degrees by both Queen's and Mount Allison universities, and she left a legacy of prizes, scholarships, and trust funds, most of them for young women, as well as her own monuments: Adelaide Hall, the women's residence at Queen's University, and, in Oshawa, Adelaide Street, a school, the YWCA, a nurses' residence, and a stained-glass memorial window in St. Andrew's Church.

Eileen died at the end of December 1959. She had spent Christmas in Bermuda, and on the flight back to Toronto she choked to death in the aircraft's washroom. Eileen was only sixty-one. In 1965 Mildred died of cancer in Florida. Mourning did not alter Sam's flamboyant life style: Parkwood, like the *Queen Mary*, steamed on at full speed. Housemaids and gardeners bustled about, the kitchen was fragrant with the aroma of smoked salmon and roast pheasant, rare orchids and prize chrysanthemums bloomed in the conservatories, and afternoon tea was served for a constant stream of visitors who kept Sam amused. Every morning he dictated a torrent of personal letters to his household secretary, Elizabeth McMullen, who, with Nursie, took over Adelaide's responsibilities, and he usually managed to go into his office at General Motors for a few hours a day: when he left, a maintenance worker swept the broadloom with a push broom to remove any trace of footprints. Sam remained on the board of the Toronto–Dominion Bank.

"He participated," says former president Allan Lambert. "He always had a useful point of view, and once he made up his mind he was bold in supporting his convictions. McLaughlin approved of our new Toronto–Dominion Centre, even though some directors thought it too big. In financial matters, he was more courageous than most people, ready to explore the limits, with a considerable amount of care. He based his judgements on people, on their style of managing. He would be exasperated if somebody brought up a problem and hadn't decided what he thought should be done. He liked to get to the point quickly and he didn't waste his time. He suffered fools badly."

Sam refused to give up hunting, and he succeeded Junius Morgan as president of the Long Point duck-hunting club when Morgan became too infirm. "Sam was a good shot," says Elgin Card, a senior Frigidaire executive who became manager of Griffith Island when Sam sold it to General Motors in 1953 for use as a management training centre. Junior executives were sequestered there during the summer; Sam opened the hunting season. "He was a cold person, self-opinionated," says Card. "He always demanded that the fireplace be lit the moment he came into the room from his afternoon sleep. Once when we were sitting down to dinner, I said: 'You sit at the head of the table, Mr. McLaughlin, and I'll take the other end.' 'You'll sit where I tell you to sit!' he barked. Sometimes he was just cruel. People were afraid of him."

Nursie, however, knew how to manage Sam. Says Card: "Sam always insisted that we have Gordon's gin. He wouldn't drink anything else. I was responsible for things like that. We went up one time with all these fancy guests, and I said to his nurse, 'Oh my God, I didn't bring any Gordon's gin!' She said, 'Did you bring gin of any kind?' I said yes. She said, 'Well, he'll never know the difference.' I said, 'I dunno.' She said, 'No, you go ahead and make up the drinks in the kitchen and have them sent in.' And so he's proposing the toast, and he says: 'I always have these drinks made with Gordon's gin. There's no other, and I can always tell.' He takes a sip, and they all take a sip. The gin was anything but Gordon's, but he didn't realize it."

Sam took a great deal of pride in being the oldest employee of General Motors, and he treasured his gold signet ring set with four diamonds representing forty-five years of company service. After twenty-five years with the company, every auto worker was presented with a ring, and a diamond was added every five years. Few workers lasted longer, but when Sam had achieved sixty-five years in 1952 he insisted on four more diamonds. There was no space on the ring, so he settled for a pair of diamond-studded cufflinks. Sam was wearin' diamonds after all, and he saw to it that his men were too.

His greatest regret was having to give up his salmon stream and Landry Camp at Cap Chat. "I don't know where anyone could go in this old earth to a nicer spot," he wrote to Pratt in August 1945.

"When I go to Heaven or to the other place I hope it will be something like the Landry Camp." Leasing rivers to Ontario millionaires was no longer popular in Quebec, and Sam was getting too frail for a canoe. "Some of the rapids were a ticklish business," says Nursie, who went along, book in hand, for the ride. "Once our canoe hit a rock. We were dumped. The lunch buckets and cushions went floating downstream, the canoes went to the bottom of the river. The stones on the riverbed were slippery, and Mr. McLaughlin fell. I caught hold of his coat and got him standing up. He still had his pipe in his mouth. Dr. Gallie said, 'I thought I'd have to gaff him.'"

Sam killed his last salmon on August 20, 1964. It weighed thirteen pounds, and it brought the season's total to forty-eight fish weighing 559 pounds. It was a relatively poor year; in 1936, the first year for which the camp logbooks have survived, 107 salmon were caught weighing a total of 1,490 pounds. The peak season was 1941, when the river yielded 221 salmon weighing 3,254 pounds. Guests took their fish home with them, and Sam shipped dozens of salmon to friends and business contacts all over North America; one fish even found its way to Sir Joseph Flavelle. Sam passed Flavelle's thank-you note on to George with the query: "I didn't send him a fish, did you?"

In his later years, Sam discovered a sport that was more fun than fishing: he played cat-and-mouse with the men who were after his money. Sam had been trying hard to unload his fortune, but it grew like a puffball on a compost heap. *The Canadian* magazine estimated it at $275 million in 1966, making Sam one of the ten richest men in Canada. Sam had built a new public library for Oshawa and a camp and swimming pool for the Boy Scouts; he took over Adelaide's charities and at Queen's he established scholarships and purchased rare manuscripts and books, including the entire library of British writer John Buchan, Lord Tweedsmuir, governor general of Canada from 1936 to 1940. Sam also influenced GM's charitable contributions, and between 1950 and 1966 General Motors of Canada gave $7 million to community services and universities across Canada.

Sam wasn't modest about his philanthropy, and the publicity attracted hordes of supplicants. "His financial man, Jack English, looked after these things," recalls C. L. Jenkins, who, as company treasurer, received copies of the requests. "This day there was a letter from the University of Alberta. They wanted some money. Mr. McLaughlin calls me in and asks, 'How much are you going to give 'em?' I said I didn't know yet. He said, 'Jack and I think we're going to give 'em $75,000. Would you think I was chintzy if I just gave 'em $75,000?' I said, 'No, Mr. McLaughlin, I don't think they'll think you're chintzy.'"

Choosing appropriate beneficiaries was difficult, and Sam took pains to project an almost puritanical public image. He enjoyed Broadway shows in New York, but when Floyd Chalmers approached him on behalf of the Stratford Shakespearean Festival, Sam replied: "I am not at all interested." Chalmers, however, was a power with the *Financial Post*, so Sam added: "You'd better come down at lunch today and we'll talk about it." Says Chalmers: "I got in my car and drove to Parkwood. I made my pitch. Among other things I told him I had just gotten $25,000 from J. W. McConnell of Montreal. He was skeptical: 'I don't believe McConnell would give money to a theatre.' He had the telephone brought to the table and asked somebody to get McConnell on the line. They dug him up at the Mount Royal Club and Sam asked him if he was giving money to the festival. He got an affirmative reply, of course.

"We continued the discussion on the lawn, over coffee, and Sam said, 'Well, I'm not really that interested but I'll give you $25,000.' I was elated. But a few weeks later I ran into a mutual friend and he said, 'Sam tells me that he expected you to ask for $100,000 and he was going to give it to you. But when you didn't ask for it, he decided just to match Jack McConnell's gift.' Later, I tried to get more money out of McLaughlin, but he turned me down, somewhat abruptly."

More timid petitioners approached the Minotaur of Parkwood through intermediaries. Jenkins recalls: "When Ted Walker was GM president he was also on the board of York University, which was just starting out, and Ted was assigned to get some money from Mr. McLaughlin. So, as a good canvasser, he said, 'I have been asked to see if you would be good enough to contribute to York.' Mr. McLaughlin never said anything. Months went by, so Ted asked him again. Mr. McLaughlin didn't say anything. Ted went to one of the university board meetings and he said he had nothing to report on McLaughlin yet. He was feeling a little embarrassed, so he went into Mr. McLaughlin and said, 'I wonder if you could let me know one way or the other.' McLaughlin said, 'Well, how much do you want?' Ted was thinking to himself, so he said, 'Well, I thought a million dollars would be pretty good.' McLaughlin never said a thing except, 'When's your meeting?' Ted said, 'Two days from now.' So the day of the meeting comes, and

Ted hasn't heard a thing from Mr. McLaughlin, and McLaughlin comes in to see him that morning and says, 'Look, if you're gonna tell 'em you've got a million dollars from me, why don't you do it in style?' And he reached down and threw all these stock certificates, bonds, etc., on his desk and said, 'Here's a million dollars. Take it to 'em in cash.'"

As his monument, Sam fancied a planetarium "bigger and better than Charlie Hayden's in New York." Planetariums were an expensive novelty, and Sam entered into a delicate *gavotte* with the Royal Ontario Museum over who would pay how much. Jack English conducted the negotiations, and after years of estimating costs, a delegation from the museum met with McLaughlin with a request for $1 million. "Do we have a million dollars, Mr. English?" Sam barked. "Yes, Mr. McLaughlin," English replied. Turning to the delegation, Sam said: "How much is the whole damn thing going to cost?" The answer: $2 million. "Do we have two million dollars, Mr. English?" Sam winked. "Not until Thursday, Mr. McLaughlin," English gravely replied. Sam wrote a cheque for $2 million plus $1 million for a maintenance fund and the museum built the McLaughlin Planetarium.

"Sam McLaughlin is a small, sturdy man, erect as a rooster," June Callwood wrote in the *Star Weekly* on the occasion of Sam's ninety-fifth birthday. "His eyes are lively in his puckish face, his manner vigorous. He wears three-piece suits, his shoes are well broken-in and his watch is ordinary looking, with a worn leather strap. Age has dimmed his hearing somewhat, and he isn't averse to being helped on the stairs. His teeth are his own. He is proud of his astonishing physique, thumping his hard abdomen with a heavy fist, displaying a bicep the texture of cordwood." Sam still went to the races at Woodbine every Saturday, and smoked like a chimney before Nursie restricted him to five pipes and one cigar a day.

"He was the king of the castle," Nursie says. Sam liked to hold court in bed, a scenario that disconcerted his visitors, and while he now wore glasses, he had not lost his eye for the ladies. In 1968, Joan Murray had just been hired as curator of Canadian art for the Art Gallery of Ontario, and her first assignment was to get a commitment from Sam to donate to the gallery his collection of Canadian art, including Clarence Gagnon's *Maria Chapdelaine* paintings. Murray was young and nervous, and for the visit to Parkwood she wore her best miniskirt. "I was ushered upstairs to his bedroom," she recalls. "He was propped up in bed with a painting of polar bears over his head. 'You're too late!' he said. 'The McMichaels came last week and I gave them away! But I'll tell you one thing, young lady, you've got a great pair of legs!'"

Ken Thomson, heir to the newspaper empire and an avid collector of Canadian art, had written Sam several letters pleading to buy the Gagnon paintings, but Sam put his sense of public duty, and his tax rebate, first. The Gagnons, along with his Group of Seven collection, became a gift to the Queen, via the Robert and Signey McMichael Gallery in Kleinburg, Ontario; the Art Gallery of Ontario had to settle for Peel's "After the Bath." Unlike his chum Eddie Taylor, however, Sam did not decamp to Bermuda or the Bahamas to evade taxes, and he repatriated his own considerable portion of GM's Canadian profits.

Sam had purchased his coffin, custom-made of white ash, and had built his mausoleum in Union Cemetery, but he was indifferent to his possessions. Parkwood's treasure was not inventoried or appraised, and although Sam never threw anything out, his company records, mementoes, and personal papers were not sorted, catalogued, or donated to an archive. Sam willed Parkwood to the Oshawa hospital with the apparent intention that it should be used as an outpatient residence or convalescent centre, and he impulsively gave things away: silverware and pieces of Parkwood furniture mysteriously turned up in Oshawa basements and antique dealers' showrooms. Sam's favourite chair was a plain Morris recliner his brother Jack had given him as a wedding present, and he liked to sit in it in front of the library fireplace. June Callwood, sitting opposite, had noticed the coat of arms over the mantelpiece and asked what it meant. Sam turned in his chair, stared up, and snorted: "Nothing, absolutely nothing."

Sam's Daddy Warbucks impersonation made him vulnerable to self-parody, and in a National Film Board documentary, *The Oshawa Kid*, Sam was cast as a small town *Citizen Kane*. "If I live to be one hundred years old, as everyone is urging me to do," Sam confessed, "I'll be one of two things, either a curiosity or a nuisance, and I don't want to be either."

He *was* a curiosity. He went for a drive every day, even in the coldest winter weather, wearing a heavy coat and his bedroom slippers, snugly tucked into the back seat of his blue Cadillac limousine. Local residents would catch a glimpse of his tiny, wrinkled face peering out the window and wave or honk their horns. Clarence Lowry, over seventy years of age, was still at the wheel. A good thing too: Sam was a lousy driver.

"When four-wheel brakes came out," Lowry recalls, "we got an

Clarence Lowry.
(*McLaughlin Public
Library*)

experimental Buick in here, the first with four-wheel brakes. Mr.
McLaughlin and I took it out – it was all dirt roads outside Oshawa in
those days – and I drove. He said, 'Let me try that, I want to see what
it's like.' So he got behind the wheel and shoved her right down to the
floor. That was the way he drove. The next thing, the left front wheel
seized up, and he just held on and never eased up on the gas. The gravel
and sand was flying in the ditch. I said, 'For Christ's sake, take your foot
off the gas!" He just ploughed a furrow up the road. The strength that
man had! I couldn't have held a car like that."

Sam could also be a nuisance. As his memory became confused, he
grew cranky and garrulous. He pawed through boxes of old photographs and sent his staff scurrying off to identify the people in them,
then took credit for being able to remember every name. "I've had
many fine friends," he told June Callwood, "but I've lost them, I've lost
them. All my chums are gone." Not quite: as Sam approached one
hundred, C. S. Mott was a spry ninety-six. "He was always putting
himself a year ahead," Mott complained. "When he turned ninety-
eight, he would say, 'I'm in my ninety-ninth year.'" Sam hated being
idle or alone, and he resented the fact that Isabel kept her own house
in Toronto and stayed at Parkwood only for long weekends. However
many visitors could be rounded up for tea or canasta, the burden of
humouring Colonel Sam fell on "the girls," Elizabeth McMullen and
Margaret Nelson.

"I would be summoned at night," sighs Nursie. "He would get upset
about anything and ring the bell. I would sit and talk to him. We had
some arguments about rest. I remember laying down the law: follow
orders or do without me, I won't stay. Then I burst into tears." Margaret

Nelson moved out into her own apartment: "Mr. McLaughlin was mad as a hatter! 'Isn't Parkwood good enough for you?' he said. It was lovely to have a day free to myself. He got over it."

"Nursie says she will take me to my hundredth birthday," Sam boasted. If Adelaide had played Wendy in Sam's *Peter Pan* psychodrama, Nursie was Tinkerbell, the good fairy who promised him eternal youth. Unlike perhaps any other person in his long life, Sam allowed Margaret Nelson to break through his crust of bluster and bombast to share his secrets. Rumours flew around Oshawa from time to time that Sam was going to marry Nursie – someone claimed to have seen them coming out of the United Church manse – but she scoffs at the speculation: "I'm sure the idea of remarrying never crossed his mind." Nursie devoted her life to the McLaughlin family – she never married – but she has no regrets. "I enjoyed Mr. McLaughlin tremendously," she says, "and it was wonderful to get to know all those interesting men. It was a far cry from real nursing!"

In the spring of 1970, a little more than a year before his hundredth birthday, Sam was operated on for bowel cancer. Coming out of the anaesthetic, his first words were: "Did I make it?" He had a colostomy, but he was never told he had cancer: Nursie feared he would die on the spot. Sam stuck to his favourite lunch of cold stewed tomatoes, melba toast, and beer, with a big mug of warm milk and garlic toast before he

Sam and Nursie, Bermuda.
(McLaughlin Public Library/Parkwood)

went to sleep. Cocktails were served before dinner, which Sam ate in bed; a card table with sawed-off legs was covered with a white linen cloth, fine china, and silverware, and each course was accompanied by the appropriate wine.

While Sam snoozed, his centennial was celebrated in Oshawa with a year-long festival of concerts, regattas, flower shows, highland games, historical displays, church services, and commemorative ceremonies. General Motors planted a circle of red oaks in a city park in his honour, and presented him with a bronze plaque mounted on a block of granite. In July, Sam came downstairs to shake hands with the directors of the Toronto–Dominion bank, who had arranged a meeting at Parkwood, and on September 8, his hundredth birthday, he was able to sit on a chair in the garden greeting friends and relatives, saluted by a parade of vintage McLaughlin–Buicks that chugged by Parkwood's front gate. On September 11, a hundred-man honour guard from the Ontario Regiment paraded to Parkwood to present birthday greetings from Queen Elizabeth II and fired a "*feu de joie*," a ceremony, according to a GM press release, "interspersing the sounds of rippling small arms fire with the playing of the national anthem and the booming of a 15-gun salute from heavy weapons, in this case the tank guns of the Ontario Regiment."

After his birthday, Sam's health failed rapidly, and his cloudy mind drifted back to the early days of General Motors. He reminisced for hours about Billy Durant, but his stories were rambling and repetitive and nobody listened. Durant had died, beggared and disgraced, on March 18, 1947. He had declared bankruptcy on February 8, 1936, listing debts of nearly $1 million and assets of $250, and on August 5 he wrote to Sam: "For the purpose outlined in my talk with you last Monday (the acquisition of a substantial interest in the well known brokerage firm of Tailer and Robinson, about to be reorganized) I am enclosing my note for $30,000 for which your check to the order of Catherine L. Durant will be greatly appreciated. Mrs. Durant with the assistance of Mr. W. E. Ditmars will handle the details until my situation in bankruptcy court in entirely cleared. The capital, which is being contributed by five of my real friends, will establish me in a business that will keep me profitably employed and if successful will enable me to retire all obligations previously incurred. It goes without saying that each of the contributors have my heartfelt thanks."

Durant promised to repay the money with 5-per-cent interest

within three years. It was a pathetic way of asking for a loan, and Sam knew his chances of seeing his money again were slim. He sent the cheque anyway, and never begrudged his loss. Sam visited Durant in New York, but Sam's maudlin reminiscences about the "good old days" caused Durant to break into bouts of uncontrollable weeping, and Catherine discouraged his visits. In 1940, Billy returned to Flint to run a bowling alley and drive-in hamburger restaurant; reporters and curiosity-seekers could find the former president of General Motors chatting with the pinboys or flipping burgers in the kitchen. Durant was as bullish and dapper as ever, and he carried an attaché case stuffed with a thousand to fifteen hundred dollars in cash, but his financial situation was so desperate that Catherine wrote to Alfred P. Sloan, offering to sell him her rope of pearls for $500,000. The pearls were all she had left. Sloan, aghast, privately arranged a $10,000 annual pension for Durant and his wife; the contributors, in addition to himself, were Charles Kettering, C. S. Mott, and Sam McLaughlin.

"We knew he was dying," Nursie says. "I'd read to him a lot. We were reading *The Last Spike* by Pierre Berton. I'd ask, 'Are you enjoying this?' and he'd reply, 'Yes, I am.'" After New Year's Day, Sam slipped into a state of semiconsciousness; Nursie sat up with him at night, and she was by his side when he died peacefully in his sleep at 2 a.m. on January 6, 1972.

EPILOGUE

Sam's estate of $37.5 million was surprisingly modest, although J. J. English estimated that Sam had given away $24 million in the last decade of his life. Sam divided $6.3 million among his descendants, and bequeathed more than $1 million to friends and employees, including $400,000 to Mr. English, $100,000 each to J. C. Fraser and Margaret Nelson, and $50,000 to Clarence Lowry. Lowry also received title to his house. All household and office employees received $200 for every year they had been on staff. Hilda inherited Cedar Lodge in Bermuda, then sold it a few years later to the gardener's son, Benjamin Rego. The Parkwood estate was left to the Oshawa General Hospital, with a legacy of $500,000 to manage it, a sum that turned out to be woefully inadequate. Today, volunteers conduct guided tours of the house and raise money to restore the gardens and furnishings.

After taxes and succession duties, the residue of Sam's estate was transferred to the McLaughlin Foundation, which currently supports hundreds of charitable and educational institutions ranging from the Clarke Institute of Psychiatry to the Ontario College of Art, the Salvation Army and the Long Point Bird Observatory. The foundation is nearing the end of its own life span: Sam stipulated that in 2001 the directors disperse its assets and wind up its affairs. "By then," he said, "nobody will remember who I am." It was a short-sighted decision. During Sam's lifetime, between 1951 and 1972, the McLaughlin Foundation dispersed $6.8 million in charitable grants; from 1972 to 1994 it gave away $74.3 million. The foundation's current assets are $66.7 million.

Wealth has not brought the McLaughlins immortality, and the younger generations have endured their share of illness and premature death, divorce, estrangement, and excommunication. "It was a family riven with feuds," sighs one disaffected cousin. "There was always a lot of screaming and fighting. The motive was never to make peace, the motive was to make war. It was very Irish. When I went to see Sean O'Casey's play, *The Plough and the Stars*, I felt instantly at home. Everything was in ferment all of the time. If there wasn't any melodrama, they'd create some. There was a great wielding of power. You could be only *so* independent, only *so* outspoken; you could go near the water, but never go in, or watch out! It was ruinous. They were a family of will-shakers: 'If you don't do what I want, and obey me, I will cut you out of my will!' And they did."

Isabel McLaughlin will not be forgotten by 2001: her paintings are cherished in galleries and private collections, and her monumental work, "Tree," hangs in the National Gallery of Canada. Had Isabel's grandfather Robert come upon her mighty tree, he would have taken his axe to its gnarled trunk and whittled the dead wood into whiffletrees; her father, Sam, and her Uncle George would have reduced it to so many board-feet of lumber. Isabel, however, records a moment in the tree's life, and transforms it into the Tree of Life. Her painting is more than symbolism: in their old age, Hilda and Isabel are planting thousands of trees in conservation areas to regenerate the rural wasteland of southern Ontario. The McLaughlin family story is coming full circle.

Car Plant #2 is still in business, and the Oshawa operation prides itself on being the biggest automotive assembly plant in North America. The Buick Regal and Chevy Lumina have been upgraded and redesigned – the two-door Lumina is now called the Monte Carlo – and in 1993 GM invested a billion dollars retooling and automating its Canadian plants. The number of employees has been reduced by 5,000 to 37,500, and both my old jobs are gone: window regulators are installed on the door line with a fraction of the time and effort, thank

God, and robots apply the black goop to the windshields. Hourly wages are up to twenty-two dollars, and while the workers welcome their hefty paycheques, mandatory overtime rips a big chunk out of their private lives. The company's annual payroll is still $1.8 billion.

When I toured the plant in the spring of 1995 with a busload of students and automotive historians, I felt right at home. The air was foul, the noise deafening. A skinhead in crypto-Nazi gear strutted as we passed, and a bush rat, naked to the waist, hoisted a fender and swivelled his hips. Radios were rocking in the chassis plant, and, because the line was crawling, a lot of workers stood around munching sandwiches or peeking at the *Toronto Sun*. Swarms of AGVs scooted around everywhere, but men in greasy coveralls were still whanging away at windows and weather stripping with rubber mallets.

Faces had changed. Howard Knapp was on sick leave, soon to retire. Perry had transferred to another department, and Gee-Gee had her old job back in stores. There were still seven thousand employees in Plants #1 and #2, and a third shift had been added in the truck plant. In February 1995, GM advertised a possible eight to twelve hundred new job openings in Oshawa; twenty-five thousand people lined up in bitter cold for three days to get application forms.

So far, the casualties of Robert Stempel's shutdown campaign have been the Scarborough Van Plant, closed in May 1993, and Stempel himself, forced to resign as chairman of General Motors Corporation in October 1992, the first GM chief executive to be pushed out since Billy Durant's stock-market spree in 1920. Canada still appears to be the best place in North America to make cars, and money: in 1994, General Motors of Canada earned a record net income of $1 billion ($730 million U.S.) "The entire North American operations of the parent company reported a net income of only $690 million [U.S.]," observed Buzz Hargrove, president of the Canadian Auto Workers union. "In short, Canada accounts for all of the profits that GM is making on car production in North America. No company struggling to improve its bottom line would dare tamper with the most profitable segment of their business."

CAW split from the UAW in 1984 to form an independent union, and it bears the ideological stamp of its radical socialist founders. Local 222 remains as fractious as ever, and Oshawa workers are as likely to vote Reform as NDP. General Motors of Canada has a Canadian president for the first time in thirty years, and Maureen Kempston Darkes is the first woman to hold this job in the company's history. Perhaps Sam McLaughlin should have trained a daughter in the business after all.

The new president of General Motors, Jack Smith, is credited with pulling the corporation back from the brink of the abyss, but not out of the ditch. GM lost $24 billion between 1989 and 1994. Its 1994 profit margin in North America – $175 a vehicle in 1994 – was one-tenth of Chrysler's $1,700, and less than 1 per cent of GM's net sales. The Canadian auto industry's brief recovery – an increase of about 5 per cent – was much weaker than anticipated, and car sales slumped again in the early months of 1995. In June, General Motors of Canada announced that an entire shift of fourteen hundred people would be laid off at the Ste-Thérèse plant on October 1. Although GM has made gains in productivity – the Oshawa car plants can produce two thousand cars a day – Oshawa vehicles lag well behind Toyota, Volvo, and Ford in terms of customer satisfaction. GM has also raised its prices. General Motors of Canada sold only eight thousand more vehicles in 1994 than it did in 1993, but it increased its profit by $700 million. The company no longer releases cost-of-production figures.

Canadian car buyers are thinking twice about spending an average of $22,000 for a disposable product, and, as incomes shrink, the amount we invest is equivalent to twenty-eight weeks of our wages. We expect our cars and trucks to last longer – more than 40 per cent are over eight years old – and work harder. The population is aging, and the North American market is diminishing to the point where the manufacturers depend almost entirely on "scrappage," selling new cars to replace the old. Demand is strongest for pick-up trucks, sports vehicles, and minivans. The era of the "utility" car has finally arrived, fifty years after Allied soldiers were driving its prototype across the deserts of North Africa, and these square, boxy vehicles bear a striking resemblance to the cars of the 1920s. They even come with running boards.

"In the electric age, the wheel itself is obsolescent," Marshall McLuhan wrote thirty years ago in *Understanding Media*. "Like penmanship or typography, the wheel will move into a subsidiary role in the culture." McLuhan was writing a guidebook to the "information highway," itself an anachronistic term. Microsoft's Bill Gates is the Billy Durant of the electric age, his car a computer. Compared to travelling in cyberspace, an asphalt freeway seems as quaint as a corduroy road.

We have fallen out of love with the car. They all look alike anyway. Nobody talks cars anymore, except to gripe. We spend more money per capita on our motor vehicles than we do for furniture or clothing, almost as much as we pay for food, and Henry Ford's promise that cars would get cheaper now seems as absurd as going for a drive to get fresh air. Canada has more cars than children, 17.5 million motor vehicles for a population of less than 30 million. Who is driving whom?

In 1970, a populist uprising in downtown Toronto stopped the construction of an expressway along Spadina Avenue. Alternative expressways were cancelled, traffic continued to increase, and the greater Toronto area has become one of the most congested and polluted in North America. Rather than give in to gridlock, planners and politicians are promoting public transit: Spadina is being equipped with a light rail service. Calgary has used LRT technology for years, and both Toronto and Vancouver are exploring "Cities Without Cars." The old electric tram is showing more signs of life than F. B. Featherstonhaugh's electric runabout.

North Americans discovered the motor car in Europe – its inventor, Otto Benz, named his most beautiful model after his daughter, Mercedes – and we are looking again to the great cities of Europe for a redefinition of civilization. Europe, however, remains a hot market for cars, and the automobile industry may be poised on the brink of another technological leap forward: a solar car, perhaps, or one that runs on compost. Why not a coin-op vehicle that plugs in like a supermarket shopping cart, or piggybacks on rail lines, or a portable model that fits together like Lego? GM has invented a "virtual car," a life-size hologram. Will it get me to the cottage?

My 1988 Pathfinder is wearing out. I can think of ways I'd rather spend my money. I could take the train to the lake, and pack stuff down the trail on my back, the way we used to do, but the train doesn't stop there anymore, and the foreman of the section gang, who had a horse and wagon, hasn't been around for years. Still, I'd rather walk than drive, and my son, who spends his money on mountain bikes and compact discs, visits his friends on the Internet.

When I was learning to walk, horse-drawn wagons clopped along city streets delivering milk and ice and bread. That era ended when I went to school. My automobile era ended on May 6, 1993. I was in Scarborough following the last van, a plain white Chevy 20, as it moved down the line. Workers wept and hugged each other, or hitched a ride on the front bumper, laughing at their bravado. A few stood hesitantly in the shadows, watching, reluctant to go home.

As the van left each section of the plant, the drag chain stopped. The lights were turned off. I walked alone through the plant in the twilight, my footsteps loud on the concrete floor. I could feel the huge skeleton of the beast twitching, warm with grease. Lockers were flung open, tattered Sunshine Girls smirking on their inside doors, and a sign on a supervisor's blackboard read: DEATH TO THE VAN PLANT AND B-SHIFT ASSHOLES!

I came upon blackened pits, the size of communal graves, where welders had worked beneath the vans, their plastic masks glowing in the sparks from their torches. The welders were gone, but they had left behind the homely little chairs they had fashioned out of scrap metal and duct tape. I felt I had stumbled on the tomb of the Industrial Revolution, the bleak world my grandfather had left behind, and as I watched the last, white van bob away in its brilliant bubble of light, I imagined his emigrant ship steaming down the Clyde, the lights of the dying shipyards fading in the mist, and heard in the ripple of the ebbing tide the cadences of Matthew Arnold's great elegy:

The Sea of Faith
Was once, too, at the full, and round earth's shore
Lay like the folds of a bright girdle furl'd.
But now I only hear,
Its melancholy, long, withdrawing roar,
Retreating, to the breath
Of the night-wind, down the vast edges drear
And naked shingles of the world.

NOTES AND SOURCES

This is the first book to be written about the McLaughlins of Oshawa and General Motors of Canada. A memoir, *Robert McLaughlin, Carriage Builder*, was written by Robert's granddaughter, Dorothy McLaughlin Henderson, in 1968, and a pamphlet, *Sam McLaughlin*, by A. Roy Petrie, was published by Fitzhenry & Whiteside, Toronto, in 1975. There is no corporate history of General Motors, and no published history of the Canadian Auto Workers union. Canadian literature on automobiles, industry, and American investment is sparse; the American literature fills entire libraries, therefore many of my sources are American. I have listed only the most relevant.

All but fragments of the records of the McLaughlin family, their companies, and General Motors of Canada have been lost or destroyed, and virtually the entire back file of the Oshawa *Reformer* and *Daily Times* was destroyed by fire in 1971. Many of the collections I consulted were unsorted and uncatalogued, and some documents had not been seen since they were locked away in vaults decades ago. Quotations that are not otherwise attributed are from my own interviews.

Introduction:

The only general history of the automobile in Canada is the illustrated *Cars of Canada*, by Hugh Durnford and Glenn Baechler, McClelland & Stewart, 1973. Within the American literature, recent useful books include: *Chrome Colossus: General Motors and Its Time*, by Ed Cray, McGraw–Hill, New York, 1980; *The Reckoning*, by David Halberstam, Morrow, New York, 1986; *Rude Awakening*, by Maryann Keller, Morrow, New York, 1989; *Paradise Lost: The Decline of the Auto-Industrial Age*, by Emma Rothschild, Random House, New York, 1973; and *Comeback: The Fall and Rise of the American Automobile Industry*, by Paul Ingrassia and Joseph White, Simon & Schuster, New York, 1994. Charlie Chaplin's movie, *Modern Times*, is essential.

Pamela H. Sugiman, McMaster University, introduced me to the Cardinal sisters, and lent me her 1991 University of Toronto Ph.D. thesis, "Labour's Dilemma: The Meaning and Politics of Worker Resistance in a Gendered Setting," an analysis of the historic role of women in the Canadian automobile industry and the auto workers' union.

Albert Lee's quote is from *Call Me Roger*, Contemporary Books, Chicago, 1988. Dr. Edwards Deming articulates his philosophy in *Out of the Crisis*, Massachusetts Institute of Technology, 1982. I sat in on a four-day Deming seminar at General Motors, Oshawa, in 1992, and unknown to me, Dr. Deming toured Car Plant #2 the week I worked there. Did my performance put a crimp in his calculations? In 1986, *The Killing Line* was published by General, Toronto; *Rivethead* by Warner Books, New York. A *Memoir of Rev. Thomas Henry*, by Mrs. P. A. Henry, was published by Hill & Weir, Toronto, 1880. The closing of the Houdaille foundry is discussed briefly in Bob White's autobiography, *Hard Bargains: My Life on the Line*, McClelland & Stewart, 1987. White's book is a rare peek into the history and politics of the CAW. Marshall McLuhan's *The Mechanical Bride* was published by Beacon Press in 1967, and *Understanding Media* by Signet in 1964.

Chapter 1:

Details about the McLaughlins in Canada are found in the land-registry and census records, Archives of Ontario. The story of John McLaughlin's dunking in the lake is told in *Robert McLaughlin, Carriage Builder*. Donald Akenson's quote is from his essay, "Whatever Happened to the Irish?" in *Canadian Papers in Rural History*, vol. 3, Langdale Press, Gananoque, Ontario. Two relevant books by Akenson are *The Irish in Ontario*, McGill–Queen's, Kingston, 1984, and *The Orangeman: The Life and Times of Ogle Gowan*, Lorimer, Toronto, 1986. Social historian Edwin Guillet has published numerous books about Canada in the nineteenth century. *The Great Migration*, originally published by Thomas Nelson, Toronto, in 1937, and in paperback by the University of Toronto Press in 1963, provides a wealth of information about Ireland, emigrant ships, cholera, and the lives of the early settlers. The quotations from Mrs. Stewart and John Howison come from

Guillet's monumental *Early Life in Upper Canada*, Ontario Publishing Co., Toronto, 1933.

J. Dunbar Moodie and Thomas Traill both failed at farming. Susanna Moodie managed to beg a patronage position for her husband as sheriff of Hastings county; the Traills moved to Peterborough. Both sisters wrote stories for British magazines to supplement their family incomes. Susanna Moodie's Canadian journals, *Roughing It in the Bush*, McClelland & Stewart, 1962, and *Life in the Clearings*, Macmillan, 1959, offer vivid accounts of pioneer life in southeastern Ontario. Mrs. Moodie's observations come from *Roughing It in the Bush*, Mrs. Traill's from her journal, *The Backwoods of Canada*, New Canadian Library, 1989.

There are numerous books about the 1837 Rebellion, among them Guillet's *Lives and Times of the Patriots*, Thomas Nelson, 1938; *The Firebrand*, by William Kilbourn, Clarke Irwin, Toronto, 1956, and *William Lyon Mackenzie*, by W. D. LeSueur, Macmillan, 1979. Thomas Conant's *Upper Canada Sketches*, William Bragg, Toronto, 1898, tells the story of the Darlington area. The Conants, Reformers from New England, were among the McLaughlins' closest friends. *Toronto of Old*, by Henry Scadding, Oxford University Press, Toronto, 1966, gives a point of view more charitable to the government.

Anna Brownell Jameson, a well-known British writer, made a brief trip to Canada in 1837 to end her unhappy marriage to Robert Jameson, the attorney-general of Upper Canada. The quotations are taken from her lively and perceptive *Winter Studies and Summer Rambles in Canada*, New Canadian Library, 1990. Mrs. Henry's account comes from her *Memoir of Rev. Thomas Henry*. Robert McLaughlin spoke about his childhood in a rare interview in the Toronto *Globe*, Nov. 25, 1919. Both Guillet and Moodie tell horror stories about "bees" that turned into drunken debauches; accidents and fistfights were common, and men died from drinking poisonous home brew. Drunkenness was a particular problem in the villages, which tended to consist almost entirely of taverns. Their cheap whisky gave a stigma to "going to town" that lasts in Ontario to this day.

Chapter 2:

The quote is from the *Globe*, Nov. 25, 1919. A photocopy of the *Financial Post* interview is in the Parkwood archives with a letter from Floyd Chalmers dating it about 1920. Robert's early life and interests are described in *Robert McLaughlin, Carriage Builder*. The Rockefeller story is told in *The Rockefellers: An American Dynasty*, by Peter Collier and David Horowitz, Holt, Rinehart and Winston, New York, 1976. Leo A. Johnson provides a detailed historical portrait of the region's economy in his *History of the County of Ontario: 1615–1875*, Corporation of the County of Ontario, Whitby, 1973.

Details of the financial affairs of John and Robert McLaughlin are found in land-registry records in the Archives of Ontario, and in the Robert McLaughlin and George William McLaughlin collections, Queen's University Archives, Kingston, Ont. Kilbourn's quote is taken from *The Elements Combined: A History of the Steel Company of Canada*, Clarke Irwin, 1960. Robert's information about the winter parties, his first cutter, and his move to Oshawa comes from the *Globe*, Nov. 25, 1919. *The Coach Maker's Illustrated Monthly* is at Parkwood. Information on James Best was provided by the Uxbridge–Scott Historical Society, Uxbridge, Ont.

Thomas Conant takes a run at tramps in *Upper Canada Sketches*, They receive a scholarly and sympathetic treatment in "'The Irrepressible Stampede': Tramps in Ontario, 1870–1880," by Richard Anderson, *Ontario History*, vol. LXXXIV, no. 1, March 1992. The quote by W. H. Graham is from *Greenbank: Country Matters in 19th Century Ontario*, Broadview Press, 1988. Graham captures wonderfully the dour, repressed lives of rural Ontario Protestants. *The Forgotten Plague*, by Frank Ryan, Little, Brown, Boston, 1993, is a recent history of tuberculosis. For information about Sarah Jane Parr I am indebted to genealogical research by Trish Hopkins of Oshawa, a descendent of both the McLaughlins and the Parrs. Sam's story comes from "My Eighty Years on Wheels," a reprint of three interviews with Eric Hutton in *Maclean's* magazine, Sept. 1; Oct. 1; Oct. 15, 1954. Robert's letter is found in his letterbooks at Queen's.

Chapter 3:

My information about Dr. James McLaughlin and Rathskamory comes from the Bowmanville Museum, Bowmanville, Ont. Dr. James served three terms, 1879–90, as a member of the Liberal government of Sir Oliver Mowat. He never achieved cabinet rank, and was known primarily for his strong stand in favour of Prohibition. He died in 1903. His house, much renovated, is now the Lions' Club.

Oshawa history is well documented. *Oshawa: Canada's Motor City,* by M. McIntyre Hood, was published in 1968 by the McLaughlin Public Library. Hood relies on two earlier histories, *Reminiscences and Recollections,* by Dr. D. S. Hoig, Mundy–Goodfellow, Oshawa, 1933, and *Historic Sketches of Oshawa,* by Dr. T. E. Kaiser, Reformer Printing and Publishing Co., 1921. A collection of early photographs is published in three volumes of *Pictorial Oshawa,* by Thomas Bouckley. The photographs are in the Thomas Bouckley Collection, Robert McLaughlin Gallery, Oshawa.

Fifty Years of Banking Services, 1871–1921, published by the Dominion Bank, 1922, gives a good history of the early years. More recent is *100 Years of Banking in Canada: A History of the Toronto–Dominion Bank,* by Joseph Schull, Copp Clark, 1958. *The History of Canadian Business, 1867–1914,* by Tom Naylor, Lorimer, 1975 (two volumes), places the Western and Dominion banks within the context of Canadian finance. *Northern Enterprise,* by Michael Bliss, McClelland & Stewart, 1987, gives brief histories of the Eatons, Masseys, and other contemporary entrepreneurs. Both Naylor and Leo Johnson in *The History of the County of Ontario* investigate railway speculation and the machinations of the Grand Trunk Railroad.

A note in Robert's ledger (Queen's) indicates that he inspected the Oshawa property in April 1877. He purchased it on July 20, and his ledgers contain details of the building's financing and construction.

Details on road construction are from *Early Life in Upper Canada* and *Toronto of Old*; Anna Brownell Jameson's quote is from *Winter Studies and Summer Rambles in Canada.* Carriage industry statistics are in *The History of Ontario County.* Sam's quotes are from "My Eighty Years on Wheels" in *Maclean's.* Robert's letters are from the Robert McLaughlin Collection, Queen's. Information about Sarah Jane, the McLaughlin children, and J. J. McLaughlin's apprenticeship in New York has been provided by members of the family. Robert's partnership agreement is in the George William McLaughlin Collection, Queen's.

For background on Oliver Hezzelwood, I am indebted to Effie Hezzelwood of Oshawa, and to his grandson, Norman Clark, and niece, Irene Dickson of Toronto. Sam's reminiscence about the horse is in a letter in the G. W. McLaughlin Collection. His cycling story is from *Maclean's*. Inventories and financial records are at Queen's; McLaughlin Carriage Company catalogues are at Queen's and Parkwood. George's New Brunswick diary and Robert's letter about Sarah are in the G. W. McLaughlin Collection, Queen's.

Sarah's will is on microfilm at the Archives of Ontario. A scrapbook with clippings of Robert's letters to the editor and an account of the fire is part of the Ewart McLaughlin collection, Oshawa. Robert's enemies, and he had many, dismissed him as "the common busy-body and scold" of the town. The street railway, financed by a $112,000 loan from the town, was built only after long and bitter opposition. "VOTE AGAINST THE RAILWAY," an 1892 handbill admonished. "If the manufacturers want it, let them build it, and not ask the Electors of the town to pay for it." Minutes of the meetings of the Oshawa town council for 1899 are part of the Oshawa municipal records, Archives of Ontario. The $50,000 by-law and the contract with the Grand Trunk Railroad are in the Ewart McLaughlin collection. *Canada, 1896–1921: A Nation Transformed*, by Robert Craig Brown and Ramsay Cook, McClelland & Stewart, 1974, gives a national overview of the era in which the McLaughlins will play a prominent role. *The History of Canadian Business* is very good on the practice of "bonusing," and the secret deals made between commercial enterprises.

Chapter 4:

Businessmen took their religion and politics very seriously in the nineteenth century, and there was no love lost between McLaughlin and Flavelle, a Methodist from Peterborough who had made an immense fortune in the Toronto meat-packing business. Flavelle was part of what McLaughlin called "The Syndicate," a group of Conservative financiers who had adopted the buccaneer style of the Rockefellers and Vanderbilts. Naylor expresses McLaughlin's opinion in *The History of*

Canadian Business, where he describes the CCM merger as "a two million dollar swindle." Says Naylor: "The only profitable part of the merger turned out to be the section that assembled automobiles on American patents from imported parts." *A Canadian Millionaire*, by Michael Bliss, Macmillan, 1978, gives a more sympathetic view of Flavelle.

The *Toronto Star* listed Oliver Hezzelwood among the guests at the CCM automobile show, and ran a photo of John Eaton in his Packard. Hezzelwood's first ride is an imaginative recreation; the quote from Henry Ford comes from the *Star*, Apr. 26, 1904. The *Star* was crusading against Toronto's inefficient electric streetcar system, run by a syndicate that was skimming $1 million a year in profits, and in April it ran a cartoon of a gravestone with the inscription: "In Memoriam. A Strapholder. Pneumonia. He waited for the next car."

Information about Ford and his first cars was supplied by the archives of the Ford Motor Company of Canada, Oakville, Ont. William Gray & Sons of Chatham made a Ford body for $17; the Dodge brothers of Detroit built the engine and chassis for $265. Ford's racing exploits are described in *The Public Image of Henry Ford*, by David L. Lewis, Wayne State University Press, Detroit, 1976. *Ford: The Times, The Man, The Company*, by Allan Nevins, Scribners, 1954, is the most authoritative biography. Hezzelwood's "flaming red" car is described by Dr. Hoig in *Reminiscences and Recollections*: "It generally stopped about every 5 minutes for repairs and made a noise like a threshing machine frightening all – and they were numerous – the animals on the road. He was the recipient of more curses than a half-pence from the farmers."

For background on the Mowbrays, I am indebted to Adelaide's brother Ralph, born the year before her marriage, and his son Milton, who currently lives in the Kinsale house.

The excerpt from *Cycle and Automobile* comes from *The Buick: A Complete History*, by Terry B. Dunham and Lawrence R. Gustin, with the staff of *Automobile Quarterly*, 90th Anniversary Edition, Automobile Quarterly Publications, 1992. I have taken my account of Buick's early years primarily from this source, including the quote about Briscoe and Albert Calver's account of production methods. *R. E. Olds: Auto Industry Pioneer*, by George S. May, William B. Eerdmans Publishing Co., Grand Rapids, Michigan, 1977, tells the story of Olds's career and finances. Olds opened his own Reo plant in

Canada in 1908. May points out that Canadian mechanics worked for both Olds and Ford.

Sam's account of his visit to Pierce and his encounter with Durant comes from *Maclean's*, 1954. Durant's story is told in detail in *The Buick: A Complete History*, as well as in *Billy Durant: Creator of General Motors*, by Lawrence R. Gustin, Craneshaw Publishers, 1984, and *The Dream Maker*, by Bernard A. Weisberger, Little, Brown, 1979. The McLaughlins' deal with the mechanics is in the George William McLaughlin Collection, Queen's, as is George's correspondence with Buick and the signed one-half page of their agreement. *Cars of Canada* tells the stories of Russell, Foss, and Featherstonhaugh, with excellent illustrations. Sam's account of the Buick deal comes from *Maclean's* and from a transcript of an interview he did for *The Oshawa Kid* in the General Motors of Canada archives. The tape and film are at the McLaughlin Public Library, Oshawa.

Chrome Colossus gives a concise account of the 1907 panic and Durant's subsequent financial career. Arthur Milbrath's arrival and departure are noted in a company ledger in the Robert McLaughlin Collection, Queen's. The incorporation documents are in the Companies Branch, Ministry of Consumer and Corporate Relations, Government of Ontario. Naylor discusses the issue of importing American patents in vol. II of *History of Canadian Business*.

Chapter 5:

Dr. Hoig's anecdotes are from *Reminiscences and Recollections*; Olds's motto from *R. E. Olds: Auto Industry Pioneer*. The story of Miss Post is told by Nevins in *Ford: The Times, The Man, The Company*. Margery Durant's memoir was published by G. P. Putnam's, New York, in a limited edition; the excerpt comes from a photocopy courtesy of the GMI Alumni Foundation's Collection of Industrial History, Flint, Michigan. Her wedding was written up in the Flint *Journal*, Apr. 21, 1906. The GMI Alumni archive also has a small file on Dr. Campbell, and a few of his letters are found in GMI Alumni's W. C. Durant collection. The Oldsmobile anecdote, one Durant loved to tell, is from *The Buick: A Complete History*. This book and *The Dream Maker* give detailed descriptions of the formation of General Motors. Sam's letter to Lee Mayes is at Parkwood. General Motors of Canada has restored a

1908 Model F McLaughlin–Buick, based on extensive research by Boyd Wood, an engineer with their experimental division. Details are in the 1908 catalogue. Restoration was done by Harry Sherry, Warsaw, Ont.

Pamphlets and historical background on J. J. McLaughlin Ltd. and Canada Dry were provided by Cadbury Beverages of Toronto and Stamford, Connecticut. The McLaughlin Public Library, Oshawa, has a few newspaper clippings. McLaughlin family members contributed their recollections and collections of McLaughlin bottles; Patricia Bishop has prepared an entry for the *Dictionary of Canadian Biography*. Two catalogues of his soda-fountain equipment are in the Special Collections room, Metro Toronto Reference Library. The invention of the automated bottle-making machine in Toledo, Ohio, in 1903 revolutionized the beverage industry just as motor-car manufacturers were exploring the possibilities of mass production. "Something Old, Something New . . . : Aspects of Prohibitionism in Ontario in the 1890s," by Graeme Decarie in *Oliver Mowat's Ontario*, ed. Donald Swainson, Macmillan, 1972, is a good, brief analysis of the temperance agitation.

The Western Development Museum, Saskatoon, Sask., has a good collection of old McLaughlin buggies and car as well as early manuals for Chevrolet and the 1912 Cadillac. Ownership statistics are from the Saskatchewan Archives. The story of the Cartercar is from *A Financial History of the American Automobile Industry*, by Lawrence Seltzer, Boston, 1928. Durant's growing involvement in the McLaughlin company is recorded in their corporate documents on file at the Companies Branch, Ontario Ministry of Consumer and Commercial Relations. General Motors of Canada published Sam's anniversary speech as a pamphlet, "75 Years of Progress."

George Gooderham's letter and John Miller's report come from the Ontario Provincial Police records, RG 23 E53, Archives of Ontario. The Manitoba Provincial Library, Winnipeg, has a complete file of *Gas Power Age*. For details about A. C. Emmett, I am indebted to his son, A. C. "Bill" Emmett of Winnipeg. A plaque honouring Ace Emmett has been erected beside the Trans-Canada highway at Kirkella, Manitoba.

Chapter 6:

W. H. Haycraft's invoices are in the collection of Ron Bouckley, Oshawa. These repairs were reasonable for the time, one reason why motorists were encouraged to buy a new car every year. Robert McLaughlin's correspondence with Laurier is in the National Archives of Canada, MG 26 G; reel C-892. McLaughlin catalogues and advertising featured the slogan, "McLaughlin – Canada's Standard Car." Although William Moyse had the title of chief engineer, he was really a local jack-of-all-trades who had a knack for tinkering with engines. According to Dr. Hoig, Moyse had repaired Oliver Hezzelwood's Ford after one of its frequent mishaps, and when the McLaughlins made their deal with Buick, Moyse was sent to Flint to learn how to put the Buicks together.

The departure of David and Tom Buick from General Motors is discussed in *The Buick: A Complete History*. Sam's purchases of Chevrolet stock are recorded in his financial notebooks at Parkwood. The complex story of Pierre du Pont's relationship with Durant and General Motors is told in the greatest detail in *The Dream Maker* and in *Pierre S. DuPont and the Making of the Modern Corporation*, by Alfred Chandler and Stephen Salsburg, Harper, New York, 1971.

Robert McLaughlin's letter to his agents is at Parkwood. Robert states that he sold his carriages and patterns to the Canada Carriage Company of Brockville, not to Tudhope. The Chevrolet Motor Company syndicate agreement, dated Feb. 18, 1916, is in the W. C. Durant papers (D 74 – 2.9), GMI Alumni Foundation's Collection of Automotive History, Flint. Sam and George acknowledged their cheques with effusive thanks.

H. J. Grasett's comments are taken from the commissioner's annual reports, Metro Toronto Police Museum. The arrival of the electric streetcar is chronicled by R. B. Fleming in "The Trolley Takes Command, 1889 to 1894," *Urban History Review*, vol. XIX, no. 3 (Feb. 1991) and in his biography, *The Railway King of Canada: Sir William Mackenzie 1849–1923*, UBC Press, 1991. Because the first street railways were privately owned and run for profit, their owners were reluctant to make repairs or improve service, and the public rightly suspected that they were being ripped off by unscrupulous speculators. *The Intercity Electric Railway in Canada*, by John Due,

University of Toronto Press, 1966, gives a glimpse of the fierce early struggle between the automobile and public transit.

Sam may have had a sentimental reason for buying Prospect Park: he had raced on its quarter-mile bicycle track. According to an 1898 brochure, the park had also featured a baseball diamond with grandstand, four tennis courts, a bowling green, and a refreshment stand. Ornamental fountains dotted the lawns, and the trees were illuminated by electric lights.

O. E. Foster appears to have sold his shares in the McLaughlin Carriage Company at the same time as Oliver Hezzelwood. Oliver remained on cordial terms with the McLaughlins, and he appeared as an honoured guest at company banquets in the 1920s. After his death, however, his name virtually disappeared from the McLaughlin legend.

Raskob's memoranda dealing with the McLaughlin purchase were filed as exhibits GTX 134 and GTX 135 in the *United States of America v. E. I. du Pont de Nemours and Company et al.*, United States District Court, Northern District of Illinois, 1949. Copies are in the Hagley Museum and Library, Wilmington, Delaware, home of the J. J. Raskob and Pierre S. du Pont archives. Raskob's memos are quoted in the "Post Trial Brief for the United States," 1953. A copy of this two-volume brief is at Parkwood. A telegram from Sam McLaughlin to Raskob, dated Feb. 3, 1919, saying "Could arrive in New York Thursday morning ready to complete transaction," is in the Hagley Museum and Library. Sam's investment and disbursement records are at Parkwood. Dorothy's memoir is from *Robert McLaughlin, Carriage Builder*. George's memorandum is in the George William McLaughlin Collection, Queen's. According to corporate records, by December 1919, the stock of General Motors of Canada had been increased to 10,030 shares valued at $1.3 million.

Chapter 7:

These excerpts are taken from *The Selected Journals of L. M. Montgomery*, vol. III, 1921–1929, ed. Mary Rubio & Elizabeth Waterson, Oxford University Press, Toronto, 1992. Marshall Pickering's granddaughter Nina Lunney of Zephyr identified his car as a Chevrolet. The Gray–Dort was a Canadian car produced by Ford's first partner, William Gray & Sons of Chatham, Ont., together with

Dallas Dort, Durant's former partner in his carriage company. Montgomery's accident illustrates the perils of driving without insurance, but in the early days insurance companies were reluctant to cover motorists: there were too many cases of fraud and bad debts.

Raskob's memorandum was the key evidence in *United States of America v. E. I. du Pont de Nemours and Company et al.* A note in the GMI Alumni Collection, Flint (D 74 – 2.2) dated June 17, 1920, shows that Durant held in trust for Sam and George McLaughlin respectively 50,000 and 11,000 shares of General Motors "no par value" common stock out of his total personal holding of 1,302,600 shares. George's correspondence with Durant and Charles Nash is in the G. W. McLaughlin Collection, Queen's.

Robert McLaughlin left an estate of $496,288, and in his will he compensated his daughters for their relatively small share of the proceeds from the sale of the company to General Motors. After providing $5,000 a year for his widow, Eleanor, unless she remarried, and making modest bequests to charities and grandchildren, Robert divided 48 per cent of his estate between Mary Jane and Elizabeth; George and Sam split the remaining 2 per cent. He left Jack's younger children, Marjorie and Roland, $5,000 each; Jack's widow, Maud, and her oldest son, Donald, got nothing. Had Maud and the children been able to hang on to a minority interest in Canada Dry, or even their 25,000 shares, J. J. McLaughlin's descendants would today be among the wealthiest people in North America.

Sam often claimed that he "designed" the bodies for the McLaughlin–Buick. By design, Sam seems to have meant that he made changes in the trim and hardware. In his National Film Board interview, Sam described the car Sloan spurned as "a D-45 six-cylinder Buick car which I had dolled up, in my own way. I had a light-coloured top. I introduced that canvas, that light-coloured top. I had a mahogany instrument board on it, recessed. It was different altogether. He [Sloan] didn't want people to see it. Ours was a much handsomer car." *My Years with General Motors* was published by Doubleday, New York, in 1964, when Sloan was nearly ninety. Sloan was only four years younger than Sam McLaughlin, but, like Pierre du Pont, he was a graduate of the Massachusetts Institute of Technology and a man of the modern age. Peter Hoskins is a pseudonym.

The handwritten minute book of the directors' meetings of the Moffat Motor Company, a poignant record of how difficult it can be to sell cars, is in the G. W. McLaughlin Collection, Queen's. Ewart, cosseted by doctors and nurses, was sent on Mediterranean cruises to restore his health; his amorous adventures, recorded in his diaries, are in the Ewart McLaughlin Collection, Oshawa.

Chapter 8:

Robert Hunter, an architectural historian with Parks Canada, provided a file of background information on Parkwood, Darling and Pearson, and F. S. Challener. Plans for the house and early photographs are at Parkwood. Moyer's quotes are from "An Office Boy Who Studied Art," *The Canadian*, August 1930. Summaries of Sam's household accounts, 1924 to 1932, are at Parkwood. *Longwood Gardens*, by Larry Albee and Colvin Randall, Longwood Gardens Inc., Kennett Sq., Pennsylvania, is a succinct illustrated history of Pierre du Pont's monumental project, now open to the public daily, 9 a.m. to 5 p.m. *A Man and his Garden*, by George E. Thompson, Sr., also published by Longwood Gardens, gives a more intimate appreciation. Du Pont began working on his gardens in 1907; he completed his outdoor theatre in 1914. Early photographs are at the Hagley Museum and Library. An unusual purple fountain grass, found both at Longwood and Parkwood, indicates that du Pont shares his plants with McLaughlin. *Canadian Horticultural History*, vol. 2, no. 3, 1990, is devoted to articles about the Dunington-Grubbs. Lorrie's quote is from her article, "Sculpture as a Garden Decoration," in *Canadian Homes and Gardens*, March 1927. This magazine also published M. E. Macpherson's article in May 1929.

Margaret Bull was the daughter of the manager of the R. S. Williams piano factory, Oshawa. *Memory's Wall*, by Flora McCrea Eaton, Clarke Irwin, Toronto, 1956, is a charming memoir by a woman of very formidable talents. Before his premature death in 1922, Sir John and Lady Eaton set the style for Ontario's *nouveau riche*. The Eatons owned not only the biggest motor cars in Toronto, but the biggest yachts on Lake Ontario and the biggest launch in Muskoka. Parkwood is a smaller and less imposing version of the Eatons' Toronto mansion, Ardwold, which also had an Aeolian player organ and a conservatory where Lady Eaton raised prize chrysanthemums. Sam's billiard table was likely made at Eaton's, as was his $10,000 Steinway piano. Sir John's former secretary. J. J. Vaughan, was part of Sam's circle of Toronto friends. Eaton, who travelled with an entourage of doctors and nurses, encouraged the fashion for invalidism.

Sam's letter is in the J. J. Raskob Collection, Hagley Museum and Library. Florida was becoming the chic place for the rich to winter, but Raskob, with eleven children, was obviously apprehensive about imitating Commodore Vanderbilt. The adventures of *Azara* and *Eleanor* are described in clippings in scrapbooks, Parkwood. Sam told *Maclean's* that he had been unable to have *Azara* registered as a Canadian boat: "Finally we learned that the only way to get the registration changed was to have the ship 'libeled' for non-payment of a liability, put up for sale and sold to a British subject," he said. "Then I could fly the blue ensign and carry supplies for the sick and ailing into any port I chose." Sam says he bought his boat back for $140. He doesn't explain why he, a British subject, had failed to get *Azara's* registration changed when he bought her, or how British registration would protect him if he was arrested for smuggling.

Sam's correspondence with Kettering is in the GMI Alumni Foundation's Collection of Industrial History, Flint. The McLaughlin–Buick General Motors of Canada built for the use of the Prince of Wales and his brother, George, Duke of Kent, during their visit to Canada in the fall of 1927 is on display at the National Museum of Science and Technology, Ottawa. Prime Minister King's correspondence with McLaughlin about his station car is in the King papers, National Archives of Canada (MG 26 J12, vol.7.) King was so pleased he traded in his Pierce Arrow for a Buick limousine, and drove Buicks and Cadillacs until his death in 1950. General Motors of Canada continued to make custom Suburbans for sale in Canada and for export to Great Britain.

Chapter 9:

The head office was demolished in 1994. The information in this chapter is based on interviews with Douglas Knapp, Harry Benson, and Clarence Lowry, as well as stories in the Oshawa *Daily Times*, formerly the *Reformer*, on microfilm at the Archives of Ontario and the McLaughlin Public Library. "Labour and Politics in Oshawa and District, 1928–1943," an M.A. thesis by James Pendergest, Queen's

University, Kingston, 1973, gives a detailed analysis of the strike. Robert McLaughlin gave his men bonuses for not drinking. Sam's correspondence with J. A. Robb is in the King papers, NAC, MG 26 J1 (101189-92). A verbatim transcript of the meeting with Miss Macphail is in the archives of General Motors of Canada. King's diary is at NAC and on microfiche. *A History of the Oshawa Generals*, by Babe Brown, Bobby Attersley, and Bill Kurelo, Chimo, Toronto, 1978, features team photographs.

Chapter 10:

Sam's financial statements are at Parkwood. The story of Durant's financial ruin is told by his biographers and by his former secretary, Aristo Scrobogna of New Jersey. A story touting Sam as Ontario lieutenant-governor ran in the *Daily Times* on July 21, 1930. Sam lost out to Dr. Herbert Bruce, an old friend of Dr. Campbell's from Port Perry. *John M. Lyle: Towards a Canadian Architecture*, by Geoffrey Hunt, Agnes Etherington Art Centre, Kingston, Ont., 1982, is a good overview of Lyle and his work. Recordings of "Canada Carries On" are at Parkwood. Scott Young describes the "Hockey Night in Canada" radio deal in *The Boys of Saturday Night*, Macmillan of Canada, 1990. The consumer survey was summarized in the Toronto *Mail and Empire*, Sept. 16, 1933.

George, falsely accused of speculating in Oshawa bonds, was defeated in the 1935 city elections. In July, Prime Minister R. B. Bennett asked him to run as a Conservative candidate in the forthcoming federal election. George replied, with some regret, "I could not possibly succeed as a candidate in this riding. I couldn't be elected as a pound-keeper for this burg and if I made application for the office of poll tax collector, I would not get it." He was wise to refuse; Bennett's government was routed. George's letter, and Bennett's reply, are in the R. B. Bennett papers, NAC, reel M-1211. A copy of "Canada as a Builder of Motor Cars" is in the collection of Harry Schoon, Oshawa.

John Lyle describes his garden in *The Builder*, May, 26, 1939. It is featured in the April 1939 issue of the British magazine, *Architecture Illustrated*. King Edward VIII's Buicks are described in *The Buick: A Complete History*. An album of photographs, with a description, is in the archives of General Motors of Canada.

Chapter 11:

Carnwith's memo and Sloan's speech are in the archives of General Motors of Canada. *John L. Lewis*, by Saul Alinsky, Knopf, New York, 1970, is a sympathetic portrait. *Sit Down: The General Motors Strike of 1936–1937*, by Sidney Fine, University of Michigan Press, Ann Arbor, 1969, gives a definitive account. Knudsen's story is told by Norman Beasley in *Knudsen*, McGraw–Hill, New York, 1947. The role of the Communists is described in *Communism, Anti-Communism and the CIO*, by Harvey Levenstein, Greenwood Press, Connecticut, 1987. *The Canadian Left*, by Norman Penner, Prentice–Hall, 1977, and *The Little Band*, by Lita-Rose Betcherman, Deneau, Toronto, provide a Canadian context. The stories told by J. B. Salsberg, Ethel Thomson, and George Burt are taken from the "Oshawa Oral History Project," by Karl Beveridge and Carol Conde, Toronto. Salsberg's papers, in the archives of the University of Toronto, show how thoroughly the Communists prepared their educational programs. Stories told by Doug Knapp, Vince Jewison, Harry Benson, and Clarence Greentree are from my own interviews.

Reports in the OPP records, General File, 1937–1938, Archives of Ontario, reveal that only two detectives, Alec Wilson and Sergeant G. E. MacKay, were sent to Oshawa. They made no attempt to conceal their identities, and spent much of their time trying to calm Mayor Hall. On the evening of April 9, Hall stormed into Wilson's hotel room and demanded he arrest Hugh Thompson for using inflammatory language; Wilson told the mayor to arrest Thompson himself. Hall then got the city solicitor out of bed, but he could see no grounds for an arrest, and, says Wilson, "I agreed with him." The detectives failed to crack Local 222, and their lone informer sent them a fifty-two-dollar bill for useless gossip. An OPP spy within the Communist Party, however, reported that the party was being torn apart by a purge of Trotskyites, and that three leading Oshawa organizers had been expelled for pocketing $964 they had collected selling subscriptions to the *Daily Clarion*. The detectives reported: "Things are quiet and orderly."

The Pendergest thesis, "Labour and Politics in the Oshawa District, 1928–1943," is a thorough, well-documented account of events surrounding the formation of the union. Pendergest points out that while the cost of living fell 29 per cent, wages were cut more than 50 per cent.

By 1937, wages were still 25 per cent below the 1928 level, although GM's profit had risen 185 per cent.

"Just Call Me Mitch": The Life of Mitchell F. Hepburn, by John Saywell, University of Toronto Press, 1991, covers the political machinations in detail. Hepburn's telegram to McLaughlin is from this source, and Saywell includes some tidbits on Jack Bickell's mistresses and friendship with Hepburn (p. 409). The *Toronto Star's* coverage of the strike is more balanced than the *Globe and Mail's* and the *Evening Telegram's*. A single surviving copy of the Oshawa *Daily Times* for Apr. 23, 1937, is in the archives of Whitby, Ontario.

Chapter 12:

Alfred P. Sloan's *Adventures of a White-Collar Man*, written in collaboration with Boyden Sparkes, was published by Doubleday, New York, in 1941. So many automobile executives, including the McLaughlins, were Freemasons that the Masonic brotherhood took on a sinister connotation among labour organizers. Sloan was succeeded as president of GM by William Knudsen, who quit abruptly in the spring of 1940 to join Roosevelt's Council of National Defense as head of industrial production.

A classic illustration of auto-worker vocabulary is the 1985 National Film Board documentary, *Final Offer: Bob White and the Canadian Auto Workers' Fight for Independence*. Cohen's minutes and correspondence are in the J. L. Cohen papers, NAC, MG30 A94. Pamela Sugiman's thesis, "Labour's Dilemma: The Meaning and Politics of Worker Resistance in a Gendered Setting," documents the discrimination women auto workers encountered. Union politics are described in detail in "From Plant to Politics: The Canadian UAW 1936–1984," by Charlotte Yates, Ph.D. thesis, Department of Political Science, Carleton University, Ottawa, 1988 (published as a book by Temple University Press, Philadelphia, 1993), and in the Pendergest thesis, "Labour and Politics in Oshawa, 1928–1943."

Sam's letter to Ewart is in the Ewart McLaughlin Collection, Oshawa. After George's funeral, Annie invited "across the road" over for tea. A maid ushered Sam and Adelaide into the parlour, and, after some time, served the tea. Sam and Adelaide drank their tea alone; Annie never appeared. In Toronto, Eric Phillips became associated with E. P. Taylor and other financiers in the Argus Group, and he became almost as rich as McLaughlin.

Reports and correspondence relating to war production are in the Department of National Defence records, NAC, RG 24 Vol. 6296. The master contracts are in PC 7691. Mackenzie King's views on Hitler and the war are expressed at length in his diaries, particularly June 1937 and September 1939. Carmichael's comments were issued as a press release on the occasion of Sam's one-hundredth birthday. According to his grandson, also named Harry J., Carmichael declined King's offer to enter politics after the war and returned to St. Catharines as a manufacturer of auto parts. He was awarded every honour the Allied nations could bestow, including the American Freedom Medal. Carmichael's boss, C. D. Howe, regularly joined the president of General Motors, Charles E. Wilson, as Sam's guests at his Cap Chat fishing lodge. A researcher for the National Film Board recalls Sam showing him a photograph of Howe on horseback, stark naked, with a mop on his head, imitating Lady Godiva.

Camp X is described in *A Man Called Intrepid*, by William Stevenson, Harcourt Brace Jovanovitch, New York, 1976, and by David Stafford in *Camp X: Canada's School for Secret Agents*, Lester & Orpen Dennys, Toronto, 1986. The camp also housed the Soviet defector, Igor Gouzenko, for a few months in 1945. *The History of the Ontario Regiment, 1866–1951*, by Captain Len Schragg, was published with the financial assistance of its honorary colonel, Sam McLaughlin. Copies of the *War-Craftsman* are in the archives of General Motors of Canada. The German communication was published as a British press release. Adelaide's letter is the only one left at Parkwood.

Chapter 13:

A copy of *The Long Point Company*, a privately published illustrated book, is at Parkwood. Clippings and other information on Griffith Island were provided by Elgin Card, Toronto. The interview with Lowry, by Philip Smith, is in the archives of General Motors of Canada. Sam's letters are quoted in the "Post-Trial Brief for the United States," *United States of America v. E. I. du Pont de Nemours and Company et al.* Copies of the documents are also at the Hagley Museum and Library.

A pamphlet, "40 Years of Philanthropy," was published by the R. Samuel McLaughlin Foundation in 1992. Information about Dr. Gallie was provided by his son, Alan Gallie, Toronto, and Dr. James Darragh of the Royal College of Physicians and Surgeons of Canada, Ottawa. McLaughlin was made an honorary fellow of the college in 1961. A memoir by R. I. Harris, "As I Remember Him: William Edward Gallie, Surgeon, Seeker, Teacher, Friend," was published in *The Canadian Journal of Surgery*, 10, April 1967. Ed Fraser loaned me the Cap Chat guestbooks.

Taylor's purchase of Parkwood is described by Muriel Lennox in *E. P. Taylor: A Horseman and His Horses*, Burns & MacEachern, Toronto, 1976. The story of Volkswagen is told in "The Car That Changed the Canadian Road," published by Volkswagen Canada, 1992. Issues behind the strike are discussed in detail in Yates's thesis, "From Plant to Politics: The Canadian UAW 1936–1984." *Hard Bargains: My Life on the Line*, by Bob White, the first president of the Canadian Auto Workers union, describes the tense relations between Canadian and American union officials.

Chapter 14:

Charlotte Yates deals extensively with this whole period in her thesis, "From Plant to Politics." The Reuther quote is from this source. George Burt's correspondence is in the archives of the Rt. Hon. John G. Diefenbaker Centre, University of Saskatchewan, Saskatoon, MG 01 vi and vii. Burt's campaign was supported by Diefenbaker's labour minister, Oshawa MP Michael Starr. *Conspicuous Production: Automobile Elites in Detroit 1899–1933*, by Donald F. Davis, Temple University Press, Philadelphia, 1988, is an historical interpretation of the American manufacturers' compulsion to build cars to be seen in. Clippings relating to the UAW investigation and the report, dated May 2, 1960, were lent to me by a former executive of the UAW.

The report of the Bladen commission and supporting documents are in NAC, RG 33 Series 45. A transcript of the verbal testimony, Oct. 24–28, 1960, is at General Motors of Canada. Halberstam's observations are in *The Fifties*, Villard, New York, 1993. Bill Graham is also the author of *Greenbank*. Jack MacLaren's grandson, Ted Enright, contributed his recollections. *The History and Development of Advertising,* by Frank Presbrey, Doubleday, New York, 1929, traces modern advertising back to Pears soap, the American Standard bathtub, and the bicycle: "If $100 bicycles could be sold to children, the sale of $1000 automobiles to adults should be possible."

Walter Gordon's views on the Autopact are given in *Gentle Patriot*, by Dennis Smith, Hurtig, 1973, and *The Life of Lester B. Pearson, 1949–1972*, by John English, Knopf, 1992. James Dykes, director of the Motor Vehicle Manufacturers' Association of Canada, provides the clearest overview of Autopact history in two pamphlets, "The Government and the Automotive Industry in Canada to 1966," and "Background on the Canada–United States Automotive Products Trade Agreement," 1977, in the General Motors of Canada archives. Beigie's analysis was published as *The Canada–U.S. Automotive Agreement: An Evaluation*.

Unsafe at Any Speed: The Designed-In Dangers of the American Automobile was published by Grossman, New York. Accident statistics come from Statistics Canada publications. Thomas Whiteside tells the story of "GM versus One Determined Man," in *The Investigations of Ralph Nader*, Arbor House, New York, 1972. The *Economist* story was reprinted in the Montreal *Gazette*, Feb. 24, 1970.

Chapter 15:

Sam's letters are in the C. S. Mott and J. L. Pratt collections, GMI Alumni Foundation's Collection of Automotive History, Flint. Clippings, press releases, and reports about the Firenza are in the archives of General Motors of Canada, as are Adelaide's "Address to the Ladies of Oshawa," a brief speech giving a clear insight into her character and motivation, and the tapes and transcripts of Philip Smith's interviews with Elgin Card, Clarence Lowry, and C. L. Jenkins. Sam's letter to Dick is at Parkwood. Parkwood, GM, and the McLaughlin Public Library have newspapers and clippings about Sam's centenary and both funerals.

Until Sam's death, GM's "twenty-five-year men" were treated to a fancy banquet at the Royal York Hotel. The banquets were discontinued, and cheap wristwatches substituted for the rings. Some of the eligible employees buy their own rings. Floyd Chalmers's recollection is in a letter at Parkwood. A copy of Durant's letter to Sam was given to me by Aristo Scrobogna, who, with his wife, cared for Catherine Durant until her death in 1974. Scrobogna attributes Durant's increasingly erratic behaviour to a head injury he suffered in a train crash in 1926: "The gambler, the dictator remained, but the direction was crazed. He gave the impression he was very mild, gentle, but that was a front. He was extremely emotional. The only way you could be happy with him was to agree with him. He was very susceptible to flattery. He thought he was omnipotent."

Durant was spared the humiliation of his daughter Margery's arrest in the summer of 1947. Margery and her fourth husband, journalist Fitzhugh Green, were charged with importing cocaine. Both admitted to being addicts: FBI agents had found $100,000 worth of the illegal drug in their Connecticut mansion. The FBI, however, was more interested in the Mafia dealers than in the victims, and Margery appears to have done her penance in a private hospital. Margery had divorced Dr. Campbell in 1923, but Campbell's luck held: he struck oil in California, and died a rich man in July 1929, three months before the Wall Street crash. Clippings are in the Durant papers, GMI Alumni Collection, Flint.

Epilogue:

R. S. McLaughlin's will is on record at the Ontario Probate Court, Whitby. The Robert McLaughlin Gallery, Oshawa, has an extensive collection of Isabel's drawings, paintings, and transcripts of interviews. An illustrated catalogue, *Isabel McLaughlin: Recollections*, by Joan Murray, accompanied a 1983 retrospective. Isabel defied the stereotype of the starving artist. "One summer I had a bad back so I went sketching in a Cadillac," she says. "That surprised a few of the artists." Usually, she drove her father's year-old Buicks. Wealth did not hurt Lawren Harris's artistic career, but as a woman, Isabel found her work was too modern for the Group of Seven, yet not abstract enough to suit American tastes. Isabel was also overshadowed by Ewart's wife, Margaret, who exhibited her vivid abstracts under the name Alexandra Luke, and it was Margaret, not Isabel, who was invited the join the popular new Toronto group, Painters 11, in 1953. Isabel never lost heart: she had a successful show and sale of her work, at the age of eighty-nine, in 1992.

Financial information for 1994 comes from the *Toronto Star*. The Canadian Automobile Association issues an annual pamphlet, "Car Costs." The Canadian Urban Institute published a study, "Cities Without Cars," in 1994. In 1991, Pollution Probe published "The Costs of the Car." There is an immense periodical literature on alternative transportation. My feature story "The Last Van" was published in *Toronto Life*, October, 1993. The lines from "Dover Beach" were taken from *Poetry and Criticism of Matthew Arnold*, ed. Dwight Culler, Houghton Mifflin, Boston, 1961.

Permissions:

The following publishers have given permission to use extended quotations from copyrighted works: from *Sit Down: The General Motors Strike of 1936–1937*, by Sidney Fine, copyright 1969 by the author, and reprinted by permission of The University of Michigan Press. From *The Dream Maker*, by Bernard A. Weisberger, copyright 1979 by the author, and reprinted by permission of Little, Brown & Co.

INDEX

Page numbers for photographs are in italics.